Geographies of Flight

Geographies of Flight

Phillis Wheatley to Octavia Butler

✦

William Merrill Decker

NORTHWESTERN UNIVERSITY PRESS
EVANSTON, ILLINOIS

Northwestern University Press
www.nupress.northwestern.edu

Printed in the United States of America

10 9 8 7 6 5 4 3 2 1

Library of Congress Cataloging-in-Publication Data

Names: Decker, William Merrill, author.
Title: Geographies of flight : Phillis Wheatley to Octavia Butler / William Merrill Decker.
Description: Evanston, Illinois : Northwestern University Press, 2020. | Includes bibliographical references and index.
Identifiers: LCCN 2020014715 | ISBN 9780810142329 (paperback) | ISBN 9780810142336 (cloth) | ISBN 9780810142343 (ebook)
Subjects: LCSH: American literature—African American authors—History and criticism. | Fugitive slaves in literature. | Escape in literature. | Space and time in literature. | African diaspora in literature.
Classification: LCC PS153.N5 D36 2020 | DDC 810.9896073—dc23
LC record available at https://lccn.loc.gov/2020014715

For Elizabeth

mi amor para siempre

They sowed in the depths the seeds of an invisible presence.

—Édouard Glissant

CONTENTS

PROLOGUE

This book addresses the geographies of the fugitive slave narrative and its descendants, the postslave and neo-slave narrative. It proceeds from a recognition of key differences in the historical experience of American space: whereas a white Eurocentric literary tradition has celebrated a continent of open horizons, westward expansion, and individual freedom represented as overland and social mobility, African American writing has commonly registered New World topography as a set of entrapments. *Geography* in this context is macro- and microcosmic: Old World slave route and coastal barracoon; sea-lane and cargo hold of the Atlantic Middle Passage; plantation and auction block; the claustrophobic alcove, indoor and out, of concealment and escape; woodland, swampland, and urban refuge; and finally, the jail cell that, over the centuries, has served the requirement of private trader, Fugitive Slave Act enforcer, and criminal prosecutor. In this broad and insistently synthetic sense, *geography* comprises affective testimonials to forced displacement (expressions of rage at oppressors, grief over separation from friends and loved ones, fear of probable death) as well as Cartesian notions of global space.[1] Accordingly, this study privileges first-person accounts of flight and resettlement in which the inscribed rapport (spatial and social) between author and reader is itself an occasion of dynamic and revisionary mapping. Just as *geography* serves as a multivalent term, so too does *flight*: referring initially to the escape and migration that carries fugitives beyond the reach of enslavers, *flight* here also adverts to the literary performance that instantiates the separation fugitives achieve between states of enslavement and the comparatively free and self-conscious performance of authorship.[2]

Geographies of Flight builds on recent scholarship that situates the study of African American testimony in hemispheric and global contexts, that reads the oral and written tradition in light of enduring structures of oppression, and that challenges redemptive readings of narratives in which the Middle Passage exists as "fall." It attends to the proposition that black subjectivities have been refashioned (if not erased) in the process of acculturating to European languages and the testimonial genres by which the fugitive speaks within and across color lines. It accepts the Afro-pessimist thesis that legacies of enslavement defy the most lucid articulations of the fugitive's predicament, the most searching indictments of a structural injustice.[3] It proceeds, however, on the assumption that while recovery of an "original free African state" is never an option, African diaspora authors, as agents involved in determining their own destinies, create spaces that do more than reflect the contours of captivity, constraint, and oppression.[4] Trusting that these genres speak generatively from what Édouard Glissant has called "the point of entanglement,"[5] this study engages in a series of readings that attempt to discern the reinvented world proceeding from the first-person pronoun. It does so mindful of the spatiotemporal divide that separates author from reader (white readers categorically, but also variously circumstanced black readers) and cognizant of the incalculable distances that fugitive authors leave unexpressed in framing a testimony intelligible to those who receive their texts in the context of a radically different experience.[6] The fugitive author, and those whose work builds on the fugitive author's testimonial example, speak from spaces Michel Foucault categorizes as heterotopic—sites not only *other than* that of the reader's here/there as measured by distance, but also *other* in the sense of standing outside the binary terms (slave/free, North/South) by which we are accustomed to map the world.[7] Accordingly, much of the discipline of reading such texts lies in maintaining an awareness of the *other than* nature of the spaces from which they arise.

In assessing the distance in space and time the fugitive's word must cross before penetrating the "free" reader's horizon, I start from the premise that there is no single spatial order that unites author and reader, no one spatiotemporal ground on which author and reader meet. The geography experienced by Frederick Douglass (say) is not a geography that applies to his white antebellum readership, much less to readers on either side of the color line in the twentieth and twenty-first centuries. Still, I hope to demonstrate that critically disciplined acts of reading, in fulfillment of the act of writing, can succeed against formidable spatiotemporal difference and the power asymmetries such difference may entail in generating a cartography by which author and reader come into intersubjective relationship.

How might we recognize the achievement of such relationship? How do we activate an "understanding" grounded in a conception of empathetic commonality while preserving a due sense of the author's distance—while resisting, in other words, such appropriation of the other's experience as even the most circumspect readings may imperceptibly effect? How, as readers, do we avoid subordinating—to adopt Jeannine Marie DeLombard's apt terminology—the witness's "testimonial authority" to the "exegetical authority" we so readily assume?[8] In "Stranger in the Village" (1953), James Baldwin speaks eloquently of the disesteemed other's "human weight and complexity," writing as the stranger whose difference from the Swiss villagers at once amuses and threatens the natives, who never comprehend him as anything but an exotic specimen whose rightful place is Africa.[9] This essay, a veritable treatise on diasporic displacement, personal but also genealogical, addresses problems of author/reader proximity in ways that will merit further examination later in this study, but its lesson is foundational to the approach I will take throughout. Relationship across cartographies begins not only with the registering of "human weight and complexity," an acknowledgment of the other's subject position, but also an understanding of how our mapmaking quite literally militates against the subject-to-subject cross-border relation and in doing so commonly reduces the other to object status, most perniciously perhaps when outreach (as Baldwin experienced it in Switzerland and the United States) is well intended. Understanding not simply how we think, hear, and read geographically but how a white supremacist colonizing atlas subtly and pervasively positions those activities is integral to the task.

Geographies of Flight is indebted to inquiries that follow the example of Henri Lefebvre (*The Production of Space*, 1974) in addressing the instrumentalist function of spatial epistemologies and in regarding all geographical description as ideologically motivated. My analysis is founded on two suppositions: first, that "space" is always a shorthand for systems of representation by which we imagine and navigate a world that can only be entered as a field of signification, and second (as a consequence), that there is no geography, only geographies, a plurality reflecting a vast diversity of travel and dwelling informed by large hegemonic forces with which individual navigators establish varied relationships of cooperation and resistance.[10] By "navigators" I mean anyone who moves through the world by volition, by coercion, or by some infinitely variable admixture thereof—and to some degree this includes everyone. To approach the dimensions of a shared world as though everyone does *not* possess the same sense of space and time is bound to seem counterintuitive, the more so given the electronic connectivity of our contemporary social eco-structure. But in view of the historical diversity with which people map and move through the world, one must reject, as David Harvey urges, "the idea that there is some 'universal' language of space, a semiotics of space independent of practical activities and historically situated actors."[11] Doreen Massey puts an even finer point on this idea: "space itself, the space of the world, far from being equivalent to representation, must be *un*representable in that latter, mimetic, sense."[12] In affirming that there is no singular order of space and time that unites author and reader, no unitary spatiotemporal ground on which author and reader meet, I emphasize that absolute time and space exceed our powers of signification and underscore the disparities of place and privilege that shape access to a navigable world.

To say that no singular spatiotemporal order applies universally to human subjects is not to deny the existence of structural parameters that shape the possibilities of collective experience. Capitalist production and reproduction of space—from the dawn of the European age of empire to the post-1989 coalescence of neoliberal economic spheres—have marked and continue to mark populations that have been uprooted and reduced to object status. "Space commands bodies," observes Lefebvre in a general proposition that gains special relevance in reference to violently deracinated peoples, "prescribing or proscribing gestures, routes and distances to be covered."[13] Those who trace their ancestry to the African diaspora appear in the contemporary geographical field as subjects whose histories embed what Orlando Patterson has called a "natal alienation" and a "social death."[14] For Frank B. Wilderson III, such histories set up a binary of "Black" and "Human," rendering the descendant's position "a paradigmatic impossibility in the Western Hemisphere, indeed, in the world."[15] This is one way to think geographically in view of the colonial and diasporic histories that generate contemporary conditions. Given, however, the irrepressible ways in which aggrieved communities produce heterotopias in defiance of catastrophic historical narratives as well as in opposition to powerful coalitions of political and corporate interests, Black/Human is not the only recourse for framing the cartographic present.[16] Moving beyond this binary—and doing so without losing sight of its instructive validity—necessitates careful intervention, beginning, in the present instance, with the interrogation of geographic paradigms that conflate a privileged ethnicity with a discrete territory, space in which a dominant group establishes large exclusionary zones even as it requires the presence of the other for the purpose of self-recognition (since identity depends on contrastive relationship) in addition to the fulfillment of subordinate economic roles. Here, such interrogation brings us face-to-face with the idea of the nation.

Everyday notions of the world's geography nearly always privilege discrete nation-states that exist as subsets of regions associated with, if not dominated by, ethnic communities and genealogies. This remains true even in a world of shifting borders and transnational populations. Such formations embed racial and gender hierarchies that wield an often invisible power with respect to who may "rightfully" inhabit a given territory, who may settle, own property, accumulate wealth, and who, if permitted access, must occupy the margins and perform a fixed set of tasks. As I address at length in this book's conclusion, such questions continue to vex U.S. nationhood two decades into the twenty-first century. Numerous scholars have contributed to the interrogation of the nation as a dominant geographical conception, exposing the politics and technologies behind its invention and demonstrating how its naturalization over time mystifies structures of privilege and exclusion. Benedict Anderson's work in this field has been foundational: this study, concerned as it is with the white supremacist assumptions of the American nation's territorial myth, is a clear beneficiary of *Imagined Communities: Reflections on the Origin and Spread of Nationalism* (1983). But study of the nation-state also entails the study of its alternatives, including nonstate notions of national community. Accordingly, my inquiry is greatly indebted to scholars of the African diaspora, notably Édouard Glissant, Stuart Hall, and Paul Gilroy, who have proposed nonwhite, supranational, heterotopic geographies in which African peoples have established cultural spaces that do more than simply counter the historically captive conditions of the diaspora—that assert, in fact, a free identity that does more than react to conditions of enslavement and exile. More recently, in *Demonic Grounds: Black Women and the Cartographies of Struggle* (2006), Katherine McKittrick has sought to highlight the agency of the black female subject by examining the ways in which a hierarchical "placing" of blackness has by no means foreclosed the subjugated individual as "integral to the production of space."[17] McKittrick is particularly helpful in the ways her reading of a text such as *Incidents in the Life of a Slave Girl* locates the microcosm of an individual's "body-space" in the macrocosm of collective resistance. My inquiry has also benefited from the challenges posed by Arlene R. Keizer in *Black Subjects: Identity Formation in the Contemporary Narrative of Slavery* (2004) and Michelle M. Wright in *Physics of Blackness: Beyond the Middle Passage Epistemology* (2015), who assess the Middle Passage as a master narrative that remains in large part dependent on Eurocentric history and that, while representing an African collective, promotes an essentialist approach to what it means to be black.[18]

For Keizer and Wright as for McKittrick, the countergeographies of the diaspora require critical intervention with respect to understanding them as inventive and elective as opposed to captive cartographies. In "Freedom Is a Secret: The Future Usability of the Underground," an essay that principally concerns Marlene NourbeSe Philip's *Harriet's Daughter* but also explicates the subterranean condition of Ralph Ellison's protagonist in *Invisible Man*, McKittrick proposes that we understand the "underground" as an oppositional epistemology that "reframes spatial knowledge" vis-à-vis "seductive and comfortable geographies of domination and ownership."[19] Although the underground forms in response to a white supremacist spatial order, and although the peril of becoming "lost" in the space of fluid refuge is ever-present, McKittrick cautions us against reading the underground as an impaired form of geographical knowledge, and therefore as evidence of an agentless condition. "Geographic ignorance is an impossibility in the underground because this strategy of subversively claiming and living unmapped routes demands that black subjects are, in fact, intimately aware of their surroundings—albeit on different terms than we may know." She suggests further that "loss of direction, *within* white supremacy" reflects a state of ignorance only as defined by the spatial order against which the underground forms.[20] To "lose direction" is a cognitively productive phase of gaining place and mobility within a reinvented frame of reference for which the invisible man's cellar serves as heuristic. The concept of *flight* that I develop in this book is compatible with McKittrick's idea of the underground, as it exhibits a double emphasis: first, on movement (under duress) away from intensities of bondage within the larger structures of oppression; second, on the written word that, while speaking as it can to other, typically isolated, denizens of the underground, would cross from an underground to an aboveground order, and that would effect an epistemic fracture of the latter in the process.[21]

By placing the assumed, inscribed, constructed readership at the inquiry's center, this study follows paths admirably established by Robert Stepto in *From Behind the Veil: A Study of Afro-American Narrative* (1979), William

L. Andrews in *To Tell a Free Story: The First Century of Afro-American Autobiography, 1760–1865* (1986), and Saidiya V. Hartman in *Scenes of Subjection: Terror, Slavery, and Self-Making in Nineteenth-Century America* (1997).[22] All three call attention to problems that inhere in the reader's reception of what the victim of slavery has to say about his or her experience: to abolish slavery or, in the postslave period, to dismantle race-based hierarchies, it is not enough for black authors to compel acknowledgment of their human status, for there remains the question of what sort of world, institutionally speaking, author and reader share, especially when their more or less abstract "common humanity" (assuming nominal transcendence of Wilderson's Black/Human binary) is separated by a color line.[23] Building on this scholarship, my readings attend minutely to the geographical situations of authors and readerships and abide by the assumption that the author (narrator) / reader dynamic is fraught with distances that are always to some degree epistemologically unbridgeable, however successful a given text may prove in moving its audience in specific affective and political directions.[24] Such unbridgeability is particularly evident when black authors address white audiences. But authors who principally inscribe black audiences, such as David Walker in his *Appeal* and Ida B. Wells-Barnett in *Crusade for Justice*, must also confront a sense of disconnection with readers at a spatial or generational remove, who can only be reached by the printed page.[25]

In the slave narrative genre (and those narratives that evolve from it), distance and difference commonly divide those who write from those who read. My discussion will therefore repeatedly return to the issue of how we hear the voices of those who are or have been situated in the space of enslavement or for whom the barracoon has figured in their genealogy. My own "position of enunciation" (to borrow Stuart Hall's useful phrase) is that of a European American of Dutch, German, and English ancestry; here, however, I propose no uniform formula as to who "we" are beyond the assumption that virtually no one who feels motivated to read in the genres generated by the African diaspora has not been profoundly shaped by that history and the color lines that determine the geographies through which we as individuals move.[26] "We" may or may not be genetic descendants of slaves or slaveholders (or both) but are manifestly the inheritors of a world built on slave labor, and thus the oldest slave testimony has something to tell us about the material order by which we find ourselves environed. Within this frame of reference my questions are as follows: What spatial and therefore ideological relationships do slave narratives and their legatees propose between first-person narrators and their inscribed readerships? By positing a "fugitive" author and "free" reader, must they reify a distance that can*not* be bridged, orientations in space unlikely to be resolved? To what degree and by what means do fugitive authors invite readers to imagine the spaces through which they move, and in what ways do such invitations expose space as configured toward racial and gender oppression? Does the fugitive corridor persuasively lead to an open space in a narrative of redemptive suffering? Does it convey readers to a counter-nation of sustainable settlement and reconciliation? In the service of wish-fulfillment fantasy, does it compel visions of a promised land? In the service of reminiscence, does it encourage utopian views of a pre-slavery past? Does the corridor extend indefinitely without release? Or does it culminate in visions of death, a more or less literal dead end?

A book about the geographies of the slave narrative and its literary descendants could expand in many directions, and it would be easy to justify parallel consideration of all sorts of writing on either side of the color line. I have narrowed my inquiry to texts that feature (with some exceptions) first-person narration, that involve geographic mobility under some species of duress, and that speak from—or of—spaces constrained by forces of oppression. Chapter 1, "Signifying Space: Geographies of Domination and Resistance," interrogates the trope of expansive free space open to white settlement promoted by figures such as Benjamin Franklin and Thomas Jefferson and celebrated by the founders of an Anglo-American literary canon and early nationalist historiography. Against this trope I provide a brief survey of the countergeographies that, beginning with *David Walker's Appeal*, arise in black literary expression. In chapter 2, "Voices from the Global South," I examine the ways in which Phillis Wheatley in *Poems on Various Subjects, Religious and Moral* (1773) and Olaudah Equiano in *The Interesting Narrative of the Life of Olaudah Equiano, or Gustavus Vassa, the African* (1789) "remember" Africa in an acquired literary English whose spatial lexicon encodes a Eurocentric colonial geography against which both must construct a testimonial personhood. Doubts that have been raised concerning Equiano's African origin (was he born in South Carolina rather than present-day Nigeria?) are in my reading immaterial to an analysis that focuses on the strategies by which both writers address a predominantly white Anglophone readership in a language that, with respect to slave travel, is always already figurative, cast in an obligatory narrative of Christian "deliverance." Although never technically a fugitive and not free during the period of her greatest productivity, Phillis Wheatley carves out a space of qualified liberty as one who adopts a tone of moral authority in her mastery of Augustan poetic conventions. Likewise appropriating a Christian authority, Equiano narrates his abduction, survival of the Middle Passage, and naturalization to a culture in which he is able to take command of first-person discursive forms and promote an understanding of "Africa" as morally and geographically continuous with an irresistibly colonizing Europe.

Pursuing the problematic of audience, I discuss, in chapter 3, "Slave State to Free," David Walker's bid to invoke a captive, geographically dispersed black audience, Frederick Douglass's rhetorical engagements of Northern white abolitionists, former slave masters, and free people of color, and Harriet Jacobs's ambivalent appeal to a Northern white female readership. In different ways, Walker, Douglass, and Jacobs all work to disrupt the easy binary of slave/free and demonstrate the degree to which writing encodes command of social space. In Douglass's three autobiographical narratives, moreover, we see a struggle for control over the fugitive slave narrative, which had come into being as a white-sponsored formulaic literary genre; this struggle is prophetic of how people of color will redraw the map of the (white) republic of letters. My attention shifts in chapter 4, "Domestic Uplift and Escape Abroad," to Booker T. Washington, *The Story of My Life and Work* (1900, 1901) and *Up from Slavery* (1901), Ida B. Wells-Barnett, *Crusade for Justice* (1928), and W. E. B. Du Bois, *The Souls of Black Folks* (1903), *Darkwater: Voices from Within the Veil* (1920), *Dusk of Dawn* (1940), and *The Autobiography of W. E. B. Dubois* (1968). Addressing readerships on either side of the color line, Wells-Barnett fashions a narrative that reprises a traditional theme of escape from rural South to urban North, whereas Washington and Du Bois (at least through *Darkwater*) propose competing visions of a black nationalist enclave, one that preserves cultural associations with the Black Belt epicenter of American slave history. My analysis frames their ideological differences as rooted in the deep geography of what they represent as their respective family histories and their own migratory paths—which for Du Bois culminates in flight to Ghana and repudiation of his American citizenship.

In chapter 5, "Notes from Underground: Richard Wright, Ralph Ellison, James Baldwin, Malcolm X," I examine the changing relationship that male mid-twentieth-century black authors, able to secure contracts with major publishing houses, establish with an expanding and predominantly white reading public, a development signaled by the Book-of-the-Month Club's promotion of Richard Wright's *Native Son* (1940) and *Black Boy* (1945). I read Ralph Ellison's *Invisible Man* (1952) as a revision and extension of *The Man Who Lived Underground* (1942) and examine James Baldwin's *Notes of a Native Son* (1955) as a variation on *Native Son* and *Black Boy*. Parallel to these discussions, I address *The Autobiography of Malcolm X* (1965) as testimony that complements that of Wright, Ellison, and Baldwin but from the perspective of an activist and nonprofessional author whose path to the printed page began in a jail cell. Following in the wake of Washington and Du Bois, these six midcentury masculinist narratives are remarkable for the ways in which they suggest the failure (if not indeed the destructiveness) of early-century uplift ideals. In their representations of lethal rural and urban space, they conjure vivid memories of enslavement and post-Reconstruction, laying the foundations of the Afro-pessimist vision of a permanent and carceral color-lineated America. At the same time, all four authors cultivate an international readership in hopes of appealing to a cosmopolitan judgment that might shame their native land onto paths of reformation. As this study shows, the history of the book (and print publication in all forms: newspaper, magazine, pamphlet, and broadside) is relevant to all phases of African American testimony; the emergence of these four authors as mass-market celebrities illuminates the larger history of the black published word.[27]

Finally, in chapter 6, "Next Worlds: Toni Morrison and Octavia Butler," I examine the genre of the neo-fugitive-slave narrative as Toni Morrison and Octavia Butler have fashioned it in view of space as occupied by men and women in mixed company, but also in view of the spatial configurations of black women's lives. While assessing themes that pervade Morrison's entire oeuvre, the discussion focuses on *Song of Solomon* (1977) and *Beloved* (1987), two novels that together comprise a range of geographies—from slave ship hold and plantation scene to the bottomlands of escape, from the prison compound to the wood-frame house of the rural black district, and from the freehold farm of Reconstruction to the twentieth-century industrial city whose black residents increasingly challenge white municipal authority. I follow with a reading of three works by Octavia Butler: first, *Kindred* (1979), an allegory of the Maryland slave past that shatters the present of 1970s Los Angeles, then, in tandem, *Parable of the Sower* (1993) and *Parable of the Talents* (1998), dystopian reappraisals of nearly every historic American geographical trope, as Butler envisions a future of intensified class conflict and increasingly complicated color lines. My epilogue, "Color outside the Lines," addresses persistent geographies of exclusion and speculates concerning future reception of the othered voice in the context of a racially fluid if also toxically divided twenty-first-century American nation. Against all that reasonably seduces us to visualize a distempered and dystopian postrepublic, however, I conclude this study mindful of what James Clifford has identified as his own commitment as a social inquirer, which may serve others seeking to define the vocation of human inquiry generally—namely, "to open space for cultural futures, for the recognition of emergence."[28] And here I read "emergence" to signify an order that defies our accumulated disappointments, our learned and fearful prognostications.

How do we hear the voices of the enslaved? How do we hear the descendent voices of those who write from spaces shaped by the African diaspora? What draws us to a testimonial archive that compels us to acknowledge the persistence of what Du Bois has called the "social heritage of slavery"?[29] Does the literary and moral achievement of this archive seem to suggest that everything will be all right in the end—that differences of race, class, region, and generation can in time be mostly set aside? By focusing on the geographical dimensions of the author/reader relationship, this study aims to preserve the otherness of the fugitive voice and to challenge readings that implicitly take these texts as evidence of the indomitable spirit of the human subject in a world that, guided by Enlightenment doctrine, universal reason, and democratic views, evolves in the direction of a secular utopia. While acknowledging the degree to which the former slave's words have become the canonized expression of a consensus democratic literary heritage, and while honoring the good-faith capacity of readers across the color line to take those words to heart, my readings look for opportunities to defamiliarize these narratives, with a view to the enduring and instructive discomfort they offer their readerships. The reader needs to hear their inscriptions of distance as well as their assertions of proximity. It will be impossible not to celebrate these texts for their manifestations of discernment, moral intelligence, and supreme human courage, but my goal is also to perceive in and through them evidence of formidable structures of oppression—structures that, to this day, operate through systems of differential geography. The antidemocracies of American space are abundantly voiced in this literature, but so too are visions of release: to freely elective movement, to possession of a fertile and sustaining earth, to citizenship in local, national, and global communities. To quote W. E. B. Du Bois, a virtuoso of the understatement, in the "Forethought" to *The Souls of Black Folk*, such visions are "not without interest" to readers who enter into partnership with these texts.[30]

Chapter 1

✦

Signifying Space

Geographies of Domination and Resistance

White Space

Before entering the constrained geography of testimonies written in the slave narrative tradition, it will be useful to examine the fabled expansiveness of the New World as it figures in white literary practice. Indeed, the term "New World," with its vigorous implication that space is available for a redemptive iteration of the Old World, serves as an apt entry point—and here we may include the whole array of *New* place names: New England, New Spain, New France, New Netherlands, New Amsterdam, New York, New Canaan, and so on. Although a revisionist scrutiny of Christopher Columbus has diminished if not dismissed his role as heroic discoverer, place names that fossilize imperial reference have not disappeared from the map of former colonies, and the idea that the Western Hemisphere is comparatively "new" lives on in narratives that look upon Europe as instigator of world-historical events. Underscoring the term's Eurocentricity and the instrumentalist cartography that it implies, I invoke "New World" in my analysis to emphasize the novelty of the Americas to migrants from Europe and Africa alike. As Édouard Glissant demonstrates, the term "new" can have ironic counternarrative application: "Our new world," he observes in *Caribbean Discourse*, "was the trader's ocean."[1] By highlighting the white supremacist ideology that pervades Eurocentric depictions of New World space, this chapter contributes to the ongoing task of denaturalizing the idea that Europeans are entitled to territories their navigation has made accessible to them. In recent decades, legatees of Euro-American privilege have been prompted (with some success) to reconsider that sense of entitlement. Given, however, the unfading nostalgia for an America abounding in "new horizons" and the perennial exaltation among entrepreneurial circles of "the pioneer spirit," entitlement remains an active element of U.S. national character.

To anyone with a critical understanding of modern world history, it can hardly come as a revelation that traditional notions of American space privilege the settler doctrine that continental interiors are there for the taking. Still, it is instructive to review articulations of this doctrine as they appear in eighteenth-, nineteenth-, and twentieth-century writing, as to do so facilitates a just recognition of its remarkable persistence. North America was by no means the only stage on which settler ideologies played out: as Mary Louise Pratt has shown, the fantasy of "free" overseas space was a structural component of the European colonial enterprise throughout the world. As much as by brute military acquisition, seizure of such space proceeded by epistemologies that reinforced the sense of entitlement supported by royal commissions and evangelical mandates. In Pratt's analysis, deep possession of overseas territory begins with aggressive systems of knowledge formation (Cartesian geometry, Linnaean taxonomy) in which "universal" concept precedes local fact. Specifically, she focuses on a phase of Europe's "planetary consciousness" arising in the first third of the eighteenth century, "marked by an orientation toward interior exploration and the construction of global-scale meaning through the descriptive apparatus of natural history."[2] European appropriation of the Americas was well under way by the close of the seventeenth century, spurred by seaboard agriculture, mineral extraction, slave trade, and fur trade, as well as by French, Spanish, and British ambitions to extend the reach of empire. Assimilation of American flora, fauna, geography, and climatology to the schema of natural history occurs in writings of Benjamin Franklin and Thomas Jefferson intended to promote inland settlement during the late colonial and early national periods. Their observations, along with those of like-minded theorists of continental expansion, provide the philosophical foundation for what John O'Sullivan in 1845 would identify as the nation's "manifest destiny."[3] As Franklin and Jefferson envisioned it avant la lettre, such destiny was emphatically agrarian and unequivocally white.

To read such texts as Franklin's "Observations Concerning the Increase of Mankind" (1751) and Jefferson's *Notes on the State of Virginia* (1785) in view of the actual racial diversity of eighteenth-century British America is to be impressed by the extent to which leading thinkers imagined a monochrome Anglo-American empire (aligned with Great Britain or not) and the ethnic exclusion required for its realization. Franklin's essay argues that it is the role of the English colonist to fulfill North America's agrarian destiny by subjecting the continent's expanse to ownership and cultivation. A laboring class that might otherwise languish in cities, unable to marry and procreate abundantly and thus reverse a statistical trend by which deaths outweigh births, may buy land cheaply and produce children who will supply the labor to work the land. This progeny in turn will marry, procreate, and repeat the pattern, contributing to the long-term project of subduing the continent, full settlement of which in Franklin's projection "will require many Ages." A slaveholder himself, Franklin deprecates slavery on economic as well as ethical grounds, although his chief moral objection concerns what he sees as its tendency to corrupt the work ethic of whites who assume the master position:

"Slaves . . . pejorate the Families that use them; the white Children become proud, disgusted with Labour, and being educated in Idleness, are unfit to get a Living by Industry." Toward the end of the essay, Franklin makes clear that his vision of a white North America is as much based on aesthetic preference as economic and moral grounds. Rejecting, among other people of color, even those Europeans "of what we call a swarthy Complexion" (curiously, the list includes Swedes, Russians, and Germans as well as French, Spanish, and Italians), he would restrict the population to Anglo-Saxons, who

> make the principal Body of White People on the Face of the Earth. I could wish their Numbers were increased. And while we are, as I may call it, *Scouring* our Planet, by clearing *America* of Woods, and so making this Side of our Globe reflect a brighter Light to the Eyes of Inhabitants in *Mars* or *Venus*, why should we in the Sight of Superior Beings, darken its People? why increase the Sons of *Africa*, by Planting them in *America*, where we have so fair an Opportunity, by excluding all Blacks and Tawneys, of increasing the lovely White and Red? But perhaps I am partial to the Complexion of my Country, for such Kind of Partiality is natural to Mankind.

"Red" in this context does not refer to Native Americans: whereas in "Increase of Mankind" Franklin conceives the indigenous population as a hunting society that could probably subsist on the margins of white settlement, in *The Autobiography of Benjamin Franklin* he envisions their disappearance entirely. Dismayed by the spectacle of drunkenness among natives he meets on the Pennsylvania frontier for the purposes of establishing settlement boundaries (his party having brought a propitiatory supply of rum to the occasion), he conjectures that alcohol may serve a higher purpose: "If it be the Design of Providence to extirpate these Savages in order to make room for the Cultivators of the Earth, it seems not improbable that Rum may be the appointed Means."[4] It is thus that Franklin contributes to the doctrine of the vanishing Indian.[5]

In *Notes on the State of Virginia*, Jefferson imagines a burgeoning agrarian nation stretching westward in accordance with principles identical with those of Franklin: the North American continent is virtually limitless and will require centuries to settle; it must be settled by a self-sustaining, landowning, Anglo-Saxon populace. Although Jefferson confines his analysis to the State of Virginia, he writes with the awareness that he sets an example for the surveying of other former colonies as well as the unorganized tracts of the Ohio and Mississippi Valleys. Unlike the Virginia of Robert Beverley, who in 1653 fixed the colony's western border at "the Californian Sea,"[6] Jefferson's Virginia terminates at the banks of the Ohio and Mississippi Rivers. But even to imagine a commonwealth comprising that much territory presages the vision of a continental nation that Jefferson, as president, will act upon in his acquisition of Greater Louisiana and his commission of Lewis and Clark to conduct an inventory of the purchase. *Notes on the State of Virginia* subjects the commonwealth of 1781–83 to geographical, botanic, zoological, sociological, and ethnographic analysis. Impressed as were many Enlightenment thinkers by the power of Linnaean taxonomy to articulate distinctions between and within species, and emboldened by its seeming applicability to the spectrum of human difference, Jefferson ventures into the domain of anthropological inquiry, and it is along these lines that he frames the more notorious pronouncements of *Notes*. His treatment of Native Americans aspires to scientific objectivity: he makes a disciplined effort to distinguish tribes according to region, language group, and way of life, and on anecdotal evidence exalts Indian skills in oratory. In proportion as he ennobles North America's indigenous population, however, Jefferson documents its disappearance: "Spiritous liquors, the small-pox, war, and an abridgement of territory, to a people who lived principally on the spontaneous productions of nature, had committed terrible havoc among them, which generation, under obstacles opposed to it among them, was not likely to make good." As though to absolve European settlement of the responsibility for this decline and situate the native's disappearance in the order of natural cause, Jefferson disputes the thesis that "the lands of this country were taken from them by conquest," insisting rather that transfer in most instances came about through "voluntary sales."[7] Jefferson's failure to acknowledge the coercions that encouraged such sales exposes the conflict of interest between the objective anthropologist and the settlement promoter who himself holds land acquired through a fiction of legitimate purchase.

Although Jefferson's treatment of Native American peoples concludes in genocidal prophecy, his discussion builds on the observations of others and thereby attempts to construct an objective frame of reference; moreover, in his defense of Native Americans against Buffon's portrait of a degenerate human subset, he identifies strengths of intellect and character that merit his culture's esteem. In Jefferson's view, those who survive the onslaught of Anglo-Saxon settlement may be readily and more or less invisibly assimilated to the new biopolitical order.[8] Ethnocentric and disciplinarily flawed as his inquiry into Native American society may be, it is not plagued by the visceral impressionism that characterizes his treatment of Virginia's (and the nation's) black population. Indeed, Jefferson's inquiry into Africans and African-descended peoples never moves beyond a matter of white obsession, namely the question of what makes black people black, and transitions from an inconclusive discussion of biology—does blackness derive from a dermatological layer or does it originate in the blood or bile?—to a fixation on the black face as illegible from the white perspective, a consideration at once aesthetic and epistemological. Jefferson concedes in effect that black is unknowable in proportion as black is *not white*: "Is this difference," he asks, "of no importance? Is it not the foundation of a greater or less share of beauty in the two races?

Are not the fine mixtures of red and white, the expressions of every passion by greater or less suffusions of colour in the one, preferable to that eternal monotony, which reigns in the countenances, that immovable veil of black which covers all the emotions of the other race?" From color Jefferson proceeds to feature, exalting the "flowing hair" and "more elegant symmetry of form" of the idealized Anglo-Saxon body over what he perceives as the animal-like appearance of blacks, citing as proof what he alleges to be "their own judgment in favour of the whites, declared by their preference of them, as uniformly as is the preference of the Oran-ootan for the black women over those of his own species."[9] The notorious orangutan reference, besides casting black people as decidedly subhuman, also brands them as territorial outsiders: although the orangutan is a Southeast Asian–Oceanian species, Jefferson and his readers would chiefly associate nonhuman primates with Africa. From phenotypical feature he proceeds to cite other alleged black differences from the white norm: a tendency to sweat more and urinate less, a greater libido and an ability to function on less sleep than white people require, memory on par with that of whites but weaker capacities of reason, a dull imagination and an affective life ruled by intense but transient emotion. Emphasizing the carnal nature of such emotion, he questions the capacity of black people to form genuinely loving attachments. Physically, intellectually, and emotionally, then, he portrays those of African descent as at best marginally human and in any case exotics in the temperate-zone nation he and his cohort endeavor to build.

As numerous scholars have noted, the urgency of black response, beginning with Benjamin Banneker, to the defamations of *Notes*, query 4, generated a voluminous and impassioned commentary.[10] No response was more passionate and forceful than David Walker's in his *Appeal* (particularly article 1), focusing as it does on Jefferson's likening of black people to apes: "Have you not, Americans, having subjected us under you, added to these miseries, by insulting us in telling us to our face, because we are helpless, that we are not of the human family?" Addressing, on the one hand, a white national readership ("Americans") in a tone of incredulous accusation, he prompts his black audience to take such cognitive action as must form the prelude to a more militant and insurrectionary response, soliciting "each of my brethren, who has the spirit of a man, to buy a copy of Mr. Jefferson's 'Notes on Virginia,' and put it in the hand of his son. For let no one of us suppose that the refutations which have been written by our white friends are enough—they are *whites*—we are *blacks*. We, and the world wish to see the charges of Mr. Jefferson refuted by the blacks *themselves*."[11] Walker's proposition that black fathers instruct black sons in the critical reading and strategic refutation of Jefferson's text is genuinely visionary: with every intention to circulate his pamphlet among an enslaved population, Walker must know that comparatively few black fathers possess the literary skills and filial relationship, much less the means to purchase the book in question, to realize this scenario. But to imagine the very possibility is a political act, one that asserts a right to literacy, family ties, and American settlement. As Robert S. Levine observes, Walker was prescient in his recognition of "the importance of print to the creation of a black nationalist consciousness."[12] Walker's discursive engagements of Jefferson are inseparable from his territorial claim—a claim that, as we shall see in chapter 3, is staked in vigorous opposition to what for Jefferson constituted a final solution: the expulsion of African-descended peoples from the North American continent.

For Jefferson, differences between white and black are irreconcilable given the toxicity of the historic master-slave relationship: "Deep rooted prejudices entertained by the whites; ten thousand recollections, by the blacks, of the injuries they have sustained; new provocations; the real distinctions which nature has made; and many other circumstances, will divide us into parties, and produce convulsions which will probably never end but in the extermination of the one or the other race." Jefferson's remedy is to undertake a program of gradual liberation and exportation of all slaves, "to declare them a free and independent people, and extend to them our alliance and protection" in a country of their own somewhere in West Africa, their place to be taken in North America by a free white labor force selectively recruited from Europe while the nation awaits a population increase from the established Anglo-Saxon stock. As vast as the American continent may be, to forestall an inevitable apocalyptic confrontation, Jefferson recommends that an oceanic distance separate black from white. He imagines such separation as mutually desirable, and that a manumitted people will want to depart rather than share even so expansive a space as North America affords: "If a slave can have a country in this world, it must be any other in preference to that in which he is born to live and labour for another."[13] Jefferson's observation here exhibits an effort to empathize with a subjectivity formed by a heritage of institutional injury, even as he concludes that political atonement cannot be achieved—that a parting of ways is the only cure for an understandable but insoluble enmity.

Like Franklin, then, Jefferson imagines North American geography in the service of apartheid at once racial and political. As with Franklin, aesthetic preference rooted in Anglo-Saxon ethnic narcissism factors irrationally into this position. His recommended exclusions pertain not only to those of African ancestry (Native Americans being likely to disappear naturally) but also to potential immigrants from those parts of Europe unacquainted with if not hostile to republican principles. In query 8, "Population," he expresses a reluctance to recruit indiscriminately from Europe, appealing to the reader's patience with the natural process by which an Anglo-Saxon community populates the land from a "single stock" whose institutions derive from "the freest principles of the English constitution, with others derived from natural right and natural reason." To permit the population to grow from an English nucleus that has rejected the monarchist preferences of the Old World would make for a polity "more homogenous, more peaceable, more durable" than otherwise.[14] For Jefferson as for Franklin, who would exclude even "swarthy" Europeans from nations of Protestant persuasion, race goes well beyond black and white. Language, religion, politics, and genetics all play a part.

Nearly every canonical Anglo-American author would reaffirm some variation of Jefferson's vision of a Protestant, antimonarchical, agrarian America in the decades before the Civil War. In *The Prairie* (1827), the third installment of the five-novel *Leather-Stocking Tales*, the first epic treatment of the western frontier and the most persistently influential, James Fenimore Cooper restates the argument Franklin and Jefferson make with respect to continental settlement and occupation. The Louisiana Purchase, Cooper observes in his opening passage,

> had made us the masters of a belt of fertile country, which, in the revolutions of the day, might have become the property of a rival nation. It gave us sole command of the great thoroughfare of the interior, and placed the countless tribes of savages, who lay along our borders, entirely within our controul; it reconciled conflicting rights, and quieted national distrusts; it opened a thousand avenues to the inland trade, and to the waters of the Pacific; and, if ever time or necessity shall require a peaceful division of this vast empire, it assures us a neighbor that will possess our language, our religion, our institutions, and it is also to be hoped, our sense of political justice.[15]

For Cooper as for Franklin and Jefferson, an American nation is not well served by diversity. Rather than affording room for a plurality of peoples, languages, and cultures, North America's vastness provides the strongest argument that the continent should be the preserve of a dominant ethnic monoculture. Memory of the rival claims of Catholic monarchical Spain and France contributes no doubt to this fear of difference: in *The Last of the Mohicans* (1826), Cooper would remind his readership of the bloody confrontations associated with the War of Empire and the foolishness of trusting even so refined a specimen of French civilization as the Marquis de Saint-Veran. But the novel also warns of the perils of diversity within the citizenry's predominantly white genome and offers Cora Munroe, who inherits from her mother a fractional and scarcely "visible" African ancestry, as an example of the sad complications of the mixed-race individual. In killing her off and thus depriving Uncas (who must also die) of a worthy mate—worthy, that is, if such a union did not further a trend toward miscegenation—he exalts the memory of the Mohicans even as he documents their genealogy's extinction. Cora and Uncas exemplify high intelligence, astute decision-making, and physical courage, but it is the pure-white weak younger sister, Alice, and the genteel, belatedly war-hardened Southerner, Duncan Hayward, who survive to marry and populate the land.[16] Their grandson, Duncan Middleton, appears early in *The Prairie* as a captain in the military detachment stationed in the Louisiana territories to oversee an orderly transition.

The opening paragraph of *The Prairie* is remarkable for another reason: the reiteration of "us" and "our" demonstrates that Cooper writes for a readership located within the monoculture he designates as rightful claimant of the future continental nation. Throughout *Geographies of Flight*, I am concerned with the cartography of a narrator-reader relationship that in the slave narrative tradition typically involves an author/narrator speaking across geo-cultural lines, from one map to another, and against many barriers to cartographic resolution. It is important, therefore, to note the ways in which an author such as Cooper positions a readership on common spatiotemporal cultural ground. In the passage quoted above, Cooper assumes that anyone reading his page will share political and religious principles pertaining to Anglo-Saxon, republican Protestantism. In the final clause of the passage he appears to concede that some readers may not share his antislavery sentiments, but such differences, in his view, are fated to be worked out within the Anglo-American community. At the time *The Leather-Stocking Tales* first appeared, an ability to read combined with the leisure to consume historical fiction would have favored this ethnic demographic. From Franklin to Cooper forward into the twentieth century, an author-reader rapport built on an assumption that "our kind" is entitled to "our space" pervades much of the writing about a national future imagined as the inevitable occupation of the continent. As the material realization of that occupation, moreover, the geographical reach of print culture made it possible for an elite to define its vision as that of a national destiny.[17] To be sure, there were variations in the way such a destiny was imagined—the biggest controversy involving the expansion of slavery into the Louisiana Territory and the lands acquired by the Mexican-American war—but even among Northerners solidly in favor of abolition, the equation of geographic space with white dominion and mobility exists as a bedrock conviction. With Ralph Waldo Emerson's *English Traits* (1856), moreover, "our space" assumes a transnational global reach founded in a doctrine of white supremacy that for Emerson and his white liberal contemporaries is so self-evident as to be invisible.

English Traits is one of several well-known American books about English national character penned by Anglo-American authors in solidarity with an ethno-literary heritage. Washington Irving's *The Sketchbook of Geoffrey Crayon* (1820), Harriet Beecher Stowe's *Sunny Memories of Foreign Lands* (1854), Nathaniel Hawthorne's *Our Old Home: A Series of English Sketches* (1863), and Henry James's *English Hours* (1905) belong to this genre; all combine accounts of travel in the United Kingdom with an impressionistic ethnography of the British people from the vantage point of an American whose Yankee identity sets the traveler at a critical if also appreciative remove from the object of study. Such perspective permits a depiction of local eccentricity but also, and more importantly, a celebration of commonalities that make the English and therefore their American descendants heroic human examples, a people whose genius finds expression in the likes of William Shakespeare, Isaac Newton, and the Duke of Wellington. As Hawthorne's title suggests, these works are published with the assumption that their readership shares the author's English ancestry and Protestant faith. Emerson's contribution to this genre is based on two visits to the United Kingdom as well as his lifelong immersion in the literature and thought of England and long-standing transatlantic contact with British luminaries such as Thomas Carlyle. His demand, in such essays as "The American Scholar" (1837) and "The Divinity School Address" (1838), for an American culture that differentiates itself from British antecedents does not prevent him from exalting English character. Rather than worship English ways and conventions, he celebrates the force of a national character that in North America has set itself to the task of creating modes of life and expression that are uniquely and heroically American. This allows Emerson to hypothesize a transnational ethnic identity that encounters no space that it hesitates to claim as its own. "The American," Emerson writes in *English Traits*, "is only the continuation of the English genius into new conditions, more or less propitious."[18] Revelatory in this remark is the geographical implication of "the continuation."

In proposing the Anglo-Saxon as the global master race, Emerson acknowledges that the English represent a fusion of several European ethnicities arriving in waves from Germany, Scandinavia, and France, but argues that the resultant hybrid has proven the most vigorous and durable as well as the most mobile type of the modern era. "The English derive their pedigree from such a range of nationalities," Emerson observes, "that there needs sea-room and land-room to unfold the varieties of talent and character. Perhaps the ocean serves as a galvanic battery, to distribute acids at one pole and alkalies at the other. So England tends to accumulate her liberals in America, and her conservatives at London."[19] Emerson's penchant for argument by analogy is on full display here and with it a tendency he shares with others to pronounce categorically on matters of race. When authors such as Franklin, Jefferson, Cooper, and Emerson affirm a white supremacist presumption, one is struck by the degree to which they assert rather than argue the truth of this position. Citing *English Traits* as a central document in white racial discourse, Nell Irvin Painter notes how frequently Emerson stumbles into contradiction as he idealizes a people whose physical beauty and intellectual acumen coexist alongside a proclivity to resolve disputes by massacring their adversaries. And as Painter emphasizes, rather than lament his tribe's homicidal tendencies, Emerson celebrates the Saxon capacity to slaughter and enslave.[20] Under no anticipated discursive challenge from those presumed to share his English ancestry, Emerson thus remarks to his reader: "It is race, is it not? that puts the hundred millions of India under the dominion of a remote island in the north of Europe."[21] He invokes thereby a mystical explanation of an asymmetric power relationship driven (as his mystification would seem to prevent him from recognizing) by greed as opposed to destiny. He suppresses, moreover, what at some level must be his awareness of the brute apparatus of the colonial enterprise beneath the ethnic sentimentality that pervades this genre of travel ethnography. Emerson the abolitionist subscribes to a theory of race that necessitates the master-slave relationship, that reinscribes that relationship wherever the English choose to settle.

Like most white Northern antislavery liberals, Emerson found himself at an impasse with respect to African-descended people and their place in an American republic. Among his casual generalizations in *English Traits* on the topic of race, his one observation concerning black people is telling: "Race in the negro is of appalling importance." In view of Emerson's sensitivity to the etymology of words, this is a resonant statement. "Language is fossil poetry," he writes in "The Poet," drawing attention to the metaphor that sleeps beneath the surface of commonplace utterance.[22] Given his encouragement that we consider a word's figurative status as we process its meaning, we must read "appall" as "to whiten" or "to make pale" as well as "to shock." The sentence thus proposes that the black person's importance consists in making white people white, in shocking the white person into a consciousness of whiteness, of one's racial identity as dependent on this binary relationship.[23] In the context of his cheerful discussion of the English community's triumphantly global eminent domain, of Anglo-Saxon self-determination through an exercise of self-justifying power, this isolated and troubled remark about black humanity suggests that Emerson senses a debt, a dependency, a guilt, perhaps, that the Anglo-American cannot easily discharge, and from which an Anglo-American literary intelligentsia seeks refuge in the free white space of an apartheid American continent.

Even when Anglo-American writers do not explicitly identify the spaces of North America as white, they employ figures of speech that assert untrammeled mobility and settler entitlement which pertain to white people exclusively. "Eastward I go only by force; but westward I go free," Henry David Thoreau observes in "Walking," invoking the narrative of European migration across an ocean and over a continent, and the deliverance from Old World monarchisms and hierarchies to a democracy of merit associated with east-to-west exodus. The fact that Thoreau's most ambitious engagement of the wild involved an eastward trek to Maine suggests the degree to which "east" and "west" serve as the poles of an entirely figurative cartography, just as, in the following passage, Thoreau sublimates brute colonization of the Western Hemisphere to the adventurous individual's pursuit, as "walker," of novelty and self-culture: "Perchance there will appear to the traveller" amid the large free spaces of the American continent "something, he knows not what, of *læta* and *glabra*—of joyous and serene, in our very faces. Else, to what end does the world go on, and why was America discovered?"[24] Thoreau was acutely aware of the fugitive migration of black people from the South and could not have failed to recognize that not all who walk can do so with the license modeled in this essay. But "Walking," directed as it is to a readership whose mobility is not subject to surveillance, assumes a geography of open horizons that need not be qualified as "white." Similarly Margaret Fuller, in *Summer on the Lakes, in 1843*, writes of her hike along the south shore of Lake Michigan: "There was a grandeur in the feeling that I might continue that walk, if I had any seven-leagued mode of conveyance to save fatigue, for hundreds of miles without an obstacle and without a change." On the Illinois prairie, Fuller and her companions are "free to imagine themselves in Elysium."[25]

Of the writers who responded to Emerson's invitation to conceive the New World as dream space conducive to the citizenry's recovery of an innate divinity and original relationship to the universe, none approached the radical egalitarianism of Walt Whitman in *Leaves of Grass*. Yet his poetry's inclusiveness and affective generosity coexist uncomfortably with the explicit racism of Whitman's Brooklyn *Daily Eagle* and *Daily Times* editorials and the observations he made as a very old man in conversation with Horace Traubel. This racism runs counter to passages in the poems that exhibit an imagination impatient with petty bigotries and celebrate a cartography of human diversity. The catalogs Whitman compiles in "Song of Myself" represent the vastness of American space by staging a synchronicity of activity extending across regional, class, gender, and ethnic lines—urban and rural, East and West, seacoast and prairie, gentry and working class, white people, black people, native Americans, good citizen and condemned felon, heterosexual and homosexual. "To the cotton-field drudge or cleaner of privies I lean," he writes in "Song of Myself,"

> On his right cheek I put the family kiss,
> And in my soul I swear I never will deny him.

In section 10 of the same poem, the poet depicts himself as offering sanctuary to a fugitive slave, nursing him to health, clothing and feeding him, before setting him on the path north, all the while treating him as equal: "I had him sit next me at table, my fire-lock lean'd in the corner." And in section 33, a fantasia of free continental and social mobility in which the poet asserts his power to "become" anyone at all on the basis of his knowledge of human joy and suffering, he appropriates a vignette familiar to readers of abolitionist propaganda:

> I am the hounded slave, I wince at the bite of the dogs,
> Hell and despair are upon me, crack and crack again the marksmen,
> I clutch the rails of the fence, my gore drips, thinn'd with the ooze of
>   my skin,
> I fall on the weeds and stones,
> The riders spur their unwilling horses, haul close,
> Taunt my dizzy ears and beat me violently over the head with whip-stocks.

One might suspect that Whitman's sympathy with the fugitive slave would be further enhanced by his experience as one whose sexuality had acquainted him with surreptitious routes, as we see in the *Calamus* poems, where lovers must tread "paths untrodden" and move "by stealth in some wood" or find refuge "back of a rock in the open air."[26] His sympathy with the oppressed speaks eloquently in the "Lucifer" passage of "The Sleepers," lines that give voice to the bondman's deep, unappeasable grievance and register what Whitman intuited as the black righteous insurrectionary presence in antebellum America.[27]

Given his affirmations, in "Song of Myself" and many other poems, of a democracy of radical inclusiveness—given moreover his discernment in the body of the slave on the auction block "the start of populous states and rich republics," a line from section 7 of "I Sing the Body Electric" that would appear to prophesy the citizenly destiny of black people[28]—the vehemence of Whitman's white supremacist views can come as a surprise. In 1847, against the extension of slavery into territories gained through the Mexican-American war, Whitman advocates on behalf of "the grand body of white workingmen, the millions of mechanics, farmers, and operatives of our country." In so doing he wishes to save the Northern worker from the embarrassment experienced by the Southern white laborer "put on a par with the negro slave mechanic." Such humiliation in Whitman's view is self-evident: "It is of no use to reason abstractly on this fact—farther than to say that the pride of the American freeman, poor though he be, will not comfortably stand such degradation."[29] It would be consoling to regard this editorial as the peculiar product of the times and the predilections of the *Daily Eagle*'s readership, and it would be convenient to read the poems Whitman writes in the course of the next decade as representing a transcendence of ethnic meanness. Perhaps, for the moments of empathy and insight they inscribe, such poems do enact a vision that has triumphed over the worst debilities of a racist reflex. But in a May 6, 1858, editorial, "Prohibition of Colored Persons," appearing in the *Daily Times* on the occasion of Oregon's application for statehood, Whitman reaffirmed that "White Labor will not demean itself to stand, walk, sit, work, or what not, side by side with the Blacks," stating his thesis as a rhetorical question: "Is not America for the Whites?"[30] Much later, moreover, in a conversation reported by Horace Traubel, Whitman's white supremacist vision of American space and futurity assumes a chillingly genocidal tone. "The nigger, like the Injun," he declares on September 8, 1888, "will be eliminated: it is the law of races, history, what-not: always so far inexorable—always to be." To this observation Traubel responds, "That sounds like Darwin," to which Whitman rejoins, "Does it? It sounds like me too."[31] Whitman proceeds to observe that the French and Spanish can reproduce successfully with Africans, as can Native Americans, but that the Southern Anglo-American cannot—or should not, despite evidence that such mixing was pervasive and irreversible. Invoking what remains for him a mystic ridding process, he maintains that U.S. racial destiny is irrefutably white. Like Franklin and Jefferson before him, Whitman projects an Anglo-Saxon America as the inevitable product of a natural order that discards the less hardy type.[32]

Four years after Whitman's offhand prediction that "the law of races" will lead to the extinction of America's people of color, Frederick Jackson Turner read "The Significance of the Frontier in American History" before a meeting of the American Historical Association at the World's Columbian Exposition, organized in commemoration of the five-hundredth anniversary of Columbus's landfall in the Americas. The event took place in Chicago, the sprawling metropolis that had rapidly arisen from the frontier town Margaret Fuller had visited fifty years before, and the temporary buildings constructed along the lakeshore in the Beaux Arts style of the French Second Empire had become known collectively as the "White City." The phrase referred to the gleaming stucco that formed the facade of the exuberant monumental structures, designed by the era's leading European-trained architects, and expressed perhaps no conscious exclusionary intent, but it is noteworthy that African American participation in the fair was a matter of contestation, and ironic that the neighborhoods adjacent to Jackson Park, the site of the exposition, would become a major center of black urban America over the course of the next half-century.[33] The exposition itself constituted an argument as to the meaning of American history, proposing a destiny no longer merely continental but global and aggressively imperial, and inviting the world to take the measure of the nation's cosmopolitan character in its principal heartland city. Turner proposed to those attending his lecture that national character and destiny had been determined by the vigorous activity of settlers along the volatile borderlands of the western frontier. "The existence of an area of free land, its continuous recession, and the advance of American settlement westward, explain American development." What has become known as the "frontier thesis" thus confirms, retrospectively, observations concerning the nation's destined expansion familiar to readers of Franklin, Jefferson, and Cooper. In keeping with his predecessors, Turner advances the supposition of "an area of free land" with little recognition of claims to the land that predate white settlement and that do not conform to Euro-American protocols of legal title. As for the African American component of "American development," the frontier thesis has little to say. Black history for Turner is confined to the closed chapter that is slavery: "When American history comes to be rightly viewed it will be seen that the slavery question is an incident."[34] In what would become a landmark spatial historiography of the United States, black America reduces to a footnote.

Turner was not the only historian to engage a spatial explanation of "American development" that foregrounded a white and chiefly Protestant populace. "Society offered the profile of a long, straggling caravan," observes Henry Adams of the post–Civil War decades, "stretching loosely towards the prairies, its few score of leaders far in advance and its millions of immigrants, negroes, and Indians far in the rear, somewhere in archaic time."[35] Adams's "few score of leaders" comprise an Anglo-American scientific elite, exemplified by Clarence King, director of the U.S. Geological Survey, in partnership with eastern industrial entrepreneurs in mining and transportation, such as Adams's brother, Charles Francis Adams II, president of the Union Pacific from 1884 to 1890.[36] Adams's cartographic metaphor is striking for its combination of space and time: visualizing a mobile American population on a westward-tending map, it locates a white elite in a modern world of their own creation while relegating people of color (including "immigrants," a term that for Adams here chiefly refers to Jews and Southern Europeans) to a premodern epoch in which they may languish or from which emerge in sudden and dangerous insurgency. Adams's frontier thesis, such as he presents it in *The Education of Henry Adams* (1918), is skeptical in ways that Turner's is not, in that he sees the Anglo-Saxon elite as vulnerable to displacement by new arrivals supposedly less scrupulous in their business dealings and more committed to private enterprise than to the welfare of an American republic. But he remains steadfast in the idea that the political and moral leadership of the nation belongs by rights to those of white Anglo-Saxon Protestant derivation.[37]

A similar association of a white American West with the nation's future global role occurs in Willa Cather's *My Ántonia* (1918), published the same year as *The Education of Henry Adams*. Here, too, that role is associated with Anglo-Saxon Protestant foresight. This narrative, based on Cather's childhood and adolescence in Red Cloud, Nebraska, presents itself as the reminiscence of Jim Burden, an attorney for "one of the great Western railways" who lives in New York and who, situated in a powerful corporate position, leverages the agricultural and mineral wealth of the U.S. inland empire. Jim comes by such power genealogically: in his portrait of the farming community of Blackhawk, Nebraska, his Protestant patriarchal grandfather stands out as the wise man among the lot of Scandinavian-Lutheran and Bohemian-Catholic settlers. "The cornfields were far apart in those times, with miles of wild grazing land between. It took a clear, meditative eye like my grandfather's to foresee that they would enlarge and multiply until they would be, not the Shimerdas' cornfields, or Mr. Bushy's, but the world's cornfields; that their yield would be one of the great economic facts, like the wheat crop of Russia, which underlie all the activities of men, in peace or war." The central character, Ántonia Shimerda, the "dark" Bohemian Catholic with whom the Protestant, upwardly mobile Jim forms a sexually confused infatuation, leads a career as a seduced and abandoned woman before undergoing rehabilitation as the wife of a fellow Bohemian immigrant and mother of ten children, locked into patterns of Old World peasantry, "somewhere," as Adams puts it, "in archaic time." Significantly, the one African American in this novel is the iterant musician, Blind d'Arnault, who arrives to lead "the gentlemen" gathered at the hotel ballroom in "some good old plantation songs."[38] The name reflects his condition. The white space of the continental nation remains the object, in *My Ántonia*, of the "clear meditative eye." Like Ántonia, the sightless black musician figures as a retrograde type, a relic of plantation days, with even less claim to an American economic future than Ántonia's rural progeny.

It would be a mistake to overlook black access to this presumably white space, be it settlement of western lands (all-black "exoduster" towns such as Nicodemus, Kansas, and Langston, Oklahoma), or the many black cowboys who worked the cattle trails (much obscured by the typically white cast of the classic western film), or the rare prospector (such as Charles P. Grove) who amassed a fortune in the gold fields.[39] In *Crusade for Justice* (1928), Ida B. Wells-Barnett writes of the migration west of a significant proportion of the Memphis black community in the wake of the "lynching at the Curve": the murder of three grocers who had encroached upon what white businessmen considered their exclusive market. Traveling toward an Oklahoma Territory recently opened for settlement, the emigrants respond in desperation to the mythic lure of free open space.[40] Toni Morrison's 1997 novel *Paradise* creates two fictional Oklahoma all-black towns in which western geography, Black Nationalist community building, individual ambition, gender and class divisions, and notions of racial purity/impurity arrive at a signal impasse in the vast American interior. African American geographies engage narratives that combine open space and liberationist themes with much greater difficulties than do their white counterparts, and often the aspiration must stand in for what is at best an only partially realized deliverance.

Countergeographies

"Much of the Afro-American literary tradition," Henry Louis Gates Jr. observes in *The Signifying Monkey: A Theory of African-American Literary Criticism*, "can be read as successive attempts to create a new narrative space for representing the recurring referent of Afro-American literature, the so-called Black Experience."[41] Reflecting varied but generally oppressive geographic placement, the "narrative space" fashioned to represent that experience has proven extensive, expansive, and adept at responding to evolving legal and political conditions. Against the white spatial imaginary by which a European and chiefly Anglo-Saxon demographic has narrated dominance over the North American continent, black authors have mapped parallel and often vibrant worlds, even as their working geographies have been conceived as a counterdiscourse—narratives and geographies of resistance and survival as well as, occasionally, insurgency, as opposed to narratives and geographies of prosperity. They have had to address an agoraphobia in both the figurative and etymologically literal sense of that term:[42] a fear not only of open spaces that expose black subjects to surveillance and abuse but to the market in black bodies and labor that continues far beyond the Emancipation Proclamation (1863) and ratification of the Thirteenth Amendment (1865). "For the black slave," Houston A. Baker Jr. observes of the African American entrance onto the North American continent, "the white externality provided no ontological or ideological certainties; in fact, it explicitly denied slaves the grounds of being." The space through which newly arrived Africans moved as objects of commerce could hardly have figured as a field of possibility. "Instead of the ebullient sense of a new land offering limitless opportunities," Baker observes, "the slave, staring into the heart of whiteness around him, must have felt as though he had been flung into existence without a human purpose. The white externality must have loomed like the Heideggerian 'nothingness,' the negative foundation of being."[43] To be sure, African Americans, enslaved and free, challenged that externality, and in doing so developed countergeographies that permitted access to North American space and with it the creation of autonomous social ontologies, but the institutional and infrastructural disposition of that space would reflect more or less visible white supremacist ideologies and reinforce historical constraints on black mobility and inhabitation.

Black representations of North American geography tell the story of the black subject's struggle to overcome the commodity status of enslavement, a condition in which a person is reduced to property and thus legally deprived of volitional movement or stasis. A shining continent of open horizons presupposes the citizen's right to free movement and settlement, but the racial basis of slavery in America served to undermine the citizenship claims of all people of African descent, whether bond or free. The identification of blackness with enslavement, and thus noncitizenship, achieved codification with Chief Justice Roger Taney's opinion in *Dred Scott v. Sanford* (1857). Affirming a supposed "universal recognition of 'slavery' as the natural relation of the races" and deprecating the "social monstrosity" of the "free negro," Taney proceeded to the ineluctable asseveration: "A free negro of the African race, whose ancestors were brought to this country and sold as slaves, is not a 'citizen' within the meaning of the Constitution of the United States."[44] A stateless entity—neither wholly person nor object—the black resident lacked a clear geographical quite as much as existential status. As Edlie L. Wong documents in *Neither Fugitive nor Free: Atlantic Slavery, Freedom Suits, and the Legal Culture of Travel*, issues foregrounded by the inevitable occasions of interstate and international transport focused attention on the fundamental question of the black subject's right to dwell: "Conflicts over the freedom of movement were explicitly about the question of black citizenship and black belonging in the United States." Wong quotes Frederick Douglass's 1852 pronouncement as to how the map should appear to black as well as white citizens: "By the constitution of the United States, every free citizen has the right to traverse the whole length and breadth of the Union as freely as if every part of it was his home."[45] But as long as race-based slavery persisted, the free black citizen was not only susceptible to the kind of abduction and enslavement that Solomon Northup famously narrates, but also had to confront such denials of citizen eligibility as Taney articulates in *Dred Scott v. Sanford*. Under this regime and well into its persistent afterlife, black claims to a home within the union would require of the claimant strategic and largely defensive spatial practices.

African American countergeographies take many forms, from the carefully plotted path of escape and Maroon encampment deep in the swamps to the all-black towns of the trans-Mississippi West and the black enclave of the Northern industrial city. They take, moreover, the form of imaginative and speculative appropriations of American space, as in Martin R. Delany's *Blake, or the Huts of North America* (1859) and Sutton E. Griggs's *Imperium in Imperio* (1899), forerunners both of Octavia Butler's Afro-futurist *Parable* series. Dating from a decade in which the Fugitive Slave Act of 1850 and *Dred Scott v. Sanford* underscored the persecuted and alien status of African-descended peoples throughout the United States, *Blake* asserted, after *David Walker's Appeal*, perhaps the most radical and visionary conception of a black militant countergeography in the antebellum period.[46] In its revolutionary protagonist, Henry Blake (also known as Henry Holland or Henrico Blacus), Delany creates a learned and physically robust avenger who uses nearly superhero capacities to move from one end of the slave South to the other, rapidly and without capture, informing an enslaved hut-dwelling population of the impending uprising and schooling individuals in the arts of escape through enemy territory.[47] In frenetic and figuratively resourceful prose, Delany projects an allegorical and indeed Bunyanesque North America, as we see when Henry describes the route north to would-be freedom pilgrims, Sampson and Dursie, residents of a plantation in East Texas: "It is the great range of White mountains and White river which are before you, and the White Gap that you must pass through to reach the haven of safety." Traversing the hemisphere himself north to Canada and south to Cuba before extending his travels east across the Atlantic to Africa and back, Henry travels "as a messenger of light and destruction." At a particularly memorable moment during his sojourn among the conjurors in the Great Dismal Swamp, he is depicted as engaging in overt subversion of the Jeffersonian vision of a white agrarian republic: "Finding ample scope for undisturbed action through the entire region of the swamp, he continued to go scattering to the winds and sowing the seeds of a future crop, only to take root in the thick black waters which cover it, to be grown in devastation and reaped in a whirlwind of ruin."[48] Delany's powerful challenge to white hegemonic territorial claims did not circulate far beyond a black Northern readership, and so the full incendiary ambition of *Blake*—like that of *David Walker's Appeal* thirty years earlier—went substantially unrealized in its occasions of initial publication.[49]

Against the reflex to flee, hide, or emigrate, black authors from David Walker to Malcolm X recurrently assert a claim to the North American continent on the basis of unacknowledged sweat-and-blood equity in the rural and urban products of black labor.[50] By this argument, the country belongs as much to the heirs of the work gangs and artisans who built it as to those who extracted that labor from them. Even Delany, who finally concluded that emigration offered the sole escape from structural white oppression and who traveled to West Africa to assess resettlement prospects, articulates in *Blake* black rights to the land: "They had inherited those regions by birth, paid for the soil by toil, irrigated it with their sweat, enriched it with their blood, nothing remaining to be done but by a dependence in Divine aid, a reliance in their own ability, and strength of their own arms, but to claim and take possession."[51] In *Back of the Big House: The Architecture of Plantation Slavery*, John Michael Vlach examines the ways in which enslaved populations asserted shadow ownership of the territories to which they had been consigned, creating their own landscapes within and beyond the boundaries of the white master's property, establishing paths in accordance with their own navigation of microlocalities that included sites of food production, leisure, and religious retreat. Vlach notes, moreover, that given opportunities to construct their own slave-quarter villages, black builders configured their habitations in ways that contested the rectilinear emphasis of plantation geometry.[52] The conviction that the land black people were forced to work belonged by rights to them is reflected in attempts on the part of former slaves to occupy and legally own that land following Emancipation.[53] Consistent with the thesis that those who inhabit and work the land are its true owners, Booker T. Washington and W. E. B. Du Bois both envision a quasi-separatist occupation of the Deep South as black possession of ancestral territory, notwithstanding their famous disagreement with respect to how willingly postslavery generations should accept the constraints white Southerners would impose on their exercise of citizenship. Responding further to the post-Reconstruction predicament, Sutton E. Griggs's *Imperium in Imperio* (1899) envisions Texas as a black-majority state within the union or, as conditions dictate, a black-separatist republic. Although the narrative concludes by rejecting (for the time being) a radically nationalist solution, Griggs's hypothesis retains a forceful appeal.[54]

With the ratification of Amendments 13 through 15 of the U.S. Constitution, questions of black personhood, citizenship, voting privileges, and rights to travel and to dwell achieved theoretical clarity: by law, to paraphrase Douglass, black people could now traverse the whole length and breadth of the union as freely as if every part of it was their home. The force of those amendments was almost instantly vitiated by measures designed to preserve white dominance over North American space: the enactment of Black Codes throughout the South but also in certain Northern states; the reduction of newly emancipated rural blacks to peonage; the fomenting of extrajudicial violence against black people in the South and elsewhere; and enshrinement of "separate but equal" in *Plessy v. Fergusson* (1896).[55] Fifty-seven years later,

Brown v. Board of Education of Topeka (1954) would reverse *Plessy v. Fergusson* but hardly eliminate the daily reality of segregation or the panoply of policies that manifested, in North and South, as "separate and unequal." *Brown v. Board of Education* served as prelude to the Civil Rights Acts of 1957, 1960, 1964, and 1968, all highly progressive in intent and effect, but to map the United States of the post–civil rights era with respect to where black people live and work and where they can travel in safety underscores the tenacity of a segregationist heritage. Even after a first U.S. African American president has succeeded in occupying for two quadrennial terms that whitest and most male of American bastions, the White House, black testimony continues to document the relegation of black people—geographically but also existentially—to the far side of a color line. In the epilogue, after tracing three centuries of such testimony, I examine the extensions of that color line into the second decade of the twenty-first century and the special geographies and spatial practices that pertain to its persistence. "The struggle for racial justice," Stephanie M. H. Camp aptly states, "would become in large part an effort to disentangle blackness from captivity, and race from place." Camp has in mind the immediate postslavery decades, but her observation has a broader relevance. Although spaces may have opened and barriers grown less obvious, that struggle continues unabated.[56]

"A story told by not telling"

Contemporary inquiry into the legacies of Atlantic slavery and the geographical displacements they have entailed repeatedly returns to the point of no return, that very real if inaccessible moment at which the enslaved, stripped of such cognitive framing as finds embodiment in shared language and kinship ties, experienced loss of the ground and scale of being—death in one form or another. Those who did not literally die had to reestablish bearings, identity, and location against the void of captivity. Recovery of that unmapped point remains largely speculative, as it involves conditions of human experience so extreme as to exceed representation—residing as it must in the silence between a natal and an acquired language. As Toni Morrison's narrator affirms in the concluding pages of *Beloved*, intoning a phrase that bundles Margaret Garner's unspeakable agonies with those of the "Sixty Million and more" to whom *Beloved* is inscribed: "It was not a story to pass on."[57] And as N. NourbeSe Philip, echoing Morrison, observes in the afterword of *Zong!* (2008), her book-length poem that conjures the subjectivities of those thrown overboard in the 1781 Zong massacre, "This story must be told by not telling."[58] That void has become the focus of considerable postcolonial fascination, particularly as it can only be imagined as *other*-worldly experience. As Glissant suggests, such radical displacement begins with "the sea, never seen from the depths of the ship's hold, punctuated by drowned bodies that sowed in its depths explosive seeds of absence."[59] And as Hortense J. Spillers observes, those aggregated as the slave ship's human cargo "were literally suspended in the oceanic, if we think of the latter in its Freudian orientation as an analogy on undifferentiated identity: removed from the indigenous land and culture, and not-yet 'American' either, these captives, without names their captors would recognize, were in movement across the Atlantic, but they were also *nowhere* at all. Because, on any given day, we might imagine, the captive personality did not know where s/he was, we could say they were culturally 'unmade,' thrown in the midst of a figurative darkness that exposed their destinies to an unknown course."[60] "Slavery annulled lives," Saidiya Hartman observes, "transforming men and women into dead matter, and then resuscitated them for servitude."[61] Countergeography begins by staking out the new *somewhere* and the selfhood (such selfhood as exceeded white appropriation) possible under those terms.

In reading the testimonies that arise from the African diaspora, one must take for granted the absent presence of the story that does not pass on. At base, the missing referent is a matter of cognitive paths and kinship genealogies shattered in the Middle Passage; it is the lost prehistory of a diasporic subjectivity birthed at what Glissant calls "the point of entanglement" and bearing the traces of a natal culture in creole amalgamation with the linguistic resources and narratives of the West. The story that does not pass on generates recurrent themes of abrupt displacement and traumatic separation, a perpetuation of the Middle Passage in the internal slave trade and the fugitive paths that may or may not eventuate in sustainable deliverance. The distance that such testimonies preserve between author and reader (especially but not exclusively when such testimony is directed across the color line) reflects the irreconcilability of the story of deliverance, which operates as a saving, celebratory release for author and reader alike, with the story that does not pass on, for in not passing on that story persists as a conspicuous silence, a chapter ineligible for assimilation.

In *Ride Out the Wilderness: Geography and Identity in Afro-American Literature* (1987), one of the first geographical treatments of the black literary tradition, Melvin Dixon examines the ways in which space as redemption, as promised land, and as home, has figured importantly in African American as well as in European American expression. With extended readings of slave songs as well as the work of authors such as Jean Toomer, Richard Wright, Ralph Ellison, James Baldwin, Alice Walker, and Toni Morrison, Dixon proposes "to show how images of journeys, conquered spaces, imagined havens, and places of refuge have produced not only a deliverance from slavery to freedom, but, more important, a transformation from rootlessness to rootedness for both author and protagonist."[62] Building on Dixon's work in *Southscapes: Geographies of Race, Region, and Literature*, Thadious M. Davis crucially demonstrates the ways in which "writers of color" have subverted "the dominant 'old' southern ideology" in an effort to "claim the very space that would negate their humanity and devalue their worth." As we will note in chapter 4, such "return to the South" is not without historical precedent and advances a long-term post-Reconstruction liberationist theme.[63] It would be inaccurate therefore to claim that black geographies exclude an emancipatory narrative or the incidental realization of something like a promised land. But in view of antidemocratic spatial regimes that perpetuate restriction and displacement, it pays to be skeptical of a redemptive, conciliatory geographical order and mindful of the continuing relevance of the story that does not pass on, a story of radical dislocation that haunts narratives of ongoing dislocation. As H. Bruce Franklin and Michael Bennett have demonstrated, the myth of the garden, the basis of the white dream of an Edenic inhabitable America, has been generally unavailable to African Americans, whose historical narratives underscore rural terror and entrapment and whose slavery-era natural refuge has been swampland and other sites offering limited degrees of impregnability.[64] Madhu Dubey has shown how thoroughly the rural/urban binary, as reflected in the work of Butler and others, has broken down, and, as she and Charles Scruggs have both demonstrated, the city in African American culture exists as both utopia and dystopia.[65]

We might more accurately view liberation as a high-maintenance work in progress—a "never-ending journey," to cite what could serve as the title of Barack Obama's second inaugural address (upbeat as all such addresses must be but not without its share of jeremiadical admonition).[66] Accordingly, the chapters that follow focus on mapping procedures by which Americans have navigated color lines that have been blurred and redrawn many times during the last five hundred years but whose persistence makes clear that the vaunted postracial nation remains very much an unachieved and, for the foreseeable future, unattainable ideal. In addition, they look at the ways in which cartographies of literary testimony engage not simply in a mimesis or reflection of a world "out there," but compel readers to rethink the map of the world we commonly occupy and, as we occupy, constantly remap. In this way, we may hope to create a spatial order that can accommodate unassimilable postmemory as well as a national demographic plurality that remains in dynamic ongoing flux and cannot but call accustomed color lines into question.

Chapter 2

Voices from the Global South

Phillis Wheatley and Olaudah Equiano

Phillis Wheatley and Olaudah Equiano are foundational contributors to the slave testimony in English, but neither qualifies as "fugitive" as that term is usually understood, and only Equiano documents a flight to freedom. Neither tells a story of harrowing and climactic escape; neither, at the moment of inscription, hides from agents legally empowered to seize and restore the property to its owner. As authors, however, both challenge the ontological status of persons who officially exist only as objects; by virtue of that challenge, both remain in perpetual flight from an objectification that turns on visible racial difference. Both raise the question of how Africans in varying conditions of liberation are to lead a life in the slave-regime West, where their presence signifies a limited number of narrative explanations. Both present the predicament of individuals situated between cultures, abductees deprived of the option to return home—people for whom "home" in an originary sense can no longer be said to exist. Both invite consideration of the degree to which acculturation perpetuates bondage irrespective of legal emancipation. To write one's own story is to exercise power over how one's story can be told, but neither Wheatley nor Equiano presents an unambiguous instance of an author taking control over the life narrative. The very titles of their works prompt one to ask whether it is possible for either to assume a subject position that affords something other than a burdened agency. In pondering their works, we must look for the ironic, subversive, unscripted utterance as a moment of breakthrough to "free" expression. As the never entirely naturalized citizens of the literary nation in which they speak (for we are ever reminded that their pages are the exceptional production of a category of people from whom little can be expected), Wheatley and Equiano remain profoundly unsettled if not literally on the run.

As participants in late eighteenth-century Anglo-African literary culture, they formed something of a nation apart with other authors of color: Ignatius Sancho, Ottobah Cugoano, James Albert Ukawsaw Gronniosaw, John Marrant, Briton Hammon, Jupiter Hammon, John Jea, and the Native American Samson Occom.[1] Coming to the occasions of authorship from diverse compass points and natal cultures, these authors witnessed colonial incursions upon their native lands and the consequent disruption of traditional communities; in experiencing removal from those communities, they were obliged to improvise a self whose conformity to Western modes served chiefly to focus their irreducible otherness. Their authorship proceeded beneath ethnic epithets ("African," "Negro," "Mohegan") or other markings indicating variance from the default expectation: that anyone writing in English is of white English genealogy (other British and European derivations perhaps factoring) and whose name and visible presence conform to an Anglo-Christian type. These authors of color all testify to a Christian conversion; several made their appearance in print as protégés of Selina Hastings, the Countess of Huntingdon, a powerful figure in Anglo-American evangelical circles.[2] For all, an acquired Christian identity represented a condition of existential compromise: it compelled, on the one hand, affirmation of the fortunate disaster that brought them within range of the Christian evangel, while, on the other, it provided the basis of antislavery witness, putting them in view of a "glorious Dispensation," as Wheatley would write to Occom in 1774, soon after securing her own emancipation, "of civil and religious Liberty, which are so inseparably united, that there is little or no Enjoyment of one without the other."[3] No longer enslaved, Wheatley speaks to Occom in happy defiance of the sympathetic white readership whose attachment to a slave economy—Hastings's implication as the absentee owner of Caribbean plantations being a prime example—discourages them from embracing emancipation.

Notwithstanding the support such writers enjoyed among a white evangelical community internally divided into anti- and proslavery camps, majority response to an emerging English literature of color was predictably condescending and dismissive. Symptomatic of white disesteem of black testimonial expression, Thomas Jefferson's assessment of Wheatley's poems and Sancho's letters exhibits clear a priori notions concerning African capacity for literary expression.[4] In Jefferson's analysis, the African's typically pietistic and emotive utterance betrays a lack of intellect and invention: "Religion indeed has produced a Phyllis Whately," he remarks, misspelling her name, "but it could not produce a poet. The compositions published under her name are below the dignity of criticism. The heroes of the Dunciad are to her, as Hercules to the author of that poem. Ignatius Sancho has approached nearer to merit in composition; yet his letters do more honour to the heart than the head." Sancho, Jefferson remarks, is capable of fluent and felicitous phrasing but is deficient in "reason and taste": "though we admit him to the first place among those of his own colour who have presented themselves to the public judgment," he ranks at bottom when compared with white practitioners of the epistolary genres. Jefferson's suspicion of African literary culture is further emphasized by the qualification with which he concludes his appraisal of Sancho's letters: "This criticism supposes the letters published under his name to be genuine, and to have received amendment from no other hand;

points which would not be of easy investigation."[5] Anticipating a future emancipation of America's enslaved population, Jefferson endorsed the idea of educational programs aimed at black people, even if he never actively worked toward their implementation.[6] But his writing on black intellectual pursuit consistently rejects the possibility that African-descended people could meet, much less exceed, European standards of achievement.

Wheatley presents the case of one whose public career began prior to her emancipation: her poems circulated in newspapers and broadsides while she was still a bondswoman in her master's Boston household. Her manumission dates from 1773, two months before *Poems on Various Subjects, Religious and Moral* appeared in London. Her narrative as a slave abducted from West Africa must be pieced together from allusions to her journey expressed in the stylized conventions of Augustan verse—the semantic unit of the heroic couplet and Latinate phrasings of a mannered diction.[7] It must be reconstructed, moreover, from a vocabulary she cannot help but derive from the global geography of European colonialism and *Felix culpa* of Christian doctrine. Similar constraints bind Equiano's *The Interesting Narrative of the Life of Olaudah Equiano, or Gustavus Vassa, the African* (1789). Equiano's prose is better equipped than Wheatley's poetry to specify the horror of abduction, separation from family members, and first encounter with the European intruder and his ocean-going vessel. Still, *The Interesting Narrative* recounts a life of travel centered in the Eurocentric geography of colonial trade to which Equiano has become the inevitable subaltern while confessing a religious conversion unfolding within a Judeo-Christian cosmography. Each constructs a narrative in which deliverance from bondage figures prominently, although as a free resident of London in the wake of the Mansfield ruling, Equiano is better positioned to address deliverance as manumission in *this* world and to engage issues pertaining to the former slave's rights of citizenship.[8] More than Wheatley, he can speak directly to the abolition of an institution that, as long as it exists, threatens the former bondsperson with reenslavement.

Both Wheatley and Equiano appear to offer the rare, vital, testimonial link between Africa and the European Old and New Worlds. There is no doubt that Wheatley was "brought," as her most famous poem phrases it, from Africa to America, whereas credible if inconclusive evidence suggests that Equiano may have been born on the Carolina seaboard.[9] *The Interesting Narrative* speaks as the firsthand witness of the Middle Passage in ways that Wheatley's poems do not, but despite the vividness of his depiction, it is possible that Equiano serves as the amanuensis-become-impersonator of oral accounts derived from those who survived the passage. Whatever his place of birth, it would be wrong to argue that Equiano submits a false life narrative inasmuch as abduction, transport, and acculturation pertain to any explanation of how, in the 1780s, a person of African descent generates autobiography in literary English.[10] Our first step toward discerning the "African experience" (however we may define that) contained in the writings of Wheatley and Equiano involves recognition of the European genres and motifs to which they were obliged to conform that experience. Such genres and motifs, the usages of a predominantly white readership and thus minimally inflected by the discourse communities of the African diaspora, leave little room for such structures of feeling associated with what Paul Gilroy distinguishes as the "expressive cultures" of the black Atlantic:[11] only on an abstract level, only in a generalized English translation consistent with the dialect of white educated readers, can Africa and the black New World be said to exist in Wheatley's poems and Equiano's prose. What affective dimensions suffered erasure in their respective conformity to the eighteenth-century literary genres cannot confidently be reconstructed, but we can and must read these writings with the certainty that erasures occurred.[12]

Both demonstrate a thorough understanding of the expectations that attach to their genres of choice as well as the metanarrative of Christian redemption that their literary practice obliges them to affirm, not least because their religious testimony empowers them to speak. In neither case is there reason to suspect anything less than sincere profession of Christian faith resulting from conversions they themselves represent as voluntary. Nevertheless there are multiple instances in Wheatley's poems and numerous passages in Equiano's *Narrative* in which religious profession exhibits deep and even sardonic double consciousness. As authors writing in deference to white sponsors in a hemispheric Christendom, both were obliged to know their place, and this required that they master the cartography of a diasporic global position. Both wrote for readerships that perceived them as having crossed from a pagan Africa to a Christian Europe and America. Both were obliged to confront the paradox that Christendom's incursion into their non-Christian worlds took the form of what they argue to be the unchristian industry that is the slave trade. For both, addressing that paradox involved entering the fissure between white people who object to slavery on Christian grounds and white people who cite biblical sanction of the practice. Unable to reconcile themselves rationally to the proposition that the slave trade beneficently seizes pagans and, if they are so favored, puts them in the way to become enlightened Christians—even as Wheatley and Equiano present themselves as examples of such redemption—both have recourse to the mysteries of Christian theodicy. Geography in their writing reflects a world map of differential theological shadings, and although the bright expanse of Christendom has clearly not been entirely won over to Christ (Wheatley and Equiano regularly perform as overt evangels in addressing their readers, particularly in itemizing the evils of slavery), both find themselves compelled to affirm that their place, such as it is, with whatever suffering it has cost them to secure it, represents an improvement over the preenslavement of their natal African condition, steeped in the "Egyptian gloom" from which they have been delivered. Argumentatively, however, such a view is ever vexed by the paradox that the goodness to which they testify necessitated the iniquity of Christendom's trade in African flesh.

"But here I sit, and mourn a grov'ling mind"

Throughout *Poems on Various Subjects, Religious and Moral*, Wheatley performs the Augustan ritual of invoking the muse to support her efforts to rise to the poem's occasion. In "To Maecenas," her prefatory appeal, she adopts the pose of the supplicant pleading the patron's indulgence, questioning her capacity to fulfill the office's lofty charge. Whereas Virgil and Horace have a Gaius Maecenas to advance their careers and social prestige, Wheatley's sponsor, the person to whom she inscribes *Poems on Various Subjects*, is Selina Hastings, the Countess of Huntingdon, an evangelical Methodist and owner of slave-worked plantations overseas, who nevertheless championed the testimony of black Christian converts, promoting the authorship of Equiano, James Albert Ukawsaw Gronniosaw, John Marrant, Briton Hammon, and Jupiter Hammon.[13] Apart from fulfilling neoclassical convention, Wheatley's self-abasements cannot help but also allude to her abject condition as slave, but to cite that condition is to challenge her readership's assumptions with respect to the slave's authority to speak, however self-depreciating that speaker may be. Given that *Poems on Various Subjects* circulated with a frontispiece portrait of a juvenile black female, pen in hand, Wheatley's African identity is very much a part of the artifact that is this book.[14] For her, therefore, to "mourn a grov'ling mind" (10), as she does in "To Maecenas," is to assert a personhood in which she defines herself as "mind," and although "grovel" may appear to reduce the intellect to a figure of bodily supplication, the phrase serves notice that she has an intellect despite the then current twofold argument to the contrary—that she is female, and that she is black. As is typically the case with such self-deprecatory gestures, it names a condition in preparation to defy it.

Wheatley's sense of place is strategically expressed in her figure of the "grov'ling mind," a phrase that occurs twice in *Poems on Various Subjects*: attached to a body that is the property of another and as such fixed in space and time, this mind has gained access to a field of activity that permits some release from the physical stultification (groveling) of enslavement. Despite the humble circumstances in which the novice poet finds herself, despite the extent to which the discourse she engages embeds the patriarchal and racist perspectives that have created the conditions of her enslavement, her poetic vocation offers some relief from confinement. Again, to speak of a "grov'ling mind" is already to move beyond that condition. Location for Wheatley exists as a set of concentric entrapments: a household in a well-to-do white neighborhood where she must abide by strictures of territory and schedule; the social, racial, and gender hierarchies of colonial Boston; the hemispheric geography of the Atlantic basin slave regime. Within these confines she seizes upon paths of qualified escape: the Anglo-American evangelical and literary circles dominated by such figures as George Whitefield, Selina Hastings, and John Wesley, as well as the vertical cartography of the Christian pilgrim.

Against the formidable constraints on what we can only imagine to have been the range of expression available to an enslaved young woman in colonial Boston, Wheatley resists a social ontology that requires her to submit to her master. For however well treated she may be in the Wheatley household, as slave she must proceed with the institutional understanding that exemption from the more abject conditions of her status neither abrogates that status nor reduces the slaveholder's power to objectify her as a marketable commodity. The white patronage by which she attains authorship has placed her within an eighteenth-century world of print culture and evolving social hierarchies. Within this world of narrow openings, defiance is mostly confined to staged pronouncements and measured phrases.

Readers familiar with *The Narrative of the Captivity and Restoration of Mrs. Mary Rowlandson* and *The Tenth Muse Lately Sprung Up in America* know that male advocacy authorized those occasions when the writings of seventeenth- and early eighteenth-century women appeared in print. Anglo-American Protestant women did not as a rule openly engage in literary activity. Only an unusual talent or circumstance warranted female publication, and the male-authored preface specified the terms of exception. By the end of the eighteenth century, amateur and professional literary activity among middle-class British and American women had largely eliminated the need for patriarchal endorsement of what had been isolated instances of female authorship, but black authorship, female or male, required certification in that the predominantly white readership remained skeptical of the African capacity for letters, and as with women in prior eras, the special instance had to be framed in such a way as to leave undisturbed the general doubt as to the black aptitude for literary culture.[15] *Poems on Various Subjects, Religious and Moral* is preceded by three explanatory documents: a publisher's preface, assuring the reader that the poems were written "for the Amusement of the Author, as they were the Products of her leisure Moments" (5) and by no means intended for publication; a letter from the master, John Wheatley, who explains that Phillis, unassisted by "School Education, and by only what she was taught in the Family, . . . in sixteen Months Time from her arrival" in North America "attained the English Language" to the degree that she could read the most difficult passages in the Bible (7); and an attestation signed by eighteen Boston gentlemen confirming that Phillis "has been examined by some of the best Judges, and is thought qualified" to have written the poems (8).[16] One might well ask: by what logic does this pietistic society, willing to concede the African's human status and salvageable spirituality but not united in an abolitionist sentiment, promote Wheatley as prodigy?[17] Beginning in 1700 with Samuel Sewall's *The Selling of Joseph* and culminating with Henry David Thoreau's 1854 "Slavery in Massachusetts" and 1859 "A Plea for Captain John Brown," white antislavery voices flourished in and around Boston. The Wheatley family could hardly have been unaware of the arguments for and against holding slaves, although to have under their protection one whom the slave trade delivered to their hands to be (in their view) Christianized, enlightened, and shielded from sexual assault must have assured them of the beneficence of what otherwise might appear as their complicity in a cruel and disreputable institution.

Such beneficence is the ostensible thesis of "On Being Brought from Africa to America," Wheatley's best-known and most controversial poem, whose first line builds upon the reader's assumed familiarity with an antislavery view—that *cruelty* is an active agent in any such extraction of Africans from their homelands:

> 'Twas mercy brought me from my *Pagan* land,
> Taught my benighted soul to understand
> That there's a God, that there's a *Saviour* too:
> Once I redemption neither sought nor knew.
> Some view our sable race with scornful eye,
> "Their colour is a diabolic die."
> Remember, *Christians*, *Negros*, black as *Cain*,
> May be refin'd, and join th' angelic train. (13)

The first four lines deploy an argument to which Wheatley would have been exposed as the member of a pious slaveholding household affiliated with an Anglo-American Methodist community that comprised both pro- and antislavery advocates. Very likely, it would have been difficult for her to say anything regarding her Middle Passage experience without first acknowledging that Providence has operated in conjunction with a blind humanity's fallen economy to put her and other Africans in the geographical and spiritual position to seek and know redemption. But Wheatley does not thereby deny that cruelty also brings her and fellow "Negros" from Africa, and it is by virtue of the first four lines that she secures the platform from which to deliver the admonition of lines 5 through 8, beginning with the imperative "Remember." Addressing forgetful and implicitly white Christian readers, Wheatley upbraids those who, on the basis of color prejudice, deny the African's spiritual capacity and redemptive opportunity, and she does so by exposing what her argument represents as the white person's false binary: *Christians* (white), *Negros* (pagan). To deny the African's spiritual capacity is to consign the *Negro* to hard earthly labor and death of the immortal soul. In line 9, Wheatley's double consciousness works through double entendre: "*Negros*, black as *Cain*" is a not overly subtle reference to the sugar plantations, far to the south of Boston but worked by bodies as black as that of the Boston maidservant, producing cane destined in refinement to appear in the Christian household as white table sugar. The last line suggests that redemption does involve "whitening," that black Africans, once Christianized, become white angels, but here again Wheatley is working within the constraints of a Western symbology: black/dark associated with evil, white/

light signifying good. The thesis that black people are fortunate to be delivered from Africa remains intact but not without Wheatley calling out the white betrayal of Christian doctrine. Grounded in her black perspectival recognition of white error and hypocrisy, she thus incarnates a paradoxical authority.

The poem thus constitutes a concise early answer to questions she would spend the whole of her brief career addressing. What can she say on the basis of her experience as a young African woman kidnapped from her homeland? What authority can she wrest from conditions that deny her testimonial capacity, that align to deprive her as woman and African of a right to define her own moral status, let alone that of anyone else? And should her pretention to speak break the bounds of her consignment to an object category, to whom might she address her seasoned words? In truth, beginning with a Maecenas who stands in for the Countess of Huntingdon, John Wheatley's prodigy addresses poems to many a genteel personage. In *Poems on Various Subjects* alone, seven poems are directed to unnamed "ladies" and "gentlemen" (including a clergyman) on the deaths of spouses, children, and other family members (in all, fourteen of the thirty-nine poems in the collection elegize the deaths of obscure and famous figures): perhaps because death visits everyone regardless of place in the racial and social hierarchy—perhaps too, as Vincent Carretta suggests, because Wheatley's Middle Passage ordeal would have acquainted her with the spectacle of death and dying—she is particularly disposed to enlarge on what, in the Christian framework to which she has become naturalized, serves as the great human leveler.[18]

The mortal condition she shares with everyone, moreover, makes those who occupy spheres beyond her social reach spiritually approachable. The last will be first: as the "last and meanest of the rhyming train" (53), she understands her priority in the "angelic train." Christian piety might well provide her with the license and duty to admonish (say) the sons of the patriarchy and to do so as one who knows from experience what it means to cross from a geography of supposed spiritual darkness to a land of Christian enlightenment:

> WHILE an intrinsic ardor prompts to write,
> The muses promise to assist my pen;
> 'Twas not long since I left my native shore
> The land of errors, and *Egyptian* gloom:
> Father of mercy, 'twas thy gracious hand
> Brought me in safety from those dark abodes. (11)

Having traversed a world and undergone a conversion that empowers her to know the gospel in ways that those who enjoy an easy and complacent access to scripture cannot, she addresses the young men who gather at Harvard College to master the geographies of a visible and invisible world:

Students, to you 'tis giv'n to scan the heights
Above, to traverse the ethereal space,
And mark the systems of revolving worlds.
Still more, ye sons of science ye receive
The blissful news by messengers from heav'n,
How *Jesus*' blood for your redemption flows.
Let sin, that baneful evil to the soul,
By you be shunn'd, nor once remit your guard;
Suppress the deadly serpent in its egg.
Ye blooming plants of human race divine,
An *Ethiop* tells you 'tis your greatest foe. (11–12)

The poem asserts the paradoxical power of the inferior to speak truth to her superior, of one who traces her origin to the "land of errors" to instruct those given "to scan the heights" and "traverse the ethereal space." Wheatley, a self-identifying courier from Africa, thus takes it upon herself to confirm "the blissful news by messengers from heav'n." Although the poet indicates from the beginning that this voice arises from the margins of her reader's accustomed world, it is not until line 28 that we come upon the explicit declaration that "an Ethiop" speaks these words.[19] For Wheatley to delay the revelation thus late in the poem reinforces two points: first, that she has mastered not only elite forms of written English but also poetic conventions (a further refinement) sufficient to pass as a native (white) practitioner of this discourse—if she does not tell us she is African, we cannot guess the fact; and second, that one who occupies the lowest scale of the social hierarchy has experience to relate and wisdom to impart that those who occupy the highest positions cannot possess.

Wheatley's boldest performance in this vein is reserved for a personage specifically invoked in the poem addressed to him: "To the Right Honourable William, Earl of DARTMOUTH, His Majesty's Principal Secretary of State for North-America, &c."[20] Although, as a member of the Hastings circle, William Legg, Earl of Dartmouth, would know the status of the poem's author—a letter accompanying the copy Wheatley sent to him apologizes "for this freedom from an African" (143)—as performer, the speaker once again strategically delays identifying herself as African and thus, presumably, a slave. Far from positioning her voice at the margins, the poet assumes the position of one who voices the consensus of bourgeois British colonial society:

HAIL, happy day, when, smiling like the morn,
Fair *Freedom* rose *New-England* to adorn:
The northern clime beneath her genial ray,
Dartmouth, congratulates thy blissful sway:
Elate with hope her race no longer mourns,

Each soul expands, each grateful bosom burns,
While in thine hand with pleasure we behold
The silken reins, and *Freedom's* charms unfold. (39)

Any member of the New England colonies who has felt the heavy-handedness of the British colonial government and lamented the autocratic behavior of parliament and crown might greet the advent of William Legg with such optimistic and vapid verses. Eight lines deep, the performance revels in an assemblage of clichés. As the poem proceeds to the next verse paragraph, however, the statement becomes something more than an exercise in courtesy:

No more, *America*, in mournful strain
Of wrongs, and grievance unredress'd complain,
No longer shalt thou dread the iron chain,
Which wanton *Tyranny* with lawless hand
Had made, and with it meant t'enslave the land. (40)

Here, the speaker identifies recent British treatment of New England as violating laws governing the relations between parent country and colony, and in doing so compares such treatment with the slave master's handling of his human chattel. As metaphor, the "iron chain" with which Great Britain intends to reduce freedom-loving British Americans to a virtual slave status is a commonplace of patriot polemics; in Wheatley's application, however, the metaphor acquires unwonted complexity because appropriated by an actual slave. To characterize the forces of enslavement as "wanton Tyranny with lawless hand" draws attention to the fact that slavery in 1774 remains lawful throughout most of the British Empire: by implication, tyranny in the form of literal enslavement is lawless in that it violates moral laws that ought to be reflected in the legal systems of Great Britain and America. In the next verse paragraph, as the speaker removes her veil, it becomes even clearer that this poem addresses the vehicle as much as the tenor of this metaphor and that its argument constitutes an indictment of both the agents of British tyranny and those who hypocritically complain of being oppressed: the slaveholding planter and merchant class of the British colonies:

Should you, my lord, while you peruse my song,
Wonder from whence my love of *Freedom* sprung,
Whence flow these wishes for the common good,
By feeling hearts alone best understood,
I, young in life, by seeming cruel fate
Was snatch'd from *Afric's* fancy'd happy seat:
What pangs excruciating must molest,
What sorrows labour in my parent's breast?
Steel'd was that soul and by no misery mov'd

That from a father seiz'd his babe belov'd:
Such, such my case. And can I then but pray
Others may never feel tyrannic sway? (40)[21]

No one, this speaker claims, has greater authority to speak on the topic of tyranny and enslavement than one who has been subject to abduction and has witnessed the sorrow the slave trade imposes on family members parted thus violently from one another. The force of this equation of slavery with tyranny, and tyranny with an absence of human empathy ("Steel'd was that soul and by no misery mov'd"), persists even beneath Wheatley's attempts to contain that argument within her concession, consistent with the ostensible thesis of "On Being Brought from Africa to America," that she has benefited from having been removed "by *seeming* cruel fate" from Africa's "*fancy'd* happy seat." To depict herself as snatched from her father's rather than her mother's arms may be a calculated appeal to the poem's patriarchal addressee, as is the attribution of the sorrow of a sundered parent-child relationship to the father—as if to inquire of the Earl of Dartmouth, how would you feel if your daughter were forcibly taken from your arms?

The final verse paragraph leaves irony and polemic mostly behind to engage once again in a rhetoric of courtesy, thanking Dartmouth for past indulgences and invoking all due blessings on an anticipated continued benevolence, but the geographical dimension of what is otherwise a collage of complimentary platitudes merits attention:

For favours past, great Sir, our thanks are due,
And thee we ask thy favours to renew,
Since in thy pow'r, as in thy will before,
To sooth the griefs, which thou did'st once deplore.
May heav'nly grace the sacred sanction give
To all thy works, and thou for ever live
Not only on the wings of fleeting *Fame*,
Though praise immortal crowns the patriot's name,
But to conduct to heav'ns refulgent fane,
May fiery coursers sweep th' ethereal plain,
And bear thee upwards to that blest abode,
Where, like the prophet, thou shalt find thy God. (40)

All souls, in Wheatley's world, are subject to transport and transformation: whereas her story involves the coerced transit by means of slave ship from Africa to the "northern clime," his story, assuming that he is the righteous man he appears to be, will culminate in transfer by means of "fiery coursers" to the "refulgent fane" in the "blest abode." By such conceit the poet, whose slave status in principle deprives her of legal authority to provide testimony, reminds Dartmouth that he too must die.

Tropes of death and migration overlap recurrently in Wheatley's poems, and the horizontal travel of earthbound displacement readily conflates with the vertical travel of the pilgrim's ascent to the afterlife. Consider, for example, the phrase "dark abodes" (antithesis of the "blest abode" to which Wheatley graciously commends Dartmouth) in the opening lines of "To the University of Cambridge, in New-England":

> 'Twas not long since I left my native shore
> The land of errors, and *Egyptian* gloom:
> Father of mercy, 'twas thy gracious hand
> Brought me in safety from those dark abodes. (11)

Compare that with the "dark abodes" in "On the Death of a Young Lady of Five Years of Age":

> FROM dark abodes to fair etherial light
> Th' enraptur'd innocent has wing'd her flight;
> On the kind bosom of eternal love
> She finds unknown beatitude above. (16)

In the first poem, "dark abodes" refers to Africa but also to the spiritual death from which the poet has been supposedly rescued in being brought "in safety" from Africa to America. In the second poem, one of many elegies written for friends and acquaintances of the Wheatley family circle, "dark abodes" refers to the earthly condition from which death has released the five-year-old girl to life everlasting in "etherial light." On this recycled phrase hinges an analogy: as Africa is to America, so earth is to heaven, although the latter migration is reserved for those who have found their way (by slave ship, if necessary, in the utmost dark abode of the slave ship's hold) to Christendom and, once arrived, have seized the opportunity to seek and know redemption. Given the parallel between Wheatley's migration around age eight and the young lady's death at age five, one cannot help but search this elegy for affective displacements of Wheatley's Middle Passage experience. In "To the Right Honourable William, Earl of DARTMOUTH," the poet voices concern for the bereaved African father's sorrow, and although that concern is expressed in a stylized locution aimed at eliciting empathy in the poem's patriarchal addressee, the African girl who becomes Phillis Wheatley almost certainly lost a family at some point in her abduction, and it is not inconceivable that her own experience of sundered ties and solicitude for those left behind finds outlet at the point in this elegy where the poet addresses the bereaved parents:

> Freed from a world of sin, and snares, and pain,
> Why would you wish your daughter back again?

> No—bow resign'd. Let hope your grief control,
> And check the rising tumult of the soul.
> Calm in the prosperous, and adverse day,
> Adore the God who gives and takes away;
> Eye him in all, his holy name revere,
> Upright your actions, and your hearts sincere,
> Till having sail'd through life's tempestuous sea,
> And from its rocks, and boist'rous billows free,
> Yourselves, safe landed on the blissful shore,
> Shall join your happy babe to part no more. (17)

Does the Middle Passage in this poem become a metaphor for anyone who must labor to the other side of life under heavy burdens? Undoubtedly—to the extent that Wheatley cannot but bring her experience to the occasion. Reading "On the Death of a Young Lady" in conjunction with "To the Right Honourable William, Earl of DARTMOUTH," however, one is aware that the spiritual consolation Wheatley offers to the girl's parents cannot be extended to her own. Here as elsewhere in Wheatley's work, one surmises a tragic education that the literary English at her disposal can never adequately express but that nonetheless lends her work authority on the topic of bereavement.

Thus far, the geography we have examined in Wheatley's writing has reflected a world divided between Pagan and Christian. By virtue of this division, the international trade in black bodies is mystified as the deliverance of African souls from the dark to the illuminated hemisphere through corridors of suffering that constitute death of the old, unregenerate self and birth of the new. In a 1772 letter to her friend and fellow African, Arbour Tanner, Wheatley could not be more explicit with respect to this favorable view of their transatlantic displacement: "Let us rejoice in and adore the wonders of God's infinite Love in bringing us from a land Semblant of darkness itself, and where the divine light of revelation (being obscur'd) is as darkness. Here, the knowledge of the true God and eternal life are made manifest; But there, profound ignorance overshadows the Land" (141–42). As a historical event, any instantiation of the Middle Passage journey is absorbed into the death and transfiguration of a conversion process dominated by the Crucifixion as master trope. It is for this reason that Wheatley's always oblique reference to her ocean crossing from Africa to America is logically and metaphorically congruent with her depiction of souls ascending to the "blissful shore" that awaits faithful Christians, be they the anonymous individuals she commemorates in her elegies or famous and powerful figures such as George Whitefield and (in her ingratiating prophecy) the Earl of Dartmouth. Not all of her poems, however, are tonally and tropologically restricted by what comports with the pietistic mood that generally prompts her effusions, and not all of her geographical representations unequivocally accrue to a redemptive Christian theodicy.

Under circumstances that remain obscure, Wheatley entered into a peculiarly sociable poetic conversation in the fall of 1774, the year after her manumission, and in December 1774 and January 1775, the *Royal American Magazine* printed the result: an exchange of poems between Wheatley, whom the editors refer to as "Philis (a young African of surprising genius)" and "a gentleman of the navy" (83), understood from references in Wheatley's poems to be John Rochfort, an Anglo-Irishman. At this point Wheatley commanded a degree of celebrity in Anglo-American reading circles, but her public definition remained "Negro Servant to Mr. John Wheatley," as the caption accompanying her frontispiece portrait in *Poems on Various Subjects* describes her. For regardless of her fame as a black prodigy and regardless of her status now as a freewoman, the association of "Negro" with bondage prevails, as does the general disdain that renders a literary African exceptional. Abolitionist at least in sentiment, the editor who prefaces the sequence (Isaiah Thomas or Joseph Greenleaf) addresses the injustice of such disdain. Having underscored Phillis's African origin and, in view of that origin, her "surprising genius," he notes that readers should not be surprised after all: human capacity is evenly distributed, and "Europe and Affrica would be alike savage or polite in the same circumstances." Having declared the equality of all people regardless of color, he proceeds to upbraid European civilization for "plundering the whole human race" to maintain an unmerited life of luxury (83). Framing the two voices as equals, then, the editor prints "To a Gentleman of the Navy" and "The Answer" in the December *Royal American*, and "Philis's Reply" in the January issue.

The three-part sequence reflects traditions of courtly address, the female voice, in this case, taking the initiative, and there is just sufficient erotic nuance in Rochfort's response to Wheatley's flattery to suggest an interracial sexual dynamic. What makes this exchange noteworthy is that the female voice very clearly reflects the African diaspora, while the male voice represents British maritime dominance; together, their poems image the Global North of Great Britain and Global South that is Africa—an Africa, moreover, that for once in Wheatley's poems does not appear as a "dark abode." No mention is made of the Atlantic slave trade, in full operation as they wrote these poems, but there is little need of such mention given the preface in which the editor reminds readers of the master position Europeans presume in their relationship to Sub-Saharan Africans. The topic is the more conspicuous for remaining unvoiced. What this sequence of poems establishes beyond its play of compliments is a hemispheric cartography fraught with racial and gender asymmetries that expose the false beneficence of a white imperial paternalism.

The first poem in the series begins and ends as a tribute to the noble merits of the British officer class that Rochfort and his colleague, Greaves, embody. But under cover of its celebratory tone, Wheatley's characterization of English naval power is remarkable for the understanding it conveys of the relationship of that power to a morally ambiguous British imperialism:

> Far in the space where ancient Albion keeps
> Amidst the roarings of the sacred deeps,
> Where willing forests leave their native plain,
> Descend, and instant, plough the wat'ry main.
> Strange to relate! with canvas wings they speed
> To distant worlds; of distant worlds the dread.
> The trembling natives of the peaceful plain,
> Astonish'd view the heroes of the main,
> Wond'ring to see two chiefs of matchless grace,
> Of generous bosom, and ingenuous face,
> From ocean sprung, like ocean foes to rest,
> The thirst of glory burns each youthful breast. (83–84)

Having limned a portrait of the island nation with forests destined to become world-roving ships, the verse paragraph glorifies Rochfort and his comrade in arms, Greaves, as types of the graceful, courageous youth drawn to such heroic enterprise. But the poem embeds an allegorical geography that tells a more complicated story. It begins with Wheatley's choice of the word *Albion* to designate the English nation: as a student of Latin (John Wheatley informs us in his letter prefatory to *Poems on Various Subjects* that Phillis "has made some Progress in it" [7]), the poet would have certainly been aware that *albus* is a Latin word for "white" and that, whatever the true etymology of *Albion* may be, anyone versed in Latin would associate the terms together. From this white world ships set forth: in her depiction of Great Britain's naval dominance, from the felling of trees to the fashioning of vessels that "plough the wat'ry main," Wheatley invests multiple suggestions of violence and sexual aggression, and those suggestions acquire mythic profile in her supernatural image of "canvas wings" that speed the ship "to distant worlds; of distant worlds the dread." There is no description of ships in such a context that does not evoke the slave ship: "The trembling natives of the peaceful plain" tremble for reasons to which the all-but-erased African child who has died to be reborn as Phillis Wheatley might abundantly testify. Well might she exclaim, "Strange to relate!" for she is narrating the story of British incursion on the African continent from the perspective of the naturalized British colonial who takes pride in the nation's power and prestige as represented by the refined heroism of an elite officer corps, as well as from the perspective of the native who sees the ships approach and reasonably dreads the sequel. To these two distinct parties Wheatley maintains contrary relations. The fact that, after the Boston Tea Party of 1773, Massachusetts residents also had reason to tremble at the approach of British ships adds another layer of complication to the picture.

Still, Wheatley removes Rochfort and Greaves from any overt adversarial context, recruiting them to what she projects as their common Christian fellowship. As she does in other poems addressed to white men in positions of power (the Harvard collegians, the Earl of Dartmouth), the poet simultaneously exalts and admonishes:

> In virtue's cause, the muse implores for grace,
> These blooming sons of Neptune's royal race;
> Cerulean youths! your joint assent declare,
> Virtue to rev'rence, more than mortal fair,
> A crown of glory, which the muse will twine,
> Immortal trophy! Rochfort shall be thine!
> Thine too O Greaves! (84)

But even as Wheatley imagines a Christian fellowship that reconciles African with European, female with male, she positions Rochfort and Greaves on the other side of a color line that is an implicit feature of a globe in which nations acquire phenotypic and gender characteristics. An "Albion" that sends out "Cerulean youths" in ships that "plough the wat'ry main" is a nation that presents itself as white, blue-eyed, and male, and such whiteness contrasts with Wheatley's own standard representation of Africa as "a land Semblant of darkness itself." Rochford's reply, while not overtly identifying Africa as a black female body, nonetheless reflects an awareness that Wheatley is a woman of color, and the poem treats its addressee not as someone who has been remade in North America as Christian bondswoman but as one who serves as the comely metonym of her country of origin. Whereas the customary European usage of African natives is subjugation and enslavement, the "Reply" extravagantly exalts its addressee. The poem's second verse paragraph reads as follows:

> Behold with reverence, and with joy adore;
> The lovely daughter of the Affric shore,
> Where every grace, and every virtue join,
> That kindles friendship and makes love divine;
> In hue as diff'rent as in souls above;
> The rest of mortals who in vain have strove,
> Th' immortal wreathe, the muse's gift to share,
> Which heav'n reserv'd for this angelic fair. (84–85)

Rochfort employs several circumlocutions to invoke Wheatley's blackness: having denominated her as "the lovely daughter of the Affric shore," he approaches the issue of color two lines later: "In hue as diff'rent as in souls above." The "difference" here cited is not the expected one between the white and black body, but between mortal human and immortal soul, although any mention of "hue" in this context automatically references the color line separating African from European, the foundational difference on which Rochfort builds his conceit. Rochfort thus playfully relocates the color line, exalting Wheatley as one who has already achieved the (white) hue of the immortal soul. His reference to Wheatley three lines later as "this angelic fair" completes the argument that she is more heavenly than earthly, and suggests that her virtue has rendered her not merely "angelic" but also "fair" in the sense of "white." Rochfort's color symbology is consistent with that which equates dark with evil and white with good, a symbology Wheatley herself has had to navigate from her earliest immersion in the English language ("Some view our sable race with scornful eye, / 'Their colour is a diabolic die'"). For a young white Englishman to describe Wheatley as "fair" differs from any occasion on which he would describe his countrywomen as "fair": in view of the fact that he addresses what participants and readers of this colloquy know to be an African, he forces his reader to process "fair" figuratively, which reinforces the color line between white and black.

If, as evidence suggests, Rochfort's tours of duty included patrols along the African Gold Coast for the purpose of defending British interests in the slave trade, he could not fail to have been an observer of captive peoples transported against their will. But his rendering of what he supposes to be Phillis's homeland is sanitized of any suggestion of mass human coercion:

> Blest be the guilded shore, the happy land,
> Where spring and autumn gently hand in hand;
> O'er shady forests that scarce know a bound,
> In vivid blaze alternately dance round:
> . . . With strains divine and true poetic fires;
> (Far from the reach of Hudson's chilly bay)
> Where cheerful phoebus makes all nature gay. (85)

Granted, the poem makes no pretense of presenting a true account of life along the West African coast: still, to address a poem to Phillis Wheatley, displaced far from her native "Affric shore," depicting her natal ground as a pastoral utopia calls attention to his omission of the economic enterprise responsible for her displacement, protection of which brings him and his Royal Navy colleagues from chilly northern latitudes to the equatorial South. Conspicuously unpeopled, Rochfort's sketch continues with its emphasis on the hospitable female character of this landscape:

> Where sweet refreshing breezes gently fan;
> The flow'ry path, the ever verdent lawn,
> The artless grottos, and the soft retreats;
> "At once the lover and the muse's seats." (85)

To which Wheatley answers:

> In fair description are thy powers display'd
> In artless grottos, and the sylvan shade;

Charm'd with thy painting, how my bosom burns!
And pleasing Gambia on my soul returns,
With native grace in spring's luxuriant reign,
Smiles the gay mead, and Eden blooms again,
The various bower, the tuneful flowing stream,
The soft retreats, the lovers golden dream,
Her soil spontaneous, yields exhaustless stores;
For phoebus revels on her verdant shores.
Whose flowery births, a fragrant train appear,
And crown the youth throughout the smiling year,

There, as in Britain's favour'd isle, behold
The bending harvest ripen into gold!
Just are thy views of Afric's blissful plain,
On the warm limits of the land and main. (87)

It is impossible to know the degree to which Wheatley draws or does not draw on her memory of Africa as she fills out Rochfort's "painting" of a pastoral Gambia, just as it would be impossible to speculate as to the relation of memory to the homeland she left behind as a preadolescent child. To the extent that geography in Wheatley's writing is theologically overdetermined, however, these verses are singular in that they portray Africa not as "a land Semblant of darkness itself," a benighted world "where the divine light of revelation (being obscur'd) is as darkness," but a bright retreat where "phoebus revels," a "blissful plain" where happiness reigns with an intensity comparable to what the faithful may anticipate on "the blissful shore" of the afterlife, a verdant and fecund land where "Eden blooms again." By locating Eden in her African homeland, even fancifully, Wheatley offers an alternative image, theologically speaking, to Africa as "dark abode": instead of a land where a fallen humanity gropes without knowledge or hope of salvation, she imagines a place of innocence regained, as though going back to a time before abduction and bondage made her the slave of the Christian redemption narrative. Admittedly, such a reading may well be bolder than Wheatley could ever have intended—the very phrase "Eden blooms *again*" may imply the inevitability of falling *again* into history and death. Still, given the insistent gloom with which Wheatley invests the idea of Africa, the application of such a term as "blissful" to a "pleasing Gambia" that "returns" on the poet's "soul" suggests a counternarrative that affirms the maternity of the remote soil on which she first drew breath.

Nevertheless, it is astonishing to see two poets, the one a former slave, the other complicit in the slave economy, collaborate in what they well know to be a false characterization of Senegambia—a depiction of the Gold Coast as distant in space and removed in time, a remnant of the Golden Age, in total denial of the exploitative relationships of a mixed company at the convergence of conflictive and irreconcilable geographies. Only in a world of make-believe can "Britain's favour'd isle" exist in harmony with "Afric's blissful plain." Perhaps Wheatley's willingness to take part in this fantasia stemmed from gratitude to Rochfort for recognizing some merit in her as an African and, in turn, beauty in her African homeland. As to any real prospects of returning to that homeland as a missionary, a proposition that John Thornton, a merchant active in Anglican evangelical circles, urged her to consider, she cannot help but express a frank horror: "Upon my arrival, how like a Barbarian Should I look to the Natives; I can promise that my tongue shall be quiet for a strong reason indeed being an utter stranger to the Language of Anamaboe. Now to be Serious, This undertaking appears too hazardous, and not sufficiently Eligible, to go—and leave my British & American Friends" (159). Thus Wheatley declined an invitation to proselytize in what is now Ghana among the multitude living in the shadow of Cape Coast Castle.[22]

"The production of an unlettered African"

The portrait of Olaudah Equiano that appears as the frontispiece in all nine editions of *The Interesting Narrative* published during his lifetime features an African of middle years dressed from an eighteenth-century English gentleman's wardrobe—a white cravat cascading through an open-necked buff waistcoat surmounted by a dark greatcoat. His posture is erect and his mien sober, and he holds a Bible open to Acts 4:12: "Neither is there salvation in any other: for there is none other name under heaven given among men, whereby we must be saved," a verse that will figure prominently in chapter 10, toward the end of his account of what he represents as his one true born-again conversion. Accosting any who should open the book, his eyes peer out from the oval frame as though to prompt readers to reflect upon their own spiritual fortunes. Equiano commissioned the miniaturist William Denton to paint this elaborately staged likeness, and its placement across from the title page indicates the degree to which he sought not only to take command over his public image but also to confront his white British readership with the arresting spectacle of exotic strangeness in familiar garb: an emissary from another world who has made himself at home as much in the sartorial as in the spiritual ways of the British evangelical gentry. The class markings of his costume contrast with those of Wheatley in her frontispiece portrait, which depict her in the humble dress of a maidservant, although any female servant who holds a pen must arrest the eighteenth-century reader's attention, and a black "servant" even more so. Like Wheatley before him, Equiano has something to say concerning the condition of those he has come to live among: Europeans with whom, "under heaven," he shares a temporal geography that culminates in a transcendent eternal home where human hierarchies cease. Like Wheatley, too, he purports to speak as the naturalized alien whose journey from pagan lands to the very center of enlightened Christendom confers an authority that native-born, passive recipients of the Gospel, prone to err in their disdain for a nonwhite humanity and in their unreflecting support of the slave trade, may not possess.

In the first two editions, the prefatory statement—"To the Lords Spiritual and Temporal, and the Commons of the Parliament of Great Britain"—directly follows the frontispiece and title page. This statement reflects *The Interesting Narrative*'s initial appearance in the spring of 1789, at the moment when debate commenced in the British Parliament over proposed legislation to outlaw the slave trade, the first major step toward the national disavowal of the one aberrant practice of what for Equiano is otherwise the paragon of civilized nations. The trade, he concedes, did place him on the path to Christian conversion and residence in enlightened, progressive England. Like Wheatley, he affirms that a divine combination of mystery and mercy brought him from his pagan land. Still, Equiano enlists his life story in the abolitionist cause to which hard trial and spiritual awakening have committed him. The "design" of the book, accordingly,

> is to excite in your august assemblies a sense of compassion for the miseries which the Slave Trade has entailed on my unfortunate countrymen. By the horrors of that trade I was first torn away from all the tender connexions that were dear to my heart; but these, through the mysterious ways of Providence, I ought to regard as infinitely more than compensated by the introduction I have thence obtained to the knowledge of the Christian religion, and of a nation which, by its liberal sentiments, its humanity, the glorious freedom of its government, and its proficiency in arts and sciences, has exalted the dignity of human nature.[23]

In the story he is about to unfold, however, he leaves little doubt that his fate was exceptional among enslaved Africans and that few blacks who make contact with the British see much beyond the monstrosity that marked his own first contact with voyagers from Christian lands.

Having stated his ambition and demonstrated the fluency with which he will tell his story, Equiano attaches what he must feel to be the obligatory self-deprecating acknowledgment of his "place," although in his efforts to accommodate white skepticism he does not sound like a man truly convinced that apologies are in order: "I am sensible I ought to entreat your pardon for addressing to you a work so wholly devoid of literary merit; but, as the production of an unlettered African, who is actuated by the hope of becoming an instrument towards the relief of his suffering countrymen, I trust that *such a man*, pleading in *such a cause*, will be acquitted of boldness and presumption" (7). Equiano justly reckoned the challenges of his task and the resourcefulness required to meet them. The narrative that follows attempts to position a white, culturally sedentary readership amid the violent and fluid transitions of the African diaspora. Specifically, it tells the story of one abducted from his native village, shipped across the Atlantic, sold and resold into conditions of servitude, immersed in new languages, literacies, religious doctrine, and the professional and domestic cultures of land and sea. Irregularly and largely self-educated, Equiano conforms to the period definition of "unlettered," but it is hard to imagine even a hostile reader doubting the proficiency of this performance. As we shall see, skepticism of Equiano's capacity to produce such a text did lead to suspicions that he benefited from white assistance, but the narrative's lexical and syntactic richness stands on its own merits.

In all editions, his prefatory statement is followed by lists of subscribers, among whom appear names familiar to readers of Wheatley and students of the abolition movement in late eighteenth-century Great Britain: the Earl of Dartmouth, Samuel Clarkson, Selina Hastings, Hannah More, James Ramsay, Granville Sharp, John Wesley, Joseph Woods. Beginning with the third edition, Equiano includes letters attesting to his character and intelligence, and that commend this book by an author whose name is always followed by the label "an African" to judicious consideration. In addition, Equiano supplements the original list of subscribers with new lists organized by place: Hull, Bristol, Norwich, Lynn, Wisbech, Dublin, and Edinburgh.[24] Beginning with the fifth edition, Equiano answers attacks on the truthfulness of his narrative published in the *Oracle* and *Star*, drawing upon the correspondence of supporters to exonerate himself from allegations of falsely claiming an African rather than a Caribbean birth. With each edition he saw through the press, from the portrait to the ever-lengthening roster of his subscribing readership, Equiano provides evidence of his integration in the lives of his fellow Britons and the depth of his naturalization. In the pages that follow, he will endeavor to define and measure the distances he has traversed before settling in England, and he will address the transformations and conversions that have made him the citizen that he is. If, as the frontispiece suggests, Equiano wishes to exhibit that aspect of his persona that remains irreconcilably alien in the white British nation, he takes care to begin his tale of exotic origin by documenting his connection with and investment in the mores and fortunes of his adopted country.

The Interesting Narrative represents several levels of Equiano's mastery of the art and technology of public testimony as practiced in British literary culture. The narrative proper reflects his command of the genres of travel, adventure, war, and sea peril as well as the discourse of spiritual conversion, while production of the book artifact demonstrates Equiano's understanding of print culture as a material practice in which an appealing commodity is mass produced and strategically distributed. As a businessman he was sufficiently astute to retain copyright and thus preserve control over the book through its subsequent editions. Any consideration of his geographic position vis-à-vis his English reader must begin by recognizing the thoroughness with which he located his testimony amid the conventional modalities by which writers and readers in English meet as intersubjective partners in recognizably common narratives. From well inside the conventions and expectations of English literary practice, Equiano proclaims a likeness to his readership that establishes the occasion for his admonitory citations of unlikeness. Drawing on biblical authority reinforced by period theories of monogenetic human origin and environmental adaptation (all humans, he asserts in chapter 1, acquire darkened complexions as they migrate toward the equator), Equiano affirms the fundamental propinquity of all people, concluding the first chapter with what would become a frequently cited verse in abolitionist literature: "God hath made of one blood all nations of men" (Acts 17:26). At other times, however, he embraces unlikeness as the foundation of experiential authority (you have never been a slave, you cannot possibly know this condition, but I have and I do). He thus situates his provocative otherness amid the British nation's first-person vernacular expressive culture.

We see Equiano actively managing this author-reader relational geography throughout *The Interesting Narrative*: rhetorically, he configures the spaces his utterance must traverse as proximity to and distance from his inscribed white British readership, and his emphasis on separation often alternates closely with his emphasis on contiguity. He begins chapter 1, for example, with general observations concerning the liabilities assumed by any memoirist: these range from "imputation of vanity" to accusations of dishonesty should events seem too "uncommon" to be believable or, conversely, censure for being tedious should the narrative too much dwell on the commonplace (31). Such often-rehearsed preliminary observations function like an exchange of familiarities, as everyone who has participated as author or reader in eighteenth-century British literary culture is likely to be aware of exactly these risks of first-person narrative. "It is, therefore," Equiano confesses, "not a little hazardous, in a private and obscure individual, *and a stranger too*, thus to solicit the indulgent attention of the public; especially when I own I offer here the history of neither a saint, a hero, nor a tyrant" (31; emphasis added). Having identified the potential embarrassment that attaches to individuals who bring obscurity (darkness, but also invisibility) and strangeness to public exposure, he proceeds to plead the terms by which the narrative might prove "interesting" in the multiple senses of that word:

> If, then, the following narrative does not appear sufficiently *interesting* to engage general attention, let my motive be some excuse for its publication. I am not so foolishly vain as to expect from it either immortality or literary reputation. If it affords any satisfaction to *my numerous friends*, at whose request it has been written, or in the smallest degree promotes the *interest* of humanity, the ends for which it was undertaken will be fully attained, and every wish of my heart gratified. Let it therefore be remembered that, in wishing to avoid censure, I do not aspire to praise. (31–32; emphasis added)

The author is not strange to the point of isolation: like James Baldwin in 1950s America, Equiano is not really a stranger to white citizens alert to the country's mixed demographics.[25] He has "numerous friends," who have encouraged him to compose a life story by which he might serve the "interest of humanity." In the full resonance of its title, *The Interesting Narrative* endeavors to engage a readership of friends and fellow citizens (strangers though they may be) as stakeholders in the large human cause.

Another example of Equiano's oscillation between proximity to and distance from a white British readership occurs at the opening of chapter 2, following his account of the native village provided in chapter 1:

> I hope the reader will not think I have *trespassed on his patience* in introducing myself to him with some account of the manners and customs of my country. They had been implanted in me with great care, and made an impression on my mind, which time could not erase, and which all the adversity and variety of fortune I have since experienced served only to rivet and record: for, whether the love of one's country be real or imaginary, or a lesson of reason, or an instinct of nature, I still look back with pleasure on the first scenes of my life, though that pleasure has been for the most part mingled with sorrow. (46; emphasis added)

The word "trespass" carries geographical but also religious implications. Equiano's gesture of apology for having overstepped the bounds of his reader's willingness to absorb information pertaining to his native African world—a world of ostensibly limited interest and relevance to the stay-at-home British citizen—conjures among truly mindful and interested readers the world-historical trespass of Europeans and their African surrogates across the boundaries of such communities as Equiano sketches in chapter 1. "Trespass" thus also invokes the Lord's Prayer as it appears in the 1662 Book of Common Prayer, where the word is synonymous with wrongdoing: "Forgive us our trespasses as we forgive them that trespass against us." Complicating the rapport that Equiano seeks to establish with his reader, however, is the fact that the first chapter largely derives from two works written in English: Anthony Benezet's *A Short Account of that Part of Africa, Inhabited by the Negroes* (1762) and James Field Stanfield, *Observations on a Voyage to the Coast of Africa* (1788).[26] Did the vale of Essaka exist under that name or another as Equiano's birthplace, or was he in fact born in South Carolina, far from the African interior? Does the phrase "whether the love of one's country be real *or imaginary*" substantially concede the fictional fabric of his remembered Africa? Whatever the truth, Equiano's descriptions of infant and childhood scenes are no less literary than Wheatley's "fancy'd happy seat" and "pleasing Gambia" or other figurations of exotic worlds that Britain's well-advanced colonial agenda had introduced to the national literature.

The only "trespass" for which Equiano might need to atone would be that of falsely impersonating one who describes Africa from the inside out, but even if he never set foot in the Kingdom of Benin, his lifelong experience as outsider in an Atlantic world dominated by white Europeans, together with his genealogical ties to the African continent, renders his factual geographical provenance somewhat beside the point.

Wheatley and Equiano both wrote at a moment in British colonial history when images of far shores and foreign peoples were anything but new to the national literary imagination. In the two centuries preceding Equiano's 1789 publication of the *Interesting Narrative*, the home reading public had been steeped in the literature of English and European voyages to oversea worlds. The ocean itself, given the vast distances routinely navigated by Great Britain's navy and merchant fleet, might well have seemed an extension of what had become the world's premiere maritime power. Richard Hakluyt, compiler of documents pertaining to British exploration, began publishing accounts of voyages and first encounters in 1582. Travel narratives in the Western tradition had always featured marvels and monsters, and the so-called true history of transoceanic exploration rarely scrupled to differentiate between fantasy and fact. By the time *The Tempest* was first performed in 1611, the exotic had become so familiar to the national imagination as to spawn genres of fabulous travel for which *Robinson Crusoe* (1719) and *Gulliver's Travels* (1726) count as late installments. The geographic reach and cartographic arrogance of the eighteenth-century British reading public find memorable expression in a letter Edmund Burke wrote to Dr. William Robertson on June 9, 1777: "When the Aegyptians call the Greeks children in the Antiquities, we may well call them Children; and so we may call all these nations, which were able to trace the progress of Society only within their own Limits. But now the Great Map of Mankind is unrolld all at once, and there is no state or Gradation of barbarism, and no mode of refinement which we have not at the same instant under our view."[27] In light of such Anglocentric attitudes, the geographies of the North and South Atlantic as well as the Mediterranean Sea could not have seemed fantastic to subscribers of *The Interesting Narrative*, and even the mysterious overland journey from his recreated Igboe village with its divagating unmapped passages had a well-established place in the genres of abduction and captivity. The novelty Equiano and Wheatley both introduce is description of the exotic world from the perspective of the exotic personage, and even if, chronologically, there is nothing new about a colonized person occupying the subject position in what remains the colonizer's discourse, Wheatley and Equiano (and how many successors who have trod the paths of the fugitive corridor?) must conquer the skepticism that arises when someone speaks and, more than that, writes from the default status of a Caliban. Unlike Caliban, whom the colonizer's language enables to curse, Wheatley and Equiano assert the power of those who have learned to bless. But as both converts show, to speak from one's faith does not preclude affirmations that carry a condemnatory weight.

Equiano's account in chapter 1 of his native village emphasizes its remoteness and inaccessibility. As he instructs readers in African geography, proceeding from the macrocosmic idea to the deep alcove of the Kingdom of Benin, he transports them to a locale (his Vale of Essaka) that in fact did not and does not exist on any map. Benin, he points out to his Global North audience,

> is situated nearly under the line and extends along the coast about 170 miles, but runs back into the interior part of Africa to a distance hitherto I believe unexplored by any traveller; and seems only terminated at length by the empire of Abyssinia, near 1500 miles from its beginning. This kingdom is divided into many provinces or districts: in one of the most remote and fertile of which, called Eboe, I was born, in the year 1745, in a charming fruitful vale, named Essaka. The distance of this province from the capital of Benin and the sea coast must be very considerable; for I had never heard of white men or Europeans, nor of the sea. (32)

Remote geographically as this site may be, his sketch of the native village, whether derived from memory or secondary sources, seeks to engage its English-speaking readership through its citation of likeness to and difference from Western social and religious custom and to describe the folkways of his home country within a frame of comparative anthropology. As anthropology, however, Equiano's depiction of life in the Vale of Essaka implicitly affirms the Rousseauean thesis that those who live in primal harmony with the natural world preserve a purity lost to more advanced, urban, mercantile, and materialist civilizations. His portrait of the African home, family, communal structure, and subsistence economy conforms to European stadialist theories that exalt the herding and agricultural phase of universal human development and lament the corruption of civilized refinement:[28]

> As our manners are simple, our luxuries are few. (34)
> Our manner of living is entirely plain; for as yet the natives are unacquainted with those refinements in cookery which debauch the taste. (35)
> Before we taste food, we always wash our hands: indeed our cleanliness on all occasions is extreme. (35)
> They are totally unacquainted with strong or spiritous liquours; and their principal beverage is palm wine. (35)
> In our buildings we study convenience rather than ornament. (36)
> As we live in a country where nature is prodigal of her favours, our wants are few and easily supplied; of course we have few manufactures. (36–37)
> Every one contributes something to the common stock; and as we are unacquainted with idleness, we have no beggars. (37–38)

By implication Equiano itemizes the ills of his readership's society: extremes of wealth and poverty, greed, aesthetic decadence, slovenliness, drunkenness. According to the narrative's chronology, he has not laid eyes on the vale for thirty years, yet in profiling his home country's ways, he writes in the present tense as though reporting from the scene, underscoring his status in England as geographic and moral outsider, which he is only able to do as one who writes from a naturalized inside position. In his depiction of the African village as aloof from historical change, he creates the impression not only that he speaks across a vast cultural and spatial gulf but also from one temporality to another. This is a world anterior *in* if not *to* time, and as Equiano delineates his society's monotheistic beliefs and patriarchal structures, citing its practice of circumcision, ritual washings, and observance of feast dates, he draws parallels between "the manners and customs of my countrymen, and those of the Jews, before they reached the Land of Promise, and particularly the patriarchs, while they were yet in that pastoral state which is described in Genesis—an analogy, which alone would induce me to think that the one people had sprung from the other" (43–44). As to the internecine conflicts that arise within this utopian world, "they appear to have been irruptions of one little state or district on the other, to obtain prisoners or booty. Perhaps they were incited to this by those traders who brought the European goods" (38–39). The disruptive trespass of the colonizing North appears on the vale's verdant periphery, but the natal scene Equiano evokes remains timelessly intact.

From an evangelical Christian perspective, this world innocent of modern corruption has languished for centuries beyond reach of the Gospel, which has only recently penetrated the African gloom as the tag-along of a corrupt, slave-trading West. Equiano's principal objective in *The Interesting Narrative* is to address this contradiction. From the frontispiece forward, he seeks to exert a corrective influence over Christian Europe's behavior toward those over whom it wields irresistible power. Toward this end he depicts the abducted child's first contact with the West. And what he represents as an initial encounter with Europeans emphasizes not their Christian role as messengers of the Word but their savage otherness juxtaposed with the innocence of the boy seized from his mother's care. Against the cruelty of the Christian slavers, he highlights the humanity of his African captors. Traumatic as his initial abduction may be, as long as he is the captive of his fellow Africans he is subject to comparatively kind treatment: he is integrated into the households where he is lodged as a slave and nowhere finds himself outside the large community of his birth language. But as he proceeds north and west, entering regions of increased European influence, he sees signs of what the adult narrator depicts as decadence: "I came among a people who did not circumcise, and eat without washing their hands. They cooked also in iron pots, and had European cutlasses and cross bows, which were unknown to us, and fought with their fists among themselves. Their women were not so modest as ours, for they eat, and drank, and slept with their men. But, above all, I was amazed to see no sacrifices or offerings among them" (53–54). Finally, when he arrives at the coast, and perceives the ocean and the vessel that will remove him even further from his native vale, his captivity takes a new and ominous turn. In describing his meeting with the non-African other, Equiano draws upon terminology by which roving Europeans have typically characterized non-European natives encountered on distant shores:

> The first object which saluted my eyes when I arrived on the coast was the sea, and a slave-ship, which was then riding at anchor, and waiting for its cargo. These filled me with astonishment, which was soon converted into terror. . . . When I was carried on board I was immediately handled, and tossed up, to see if I were sound, by some of the crew; and I was now persuaded that I had gotten into a world of bad spirits, and that they were going to kill me. Their complexions too differing so much from ours, their long hair, and the language they spoke, which was very different from any I had ever heard, united to confirm me in this belief. (55)

The frightened boy asks the black people employed to load the ship "if we were not to be eaten by those white men with horrible looks, red faces, and loose hair" (55). Perhaps Equiano at this or some other point in his life genuinely feared cannibalism, but as narrator he plays significantly on a motif that pervades the literature of colonization, in which the dread of being killed, dismembered, and consumed betrays a larger fear that a cultural and environmental otherness has the power to assimilate the captive to its exotic ways, prevailing against what may be the captive's merely token resistance.[29] Equiano sets the scene of first encounter against the knowledge that he would master the language and navigational technology of this new world; would spend a large portion of his life on the ocean, which he would come to know in cartographic detail; and would be involved henceforward in the lives of white people to the point of speaking and worshipping as they do and marrying an English woman with whom he would have two children. Whatever relation his narrative bears to what he remembers, and whatever relation memory bears to the life he led as a boy, the naturalized citizen must invent this recollection in an acquired language for a narrative occasion that renders the lost child a figure of speculation for author and reader alike.

The acquired language, the narrative's irreducible medium, is never far from the thematic foreground, where it at once reflects and expresses Equiano's proximity to and distance from a native-speaker readership. The dramatic development of *The Interesting Narrative* consistently unfolds in conjunction with Equiano's increasing command of spoken and written English and what he is able to achieve by virtue of his eventual proficiency. This theme emerges from what he depicts as the languageless state—or isolation from anything like a language community—that defines his condition of Middle Passage distress: "I was now exceedingly miserable, and thought myself worse off than any of the rest of my companions; for they could talk to each other, but I had no person to speak to that I could understand" (62).[30] In chapter 3, after he has been transferred from Barbados to Virginia, bought by Michael Henry Pascal, and put on a ship to England, his adjustment to post-African life corresponds to his acquisition of English.[31] He comes to understand that he is not to be eaten or sacrificed and is able therefore to dismiss his overwhelming fear of death: "I could smatter a little imperfect English," and this gives him confidence, even though such was inadequate "to conjecture my destiny" (64). Befriended by Richard Baker, "my best interpreter" (68), he acclimates to the ways of white people and is introduced to the Bible, churchgoing, and the Christian God. In chapter 4, after seeing nearly two years' wartime service on the *Namur* as Pascal's servant, he is baptized in London and under care of Pascal's cousins makes progress in the acquisition of literacy skills that he already associates with liberation and empowerment: "I thought now of nothing but being freed, and working for myself, and thereby getting money to enable me to get a good education; for I always had a great desire to be able at least to read and write" (91). As a baptized and increasingly literate individual, Equiano imagines himself exempt from further enslavement and looks forward to a life of freedom in England at the conclusion of the Seven Years' War. When, arriving at Gravesend, Pascal sells him to James Doran, captain of the *Charming Sally* bound for Montserrat, he protests in vain: "I have been baptized; and by the laws of the land no man has a right to sell me" (93–94). In response, Doran tells him that he "talks too much English": if he "did not behave . . . and be quiet," this captain "had a method on board" to force the issue (94). In Virginia, Equiano had seen a slave woman with an iron muzzle who "could scarcely speak" (63), so he was well acquainted with the repertoire of methods.

Along with suppression of what he had become accustomed to as a free expressiveness that extended to the fashioning of arguments in support of his human rights, Equino's subsequent West Indian enslavement reacquaints him with the spatial confinement to which the slave master customarily relegates his objects of trade. The graphic description in chapter 2 of the claustrophobic slave-ship hold establishes early in the narrative the existential condition of enslavement with respect to one's embodiment in space; so insupportable is the condition, as Equiano shows, that life itself becomes unendurable: "I was soon put down under the decks, and there I received such a salutation in my nostrils as I had never experienced in my life: so that with the loathsomeness of the stench, and crying together, I became so sick and low that I was not able to eat, nor had I the least desire to taste any thing. I now wished for the last friend, Death, to relieve me" (56). This passage comes back more than once to haunt the reader, for, in addition to silencing Equiano, Doran confines him for a period "under the deck" (96), a site that not only recalls the slave ship that brought him to Barbados but also anticipates the predicament of

Africans in the cargo hold of a sloop on which Equiano later serves as steward to the incompetent Captain William Phillips. When the sloop founders on the rocks, Equiano must prevent Phillips from nailing the hatches to the hold, entrapping the vessel's "live cargo" (133). The theme of spatial entrapment pervades Equiano's testimony, and his narrative cites numerous examples in which the enslaved subject is deprived of mobility. We learn that in the West Indian "land of bondage" (98), a common punishment for slaves who would escape is to be pinned to the ground and tortured and then imprisoned for some time in a casket-like box (106–7). In another instance that bears tacit reference to Equiano's social mobility in England, where, as he tells the reader at the book's conclusion, he has married an English woman, he speaks of witnessing in Montserrat "a negro-man staked to the ground, and cut most shockingly" because of his relations with "a white woman who was a common prostitute" (104). As though to underscore the turpitude of white male sexual practice, at various points in the narrative Equiano reminds readers of the free access the enslavers exercise to African women and girls.

Equiano's West Indian enslavement is mitigated by his sale to the Quaker merchant Robert King. Recognizing Equiano's aptitudes, King enlists him in various capacities as clerk and ship's steward. Such employment leads to a life of constant travel among Caribbean islands and the North American mainland and provides Equiano with occasions to acquire skills as a navigator. *The Interesting Narrative*'s extensive catalog of cruelties visited upon the enslaved proceeds from Equiano's mobility as an agent in and witness to the trade. His complicity as participant-observer is a source of distress to the narrative inasmuch as he who has documented life below deck must locate himself significantly above it. "I used frequently to have different cargoes of new negroes in my care for sale," he reports, but such care affords little authority when whites are of a mind "to commit violent depredations on the chastity of the female slaves" (104). Chapters 5 and 6 portray a highly valued bondsman whose opportunities to learn the business of Atlantic shipping and to conduct his own small-scale merchant operation—profits from which he will apply to purchasing his own freedom—contend with the guilt he feels (but never entirely articulates) for his enforced betrayal of fellow Africans as well as with the constant "impositions" of white people who wish to abduct or cheat him or make him the object of violent attack. Equiano depicts himself prior to his manumission as constantly balancing the urge to escape against the slow and "honest" process of saving sufficient money to buy a legal release, although once free he will still be liable to illicit enslavement, a practice immune from legal redress given the association of blackness with bondage and the ineligibility of black people to contest the testimony of whites.[32]

As Equiano represents it, then, the hellishness of the West Indies consists not only in the confinements of the enslaved but, with respect to his acquired language, the powerlessness of even the most articulate African to obtain redress inasmuch as "throughout the West Indies no black man's testimony is admitted, on any occasion, against any white person whatever" (162). Although Equiano contemplates running away prior to his emancipation—and running away always means finding his way back to London—his life as a fugitive properly begins only after Robert King signs his manumission, for he quickly learns that emancipated slaves "live in constant alarm for their liberty." They cannot protect themselves against kidnapping and return to bondage "for such is the equity of the West Indian laws, that no free negro's evidence will be admitted in their courts of justice" (122). Verbal proficiency alone makes the black speaker liable to attack: in Savannah, as Equiano relates, he is physically threatened by two white men enraged because he "talked too good English" (159). A black person may carry documents designating the bearer as free but, unable to make a first-person claim, the emancipated individual remains a mute third person, and white people are not bound to respect such documents in the absence of the statement's signatory. The white master class's insistent conflation of African origin and slave status precludes any African's first-person claim to be free. From cover to cover, *The Interesting Narrative* implicitly presents itself as a counter to West Indian laws (and such British sentiment as would support those laws) that invalidate the African voice on the basis of ethnic disesteem.

Long before its conclusion, *The Interesting Narrative* achieves a degree of formal resolution in chapter 9, when Equiano parts from his former master and boards a ship for London:

> With a light heart I bade Montserrat farewell, and never had my feet on it since; and with it I bade adieu to the sound of the cruel whip, and all other dreadful instruments of torture! adieu to the offensive sight of the violated chastity of the sable females, which has too often accosted my eyes! adieu to oppressions (although to me less severe than most of my countrymen!) and adieu to the angry howling dashing surfs! I wished for a grateful and thankful heart to praise the Lord God on high for all his mercies! in this extacy I steered the ship all night. (164)

Readers may be forgiven for taking this last clause literally. Equiano steers in this voyage the figurative ship of his self-possession, although the metaphor builds on what had become an expertise tested, at the end of chapter 7, in his piloting of King's sloop *Nancy* to port in Montserrat after the onboard death of Captain Thomas Farmer. In relating that incident, Equiano bestows on himself the epithet "sable captain" (144), and it is with a captain's frame of mind that he arrives in London with a very particular score to settle. The control he has been gaining over his own destiny reaches a climax in chapter 9 with his confrontation in London of Captain Pascal, from whom he demands the prize money Pascal had stolen from him, threatening Pascal with a lawsuit if he does not return the sum voluntarily. Out of courtesy to Pascal's cousins, Equiano never follows through with this threat, but his expressed willingness to engage the judicial process in obtaining restitution signals his recognition of having passed from the colonies, where he has no voice and defensible rights, to the home country, where he is entitled to press a claim.

Formally, *The Interesting Narrative* might have concluded with Equiano's confrontation of Pascal and his assertion of their equality before the law: a scene marking Equiano's splendid reversal of Pascal's attempt to banish him deeply in a geography of bondage and thus to silence what had become his argumentative voice. However, there is more life to narrate. In chapter 9 alone, Equiano has much to report concerning settlement in London, finding work as a barber and hairdresser, and taking jobs on ships bound for Turkey, Portugal, and even the West Indies (Grenada and Jamaica), to which he had bid a florid adieu in the previous chapter. His very evident craving for adventure that requires vast geographic mobility tests planetary limits in his attempted voyage to the North Pole in the company of his employer, Dr. Charles Irving; this excursion frames his career as global traveler between tropical and arctic extremes. Besides recounting additional travels, chapter 10 highlights what Equiano considers to be his spiritual conversion from the baptized, nominal, but not very religious Christian he had been through much of his life to one who feels confident in his justification. For Equiano, this is the most important life event and the warrant of a testimonial authority that is spiritual before it is legal or literary. Chapter 11 enumerates further travels to Spain, followed by an account of yet another foray to the Caribbean and the Central American coast in a venture to establish a plantation in partnership with Irving. Equiano's only very gradual gravitation to the position he establishes in the preface to the book—that the slave trade and slavery must both be abolished—becomes evident in this chapter, as Equiano and Irving purchase slaves to work their plantation. Following the complete collapse and failure of this project and additional accounts of abuse he encounters in the West Indies, Equiano takes final leave of the Caribbean basin.

Chapter 12 concludes the volume with brief mentions of further voyages to New York and Philadelphia as well as accounts of two attempted reengagements with Africa that end in disappointment. The first involves a ministry to Africa, as proposed by his friend Matthias Macnamara, a former governor of the British colony of Senegambia. Never particularly well defined, the idea is abandoned when the bishop of London declines Equiano's petition that he be ordained. The second abortive reengagement concerns his ill-fated appointment as commissary agent in the project to resettle England's black and brown poor in Sierra Leone, a proposal that beneath a charitable veneer sought to purge nonwhite indigents (Africans and East Indians) from the nation's city streets. Equiano was tasked with provisioning the settlement party but before the three ships could sail was relieved of his duties. Given that he had been accused of mismanagement of his responsibilities, Equiano takes this opportunity to vindicate his name and to offer suggestions as to the true authors of malfeasance. The delayed departure of the would-be settlers resulted in their badly timed arrival in Sierra Leone just at the start of the rainy season; for this and additional reasons, the colony met with a short-lived and disastrous fate.[33]

Whatever the likelihood he might serve in some future ambassadorial role in Europe's relations with Africa, Equiano envisions the integration of the two continents spiritually and economically, and he applies his vision of integration to his overall argument that the slave trade must be outlawed and slavery abolished. He calls on Great Britain, as the moral center of Christian Europe, to recognize that both the nation's spiritual authority and its economic self-interest require an end to the traffic in and exploitation of black bodies: "May Heaven make the British senators the dispersers of light, liberty and science, to the uttermost parts of the earth: then will be glory to God on the highest, on earth peace, and good-will to men.—Glory, honour, peace, &c. to every soul of man that worketh good; to the Britons first, (because to them the Gospel is preached), and also to the nations" (233). To this portrait of London as spiritual center and its colonies east and west as "the uttermost parts of the earth," he appends an economic forecast of the prosperity that awaits a postslavery colonial order: "As the inhuman traffic of slavery is now taken into the consideration of the British legislature, I doubt not, if a system of commerce was established in Africa, the demand for manufactures would most rapidly augment, as the native inhabitants would insensibly adopt the British fashions, manners, customs, &c. In proportion to the civilization, so will be the consumption of British manufactures" (233). Equiano presses the argument for abolition in ways that flatter the spiritual self-regard and reinforce the economic presumption of the metropolitan perspective. He has come a long way from what he presents in the first two chapters as an Afrocentrist view of the world.

Beginning with the fifth edition, the narrative concludes with an account of Equiano's marriage to Susan Cullen, a personal detail that adds weight to the argument that Europeans and Africans should embrace one another in economic partnership and spiritual equality, notwithstanding that Western imperialism and Christianity form the frame of reference for such postslavery—but hardly postcolonial—relations. As Vincent Carretta has argued, *The Interesting Narrative* in its nine editions served in multiple generic capacities. Whereas in its first, strategic appearance in spring 1789, it functions as a petition to the British Houses of Parliament just as they enter debate over the proposed abolition of the slave trade, subsequent editions (as reflected in expanding subscriber lists) are overtly directed at a general public.[34] As Equiano engages a national audience, his autobiography functions as apologia, permitting him to address the charge that his narrative falsifies his birthplace and early upbringing and to provide a counterexplanation of what led to his dismissal as commissary of the Sierra Leone colonization project. One measure of his book's success is the financial return it brought him over the course of its nine printings—a success that, along with his marriage, is further evidence of his thorough naturalization. Contemporary reviews, however, even when complimentary, condescend in commenting about a literary performance whose excellence is deemed relative to its inherent inferiority as the product of a dark-skinned alien. "The life of an African, written by himself, is certainly a curiosity," writes Mary Wollstonecraft, and while she concedes the power of the *Narrative* to incite indignation in the sympathetic reader, she does not find the work to demonstrate the "extraordinary intellectual powers" necessary to refute the association of blackness with inferiority. Richard Gough, echoing Wollstonecraft, observes that Equiano's "memoirs, written in a very unequal style, place the writer on a par with the general mass of men in the subordinate stations of civilized society," while the anonymous commentator in the *Monthly Review* is willing to credit "the authenticity of this very intelligent African's story" but thinks it probable that an "English writer had assisted him in the compilement."[35] Equiano's appeal for recognition as a citizen of the literary nation ever encounters the condemnation of qualified praise.

For Equiano is ever "the African," even in his self-subscription. He is "Olaudah Equiano, or Gustavus Vassa, the African," on the frontispiece and title page (2–3), a man known by two names: the European alias bestowed on him (with racist irony) after the Swedish popular hero, and what he invokes as his reclaimed birth name. He is "an African," as the Reverend Dr. Peckard styles him in a letter quoted in the preface (8); he is "an enlightened African, of good sense, agreeable manners, and of an excellent character" (10), as the American Thomas Digges describes him in another letter; and he is "the enlightened African" (11–12), as William Langworthy refers to him in yet another. Equiano's successful acculturation to the British nation carries an asterisk forever identifying him as one permanently displaced. To be "an African" in these contexts is to be identified with a country that does not exist: only outside of Africa, a continent comprising many localities, ethnicities, languages, can one be identified as such. In the vast English ignorance of the multiplicity of African places and peoples, to be "African" is simply to be other; to exist, in England, as African, is to be a stateless resident. As is the case with Phillis Wheatley, place of origin can no longer be said to exist. These voices from the Global South emanate from a fantasy of difference that each has crafted from metropolitan and evangelical geographies that have made it possible for them to speak at all. In reading Wheatley's poems and Equiano's prose, one must be aware of the forces that have all but succeeded in silencing what they have to say in order justly to appreciate the moments of assertion and resistance they are able to inscribe in the tongue circumstance compelled them to acquire.

Chapter 3

✦

Slave State to Free

David Walker, Frederick Douglass, Harriet Jacobs

Between ratification of the U.S. Constitution (1788) and ratification of the Thirteenth Amendment (1865) the distinction between slave state (or territory) and free state (or territory) remained fluid and contested. During the colonial era, slavery existed all along the Atlantic seaboard, with antislavery sentiment strongest in the Northeast and Middle Atlantic. Before unification under the Constitution, five of the former colonies adopted a gradualist approach to end the practice within their borders: Pennsylvania, 1780; Massachusetts and New Hampshire, 1783; Rhode Island and Connecticut, 1784. Rather than enacting an immediate and unconditional emancipation, these states abolished slavery by phases, typically honoring slaveholder claims to the productive years of those currently held in bondage. Whereas the Society of Friends and other Christian denominations presented ethical arguments for abolition, white laborers and artisans fearing for their livelihood also enlisted in the cause. In providing for the emancipation of what was becoming an economically insignificant slave population, legislators were as concerned with the financial interests of slaveholders as the human rights of the enslaved.[1] In Northern states, emancipation conferred a second-class citizenship already in place for free people of color: property rights and access to public space were limited and voting rights restricted if not prohibited.[2] On the map, the 1789 nation was a patchwork of slave and free, but at ground level there were few clear lines and no open spaces where people of color were not subject to harassment. Although the Thirteenth (1865), Fourteenth (1868), and Fifteenth (1870) Amendments later provided some legal clarity, they could hardly resolve the complicated geographies black people navigated as subjects only nominally equipped with full rights of citizenship.

As the nation acquired western territories and admitted new states to the union, slave state and free state became a matter of competing demographics and economic hegemonies, with parties on both sides employing different strategies for attaining or preserving leverage within the federal scheme. Among other legislative initiatives related to the political organization of the vast expanse gained through the Louisiana Purchase and the Mexican-American War, the Missouri Compromise, the Compromise of 1850, and the Kansas-Nebraska Act delayed resolution of the slavery question as it related to national policy. Compromise in various forms put off the moment at which the nation would fracture and become embroiled in the full-scale armed conflict to which slave revolt, urban riot (now white, now black), border skirmish, massacre, and insurrectionary incident were but the prelude. Throughout the antebellum period, the Mason-Dixon and Missouri Compromise Lines served as cartographic expressions of the border distinguishing slave state from free, but the Fugitive Slave Laws (especially those of 1850) extended the reach of the slave power into supposed safe havens in the North. With the secessions of 1861, vague and shifting militarized boundaries and active battle lines appeared between and within North and South, but even with the 1863 Emancipation Proclamation, slavery persisted in the nonseceding slave states, and movement across borders was no less ambiguous than it had ever been. Slave state and free state, in short, never conformed to a settled map, and even when borderlines appear in the narratives as significant thresholds, the public status and inward state of the fugitive remain in flux.

David Walker, Frederick Douglass, and Harriet Jacobs all write from the perspective of individuals who have migrated from microcosms in which an enslaved population and free people of color are subject to coercive placement, systematic surveillance, and unchecked abuse. In the course of migrating from the South to the North, all acquire the sense of a large geographical context that enables them to see the slave-state microcosm as a social arrangement with a distinct political and cultural history. As one who always enjoyed the legal status of a freeman, Walker speaks to and on behalf of an African American community for whom the distinction between slave and free is blurred by the race-based foundation of American slavery. The assumption that people of African origin are an ordained underclass rendered even free black Northerners second-class citizens susceptible of abduction and enslavement: in addressing deeply ingrained prejudicial attitudes that spill over the North-South boundaries, Walker anticipates issues Douglass and Jacobs face first as fugitives and then as free persons in the North. Walker's references to classical texts and his engagement of Jefferson's *Notes on the State of Virginia* exhibit a cosmopolitanism that affords him perspective on the phenomenon of American slavery, whereas Douglass and Jacobs come to know their former status through self-education supplemented by international travel. As memoirists, Douglass and Jacobs develop detailed portraits of the slave-life microcosm and document the process by which bound individuals, from early childhood forward, cognitively map a world in which oppressive routine and dictatorial rule dominate the organization of space but never quite foreclose the establishment of counterspaces for communal memory, story, song, worship, literacy, conspiracy, and other forms of resistance and concealment. Such counterspaces nourish the imagination of escape, even when escape means traversal of a hostile rural world, mapped sketchily if at all, where fugitives risk notice among glaring vacancy and dark recess, the North Star figuring as the one source of directional certitude.

"Having travelled over a considerable portion of these United States"

David Walker's passionate lay sermon combines the voice of one crying in the wilderness with the arguments of an autodidact alert to the resource of Enlightenment thought. From the cosmopolitan perspective he derives from that thought, he proceeds to build his radical critique. The pamphlet's full-length title articulates a global vision as well as a sense of black statelessness prefiguring (among others) W. E. B. Du Bois and Malcolm X: *Walker's Appeal, in Four Articles; Together with a Preamble, to the Coloured Citizens of the World, But in Particular, and Very Expressly, to Those of the United States of America. Written in Boston, State of Massachusetts, September 28, 1829*. Dramatically invoking a borderless public, the title highlights Walker's educational mission and his strategy to connect with readers and hearers in remote localities where awareness of a national or international context would be difficult to achieve. Given the rural isolation of much of his target audience, Walker developed an elaborate scheme of distribution whereby the tract might successfully reach secluded pockets of African Americans in the Deep South, many of whom he imagined receiving his word read aloud by the one black person in twenty who could do so.[3] His title calls on the world to witness the crimes taking place in the United States, while assuring hostages of the slave-state microcosm that their sufferings are duly noted—indeed, that their struggles unite them with people worldwide who find themselves resisting European colonialism and such white supremacist attitudes as Jefferson expresses in *Notes on the State of Virginia*. Anticipating many future black authors in his wish to indict the United States in an international court of opinion, and foreshadowing Du Bois specifically in his recognition that color line conflict far exceeds the boundaries of one nation, Walker assures his variously situated audiences of color that their liberation "shall never be fully consummated, but with the *entire emancipation of your enslaved brethren all over the world*."[4] Walker is concerned that his auditors understand the magnitude of the struggle and the need to end infighting and betrayal among those determined to resist.

As sermon and manifesto, the *Appeal* presents an expository treatment of the oppression of black people rather than a narrative of Walker's own journey from the Carolinas to Boston, although he alludes to that journey now and again. The son of a free black woman, Walker was able to migrate north without becoming a fugitive. Born in Wilmington, North Carolina, he resided in Charleston, South Carolina, before settling in the small African

American neighborhood on Beacon Hill, close by the North End wharf district, where he ran a used clothing business for several years before dying under peculiar circumstances shy of his thirty-fourth birthday. Little documentary evidence exists to verify Walker's whereabouts or activities prior to his Boston residence, although the certainty that he was in Wilmington and Charleston during childhood and young manhood makes it possible to speculate about formative influences. Walker's early years in Wilmington would have acquainted him with a black population, mostly enslaved, involved in the production of lumber and turpentine, the basis of the region's economy, and whose employment in the building trades and as navigators of the Cape Fear estuaries accustomed them to unusual mobility. In addition to a comparative freedom of movement, black people in Wilmington preserved a living memory of having rebelled against area slaveholders during Cornwallis's 1781 occupation of the city. The long-standing existence of Maroon camps among the Cape Fear swamps suggested, moreover, the viability of nonwhite communities subsisting in defiance of a white territorial polity. Early nineteenth-century Charleston, where a skilled and often literate free black community cohabitated with the enslaved population, further encouraged Walker's defiant tendencies. With a militant African Episcopal Methodist Church providing a liberationist interpretation of Christian theology, the city served as fertile ground for Denmark Vesey's conspiracy. As evinced by the Gabriel conspiracy (1800) and Nat Turner's rebellion (1831), the coastal Carolinas and Virginia Tidewater fostered and sustained an insurrectionary mood. Given this environment, it is not surprising that the *Appeal* expresses lavish indignation and calls for revolutionary action.[5]

Although chiefly expository and lacking an account of crossing the threshold of slave state to free, the *Appeal* is not without narrative moments, beginning with the first sentence of Walker's preamble:

> Having travelled over a considerable portion of these United States, and having, in the course of my travels, taken the most accurate observations of things as they exist—the result of my observations has warranted the full and unshakable conviction, that we, (coloured people of these United States,) are the most degraded, wretched, and abject set of beings that ever lived since the world began; and I pray God that none like us ever may live again until time shall be no more. (1)

The nonspecific reference to his travels and the withholding of anything like a distinction between bondsman and freeman contribute to his argument that the condition of African Americans is firmly founded in racial identity irrespective of person and place. In Article II Walker invites readers to infer that his extensive travels have exposed him to a range of harassments: "If any of you wish to know how FREE you are," he advises his black audience, those who are free and those who aspire to freedom, "let one of you start and go through the southern and western States of this country, and unless you travel as a slave to a white man (a servant is a *slave* to the man whom he serves) or have your free papers, (which if you are not careful they will get from you) if they do not take you up and put you in jail, and if you cannot give good evidence of your freedom, sell you into eternal slavery, I am not a living man" (28). On no terms, in other words, and by no effective documentation, can persons of color be free anywhere in the United States under its inherently racist regime.[6] Walker's refusal to acknowledge a distinction between slave state and free state (he nowhere cites the Mason-Dixon Line) supports his charge that the nation as a whole colludes in the institutions of Southern slavery. Allusion to his current Boston residence and brief mention of experiences in South Carolina and North Carolina suggest that he could identify differences between regions were they to figure among his "accurate observations." But clearly they do not, and expectations that the North provides a difference of kind are not realistic. "Even here in Boston," Walker reports, "pride and prejudice have got to such a pitch, that in the very houses erected to the Lord, they have built little places for the reception of coloured people, where they must sit during meeting, or keep away from the house of God" (40). Restrictions on movement and settlement reappear even before a supreme being said to be no respecter of persons.

That the antebellum church, South or North, should enforce the color line is hardly surprising, but the *Appeal* cites such prejudicial treatment of black parishioners in its larger effort to contest the slave power's appropriation of the Gospel. In one of his few extended narrative episodes, Walker writes of attending "a Camp Meeting in South Carolina, for which I embarked in a Steam Boat at Charleston, and having been five or six hours on the water, we at last arrived at the place of hearing." Walker identifies no other circumstances relating to this meeting, although it is clear that the preacher is a white man speaking to black congregants:

> I fixed myself in a complete position to hear the word of my Saviour and to receive such as I thought was authenticated by the Holy Scriptures; but to my no ordinary astonishment, our Reverend gentleman got up and told us (coloured people) that slaves must be obedient to their masters—must do their duty to their masters or be whipped—the whip was made for the backs of fools, &c. Here I pause for a moment, to give the world time to consider what was my surprise, to hear such preaching from a minister of my Master, whose very gospel is that of peace and not of blood and whips, as this pretended preacher tried to make us believe. (39)

The scenario of a white preacher holding forth to a black congregation on the topic of "Servants, obey your masters!" recurs in *Incidents in the Life of a Slave Girl*; in Douglass's 1845 *Narrative*, Hugh Auld paraphrases the scripture in explaining why Sophia's tutoring of Frederick must stop.[7] By contrast, black preachers in African American literature convert the camp meeting into a sacred space, a locus of recovery: a rare, hospitable, natural site in an American landscape generally inimical to black travel and settlement. Assuming throughout the *Appeal* a ministerial authority, Walker establishes a counter-interpretation consistent with the Gospel as preached in the Charleston AME of the Vesey era. Walker most likely imagined the *Appeal* to be read aloud in the seclusion of a camp meeting setting, one of the few venues in which black people could share such seditious and inflammatory material.

A central topic of the *Appeal*, in fact, is the black right-to-land on the North American continent, and this concern develops particularly in Walker's critique of the American Colonization Society's project to relocate African Americans to West Africa. Even before Walker confronts what he believes to be the false premises of a Liberian homeland, he has identified free movement and free settlement as privileges denied to black people regardless of legal status. "I have known a poor man of colour, who laboured night and day, to acquire a little money," Walker writes in Article I, "and having acquired it, he vested it in a small piece of land, and got him a house erected hereon, and having paid for the whole, he moved his family into it, where he was suffered to remain but nine months, when he was cheated out of his property by a white man, and driven out of door! And is not this the case generally?" (9–10). In turning his attention to the activities of the American Colonization Society, Walker takes on the larger issue of a whole demographic, namely, free people of color in the United States, "driven out of door." As a critical reader of *Notes on the State of Virginia* (much of Article I is written in response to Jefferson's obsessive disesteem of the black body and intellect), Walker knows that much of the black expulsion initiative begins with Jefferson. Concerned with what he perceived as the irreconcilably embittered relations between white and black, master and slave, and understanding that general emancipation must occur sooner or later, Jefferson had surmised, "If a slave can have a country in this world, it must be any other in preference to that in which he is born to live and labour for another."[8] A principal objective of the American Colonization Society was to insulate an enslaved population from free people of color whose proximity must have a subversive effect on the supposed docility of those held in bond, but the idea of gradually repatriating all black Americans to a theoretical homeland appealed at once to slaveholders who, like Jefferson, recognized the dangerous unsustainability of the institution, and abolitionists concerned with the slave's human rights and convinced that those rights would enjoy optimal protection in a black republic at an ocean's distance from North America.

To the proposition that black people are aliens in a white North America, however, Walker responds forcefully, and as indignant as he is with white Southern supporters of expulsion such as Henry Clay and John Randolph, he expresses deeper frustration with black people who have been drawn into the scheme: "What our brethren could have been thinking about, who have left their native land and home and gone away to Africa, I am unable to say. This country is as much ours as it is the whites['], whether they will admit it now or not, they will see and believe it by and by" (55). In admonishing a black audience scattered over thousands of square miles, Walker seeks constantly to instill an idea of group resistance founded in critical-mindedness. "Can we not discern the project of sending the free people of colour away from their country?" he writes incredulously. "Is it not for the interest of the slave-holders to select the free people of colour out of the different states, and send them to Liberia? Will it not make their slaves uneasy to see free men of colour enjoying liberty?" (57). As for efforts to deterritorialize a black population that has resided in North America for generations, "let no man of us budge one step, and let slave-holders come to beat us from our country. America is more our country, than it is the whites[']—we have enriched it with our *blood and tears*. The greatest riches in all America have arisen from our blood and tears:—and will they drive us from our property and homes, which we have earned with our *blood*?" (65). The *Appeal* is fascinating from a geographic perspective in that it speaks to a much oppressed people bound in rural isolated areas where freedom to move and settle is radically abridged even as it presents a claim to the land that surpasses that of the white plantation gentry. In this regard Walker anticipated a motif that reappears in the work of many black authors, most memorably in lines toward the end of *The Souls of Black Folk*, where Du Bois accosts the white reader thus: "Your country? How came it yours? Before the Pilgrims landed we were here."[9]

In his bid to counteract what he looks upon as the formidable threat of ethnic expulsion under the ostensibly benign cover of colonizing West Africa and founding a black, self-governing republic, Walker implores his black audience not to be deceived and to enter into a consciousness of American space as black space. Mindful, however, that his text (beyond the readership his title names) will be intercepted and read by whites, most of whom will prove hostile, while a few perhaps may harbor some sympathy or anxiety that he might productively engage, he holds out the possibility that white and black people can coexist and co-occupy land within a common set of cartographic coordinates. Do white people wish to do right by the principles they profess as Christians? Do they wish to avoid a violent physical confrontation with an aggrieved people? "Throw away your fears and prejudices then, and enlighten us and treat us like men," he enjoins the white reader, "and we will like you more than we do now hate you, and tell us now no more about colonization, for America is as much our country, as it is yours.—Treat us like men, and there is no danger but we will all live in peace and happiness together. For we are not like you, hard hearted, unmerciful, and unforgiving. What a happy country this will be, if the whites will listen" (70). In the last sentence, Walker redirects his address to a mixed readership, straddling what Elizabeth McHenry has called "the two public spheres" the *Appeal* seeks to engage while modeling the speaking of truth to power for the benefit of his primary audience.[10] But as he proceeds, as McHenry argues, on the proposition that any hope of genuine black citizenship necessitates strategic and vigorous resistance, he entertains few illusions, from beginning to end, as to the possible result of his speaking thus freely and forcefully: "I do not only expect to be held up to the public as an ignorant, impudent and restless disturber of the public peace" but also "perhaps put in prison or to death, for giving a superficial exposition of our miseries, and exposing tyrants" (2). Here, as in so many other African American geographies, the prison cell looms as a probable destiny.[11]

"Instead of being here seated by my own table"

The spatial politics of *The Narrative of the Life of Frederick Douglass, an American Slave, Written by Himself* begins with the title, which announces to a white, predominantly Northern audience that the text concerns the exotic experience of a black person who has escaped the slave South and who has likewise escaped the unlettered state associated with enslavement and blackness generally. As one who has written his own narrative, Douglass distinguishes himself from the mass of enslaved or formerly enslaved people by having entered—in addition to the free-state North—the republic of letters. Although by 1845 an active and distinguished black intelligentsia had established a solid foothold in the North, the *Narrative*'s full title calls attention to the fact that illiteracy figured as a presumed component of the enslaved person's existential condition. If, as a rule, to be black was to be enslaved, to be black was likewise to be illiterate. Douglass's first book presents Frederick Douglass as the exception that proves the rule. As the exception to the condition of black illiteracy, Douglass also appears as an abolitionist movement client: the 1845 *Narrative* appears under the imprint "The Anti-Slavery Office," identifying it as a publication of William Lloyd Garrison's Boston-based New England Anti-Slavery Society. Occupying page space furnished by *The Liberator*'s white editor, Douglass's testimony is placed and packaged in ways consistent with Garrison's then-subordination of the society's star orator. Douglass's voice is the third we hear as we proceed from title page to preface, from preface to the letter from Wendell Phillips, Esq., and from the letter to the narrative itself—a sequence in which Douglass figures as third person in Garrison's reminiscence of their first meeting, second person as Phillips's epistolary addressee, and at last as first person assuming control over Frederick Douglass as bildungsroman protagonist.

To be sure, Douglass's voice dominates the assemblage of texts that constitutes the 1845 *Narrative*, but in light of his ultimate estrangement from Garrison, the Anti-Slavery Society, and the strategy of pacifist moral suasion, we can see these voices contesting for expressive dominance in the short book's expanse.[12] The matter is inherently geographical and reflects irreconcilable if not adversarial cartographic understandings of the antebellum nation.[13] Garrison's preface tells his own story of attending the antislavery conference on Nantucket Island, where he met and "discovered" Douglass, a New Bedford resident who had recently escaped "the southern prison-house of bondage."[14] Garrison's "prison-house" metaphor may aptly invoke the carceral status of black people in the South, but it also exemplifies the florid prose by which he maps a polarized world: Douglass, in this figure, arrives from a generalized rather than a specific place. Garrison will later depart from blanket generalization in drawing valid if conventional distinctions between Upper and Deep South, emphasizing that, bad as life was in Maryland for Douglass, it would have been worse to the south and west, but the detailed geography of the Eastern Shore and Baltimore counts for little in his characterization of the fugitive. In his patronizing and self-congratulatory characterization of their first encounter, Garrison recalls a Douglass who could be any fugitive, "trembling for his safety, hardly daring to believe that on the American soil, a single white person could be found who would befriend him at all hazards, for the love of God and humanity!" (4). Tremble though he may, Douglass in Garrison's account seizes the opportunity to speak of his experience, giving "utterance to many noble thoughts and thrilling reflections" (4). Much given to self-dramatization, Garrison reports that he rose immediately to inform the audience that Patrick Henry himself "never made a speech more eloquent in the cause of liberty" before extracting a promise that Douglass's first auditors would never betray the vulnerable fugitive:

> "Will you succor and protect him as a brother-man—a resident of the old Bay State?" "YES!" shouted the whole mass, with an energy so startling, that the ruthless tyrants south of Mason and Dixon's line might almost have heard the mighty burst of feeling, and recognized it as the pledge of an invincible determination, on the part of those who gave it, never to betray him that wanders, but to hide the outcast, and firmly to abide the consequences. (4–5)

Garrison's generalized geographical expression leans toward the verbal cartoon. Unable to think of the tyrannical South except as the antithesis of the noble-hearted North, he insists on portraying the fugitive as victim and child seeking the North's patriarchal protection, and even if the fugitive is supremely gifted, according to this portrait, his limited knowledge and agency will require mentoring and direction.

Garrison proceeds to relate how he was able to conquer Douglass's "unfeigned diffidence" (5) and enlist his services as antislavery speaker. His account of launching Douglass's career celebrates his own eye for new talent as well as the noble vision of the cause and heroic character of those pledged to it. He recounts Douglass's transformation from trembling fugitive to oratorical prodigy, but inasmuch as Douglass remains a fugitive even as the book is released, Garrison implicitly presents himself as Douglass's patron and protector. In highlighting the abstract evils of slavery and drawing the reader's attention to the *Narrative*'s most sensational episodes (those in which slaves are sold, whipped, and shot), Garrison disregards the enduring propinquity Douglass expresses with respect to family and friends still in bondage. He concludes the preface with his well-known slogan, "No union with slaveholders!" (10). The idea is fundamentally secessionist: if the South cannot be compelled to abolish slavery, the North will have to form its own nation. Douglass would give lip service to this idea in the years ahead, but he must have recognized from the start that any realization of this doctrine would mean abandoning to the slave power a multitude among whom he counted siblings and intimates. It was over this specific geopolitical doctrine, among other reasons, that Douglass would break with Garrison.

The letter from Wendell Phillips, Esq., contrasts with Garrison's preface in that it addresses Douglass in the second person ("My Dear Friend"), and the performance of one man speaking to another serves as the vehicle of Phillips's characterization of Douglass. Epistolary expression (whether or not it involves a communication that actually crosses the space between noncontiguous correspondents) always signals some form of geographic separation between addresser and addressee. Phillips's dateline, "Boston, April 22, 1845," inevitably raises the question of where geographically Douglass may be. The answer comes at the conclusion of Douglass's appendix, where he subscribes himself above the line, "Lynn, Mass., April 28, 1845." But Garrison and Phillips insistently frame the *Narrative*'s author as a man in flight, living under the Anti-Slavery Society's protection, surrounded by people willing to engage in acts of civil disobedience to thwart attempts to return him to bondage. In addressing Douglass as "you," Phillips reaffirms the fugitive's literacy, and by remarking in his opening line, "You remember the old fable of 'The Man and the Lion'" (11), he calls attention to Douglass's erudition. The fable to which Phillips alludes (also known as "The Lion and the Statue": it appears in the Harvard Classics edition of *Aesop's Fables* under that name) proffers the moral that a man may think himself more clever than a lion, but the lion will naturally think of himself as stronger and more clever than the man. By referring to the fable, Phillips makes the point that slaveholders inevitably paint a favorable portrait of the peculiar institution, but what they present must be viewed alongside the testimony of those who have been enslaved. Phillips's analogy, however, reprises a condescending and indeed white supremacist attitude in that it projects the "you" (Douglass) as the lion, anthropomorphized but not quite human. In addition, it associates Douglass with an exotic beast, native to Africa and Asia—geography apart from the Massachusetts that Garrison and Phillips lose no opportunity to exalt.

In commending Douglass's account of slavery in the Upper South, Phillips repeats the truism that, bad as slavery is in Maryland, it is worse the farther south one goes (a trope that will achieve a sort of climax seven years later with Harriet Beecher Stowe's depiction in *Uncle Tom's Cabin* of Simon Legree's Red River plantation): "You come from that part of the country where we are told slavery appears with its fairest features. Let us hear, then, what it is at its best estate—gaze on its bright side, if it has one; and then imagination may task her powers to add dark lines to the picture, as she travels southward to that (for the colored man) Valley of the Shadow of Death, where the Mississippi sweeps along" (11–12). Like Garrison, Phillips relies on generalized phrases: "the colored man," the "dark prison-house" (13). On the other hand, despite his reliance on the clichés of abolition movement geography, Phillips, like Garrison, does express a just if ever abstract understanding of the degree to which American space withholds protection from, and forbids accommodation to, a whole segment of the population: "In all the broad lands which the Constitution of the United States overshadows, there is no single spot,—however narrow or desolate,—where a fugitive slave can plant himself and say, 'I am safe' " (12–13). Like Garrison, however, Phillips affirms the doctrine "no union with slaveholders" and does so with a sanitized notion of the Bay State's historical record of tolerance and accommodation:

> New England, cutting loose from a blood-stained Union, shall glory in being the house of refuge for the oppressed;—till we no longer merely "*hide* the outcast," or make a merit of standing idly by while he is hunted in our midst; but, consecrating anew the soil of the Pilgrims as an asylum for the oppressed, proclaim our *welcome* to the slave so loudly, that the tones shall reach every hut in the Carolinas, and make the broken-hearted bondman leap up at the thought of old Massachusetts. (13)

To present the Pilgrims as asylum keepers of any but their own Anglo-Saxon dissenter kind is greatly to distort the historical record. Moreover, as Douglass will document in *My Bondage and My Freedom*, the welcome Massachusetts tendered to fugitives, not to mention free people of color, was distinctly qualified. When it is his turn to speak in the *Narrative*, Douglass's task is to fill in the outlines suggested by the sounding metaphors and large generalizations dominating the free-state/slave-state geography that flourishes in abolition-movement rhetoric as exemplified by Garrison and Phillips. In addition, it is to call attention to those who, as the volume is published in 1845, remain under the Southern slave regime with no realistic prospect of escape, a multitude that New England, in "cutting loose from a blood-stained Union," would effectively abandon.

A remarkable if ephemeral feature of the antebellum slave narrative is its urgent engagement of slavery as a live and polarizing issue, its enactment of protest and advocacy at a moment in which the debate remained unresolved and author and reader entered a relationship framed by a national crisis. Today, we read the *Narrative* as the historical testimony of a long-deceased author, a reading experience qualitatively different from the experience of the *Narrative*'s first audience. Those who read it in 1845 and for the sixteen years following could act (or not) in response to Douglass's depiction of a clear and present evil. For readers in the twenty-first century, the status of Douglass's writing as time-sensitive political intervention is understandably obscured by the longtime abolition of chattel slavery, and although enduring issues of racial injustice, along with the *Narrative*'s literary merit, amply sustain interest in this work, readers today must actively imagine the intensities associated with its initial appearance. How does this text address a now bygone world in which the white enslavement of Africans and African Americans seems hopelessly entrenched, in which fugitives who have come north (but also free people of color) are in danger of being remanded to Southern masters, and in which the young man who has authored the text is alive and liable to answer for the crime of stealing himself? Again, Garrison and Phillips underscore Douglass's fugitive condition and dramatize his jeopardy. Publication of the *Narrative* carries large risks that Phillips acknowledges in the following statement: "I am free to say that, in your place, I should throw the MS. into the fire" (13). A geographically oriented reading must consider how the 1845 readers imagined themselves in cartographic as well as social relationship to this author. He is somewhere in the North, and perhaps one has just seen him speak at a local auditorium, but in reading the *Narrative* one might well wonder where he might be, and in what condition.

For his part, the Douglass who speaks in the *Narrative* expresses little concern for his personal safety. He conveys the conviction that he has escaped enslavement once and for all and will die before anyone succeeds in dragging him back to his legal owner. In contrast with the Frederick Douglass of Garrison's preface and Phillips's letter, the first-person Douglass of the *Narrative* performs as one whose self-possession (literally and figuratively) is beyond question. From the first paragraph forward he writes of his former condition as though viewing it through a telescope and prompts the reader to take instruction as he presents the spectacle of his life as a slave. The highly wrought first paragraph introduces the reader to a narrator who combines irony with indignation and who establishes right away the patterns by which this story will be told:

> I WAS born in Tuckahoe, near Hillsborough, and about twelve miles from Easton, in Talbot county, Maryland. I have no accurate knowledge of my age, never having seen any authentic record containing it. By far the larger part of the slaves know as little of their ages as horses know of theirs, and it is the wish of most masters within my knowledge to keep their slaves thus ignorant. I do not remember to have ever met a slave who could tell of his birthday. They seldom come

> nearer to it than planting-time, harvest-time, cherry-time, spring-time, or fall-time. A want of information concerning my own was a source of unhappiness to me even during childhood. The white children could tell their ages. I could not tell why I ought to be deprived of the same privilege. I was not allowed to make any inquiries of my master concerning it. He deemed all such inquiries on the part of a slave improper and impertinent, and evidence of a restless spirit. The nearest estimate I can give makes me now between twenty-seven and twenty-eight years of age. I come to this, from hearing my master say, some time during 1835, I was about seventeen years old. (15)

This paragraph and chapter 1 as a whole reflect a familiarity with life narratives such as *The Autobiography of Benjamin Franklin* that open with birth, parentage, and genealogy.[15] In keeping with period conventions of biography and autobiography, Douglass likewise begins with the circumstances of his birth, as this provides a first opportunity to discuss how the norms of slave life differ from the norms of his white readership. He can state where he was born and assist the reader in locating the remote site on a map. But he is unable to say *when* he was born, which prevents him (as he would have his reader notice) from fulfilling normal autobiographical genre expectations. In emphasizing the unknown status of this datum, he inaugurates one of his major themes: to be enslaved is to be subject to enforced ignorance and cognitive quite as much as social death. Of the paragraph's eleven sentences, eight concern the unresolved mystery of his date of birth, how the "want of information" is a common feature of slave life, how he suffered as a child from this suppression of knowledge, and how his natural curiosity marked him, a subject ever under slaveholder surveillance, as possessing a "restless spirit"—a person ill suited to stay in place. A white autobiographer might state place and date of birth in one sentence. Douglass counts on his readership to note that it requires a whole paragraph for him to explain why he can cite place but not date. In the paragraphs that follow, he will similarly demonstrate that he can state the facts of his maternity, but paternity for him remains a mystery that requires a sociological disquisition.

The first paragraph balances narrative with exposition in ways that typify Douglass's account of his life as a slave. In order to convey the exceptional experience of the individual who escaped, he must tell the story of the vast majority who remain enslaved and whose bondage will terminate only as a result of such moral recognition and political action as the *Narrative* would incite. Telling these stories requires that he provide a geography and sociology of plantation life of the Eastern Shore and, later, of city life in Baltimore, where slave and free labor commingle: to set the scene for extraordinary events, he must document ordinary conditions. He thus devotes many passages to local topographies, family structure, and the means by which a white slaveholding class dominates the lives of the people (whites as well as blacks) who work the plantations. In addition to a sociological account of life on the Eastern Shore and in Baltimore, he also provides a psychology of white people caught up in the master/slave relationship, and not only does he develop the obligatory rogue's gallery of slave masters, slave mistresses, overseers, and preachers, he also highlights what he looks upon as the innate goodness and generosity of whites caught up in a system that in time coarsens and destroys their human sympathies.

In narrating these experiences to a predominantly white audience, Douglass predictably recruits the oratorical phrasings by which he had been telling his story as an Anti-Slavery Society speaker in the four years prior to the book's publication and which had become the conventional language of abolitionist discourse, reflecting the spoken-word, performative occasions of abolition-movement activism. Although more constrained in his use of generalizing tropes than Garrison and Phillips, and using them in any case with an authority his sponsors cannot command, Douglass himself deploys the phrase (but only once) "prison-house of slavery" (71) and famously exhibits a fondness for chiasmic constructions: "You have seen how a man was made a slave; you shall see how a slave was made a man" (60).[16] In concluding the account of his fight with the slave breaker Covey, "the turning-point of my career as a slave," he describes his victory in conventionally religious language: "It was a glorious resurrection, from the tomb of slavery, to the heaven of freedom" (65). Such phrasing interposes a distance between the autobiographical event and the occasion of its telling, subordinating "experience" to the narrative performance of public recollection. At least some of Douglass's early readers would have first encountered him in a lecture hall, sharing a public space in which the partnership of audience and performer supports illusions of intimacy. Later, those attending his performance of "What the Fourth of July Means to the Slave" (1852) would be subjected to a spectrum of relational verbal gestures—everything from apology for his inadequate training to an accusation of exposing him to the awkwardness of speaking on such a topic to (finally) an assurance of mutual goodwill and dedication to making good America's egalitarian promise. At that point, however, he is no longer a fugitive and no longer employed by the Anti-Slavery Society. As a free agent and editor based in Rochester, New York, he can hector and seduce an audience to his own satisfaction. The *Narrative*, by comparison, is expressively circumspect, the narrator sustaining a reserve by virtue of well-rehearsed oratorical gestures, hopeful but not quite certain that there will materialize for him across the color line such genuinely attentive if inconspicuous auditors as exist, say, for Madison Washington, protagonist of *The Heroic Slave* (1852), Douglass's one published venture into narrative fiction, in the person of Mr. Listwell.

As the testament of an author who remains on the run, the *Narrative* generates numerous locational gestures, precise in some respects, elusive in others. One of the earliest of such gestures addresses what he recognizes as the epistemology he brings to his former life as a slave. Toward the end of chapter 2, having explained that field hands on satellite farms were regularly dispatched to the Great House Farm to collect the monthly allowance of provisions, he recollects what it was like to hear these sorrowful men sing as they took delight in the privilege of walking through the woods, a welcome break under any circumstances from the routine of field work. "They would compose and sing as they went along, consulting neither time nor tune. The thought that came up, came out—if not in the word, in the sound;—and as frequently in the one as in the other. They would sometimes sing the most pathetic sentiment in the most rapturous tone, and the most rapturous sentiment in the most pathetic tone" (23). This passage is noteworthy from the standpoint that it places Douglass and his reader outside of—but proximate to—the expressive culture of Eastern Shore black life. As one formerly situated inside that world, Douglass can interpret the meaning, but only as someone who has achieved a position exterior to it: "I did not, when a slave, understand the deep meaning of those rude and apparently incoherent songs. I was myself within the circle; so that I neither saw nor heard as those without might see and hear" (24). His affective response, however, even as a child (the child the adult strategically recalls), prepared him for the recognitions that come with age and distance:

> The hearing of those wild notes always depressed my spirit, and filled me with ineffable sadness. I have frequently found myself in tears while hearing them. The mere recurrence to those songs, even now, afflicts me; and while I am writing these lines, an expression of feeling has already found its way down my cheek. To those songs I trace my first glimmering conception of the dehumanizing character of slavery. (24)

The voices pursue him across the geographical and temporal expanse that separates him from Colonel Lloyd's plantation: "Those songs still follow me, to deepen my hatred of slavery, and quicken my sympathies for my brethren in bonds" (24). The anguish in this passage measures the degree to which he cannot distance himself from his origins. Thought of his brethren, as he writes those lines, induces what appears to be a spasm of survivor's guilt.

This passage is significant for the way it situates Douglass in the 1845 present, "writing these lines." It is one of three moments in the *Narrative* in which Douglass depicts himself in the present tense as Man Writing. The other two occur in chapter 5, where he chronicles his departure from Colonel Lloyd's plantation for Hugh Auld's household in Baltimore. At the chapter's beginning Douglass continues his account of early and middle childhood, describing the light duties assigned to him and noting that he "was seldom whipped by my old master, and suffered little from any thing else than hunger and cold" (33). Yet to be "kept almost naked" in cold as in hot weather has left a vivid memory of bodily duress: "My feet have been so cracked with the frost, that the pen with which I am writing might be laid in the gashes" (33).[17] The gashes have presumably closed, but the recollecting movement of the pen demonstrates how injury persists beneath the healing. The pen with which Douglass writes might be laid in any number of gashes on the bodies of enslaved men and women to which the *Narrative* bears witness, many if not most inflicted by active malevolence directed against the enslaved body rather than by the passive action of heat and frost. The pen's recollecting movement reinforces Douglass's sense of being "here" rather than "there" (the place of confinement and injury) and the importance of his removal to Baltimore in the diegetic arc that culminates in the present moment, the eternal literary *now* in which Douglass, rather than the lot of enslavement, writes his life's narrative: "I look upon my departure from Colonel Lloyd's plantation as one of the most interesting events of my life. It is possible, and even quite probable, that but for the mere circumstance of being removed from that plantation to Baltimore, I should have to-day, instead of being here seated by my own table, in the enjoyment of freedom and the happiness of home, writing this Narrative, been confined in the galling chains of slavery" (35). For in Baltimore he learns to write, first under tutelage of Sophia Auld, and later, after Hugh Auld puts an end to the lessons, by his own autodidactic ingenuity. In Baltimore he is first exposed to books, such as *The Columbian Orator*, that allow him to frame his struggle against bondage within a liberationist narrative that transcends slavery in America.

As he writes "in the enjoyment of freedom and the happiness of home," he is still technically subject to reenslavement, to confinement in galling chains and the physical abuse of which he provides an extensive inventory in his three autobiographies. The image of Douglass as Man Writing in utopian domestic space does not yet reflect a secure and sustainable end point to his journey. At the *Narrative*'s conclusion, the author subscribes himself "Frederick Douglass, Lynn, Mass., April 28, 1845," almost as an invitation to federal marshals to apprehend him on behalf of Hugh and Thomas Auld. At the moment of publication, however, Douglass was en route to Great Britain and would not return for twenty-one months. By that time his British benefactors had taken up a collection and purchased his freedom.

"I understood the pathway from slavery to freedom"

The Narrative of the Life of Frederick Douglass, an American Slave, Written by Himself relies throughout on that most common of narrative metaphors: life-as-journey. Writing in a Protestant literary tradition for which *The Pilgrim's Progress* provides the paradigm and *The Autobiography of Benjamin Franklin* its American secularization, the journey trope comprises motifs of losing and recovering one's way, condemnation and redemption, descent to hell and ascent to heaven, as well as dystopian embarkation and utopian arrival. Douglass introduces the metaphor at the close of chapter 1, as he prepares the reader for the graphic account of young Frederick watching Captain Anthony whip Aunt Hester.[18] In accord with the *Narrative*'s retrospect, the traumatic spectacle represents Douglass's egress from an Edenic if impoverished geography situated on the maternal "outskirts of the plantation" (19) to an underworld marked by outbursts of inexplicable madness, as white people vent their fury against the bodies of black people: "It was the blood-stained gate, the entrance to the hell of slavery, through which I was about to pass" (18). In chapter 5, recounting the turn of events that resulted in his being sent to live with Hugh and Sophia Auld, his first excursion beyond plantation horizons, Douglass (sounding very much like Benjamin Franklin) again enlists the figure of the gate: "Going to live at Baltimore laid the foundation, and opened the gateway, to all my subsequent prosperity" (36). In both examples, events involving geographical displacement contribute to the figurative expression: in the one, a five-year-old Douglass has recently moved from his grandmother's house to the residence of Old Master (the whip-wielding, profanity-spewing man we are encouraged to suspect may be Douglass's father); in the other, an eight-year-old Douglass relocates from rural backwater to bustling international urban port.

Having shifted the scene to Baltimore, the narrative employs the journey trope to depict the internal, brooding, cognitive travel instigated by Sophia Auld's tutorials in basic literacy and Hugh Auld's traumatic but more powerfully instructive interdiction of his wife's lessons. Douglass reports overhearing the husband inform his wife that "if you teach that nigger (speaking of myself) how to read, there would be no keeping him" and proceeds to dramatize how that simple explanation demystifies a system in which a numerically and thus physically inferior white population dominates a numerically and physically superior black population. Sudden enlightenment leads to discernment of a path: "It was a new and special revelation, explaining dark and mysterious things, with which my youthful understanding had struggled, but struggled in vain. I now understood what had been to me a most perplexing difficulty—to wit, the white man's power to enslave the black man. It was a grand achievement, and I prized it highly. From that moment, I understood the pathway from slavery to freedom" (37–38). Douglass presents this moment as his first intimation that a path *out* exists. It follows his recognition that power proceeds not so much from brute force as from a social hypothesis put into practice, ideologies by which some people are assigned active while others are assigned passive roles. Once one understands how one came to be enslaved, one can set about plotting escape.

But his inner conviction that he is on a path of self-emancipation must contend with a sense of the nation's expanse as a geography in which the number and variety of entrapments preponderate over the corridors that lead to "freedom," in whatever qualified form the latter materializes north of the Mason-Dixon Line. Soon after recounting what has come to him as the "new and special revelation," he relates an anecdote in which he assists two Irishmen unloading a scow at Fell's Point: they ask him if he is a slave and, when he says yes, observe that "it was a pity so fine a little fellow . . . should be a slave for life" (43). The phrase, "slave for life," had surfaced earlier in his colloquy with the white boys of Philpot Street (41). Already encouraged by his reading (*The Columbian Orator* had come into his possession) and spurred by increasing restlessness, the resonant phrase in its reiteration gives additional urgency to his conviction that he is destined to escape: "From that time I resolved to run away" (44). This resolution meets with setbacks, particularly after he is rusticated to the plantation, and even more so when he is farmed out to the slave breaker Edward Covey. Douglass's climactic defiance of Covey and the physical and psychological triumph over arbitrary power that his defiance symbolizes lend the narrative a necessary catharsis, one that does not occur in his account of finally escaping to the North (the details of which he strategically withholds), but the episode leaves unaddressed the problem of how to exit the plantation microcosm or even a slave-worked port city where paths of escape are more numerous. "This battle with Mr. Covey was the turning-point in my career as a slave," he observes. "It was a glorious resurrection, from the tomb of slavery, to the heaven of freedom" (65). But before he can close the book on his career as a slave (technically this occurs ten years later with *My Bondage and My Freedom*), he has to narrate his two attempts to escape, and to do so involves recitations of what it was like to find oneself immobilized in plantation country, faced with the prospects of overwater or overland travel across cartographies that far exceed the traveler's understanding.

In a memorable passage that precedes his account of the fight with Covey, Douglass portrays himself at the edge of Chesapeake Bay contemplating the free movement of the clipper ships. At this point he has been considering the bay as a possible escape route for some time: when he is sent back to St. Michael's after his eight-year residence in Baltimore, he pays "particular attention to the direction which the steamboats took to go to Philadelphia" (49). But as Paul Gilroy has suggested, if the clippers figure as emblems of liberation, they also mark the irrepressible memory of the Middle Passage past, hardly an encouragement to imagine a New World geography that serves a personally emancipatory purpose:[19] "Those beautiful vessels, robed in purest white, so delightful to the eye of freemen, were to me so many shrouded ghosts, to terrify and torment me with thoughts of my wretched condition. I have often, in the deep stillness of a summer's Sabbath, stood all alone upon the lofty banks of that noble bay, and traced, with saddened heart and tearful eye, the countless number of sails moving off to the mighty ocean" (59). His "apostrophe to the moving multitude of ships" meditates on the theme "You are loosed from your moorings, and are free; I am fast in my chains, and am a slave!" (59). Douglass here develops his most impassioned statement as to the sense of paralysis that descends upon the slave amid territories that afford unlimited mobility to those who possess the means and privilege to move.

With a spirit revived by his successful challenge of Edward Covey and opportunities to form communal bonds on the plantation of William Freeman, Douglass transitions from viewing the immensities of water and land as absolutely forbidding to regarding such expanse as space that admits movement to those who plan and dare. Given their limitations of cartographic knowledge and impossible foreknowledge as to what awaits at each new turn, the strategy of the first attempt—to traverse the bay north by canoe, thereby avoiding the interrogation of random whites at every bend in the road and leaving no trace for the bloodhounds—does little to reduce the anxieties that beset the geography of flight. In a passage that first appears in the *Narrative* and reappears in both *My Bondage and My Freedom* and *Life and Times of Frederick Douglass*, Douglass characterizes that geography as he and his companions contemplated it in advance of their aborted attempt:

> Our knowledge of the north did not extend farther than New York; and to go there, and be forever harassed with the frightful liability of being returned to slavery—with the certainty of being treated tenfold worse than before—the thought was truly a horrible one, and one which it was not easy to overcome. The case sometimes stood thus: At every gate through which we were to pass, we saw a watchman—at every ferry a guard—on every bridge a sentinel—and in every wood a patrol. We were hemmed in upon every side. (73)[20]

In this passage Douglass creates a double vision of American space, private and public, rural and urban, overlaid with the rudiments of transportation infrastructure. On the one hand, such space, with its gates, ferries, and bridges, invites the flow of free citizens: such flow would be celebrated in the coming decade by Henry David Thoreau and Walt Whitman, who build on long-standing ideas of the North American continent as open to white travel, adventure, and settlement. On the other hand, for people of color (the fugitive slave, but really all whose nonwhite status relegates them to a place outside the current of free white movement), American space subdivides into zones of probable surveillance and entrapment. Rural America, the foundation for Jefferson of the agrarian republic and the spiritual refuge of Emerson, Thoreau, Fuller, and Whitman, presents special dangers to nonwhite travelers. In order to move from slave state to free, the fugitive must conquer the apprehension of always being watched, always being objectified by the inimical gaze of watchman, sentinel, patrol.

In *My Bondage and My Freedom*, Douglass elaborates on the geographical challenge related to an attempted escape. Even before setting foot off the plantation, the would-be fugitive confronts problems cognitive and psychological. "The real distance was great enough, but the imagined distance was, to our ignorance, even greater" (310). To move beyond the plantation microcosm required one to overcome the immobilizing conception of geography that the slave regime instilled in the enslaved. "Every slaveholder seeks to impress his slave with a belief in the boundlessness of slave territory, and of his own almost illimitable power" (310). The 1850 Fugitive Slave Act did much to substantiate that doctrine, but even before its passage the judicial and extrajudicial recovery of fugitives and enslavement of free people of color (Solomon Northup being the best-known example) confounded distinctions between slave and free state. "The nearer are the lines of a slave state and the borders of a free one, the greater the peril" (310). Writing in 1855 as a freeman, Douglass assures his white Northern readers that they "can have little idea of the phantoms of trouble which flit, in such circumstances, before the uneducated mind of the slave" (311). As a former slave whose mind has been educated in the schools of experience and self-directed study, Douglass is in a position to identify the realities that justify the fugitive's intuitions of danger. In all three autobiographies he makes the point that his arrival in New York, far beyond the Mason-Dixon Line, was accompanied by euphoria that rapidly gave way to paranoia—fear emanating from an unspecified but just apprehension of the menace encompassing him as an undocumented black street person. Temporary refuge provided by David Ruggles, followed by departure for the comparative safe haven of New Bedford, mitigates for Douglass the risks of reenslavement, but it is only the trip abroad that marks his outdistancing of the reach—fancied or real—of his old master.

My Bondage and My Freedom (1855), published a decade after *Narrative of the Life of Frederick Douglass, An American Slave, Written by Himself*, represents a Douglass who in ten years' time has not only acquired freeman status but has survived and prospered from an emancipatory rupture with his first sponsors. His ocean crossing and lengthy sojourn in Great Britain have expanded his geographical frame of reference. His return to the United States as one whose freedom has been secured relieves him of the epithet "fugitive slave": he no longer resides and travels as an object of legitimate pursuit and can move among the nation's private and public spaces without the fugitive's crippling agoraphobia. To enjoy a qualified right of free passage after a lifetime of regimented and imperiled mobility requires a fundamental alteration of the process by which one knows and maps the world. To be sure, for the rest of his life color-line constraints annoyed and occasionally threatened Douglass, but his freeman's status and increasing celebrity permitted him to challenge discrimination head-on (increasingly, he would take seats in railroad carriages reserved for whites and enter restaurants where blacks were known to be unwelcome). Settling in Rochester, New York, across Lake Ontario from Canada, he operated at a significant distance from the seat of Garrison's organization, establishing himself as the editor of his own paper. The world was a different place, and the personal autonomy that made it different may be seen in the features of *My Bondage and My Freedom* that set it apart from the *Narrative*.

Three features immediately distinguished *My Bondage and My Freedom* from the *Narrative*. Whereas the frontispiece portrait of the *Narrative* presents the conventionally reserved and abstracted head and shoulders of a young, well-dressed, and obviously biracial man, the portrait greeting the reader in *My Bondage and My Freedom* showcases the head, shoulders, and torso of a still young but more mature man whose eyes beam horizontally. Arms akimbo, neither rigid nor at ease, he rests his half-clinched fists on the table before him. The eyes at first appear to meet the reader's directly, but his attention clearly lies elsewhere. The face projects a degree of inaccessible personhood. It seems possible that visitors have caught him in a phase of intense introspection and that his vision does not register their presence. From the facial expression it is difficult to tell what relationship this author bears to his readership.[21] That he qualifies as an extrovert among similarly committed partisans, however, becomes clear with the second front-matter feature: a florid inscription to the upstate New York abolitionist and Free-Soil politician, Gerrit Smith, whose view of the Constitution as a document inherently condemnatory of slavery contested the reading Garrison had made foundational to his campaign. In the words of Douglass's tribute, Smith denies slavery "either a legal or constitutional existence" (104). The abolitionist's true mandate, consistent with a right interpretation of the nation's founding compact, is not disunion but the abrogation of slavery throughout the geographical extent of the United States and its territories. Like David Walker, Douglass is averse to any resolution that concedes space anywhere to slaveholding, for as long as an institution built on white supremacy persists, those marked as inferior are susceptible anywhere to abduction, enslavement, and abuse, not to mention the disesteem that discourages recognition of full rights of citizenship even in places where slavery has been abolished. Accordingly—as he will state in the words that conclude *My Bondage and My Freedom*—his lifework's goal is "the universal and unconditional emancipation of my entire race" (398).

The third feature is the introduction, generally reserved in the slave narrative genre for the certifying statement of a known and trusted white abolitionist, but not in the manifesto Douglass intends *My Bondage and My Freedom* to constitute. Not Garrison, not even Gerrit Smith, performs the honors, but rather James McCune Smith (1813–1865), a freeborn African American physician who received his medical degree from the University of Glasgow and was active in New York abolitionist circles.[22] If the displacement of an expected white sponsor by a member of the black intelligentsia were not already obvious, McCune makes it more so by quoting from one of Douglass's addresses, in which he rejects "Garrrisonian views of disunion" (133) as a doctrine that would serve to perpetuate slavery. Even more to the point, McCune identifies Douglass's strong sense of self as permitting him "to measure strength with Mr. Covey" as well as "to wrench himself from the embrace of the Garrisonians" (137). Toward the end of *My Bondage and My Freedom* Douglass would have his own more tempered grievances to air concerning his association with the New England Anti-Slavery Society, and would find ways to express what would remain, for all their differences, his enduring affection for Garrison and Phillips. To McCune as surrogate, however, falls the task of delivering the harshly worded repudiation. Finally, as a mixed-race individual who, like Douglass, has had to contend with those who, in deprecation of his African heritage, attribute his talents to Anglo-Saxon ancestry, McCune draws attention to passages in *My Bondage and My Freedom* in which Douglass expressly identifies his literary gifts as a maternal inheritance.

Much of *My Bondage and My Freedom* covers ground familiar to readers of the *Narrative*. In several instances, Douglass imports whole passages from the first book. The fight with Edward Covey again serves as the narrative's cathartic moment; he has no more to say in *My Bondage and My Freedom* as to how he made his successful escape than he does in the *Narrative*. One significant difference between the first and second iteration of early childhood is the portrait of his mother. "I never saw my mother, to know her as such, more than four or five times in my life; and each of these times was very short in duration, and at night" (16). So Douglass observes in the *Narrative*, where he cites her minimal presence in his life as evidence of slavery's unnatural disruption of primary family relationships. In *My Bondage and My Freedom*, knowledge of his mother remains "very scanty" but in certain respects is "very distinct" (151). He testifies to retaining a strong visual image of someone "tall, and finely proportioned" and who, in contrast with the unknown white father, possesses a "deep black, glossy complexion" (152). Her fierceness on those rare occasions in which she has the opportunity to protect her children is made evident in the account of her confrontation with the abusive Aunt Katy, an anecdote that does not appear in the *Narrative*. Nor does he mention in the earlier work that his mother "was the *only* one of all the slaves and colored people in Tuckahoe" who could read (155), whereas in *My Bondage and My Freedom* he inserts the following encomium: "I am quite willing, and even happy, to attribute any love of letters I possess, and for which I have got—despite of prejudices—only too much credit, *not* to my admitted Anglo-Saxon paternity, but to the native genius of my sable, unprotected, and uncultivated *mother*—a woman, who belonged to a race whose mental endowments it is, at present, fashionable to hold in disparagement and contempt" (156). Homage to the mother is in keeping with the book's overall strategy of renarrating the life from an uncompromisingly black perspective.

It is a perspective that reflects his current residence west of the Appalachian plateau in the young and socially eclectic city of Rochester, a hub of both aboveground and underground railroad traffic and a point of embarkation for Canada, a day's journey across Lake Ontario. This deliberately chosen seat of operations reflects the distance he has put between himself and his Eastern Shore origins, as well as his subsequent residence among the New England abolitionists. The angle of vision he brings to retelling the Frederick Douglass story is one he assumes having sojourned far from the bound horizons and intense localities of plantation Maryland and antislavery Massachusetts and having broadened, during that sojourn, his circle of colleagues and supporters. His revisitation, in the opening paragraphs of *My Bondage and My Freedom*, of his Eastern Shore birthplace does not convey a sense of imaginative homecoming common to the literary reminiscence of childhood scenes so much as a recollection of an alien world the mere thought of which he is determined to set as far from his current life as possible: "In Talbot County, Eastern Shore, Maryland, near Easton, the county town of that county, there is a small district of country, thinly populated, and remarkable for nothing that I know of more than for the worn-out, sandy, desert-like appearance of its soil, the general dilapidation of its farms and fences, the indigent and spiritless character of its inhabitants, and the prevalence of ague and fever" (139). Identifying Tuckahoe as "the name of this singularly unpromising and truly famine stricken district," he speculates facetiously that the name commemorates an instance in which someone "had been guilty of the petty meanness of stealing a hoe," explaining that "tuck" is the regional pronunciation of "took" (139). This gesture permits him to call attention to the fact that, among other measures, he calculates the distance he has put between himself and his home turf by his mastery of standard written and spoken English, an issue that resurfaces late in the book when he expresses his resentment of white abolitionists who in his early days as a speaker urged him to exhibit some "plantation manner of speech" (367) in order to seem credible to his antislavery audience. In the pages that follow, he will reprise his life events with an irony more pronounced and more freely expressive of unresolved anger than he was in the position to cultivate in the shorter *Narrative*. The sentence concluding the opening tableau of his unlovely birthplace evinces a causticity mostly confined in the previous book to the overtly sarcastic appendix: in "this dull, flat, and unthrifty district," he writes, "surrounded by a white population of the lowest order, indolent and drunken to a proverb . . . I—without any fault of mine—was born, and spent the first years of my childhood" (140).

It would be understandable to compare the opening paragraphs of the *Narrative* and *My Bondage and My Freedom* and conclude that the one is simple and straightforward whereas the other is ironic and given to sardonic and satiric flourish. As we have seen, however, the *Narrative* in its seeming simplicity is deceptively artful in the way it sets up the life as a voyage to self-knowledge and the self-emancipation that comes as a result. In both, Douglass establishes himself as cognitively and critically aloof from his life as a slave, although in *My Bondage and My Freedom* he is freer to express contempt for the stultifying conditions of early childhood. Stylistically, he positions himself a world apart from the Eastern Shore of infancy and childhood, as though from start to finish the book must testify to the success with which he has escaped the environmental pressures that degrade whites and blacks alike, and that gave the enslaved occasion to utter "'*Oh, what's the use?*' every time they lifted a hoe" (140). But distant as he positions himself stylistically, his second narration of childhood and youth abounds in details absent from the *Narrative*. Expanded treatment of his mother, Harriet Bailey, is one example, as is his portrait of "Grandmamma Betty" as one skilled in folk medicine, net-making for the harvesting of fish, and the proper planting and preservation of potatoes. The account of his grandmother escorting six-year-old Frederick to the residence of Aaron Anthony when the time had come for him to live with Old Master records a trauma that precedes what Douglass marks in the *Narrative* as the initiation into slave life ("the blood-stained gate") that coincides with his witnessing Aunt Hester subjected to the whip. In addition, *My Bondage and My Freedom* goes into far greater detail in its depiction of the white master Edward Lloyd and his Wye House estate, a site that with woodland, water, and gardens afforded "pleasant resort" (161): broad margin for childhood pleasures, adventures, and companionships. Although *My Bondage and My Freedom* has little more to say of Captain Anthony, it provides a fuller picture of the favor and friendship of Lucretia Anthony Auld. Likewise, it deepens our sense of his aggravated relations with Lucretia's husband and Douglass's final master, Thomas Auld, as well as relations with the foster family he finds in Hugh, Sophia, and Tommy Auld.[23]

Stationed a world apart from the Eastern Shore of infancy, childhood, and adolescence, Douglass has much to say about the enslaved population's attachment to the plantation microcosm, an attachment that coexists with a constant dread of seeing friends, partners, parents, and children sold and shipped to the unmapped void of the Deep South, a bereavement worse than losing a loved one to death. In a chapter titled "Vicissitudes of Slave Life," which addresses the valuation and division of property that occurred at the decease of Aaron Anthony and the involuntary displacement that such legal procedures typically entail for the human portion of an estate, Douglass speculates that "people of the north, and free people generally, I think, have less attachment to the places where they are born and brought up, than have the slaves" (238). His observations respecting the liberty of movement enjoyed by Northerners and "free people generally" apply more obviously to white people: whereas free black Northerners are seldom subject to the enslaved population's enforced immobilization or the involuntary travel associated with sale, Douglass's own experiences as a segregated passenger (cited especially in chapters 24 and 25) demonstrate the restrictions and risks incurred by free people of color attempting to exercise unobstructed right to travel. In view of the restrictions African Americans have historically experienced as travelers along public corridors and as would-be settlers among civic configurations that materially embody white supremacist ideology, his remarks point to core distinctions between white and black constructions of North American geography. Those for whom the open road provides access to an unbounded continent navigate a world distinctly different from that navigated by even as mobile an African American as Douglass. "Their freedom to go and come, to be here and there, as they list, prevents any extravagant attachment to any one particular place, in their case. On the other hand, the slave is a fixture; he has no choice, no goal, no destination; but is pegged down to a single spot, and must take root here, or nowhere. The idea of removal elsewhere, comes, generally, in the shape of a threat, and in punishment of crime" (238). The post–Civil War mobility of newly emancipated black people that Toni Morrison portrays in *Beloved* supplements that geography—as we shall see in chapter 6—with the spectacle of impoverished people caught up in a condition of radical placelessness.

Douglass's observations concerning the enslaved community's attachment to place draw attention to his own enduring attachment to a remembered Eastern Shore as someone who escaped and can now move (with some restrictions) of his own free will. He recalls that the eight-year-old dispatched to Baltimore felt no regret at having left Wye House behind. "I was greatly excited," he writes of the child anticipating his voyage aboard the *Sally Lloyd*, "and could hardly consent to sleep, lest I should be left. The ties that, ordinarily, bind children to their homes, were all severed, or they never had any existence in my case, at least so far as the home plantation of Col. L. was concerned" (210). Yet his return to scenes of childhood in the pages of all three autobiographies demonstrates subtle and continuing affection. And among those hard-to-sever bindings is his unresolved relationship to his Eastern Shore master, Thomas Auld, for whom he cannot feign indifference.

In the appendix to *My Bondage and My Freedom*, Douglass includes his "Letter to His Old Master: To My Old Master, Thomas Auld." The title under which Douglass reprints this letter, which originally appeared in the North Star on September 3, 1848, is interesting for the way he figures as both third and first person; it thereby invites readers to participate in a discourse that combines, as Celeste-Marie Bernier observes, "the intimate tone of the 'private correspondent' with the denunciatory invective of the public figure."[24] An asterisk attached to the title directs readers to an editorial comment Douglass sets down in the voice of an informed bystander: "It is not often that chattels address their owners. The following letter is unique; and probably the only specimen of the kind extant. It was written while in England" (412). One may dispute the uniqueness of this document: slaves and former slaves, along with those who, by virtue of their African ancestry, were at risk of illegal enslavement, had for some time more or less directly addressed slaveholders and their supporters, and in this book already we have seen Wheatley, Equiano, and Walker speak in a similarly accusatory mode. Into this letter addressed to his last master Douglass distills material he has drawn upon in crafting his many orations as well as his two autobiographies. What is unique about the document is that it names the one person to whom Douglass has been most consistently speaking in the ten years since making his escape. His inscription of the letter in England (it is important to Douglass for his reader to know that he composed this screed a continent away from the plantation microcosm) on the tenth anniversary of his escape defines the spatiotemporal distance he has put between himself and his life as a slave. Yet the need to speak his by now oft-repeated grievances to the person who, until 1846, held title to his person confirms the power of unresolved conflict to command an injured party's imagination irrespective of a decade's lapse and an ocean's distance.

Douglass begins the letter on an intensely familiar and adversarial note, one that bears witness to a relationship whose deep and evidently mutual aggravation forecloses the possibility of a clean and purgative break: "SIR—The long and intimate, though by no means friendly, relation which unhappily subsisted between you and myself, leads me to hope that you will easily account for the great liberty which I now take in addressing you in this open and public manner" (412). Douglass acknowledges that this is not the first time he has named Auld before a public tribunal, but in marking the ten years since his self-emancipation, he wishes to make good on a long-held thought—as he states in a phrase that conveys the affect of a filial relationship—"to explain to you the grounds upon which I have justified myself in running away from you" (413). The explanation follows the outlines of his two autobiographies but foregrounds a persistent turmoil over the inscrutable ontology that made him a slave and documents an education that predates his introduction to letters. Hearing from "some of the old slaves" that their parents had been "stolen from Africa by white men, and were sold here as slaves," he understands the original sin behind the peculiar institution and the ongoing felony of his existential status. Soon afterward, as he reports, the successful flight of Aunt Jinny and Uncle Noah acquaints him for the first time "with the fact, that there were free states as well as slave states," and with that knowledge he at once resolves that he "would some day run away" (414). Beginning with his residence in Baltimore and continuing with his unhampered efforts at self-improvement in New Bedford, Lynn, and Great Britain, he has achieved literacy and standing as a public intellectual, but in this letter he attests to the flow of information and occasions of instruction occurring on the plantation among black people who did not require literacy to comprehend the criminal circumstances of their enslavement.

Douglass's citation of what he learned as one immersed from infancy in the archives of an oral tradition speaks to what this letter, written supposedly at a transoceanic remove, everywhere confesses: an attachment to the scenes of his by turns miserable and euphoric childhood. "You may perhaps want to know how I like my present condition," he remarks to Auld, and explains that his preference for his current residence principally derives from the freedom it permits him to enjoy. However, he is quick to affirm that his native Maryland, with its natural beauty and rich resources, is "a very desirable abode for any man" and dismisses the supposition that a mass migration to the North would follow universal emancipation in the South. Those, like himself, who have sought refuge in the North would be eager to return. "We want to live in the land of our birth, and to lay our bones by the side of our fathers" (414–15). Douglass's assumed white paternity makes the last word in this phrase stand out, and the fact that the never-to-be-identified Caucasian father might in fact have been Thomas Auld invests the remark with all manner of family drama.[25] Passages in the missive at times assume the tone and phrasing of the conventional letter home, particularly when he speaks of his "four dear children—the oldest a girl of nine years, and three fine boys, the oldest eight, the next six, and the youngest four years old. The three oldest are now going regularly to school—two can read and write, and the other can spell, with tolerable correctness, words of two syllables. Dear fellows! they are all in comfortable beds, and are sound asleep, perfectly secure under my own roof" (416). But what in the average letter home would be the bland citation of happy domestic details acquires here the polemic force of the former slave describing what he could not claim back in Maryland: the tranquil geography of nuclear family life in the inviolability of the patriarchal home in which, moreover, children enjoy the birthright prerogatives of parental care and an education in letters. "Oh! sir," Douglass writes, lest inadequate reserves of empathy prevent Auld from comprehending his meaning, "a slaveholder never appears to me so completely an agent of hell, as when I think of and look upon my dear children" (416).

But Douglass proceeds to put an even finer point on his argument. If this portrait of the slaveholder seems excessively harsh, how, he asks Auld, "would you look upon me, were I, some dark night, in company with a band of hardened villains, to enter the precincts of your elegant dwelling, and seize the person of your own lovely daughter, Amanda," and subject her to all the consequences of enslavement: coerced labor, inadequate food and clothing, whippings to her "naked back," consignment "to the brutal lust of fiendish overseers," and so forth (417–18). Douglass's combination of intimacy and aggressive animosity in this sketch of a father's worst nightmare, invoking the daughter by name and casting himself in the role of ravisher, measures the degree to which the letter is much more than a public illustration of the evils of slavery. This document seeks to open a new chapter in an old and complicated human relationship that crosses the color line. Far from a tirade directed at having the last word in a conversation, the letter invites response: "You shall hear from me again unless you let me hear from you" (418). Its conclusion is remarkable for the way that Douglass expresses hostile intent and unappeased rage but at the same time would rise above personal animus and even imagine a space of reconciliation. "I shall make use of you," he warns a Thomas Auld who at this point needed no such warning,

> as a means of bringing this guilty nation, with yourself, to repentance. In doing this, I entertain no malice toward you personally. There is no roof under which you would be more safe than mine, and there is nothing in my house which you might need for your comfort, which I would not readily grant. Indeed, I should esteem it a privilege to set you an example as to how mankind ought to treat each other.
>
> I am your fellow-man, but not your slave. (418)

Douglass affirms that, were Auld to appear at his door, he would cheerfully fulfill classical obligations of hospitality, casting himself and Auld as fellow men, each of whom should be willing to provide roof and refuge to the other in the patriarchal geography of the detached house. This vision of the inviolable home contrasts with the slave household with its unprotected, permeable borders; to convey that idea to Auld, Douglass urges him to consider his own home as subject to invasion and his daughter's body as object of forced entry. The open invitation his final remark tenders to Auld builds on his request that Old Master put himself in the slave's place: Douglass's roof had sheltered numerous fugitives on the eve of a water crossing to Canada.

Thomas Auld would never enter Douglass's house, but in 1877, returning to the Eastern Shore for the first time in over four decades, Douglass entered the Auld residence, invited to do so by the eighty-year-old man who lay on what was thought to be his deathbed. Robert S. Levine encourages us to resist the pat reconciliation of Douglass's "reunion narrative"; David W. Blight reads this episode as indicative of the memoirist's need to set aside an old and exorbitant grievance.[26] In any event, chapter 16 of *Life and Times of Frederick Douglass* (1882), "Time Makes All Things Even," depicts a scene that contrasts starkly with the scenario in which Douglass crosses the threshold to rape the master's daughter. He had made Auld's name "in four different languages" a byword for slaveholder cruelty, "yet here we were," Douglass writes,

> after four decades, once more face to face—he on his bed, aged and tremulous, drawing near the sunset of life, and I, his former slave, United States Marshal of the district of Columbia, holding his hand and in friendly conversation with him in a sort of final settlement of past differences preparatory to his stepping into his grave, where all distinctions are at an end, and where the great and the small, the slave and his master, are reduced to the same level. (875)

The account of their meeting gives Douglass the opportunity to recant his earlier misrepresentations as to Auld's treatment of Douglass's grandmother (Auld, we are told, rescued her from the poverty and isolation to which

Douglass thought she had been abandoned) and to quote Auld as saying that he always knew Frederick was too smart to be a slave and that he would have fled to the North had he been in Douglass's position. The old man's imminent death (Douglass asks us to visualize this demise as Auld "stepping into his grave") permits Douglass to consign former master and former slave, after long travels through diverse geographies, to a common destination. Acting in the capacity of an Auld family member, Douglass would also maintain contact with Thomas's daughter, Amanda Auld Sears, and visit her at her deathbed in Baltimore a year later.

Chapter 16 extends the theme of reconciliation in its account of Douglass's visit to Wye House. In *My Bondage and My Freedom* he had written of his "strong aversion to the great house farm" (211) and his hope, on leaving it at age eight, never to see it again. At age sixty, however, he confesses that "when long distances of time and space have come between him and his point of departure, it is natural that his thoughts should return to his place of beginning" and that "seized with a strong desire to revisit the scenes of his early recollection" he should "live over in memory the incidents of his childhood" (879). Arriving by prior arrangement with descendants of Edward Lloyd, the United States Marshal of the District of Columbia steps off at St. Michael's from a government cutter and tours the grounds of the Great House as a distinguished guest. In total command of his itinerary, able to effect a state visit, he can freely recall Aunt Katy, William Sevier, Austin Gore, and James Hopkins, inspect the kitchen where he last saw his mother, and note that renovations have removed the closet from which he observed Captain Anthony whip Aunt Hester, and he can do so without dwelling on the associated traumas described in his previous narratives. At the conclusion of this visit, Douglass joins the Lloyd descendants in the Wye House dining room "to refresh ourselves with wine of most excellent quality" (883). In the years ahead, Douglass continued to exercise a mobility that defied the prospects of the recollected child in his return to Tuckahoe, Easton, and St. Michael's, traveling regionally for speaking engagements, embarking on a grand tour that in contemporary fashion culminated in a visit to Egypt. For the last twenty-five years of his life he would make his home in Washington, D.C., and, shortly before his death, construct a summer home south of Annapolis on the western shore of Chesapeake Bay.

"Pit of abominations"

When Frederick Douglass writes Thomas Auld and asks him to put himself in the place of the slave, he enlists a rhetorically aggressive heuristic: he invites Auld to imagine Douglass invading his home and seizing his daughter, Amanda, and then subjecting her to various forms of abuse—dressing her in scant clothing, whipping her naked back, surrendering her to "the brutal lust of fiendish overseers." Gang rape, in Douglass's scenario, figures as the ultimate metonym of a toxically asymmetrical human relationship. Such asymmetry reflects a condition in which some have property rights, and thus rights to the space their bodies occupy, whereas others are deprived of such rights absolutely, lacking sovereignty over the body itself.

The former slave's epistle forces the master to reconceive space to accommodate evidence that a slave, become former slave, has detached altogether from the master's will and in discrete personhood is now a speaking subject with the power to command the master's attention. By writing Auld from a remote point, access to which he has had to seize by guile, if not by force, Douglass illustrates the geography of this relationship through a sequence of distinct zoom settings. The zoom farthest out displays slave state, free state, Canada, and Great Britain, with Douglass freely expressing himself as one who composes a letter in England and then publishes it openly in the paper he edits in Rochester, New York, close to the international border, counting on the letter's arrival before his Maryland reader through channels of communication linking the adversarial regions. The territory this letter traverses includes Douglass's free-state and Auld's slave-state residences, appearing in detail as we zoom inward, each residence conforming to expectations of the father-headed household with its stout roof and tight borders. Douglass and Auld—in what Douglass imagines as their man-to-man peerage, the imaginary symmetry of ex-master and former slave conceived in conformity with the slave master's patriarchal rule—reign supreme in their respective homes.[27] Within each household dwell dependents whose bodies are imagined as perfect and innocent. Under the abusive regime of chattel slavery, as Douglass proposes in his graphic inversion, those same bodies would be subject to violation. Were Douglass the slave master and Auld the slave, nothing in Auld's power could legally prevent Douglass from crossing his threshold, abducting his daughter, and violating her body's perimeters. The hypothetical ravishment Douglass depicts returns us to his account of Captain Anthony whipping Aunt Hester, "the blood-stained gate, the entrance to the hell of slavery," which concludes chapter 1 of the *Narrative*. As Douglass compels master and third-party reader to consider slave life in the microcosmic frame, the close-grained feature of slave-state topography is the human body: scarred, violently entered, and bearing in the signs of genetic mixing evidence of whole cycles of coercion.

In much slave testimony, the female body serves preeminently but by no means exclusively as the point of focus in the documentation of physical and sexual abuse. Douglass makes few but memorable references to the marks enslavement has inscribed on his own body. Some of those marks persist by virtue of the indelibility of his memory of them: thus "the pen with which I am writing might be laid in the gashes" that exposure to the elements have opened in the child Frederick's feet. But some marks, he suggests, would be visible to anyone who should inspect his body, and a reference to still-visible scars occurs in his letter to Auld: "You well know that I wear stripes on my back, inflicted by your direction" (417). But physical and specifically sexual abuse have done far more than leave visible and invisible traces on the individual bodies that have borne direct impact. European violence against Africans has resulted in the enslaved body's mixed genetic heritage. At the outset of each of his autobiographies, Douglass addresses the mark of enslavement ingrained in his body by virtue of his mixed-race parentage, and although he calls attention to the fact that his complexion is lighter than that of most of his fellow slaves on the Lloyd plantation, he is far from alone in his biraciality: "A very different-looking class of people are springing up at the south, and are now held in slavery," he observes in chapter 1 of the *Narrative*, "from those originally brought to this country from Africa" (17). The invasive force of a white forefather is a crime that enters into the ontology of those whose European ancestry is evident.[28] A century after Douglass commented upon the "different-looking class of people" arising in the South, Malcolm X would invoke the rapist memorialized by his red hair.[29]

In turning our attention to the geographies that Harriet Jacobs develops in *Incidents in the Life of a Slave Girl*, we meet with the familiar opposition of free state to slave state and a predictably close attention to borders, thresholds, and confinements, but we do so from the female perspective of Jacobs's alter ego, Linda Brent, and the female's enhanced consciousness of possessing a permeable body. In following Linda's career as a slave, we are introduced to many instances of microcosmic space, all of which are subject to white male intrusion. The interiors of built structures figure prominently: the two-parent "comfortable home" of earliest memory, the cabin Dr. Flint proposes to build in order to isolate Linda in concubinage, the grandmother's house of fragile sanctuary, the cellars and attic bedrooms that serve as way stations in Linda's flight, the jail to which her brothers are confined following aborted attempts to escape and to which her children are likewise confined in the process of being sold, the garret in which she reposes for seven years, the ship's hold in which she escapes from the South, the temporary lodgings she finds in Northern cities in abolitionist safe homes or residences of Northern employers who take on the risk of harboring her, and finally the longed-for but still unachieved "hearthstone" with which the narrative concludes.[30] This immersion in the microcosmic sites of Southern enslavement and Northern fugitive slave life takes place within the macrocosmic slave-state and free-state frame of reference. Within that shared frame, Jacobs pointedly reminds readers of the privilege and security they take for granted in the microcosmic North. As a testament that very specifically inscribes a readership, primarily Northern middle-class white women, secondarily their husbands, sons and fathers, *Incidents* regularly invokes what Jacobs imagines as the snug, untroubled scene in which her book is read: the mother-centered patriarchal household for which laws of marriage and property theoretically constitute a shield of protection.[31]

As the testimony of one destined to be perceived as a "fallen woman," Jacobs's narrative engages periodically in self-deprecatory gestures but aims to speak to a female readership from a position of gender commonality, if not social equality, and to assume an authority that can credibly formulate moral imperatives leading to political action. In editing *Incidents* for its 1861 publication, Lydia Maria Child promotes Linda Brent's intimate rapport with her reader by placing the author's preface before the introduction she has penned in her role as the standard white editor. Certification by a second white friend, Amy Post, is discretely placed as the narrative's afterword. In the book's first appeal to its readership, Linda speaks for herself and in doing so confesses her reluctance to tell her story: "It would have been more pleasant to me to have been silent about my own history" (1). Far from emphasizing the personal dimensions of that history, she disavows any wish

> to excite sympathy for my own sufferings. But I do earnestly desire to arouse the women of the North to a realizing sense of the condition of two millions of women at the South, still in bondage, suffering what I suffered, and most of them far worse. I want to add my testimony to that of abler pens to convince the people of the Free States what Slavery really is. Only by experience can any one realize how deep, and dark, and foul is that pit of abominations. (1–2)

This paragraph cites regional differentiation, "women of the North" and "women at the South," without reference to the color line. Women of both regions comprised by the macrocosmic national geography have in common vulnerabilities that attach to gender; commonality of victimhood (rampant in the South but a frequent if unacknowledged occurrence in the North) accordingly is greater than racial difference, particularly since, as Jacobs will emphasize, many of the enslaved have such a preponderance of Anglo-Saxon ancestry that they can pass for white. The attenuation of such racial difference as would place a "black" author at an unbridgeable distance from a "white" reader is reinforced in Child's conspicuously short introduction, in which she explains why she has assisted in the publication of a book containing "indelicate" sexual material:

> I do this for the sake of my sisters in bondage, who are suffering wrongs so foul, that our ears are too delicate to listen to them. I do it with the hope of arousing conscientious and reflecting women at the North to a sense of their duty in the exertion of moral influence on the question of Slavery, on all possible occasions. I do it with the hope that every man who reads this narrative will swear solemnly before God that, so far as he has power to prevent it, no fugitive from Slavery shall ever be sent back to suffer in that loathsome den of corruption and cruelty. (4)

Sisterhood, in Child's fervent conclusion to her remarks, knows no color line. And although enslaved "women at the South" were far more susceptible to abuse than women of the North, Child undoubtedly writes with the recognition that abuse is far from unknown among white middle-class women who supposedly live among patriarchal safeguards; such practical knowledge of sexual vulnerability as they must certainly possess might motivate such women to come to the aid of their enslaved sisters. Child's allusion to male readers in the last sentence acknowledges that men have a power to take direct political action that women do not, but in exerting "moral influence" within the home circle, the wife, sister, or mother might open a conversation of far-reaching consequence.

In Linda Brent, Jacobs creates a character whose location relative to the Northern reader is always spectral. Since escaping the slave South, Brent tells us in her preface, she has worked diligently to support herself and to provide educational opportunities for her children (1). Child informs us that Brent has lived in the North for seventeen years, "the greater part of the time with a distinguished family in New York" (3). Readers are given to understand that she has been employed in domestic service with honorable white people; this association, along with Child's and later Post's character references, attests to the worthiness of a person whose history is first and foremost a sexual history so far as it compels public attention. Readers might speculate that she still resides somewhere in New York City, but because she has "concealed the names of places, and given persons fictitious names" (1), they are unable to place her positively.[32] Socially, as an unmarried, middle-aged woman of color, she resides amid a shadowy underclass stratum of people who work in the homes of affluent and enlightened professionals. To the degree that "we" (as 1861 readers) identify with that class, we might visualize her in the next room minding the children or engaged in housework somewhere upstairs. Having escaped from her grandmother's garret, she still leads a life that hugs the margins and strives to remain invisible. Relative to a Northern readership that possesses the leisure to read and to think about social issues, *Incidents* positions Linda as the "not-us" whose victimhood affords her an authority to speak from below her readership's station—she has, after all, known firsthand the "pit of abominations"—but in whom the white female confidante may be coaxed to perceive a remote reflection.

The narrative's first paragraph pushes back against the stigmatized otherness with which preface and introduction position Linda Brent. "I was born a slave," she begins her testimony, "but I never knew it till six years of happy childhood had passed away" (5). In six years' time, she implies, she formed a personality that repelled notions of subjugation, particularly as that formation took place among a seemingly freestanding family unit. With respect to that unit, Jacobs sketches a "comfortable home" that presumably resembles the homes of her readers in that her parents, duly married, reside together in a patriarchal household that functions with virtual autonomy. Although technically a slave, her father is a skilled artisan whose mistress permits him to hire out his time; the proceeds from his work as carpenter and project manager support the family. As though to enhance the degree to which this original home situation mirrors white middle-class norms, Linda reports that her parents possessed the light complexions that marked them as people "termed mulattoes" (5). The grandmother who will play such a central role in this narrative is likewise depicted as occupying terrain between white and black. The daughter of a South Carolina planter who manumits his slave family, she is captured along with her mother and siblings as the family travels to join relatives in Florida. Sold to a hotel keeper, she becomes, as cook and seamstress, indispensable to the hotel's operation. On her growing reputation as a baker, she sets up her own profitable business with a view to buying her children's and her own freedom. Enterprising as the grandmother is, she cannot prevent the sale of her youngest son when the master dies and the property is divided among the heirs. Although she is unable to intervene in the sale of her "nearly white" (6) ten-year-old son for $720, she is nevertheless known as a woman of superb economy, and Linda highlights occasions on which she has become creditor to mistress and master, who, under no obligation to honor a slave's claim, unsurprisingly default on their loans.

The "nearly white" condition of Linda Brent and her family is emphasized throughout the narrative. Whether or not Jacobs thereby expresses an intra-ethnic prejudice against color, her insistent foregrounding of the family's biraciality is a clear appeal to the white reader to identify with Linda's predicament. Lydia Maria Child and Harriet Beecher Stowe had developed the trope of the "nearly white" slave, and when Jacobs writes the following, a description of her mother's relation to her mistress, she adopts language long familiar to readers of abolitionist literature: "My mother's mistress was the daughter of my grandmother's mistress. She was the foster sister of my mother; they were both nourished at my grandmother's breast. In fact, my mother had been weaned at three months old, that the babe of the mistress might obtain sufficient food. They played together as children; and, when they became women, my mother was a most faithful servant to her whiter foster sister" (6–7).[33] In such pairings, the siblings on either side of the color line more commonly share a father. Elsewhere, however, Jacobs makes reference to the "tangled skeins" (78) of biracial genealogy, and given the "nearly white" genetics of Linda and her family, the bond of milk is as strong, or more precisely, as weak, as the bond of blood.

Jacobs has additional means of demonstrating Linda's propinquity to a white readership. Although in the preface the self-deprecating author makes reference to the "deficiencies" of education that she brings to the task, her written and (where she depicts herself in dialogue) spoken English exhibit a mastery of standard form that evidently owes very little to Child's editing.[34] Her conversation and that of her grandmother, brothers, and uncles all conform to educated norms, whereas in dialogue with Sally, Old Betty, Jenny,

Old Addie, Uncle Fred, and Luke, Linda speaks standard English while her interlocutor speaks a stylized plantation dialect. The same disparity in language use also occurs across the color line when Linda converses with poor white Southerners who invade her grandmother's house and later when she negotiates with an Irish cabdriver who attempts to cheat her upon her arrival in New York City. In both cases the disparity aligns her with her genteel Anglo-Saxon reader. The earlier representation of white nonstandard English particularly merits close examination, as it challenges the white supremacy of people the text instructs us to view as Linda's social inferiors. In chapter 12, "Fear of Insurrection," militias assembled of "low whites, who had no negroes of their own to scourge" (64) are assigned the task of searching black homes for evidence of conspiracy in emulation of Nat Turner's recent revolt. Language use as a class marker is visible in the following exchange (the militia men have invaded the grandmother's house, but their fury is checked by the presence of an unidentified white "gentleman" friend of the family):

> My grandmother had a large trunk of bedding and table cloths. When that was opened, there was a great shout of surprise; and one exclaimed, "Where'd the damned niggers git all dis sheet an' table clarf?"
>
> My grandmother, emboldened by the presence of our white protector, said, "You may be sure we didn't pilfer 'em from *your* houses." (65)

At such moments, the author asks her readership to join her in her disdain for the white underclass roused by the local slaveholding elite to act the part of race persecutor. Like the Northern white reader, Linda and her grandmother live in a home of decent furnishings where refined language is customarily spoken. In such genteel settings, as Linda's story will show, people will internalize the expectations of those who can choose to conduct their lives in a particular manner. A clean, well-appointed house is consistent with an ideal of self-respect that preeminently expresses itself in sexual propriety. Even a grandmother who knows better might dream that her granddaughter will be able to conduct herself in a way that preserves her "purity." Whether Jacobs's grandmother actually succumbed to the self-deception depicted in *Incidents*, the narrative is committed to presenting Linda as a girl whose desire to lead a life of chastity and probity is equal to that of a readership whose sexuality has benefited, at least on the surface, from the oversight and protection of patriarchal rule.

"Perilous passages"

From first to last, Linda Brent focuses her reader's attention on what it is like to function as a self-respecting human subject among constraints imposed by a legal status that defines her as a commodity susceptible to immediate sale in addition to all manner of physical exploitation. The innocence of her first six years consists in her blissful ignorance of that status: "I never dreamed I was a piece of merchandise" entrusted to her parents "for safe keeping, and liable to be demanded of them at any moment" (5). Given what she represents as the delayed consciousness of her enslaved condition, she has formed an inalienable sense of herself as a free subject, or so it is important for her to argue in building a bond with her white Northern readership. From the illusion of leading what her reader would regard as a normal home life, she is first awakened on the occasion of her mother's death. At this point she learns of her slave status, but under the mild regime of a kind mistress she lives an additional six years among adults, on both sides of the color line, who provide affectionate support. When at age twelve Linda loses her mistress, she learns a first lesson in betrayal as it becomes clear that this loving figure did not fulfill the pledge she had made to Linda's mother to free Linda and her brother, William, at her death. Instead, her mistress has bequeathed Linda to a five-year-old niece, the daughter of Dr. Flint. When Linda is thirteen, her father dies, and beginning with chapter 5, "The Trials of Girlhood," she becomes Dr. Flint's obsessive object of pursuit. In broaching the topic of her preadolescent sexualization, Linda signals her departure from a girlhood she heretofore presumed to resemble that of her reader, and in doing so defines what she fears must remain an unbridgeable distance between herself and her audience.[35]

Jacobs begins the project of distinguishing her lot from that of her readers in the first of what might be described as three ethnographic chapters devoted to an exposition of life in the slave South. In chapter 3, "The Slaves' New Year's Day," she describes the geographic redistribution of the enslaved population that takes place on January 1, hiring day in the South, and the dismemberment of families as traders descend to conduct business. "O, you happy free women," Linda admonishes her readership, "contrast *your* New Year's day" full of family joy and the exchange of gifts "with that of the poor bond-woman" who must watch as her sons and daughters are dispatched to undefined and trackless distances (16). But the "bond-woman" at this point in the narrative is something of an abstraction. Beginning with chapter 5, "The Trials of Girlhood," Jacobs documents her initiation into that role—specifically, the role an enslaved teenage female is expected to play within the slaveholder patriarchy. In the first stages of that initiation, she is the portrait of innocence under assault: "My master began to whisper foul words in my ear. Young as I was, I could not remain ignorant of their import" (27). Superficially, such moments may recall scenes in a Richardsonian tale of seduction, but the sociology of *Incidents* bears little resemblance to that of *Clarissa*. Young as Linda is, her master's behavior continues an education that has gone on for some time:

> Every where the years bring to all enough of sin and sorrow; but in slavery the very dawn of life is darkened by these shadows. Even

> the little child, who is accustomed to wait on her mistress and her children, will learn, before she is twelve years old, why it is that her mistress hates such and such a one among the slaves. Perhaps the child's own mother is among those hated ones. She listens to violent outbreaks of jealous passion, and cannot help understanding what is the cause. She will become prematurely knowing in evil things. Soon she will learn to tremble when she hears her master's footfall. (28)

By chapter 5, Linda has already marked herself off from her white Northern female readership by detailing an early exposure to sexual harassment from which she presumes (or pretends to presume) her readership to be exempt, but it is not until chapter 10, "A Perilous Passage in a Slave Girl's Life," that Jacobs has her narrator embrace the stigma that defines Linda as victim and pariah.

In proceeding with her story, Jacobs confronts a difficult task: how to frame Linda's admission that at age fifteen she consented to an affair with Mr. Sands as a way to avoid losing her virginity to Dr. Flint?[36] Mindful of the shock that such a revelation is supposed to produce to the sensibility of women who live a narrative (true, false, or somewhere in between) of maiden chastity and married fidelity, she halts her account of events long enough to pledge that she will tell of events as they truly fell out but do so with the appropriate remorse:

> And now, reader, I come to a period in my unhappy life, which I would gladly forget if I could. The remembrance fills me with sorrow and shame. It pains me to tell you of it; but I have promised to tell you the truth, and I will do it honestly, let it cost me what it may. I will not try to screen myself behind the plea of compulsion from a master; for it was not so. Neither can I plead ignorance or thoughtlessness. For years, my master had done his utmost to pollute my mind with foul images, and to destroy the pure principles inculcated by my grandmother, and the good mistress of my childhood. The influences of slavery had had the same effect on me that they had on other young girls; they had made me prematurely knowing, concerning the evil ways of the world. I knew what I did, and I did it with deliberate calculation. (53–54)

Linda concedes that all the extenuating circumstances in the world do not combine to absolve her from the actions she undertook. As Saidiya Hartman observes, the "identification of the slave girl as 'victim' does not negate her role as agent."[37] But any agency she commands as a sympathetic protagonist desperate to avoid entrapments and coercions must count as a virtue within her narrative's economy, and thus the same action for which she must be willing to accept blame qualifies her by other criteria as a strong heroine who refuses to succumb to soul-death passivity. Her apology is fraught with ambivalence, and readers to whom she presents herself at the bar of judgment are all but informed that they have no right to judge the slave girl—indeed they have lost this right, her statement implies, because they have not done everything in their power to bring an end to the system responsible for her persecutions:

> But, O, ye happy women, whose purity has been sheltered from childhood, who have been free to choose the objects of your affection, whose homes are protected by law, do not judge the poor desolate slave girl too severely! *If slavery had been abolished*, I, also, could have married the man of my choice; I could have had a home shielded by the laws; and I should have been spared the painful task of confessing what I am now about to relate; but all my prospects had been blighted by slavery. I wanted to keep myself pure; and, under the most adverse circumstances, I tried hard to preserve my self-respect; but I was struggling alone in the powerful grasp of the demon Slavery; and the monster proved too strong for me. (54; emphasis added)

The incrimination of Linda Brent is only valid if she had possessed the opportunity to preserve her virginity in accord with the ideals of her readership's middle-class culture—and that she did not possess that opportunity incriminates the reader. Amid the flurry of apologies and qualifications of those apologies, she offers dispassionate arguments as to why someone in her position might reasonably enter into a sexual relationship. First, there is the matter of choice: "It seems less degrading to give one's self, than to submit to compulsion" (55). Secondly, at a time when a teenage female's heterosexual activity almost certainly will lead to pregnancy, there was forethought regarding issue. "Of a man who was not my master I could ask to have my children well supported; and in this case, I felt confident I should obtain the boon. I also felt quite sure that they would be made free" (55). Her contention that the slave girl's experience is different from the experience of her nonslave counterpart is well founded. As she proceeds in what she perceives as an obligatorily self-incriminating mode, she will not refrain from expressions of anger that she should be put under such obligation:

> With all these thoughts revolving in my mind, and seeing no other way of escaping the doom I so much dreaded, I made a headlong plunge. Pity me, and pardon me, O virtuous reader! *You never knew what it is to be a slave*; to be entirely unprotected by law or custom; to have the laws reduce you to the condition of a chattel, entirely subject to the will of another. You never exhausted your ingenuity in avoiding the snares, and eluding the power of a hated tyrant; you never shuddered at the sound of his footsteps, and trembled within

> hearing of his voice. I know I did wrong. No one can feel it more sensibly than I do. The painful and humiliating memory will haunt me to my dying day. Still, in looking back, calmly, on the events of my life, I feel that the slave woman ought not to be judged by the same standard as others. (55–56; emphasis added)

But whether *this* slave girl should be judged by modified or wholly different standards, she does not venture to say.

It is impossible to know what orders of shame Jacobs experienced as a result of bearing two children with Samuel Tredwell Sawyer, the Mr. Sands of *Incidents*. Did Molly Horniblow, Jacobs's grandmother, raise her granddaughter with the expectation that she could lead a life of maiden chastity, wed a man to whom she felt united in love, and live ever after in a married state recognized and respected by a white slaveholding Southern patriarchy? Did the grandmother banish Harriet from the house on learning that she had become pregnant? Did Jacobs experience the humiliation Linda claims she experienced as a result of her actions, first in private, and then when forced to reveal her pregnancy to her grandmother? Was this humiliation experienced anew when she told her story to the Reverend Jeremiah Durham in Philadelphia? Or does the shame Linda expresses pertain to the public confession she makes in publishing her life story, a shame that has little to do with internalized values but rather with how any person is compelled to speak publicly of one's sexual past? Jacobs had to know that free white women were not unacquainted with sexual harassment. Did she not anticipate that some white readers would resonate to her reference to the master's snares, footstep, and voice? Child and Jacobs both invoke a sisterhood that binds women in the North to women in the South. Patriarchal sexual oppression, in North and South, is the implied basis of this bond, but there were limits to what either woman could say about predatory sexual practices in the free states.

In chapter 14, "Another Link to Life," Linda accounts for her second pregnancy as a natural occurrence in the life of a young woman who has chosen a certain path and cannot reverse course. Upon receiving news of this pregnancy, evidence of his slave's continuation of an unauthorized liaison, Dr. Flint is enraged to the point of savagely cutting her hair, an assault that substitutes for the rape Linda ostensibly manages to avoid, but the advent of another child produces no new rupture with the grandmother who evidently has accepted the fact of her granddaughter's compromised virtue. Now that the great conflict in her life has shifted from resisting the overtures of Dr. Flint to putting her children beyond reach of the slave trader—an imperative that for her becomes even more urgent with the birth of the second child, a daughter—Linda's identity transitions from that of shamed pregnant unwed teenager to heroic mother for whom no sacrifice is too great to protect her children from ill usage as marketable commodities. In the aftermath of her fall into procreative sexuality, she has reconciled herself to the idea that "there was no chance for me to be respectable" (76), and although she will periodically advert to occasions in which she is made to feel shame as a single mother, Jacobs stakes the rehabilitation of Linda Brent on two goals that she is almost but never quite able to attain: first, her successful resistance to a system that, short of dragging her back to Southern bondage, would confirm her abjection by extorting money to legalize her freedom; and second, the rescue of her children from the cruelties and exploitation that blighted her own youth, and recuperation of the family in a home of their own under protection of law. If the sanctified patriarchal home she ascribes to her readership is ever beyond reach—"My story ends with freedom," she tells us in her penultimate paragraph, "not in the usual way, with marriage" (201)—she aspires nonetheless to its near approximation.

Linda's career as a mother in quest of domestic space for herself and her children free from incursions of the slave patriarchy plays out among the claustrophobic scenes of her initial flight and seven-year refuge in the garret her uncle Phillip constructs for her under the eaves of her grandmother's house. Her escape path leads down dark, rainy roads and in and out of houses at night. She endures a series of suffocating concealments, with never a map and seldom a clear vision of how to move beyond the impasse of the moment. On those occasions when she must quit an indoor hiding place, her outdoor refuge offers little relief, as she finds herself in snake-infested bushes or swamplands. Caught between claustrophobia and agoraphobia, however, she prefers closed to open spaces; immobilized in her garret, she summons what powers she can. Closeted in a house that is closely watched, she nevertheless vanishes from surveillance, and after she has punched a peephole in the side of the garret, she can conduct surveillance of her own. Invisible in the midst of her pursuers, she applies her skill as a literate woman to disinform her adversary concerning her whereabouts: by writing a letter to Dr. Flint datelined New York with reference to her life in Boston, she induces him to travel north on a fool's errand. She follows this ruse with subsequent letters that she arranges to have sent from other free states and Canadian locations, thus creating the impression of frequent and evasive movement. Her scheme is to convince Dr. Flint that she is no longer his captive, thereby softening his resistance to selling her children to Mr. Sands, who has promised to set them free—and in guessing that Dr. Flint will want to disburden himself of their care she is correct. But the power she exerts from her retreat has its limits, and when Mr. Sands fails to fulfill his promise after having sent the children north, it is time for Linda to leave the space she has variously called her retreat, den, dungeon, hole, and prison.

Linda's occupation of the garret for the biblically resonant term of seven years constitutes the book's most memorable narrative feature.[38] Her characterization of this period combines depiction of physically agonizing confinement and emotionally anguishing separation from her children with the portrait of a woman absenting herself from what she deems a condition of worse sufferings, as well as exercising powers of oversight and stagecraft unsuspected by Dr. Flint. The situation is remarkable because it conflates elements of imprisonment and freedom, compulsion and agency. "It seemed horrible to sit or lie in a cramped position day after day, without one gleam of light," Linda observes. "Yet I would have chosen this, rather than my lot as a slave" (114). "Would have" is not quite equivalent to "did choose," but her decision not to abandon her immurement and acquiesce to the demands of Dr. Flint confirms her garret residence as an option reluctantly elected. Her concealment allows her to elude, as Katherine McKittrick argues, the "white masculine knowledge and the logic of visualization" according to which "her place and body are seen to be, and understood as, naturally subordinate to whiteness and masculinity"; in addition, it disrupts "Dr. Flint's sense of place" as a representation of the patriarchal slaveholding order, dependent as this order is on the "seeable presence" of the slave as a sexually available commodity.[39] Her literacy empowers her to compose letters that plant false leads as to her whereabouts, which in turn allows her to move Dr. Flint from slave state to free in futile quest of the body lying prostrate aloft in Edenton.[40] The concealment she adopts in her garret refuge extends to the moment in which she inscribes her narrative: her determination to leave her reader ignorant as to her precise whereabouts in the North replicates the ways in which she eludes Dr. Flint's efforts to map her movements and fix her location. At the price of great physical and psychological suffering, Linda achieves an unplaced existence: "Everywhere and nowhere," as McKittrick observes, "north and south, unvisibly present across the landscape, in the last place they thought of."[41] By sacrificing her body, she has established an out-of-body existence, wresting a degree of permanent control over the master/slave cartography.

Even after she has vacated her garret, we still find Linda typically within walls and behind doors: on board the ship that takes her to Philadelphia, she occupies a "little box of a cabin" (156) and has to be encouraged to take fresh air on deck; on the packet from Brooklyn to Stonington, she seeks relief from the open deck for herself and her daughter, Ellen, by pleading successfully for a berth below. When running errands for the Bruce family in New York City, she moves hurriedly "through back streets and by-ways" (191). In general, Jacobs does not write favorably of spatial expanse. Except for a brief expression of joy to be "fairly sailing on Chesapeake Bay" (158) in her passage to the free states, Linda is averse to the spectacle of the long view and open horizon. Chapter 37, "A Visit to England," is curiously devoid of description of what for her would have been the novel sights and sounds of an ocean crossing; she has, moreover, nothing to say about the English countryside. Perhaps what she observes to be the absence in England of color prejudice relieves her of the task of noting the geographies of her interurban travels. The return voyage excites prospects of fear: "From the distance spectres seemed to rise up on the shores of the United States. It is a sad feeling to be afraid of one's native country" (186). Upon landing in New York, she resumes her career as fugitive. With Ellen, she resides for two years in Boston, dwelling comfortably together in "two little rooms" (188), and when Ellen goes off to school, she lives for a year with Isaac and Amy Post in Rochester, New York, managing a bookstore and reading room. For all this travel, she provides no description of space traversed and place inhabited beyond noting the fact that she shared quarters with specific people. Her prose scrupulously avoids registering the open spaces that threaten her exposure.

Incidents in the Life of a Slave Girl concludes with Linda's emancipation in New York City at a time when the 1850 Fugitive Slave Act had rendered the distinction between slave state and free state all but meaningless. Much of the cumulative power of *Incidents* resides in the climactic defeat her manumission represents, as the Flint heirs' quitclaim proceeds from a monetary settlement. In the final chapter, "Free at Last," Linda learns that her benefactress, the second Mrs. Bruce, has put an end to her perpetual flight by entering into the transaction that confirms her status as "a piece of merchandise"—the words "free" and "sold" thus bound together in sickening compromise:

> So I was *sold* at last! A human being *sold* in the free city of New York! The bill of sale is on record, and future generations will learn from it that women were articles of traffic in New York, late in the nineteenth century of the Christian religion. It may hereafter prove a useful document to antiquaries, who are seeking to measure the progress of civilization in the United States. I well know the value of that bit of paper; but much as I love freedom, I do not like to look upon it. I am deeply grateful to the generous friend who procured it, but I despise the miscreant who demanded payment for what never rightfully belonged to him or his. (200)

If Linda's public narration of an errant sexual past has erected one barrier between herself and her readership, the condition of having been sold erects another insofar as her ontology as a free human being is impugned by "that bit of paper" testifying to her once-and-forever monetization.

Her status as a conditionally free human being is reinforced by the fact that she still lives unequally as Mrs. Bruce's protégé, dependent on the white woman's charitable disposition. The stigma of unwed motherhood continues to haunt her. "Reader, my story ends with freedom; not in the usual way, with marriage" (201). The line serves to juxtapose the narrative arc of *Incidents* with that of *Jane Eyre* and Jane's status as foster child, governess, young woman potentially compromised at the hands of an older married man, and her final reward for steadfastness: "Reader, I married him." But if, in juxtaposition, Linda is a Jane whom fortune has failed, she is more permanently a Bertha Mason Rochester, confined to the categories reserved for women marked by color and scandal.[42] Like Bertha, Linda lives a life of exile; her last thoughts concern her "tender memories of my good old grandmother, like light, fleecy clouds floating over a dark and troubled sea" (201), a sea she has crossed in her flight north from a home to which she cannot imagine returning, at least while slavery persists, and in any event never again to see her grandmother, who is now deceased. By her literary practice, however, she reorders the space of her persecutions and compels her audience to reconsider their world from the margins to which she has been consigned. However belatedly, with Jean Fagan Yellin's 1987 edition and recertification that this book "is no fiction" (1), readers are able to accept and celebrate the moral authority Harriet Jacobs made bold to exert.[43]

Chapter 4

✦

Domestic Uplift and Escape Abroad

Booker T. Washington, Ida B. Wells-Barnett, W. E. B. Du Bois

In the transitional period between the Emancipation Proclamation (1863) and ratification of the Thirteenth Amendment (1865), the occasion for composing and publishing texts that strictly qualify as fugitive slave narratives ceased to exist. Narrowly defined, such narratives are the testimony of authors in flight from the property claims of masters, mistresses, and their heirs—or, if ransomed from their slave status, of authors burdened by the memory of such flight and the chattel objectification they sought to escape. With white readers specifically, slave narratives sought to construct a relationship that would materialize in action along a broad spectrum of political expression: ballot box, petition, letters to editors and elected representatives, street protest, and (not least) conversation among family members in the privileged recess of domestic space, as when sister, wife, and mother encourage brother, husband, or son to speak and vote against the slave power. After 1865, the terms "fugitive" and "flight" enter altered fields of signification: slavery per se, along with other forms of involuntary servitude not associated with a penal code, has been at least nominally abolished. The Fourteenth Amendment (1868) with its broadened definition of citizenship and the Fifteenth Amendment (1870) guaranteeing voting rights would soon follow. At the state level, however, the de jure status of black people would remain vexed, fluid, and frequently overmastered by their de facto status, and the white supremacy of the Southern statehouse not only would prove resistant to federal legislation but also would find support in U.S. Supreme Court rulings.[1] Black testimony need no longer contend with the legality of chattel objectification but must still press back against forces that would deny a liberated people's human and citizenly rights and persist in classing the nonwhite person as existentially inferior to the white.

In short, such testimony had to contend with what Du Bois, in *Dusk of Dawn*, would call the "social heritage of slavery" (59), a legacy that from one generation to the next replicates the color line under evolving demographic conditions. To be sure, *Brown v. Board of Education of Topeka* (1954) and federal legislation associated with the civil rights era would mitigate that heritage, as would affirmative action policies implemented at federal, state, and local levels. Moreover, the 2008 election of the nation's first African American president would appear to signal the advent if hardly the achievement of a new era in the United States. But the persistence of the past may be read in the social geography of twenty-first-century urban, suburban, and rural America; it may be heard loud and clear in the intensified discourse of race in which a fearful white nationalist contingent rails against communities of color disproportionately subject to racial profiling and police violence. It is no wonder that such probing, analytical, and global thinkers as Douglass and Du Bois continue to speak to us today.

Among African American authors of first-person testimonies that build on the slave narrative genre, Ida B. Wells-Barnett, Booker T. Washington, and W. E. B. Du Bois do much to frame for succeeding generations the postslavery and post-Reconstruction predicament of black people and the confined geographies of a second-class citizenship. In *Crusade for Justice*, Wells-Barnett develops a narrative in which she seeks sanctuary in the North and assistance in Great Britain after running afoul of the Memphis city fathers, whose lynch-law tactics she had brought to national attention. Flight along lines of a slave-narrative cartography thus figures in her story's plot. For his part, Washington begins *Up from Slavery* as a studied revision of the opening paragraphs of Douglass's 1845 *Narrative*, but neither he nor Du Bois structures his story as a South-to-North migration—on the contrary, both gravitate to the Deep South, as to the site of compelling need as well as, by numbers, a viable black nationhood.[2] In the context of their respective narratives, *flight* pertains to the material and spiritual oppression of black Americans, and in both cases escape from oppression remains a work in progress. That much they have in common, but nothing, of course, could be more incompatible than the respective responses of Washington and Du Bois to the legacies of the recent slave past. Even as they lived, their careers were understood as binaries, given their radical unlikeness in nearly every respect: regional origin, educational and travel experience, temperament, intellectual and aesthetic susceptibilities, and so forth. Although Washington's Southern circumstances conform to a generalizable black experience in ways that Du Bois's Northern circumstances do not, their diverse paths articulate a range of experience within a heritage that places them alike on the same side of the cultural-historical color line. The careers of these three authors reflect dramatic and personally transformative shifts in geographic location, and each develops a national if not international perspective on the harsh conditions black people experience in microlocalities north and south. For each, moreover, ameliorative possibility consists not simply in the specific remediations they propose but in the relationships they would form with black and white readerships as they seek to redefine the fraught public space of post-Reconstruction America.

"Tight places"

Of the three, Booker T. Washington alone sought primary support from the other side of the color line. Promoted by Northern philanthropists and their political allies, his national profile overshadowed the public presence of Wells-Barnett and Du Bois in the years between the Spanish-American and First World Wars. In the view of ruling-class white Americans, the mantel of black leadership had passed from Frederick Douglass to the Wizard of Tuskegee. However, beginning with critiques that date from Du Bois's "The Evolution of Negro Leadership" (*The Dial*, July 16, 1901), Washington's accomplishments would be subject to question and his influence increasingly contested. His notorious reference in *Up from Slavery* to African American bondage as "the school of slavery" and his proposition that "the black man got nearly as much out of slavery as the white man did" retain the power to offend readers more than a century after the book's publication.[3] Despite the genuine achievement represented by his founding of Tuskegee Institute, the era's black industrial schools with their extensive capitalist web of support remained, in Kevin K. Gaines's words, "deeply implicated as bureaucratic instruments of segregationist state power."[4] The present discussion need not dwell on the familiar charges leveled against Washington as a leader who promoted a subservient and depoliticized role for a Southern black populace. My aim, rather, is to examine how Washington, in his twin and nearly simultaneously published autobiographies, connects with established traditions of slave testimony and, in so doing, maps his progress from origins in rural poverty to the occasion of composing a life story in the light of a publicly celebrated success. Granted, his autobiographies convey the impression of one who has acquired spheres of influence at a heavy price: specifically, any insistence that white people honor those rights guaranteed in the Fourteenth and Fifteenth Amendments. But that does not mean that Washington manifests no signs of unease with the accommodation for which he figures as master of ceremonies. Amid the many refractions of the public man that appear in his narratives, the mobile inscribing subject who writes and revises the life story illuminates unique dimensions of the nation's postslavery geographies.

Washington's two autobiographies, *The Story of My Life and Work* (1900, 1901) and *Up from Slavery* (1901), reflect efforts to reach two distinct audiences. *The Story of My Life and Work* was composed at the suggestion of J. L. Nichols and Company, a publisher specializing in the door-to-door marketing of books to black people, and produced with the assistance of two ghostwriters.[5] *Up from Slavery* represents a recasting of material from the earlier narrative at the encouragement of Lyman Abbott, a white Congregationalist minister and editor who serialized Washington's story in his weekly magazine, *The Outlook*, and Walter Hines Page, a white journalist and partner in the firm Doubleday and Page, which would publish *Up from Slavery* for a general audience. Whole passages of the one reappear in the pages of the other, and yet the differences between the two texts are significant. The most obvious difference is that *The Story of My Life and Work* contains sixty illustrations directed at promoting the myth of Washington as one whose personal merit attracted notice and favor from an early age (examples: "Little Booker a Favorite with His Master—Is Allowed to Peep into the Parlor of the Big House"; "Booker T. Washington Rehearsing His Graduating Oration at Hampton"; "President Eliot Conferring Honorary Degree upon Mr. Washington at Harvard University, June 24, 1896"). *Up from Slavery*, by comparison, features seven illustrations with little narrative continuity, aimed as it is at a predominantly white audience regarded perhaps as less dependent on pictorial cues than a black readership emerging from illiteracy. But in addition to its wealth of illustrations, *The Story of My Life and Work* narrates one experience in particular that could not but speak powerfully to an audience for whom antebellum bondage remained a living memory: "The thing in connection with slavery that has left the deepest impression on me was the instance of seeing a grown man, my uncle, tied to a tree early one morning, stripped naked, and someone whipping him with a cowhide. As each blow touched his back the cry, 'Pray, master! Pray, master!' came from his lips, and made an impression upon my boyish heart that I shall carry with me to my grave."[6] What Washington here presents as a deeply scarring incident finds no iteration in *Up from Slavery*. Indeed the word "whip" never occurs in the second autobiography. Conversely, *The Story of My Life and Work* makes no mention of "the school of slavery." Both narratives stress Washington's determination to achieve rapprochement with the white South and to establish a secure economic niche for a black impoverished populace, and both identify the 1895 Atlanta Exposition Address as a climactic moment in the arc of his career. Nevertheless, if we accept this account of his uncle's whipping as the active memory Washington claims it to be, rather than dismissing it as an obligatory set piece modeled on incidents in any number of slave narratives, *The Story of My Life and Work* suggests that Washington can never be entirely reconciled to a rhetoric of forgiveness.

The spectacle of an uncle's whipping that leaves an indelible mark on a "boyish heart" mirrors scenes (such as the whipping of Aunt Hester) from Douglass's accounts of childhood. But Washington opens *Up from Slavery* with an even more obvious reference to *The Narrative of Frederick Douglass, An American Slave*, although, in doing so, he distances his persona from that of his powerful literary progenitor in what Henry Louis Gates Jr. has identified as a "signifying" verbal gesture.[7] With a few deft strokes Washington intimates that the antebellum grievances Douglass classically formulated have been or are in the process of being addressed if not rectified. The first clause of *Up from Slavery* repeats the first clause of Douglass's *Narrative*, then introduces an ironic if not facetious turn of phrase: "I was born a slave on a plantation in Franklin County, Virginia. I am not quite sure of the exact place or exact date of my birth, but at any rate I suspect I must have been born somewhere and at some time."[8] Washington thus adroitly signals that he is not a man whose self-possession requires inquiry into the circumstances of birth or the settling of genealogical questions. On the contrary: his confident presence-to-himself in the moment of inscription repels the validation of knowledge with respect to origins. For Booker T. Washington, principal of Tuskegee, it suffices to know that he possesses, personally and professionally, an identity of achieved destination if not one of origin; the generic nature of his Southern late-antebellum beginnings is knowledge enough. With Douglass, the "want of information" concerning his time of birth "was a source of unhappiness" in childhood as in adulthood, but Washington neither recalls nor evinces cognitive misery related to the mysteries of birth.

As to what can be known of Washington's ancestry, "I have been unsuccessful in securing any information that would throw any accurate light upon the history of my family beyond my mother" (*Up*, 2) but such "want of information" causes, again, no apparent distress. And as to the paternal line specifically,

> of my father I know even less than of my mother. I do not even know his name. I have heard reports to the effect that he was a white man who lived on one of the near-by plantations. Whoever he was, I never heard of his taking the least interest in me or providing in any way for my rearing. But I do not find especial fault with him. He was simply another unfortunate victim of the institution which the Nation unhappily had engrafted upon it at that time. (*Up*, 2–3)

For Douglass, the unspoken anguish of his white parentage is not simply his inability to identify a person—was it an Anthony, a Lloyd, an Auld, a man with whom he may have experienced close spatial proximity?—but the certainty that he is the issue of an asymmetrical relationship if not, indeed, rape. Captain Anthony's whipping of Aunt Hester stands in for what he cannot openly speculate about the scene of his inception. But just as "whip" never occurs in *Up from Slavery*, neither does "rape." Whatever grievance Washington may associate with his biracial status is suppressed, along with the entire topic of sexual relations—antebellum or postbellum—across the color line.

The erasure of slaveholder cruelty that *Up from Slavery* perpetrates (what happens to the "impression" that he previously said he would carry to his grave?) draws attention to the principle of repression that operates in both books but fulfills its task more completely in the second. Washington begins both narratives from the position of one whose success has compensated for whatever suffering he has incurred as a black person in America—if, in fact, he requires compensation for circumstances that induced him to develop the self-empowering, Franklin-like character that led to his dramatic rise. Liberation associated with a northward trek from slave state to free state, the staple theme of the slave narrative tradition, is conspicuously absent from

Washington's autobiographies. His journey begins in Virginia and concludes in Alabama, and nowhere does he express a wish to escape the boundaries of the erstwhile Confederacy. Yet the celebrated educator who composes both narratives is a well-traveled man whose professional activities involve frequent trips to the Northeast and Midwest as he fulfills his duty as Tuskegee's indefatigable fundraiser. His reminiscences, he tells us, are the byproduct of a crowded and largely itinerant schedule: "Much of what I have said has been written on board trains, or at hotels or railroad stations while I have been waiting for trains, or during the moments that I could spare from my work while at Tuskegee" (*Up*, vii–viii). Washington in fact regales his reader with evidence that he commands a geographic and social mobility that defies expectations pertaining to individuals of hardscrabble origin and persecuted caste. He has managed even to cross the Atlantic, and devotes a chapter in both autobiographies to his European sojourn, although the excursion conforms more to the grand tour associated with the achievement of bourgeois status than to the pattern of black Americans seeking financial and moral support, if not refuge, abroad. Despite what he represents as a life in perpetual motion, Washington remains a man of rural microlocalities, both in his account of the geographies of birth, childhood, and higher education, as well as in his establishment of the Tuskegee campus as a freestanding mini-empire.

Washington derives great satisfaction from the Southern occupation Tuskegee represents. In his view it is ideally situated "in the centre of that part of our country that was most devoted to slavery," where "no Negro could be taught from books without the teacher receiving the condemnation of the law or of public sentiment" (*Up*, 146). At the time Washington writes, however, Tuskegee, as he knows, is anything but truly freestanding. The campus could not prosper without the financial support of Northern industry and its philanthropic industrialist-oligarchs, so that the model of rural self-subsistence remains dependent on the national and global economy of post–Civil War American capitalism. Similarly it could not survive without Southern white protectors convinced (as many white Southerners were not) that Tuskegee affirms rather than threatens a white supremacist culture.[9] Overtly at least, the institute poses no immediate challenge to the post-Reconstruction status quo. Its curriculum equips its graduates for artisanal vocations in the rural and small-town South rather than for a successful transition to professional life in urban industrial and administrative centers. In recollecting what he represents as the dependent and vulnerable condition of blacks who had migrated to Washington, D.C., during Reconstruction, Washington expresses the wish "that by some power of magic I might remove the great bulk of these people into the country districts and plant them upon the soil, upon the solid and never deceptive foundation of Mother Nature, where all nations and races that have ever succeeded have gotten their start" (*Up*, 90). This sentiment dovetails with Jefferson's vision of an agrarian republic, except for the fact that Washington de-emphasizes the role of political citizenship. Beyond agricultural vocations, the Tuskegee degree might lead to a career in such service professions as nursing or teaching but not to the law or to advanced positions in medicine or the academy. That any Tuskegee career path should lead to an engagement of local, state, or national politics (at least in the near term) was totally contrary to what Washington professed as his institution's mission.

So absorbing of Washington's energies is that campus and so dependent is his success on the largesse of Northern oligarchs and the goodwill of Southern planter-class heirs that his attention strays very little from the present moment, in which he must solicit contributions and make the concessions that will perpetuate his success. In this regard he is (as he admits) an improbable autobiographer, or at least an autobiographer reluctant to include material that does not accrue to current projects and commitments. Unlike Douglass, unlike Du Bois, Washington expunges as he can historical awareness from his spatiotemporal frame of reference: he conjures the past mostly to affirm that it must not dominate the present. In writing of family in both autobiographies, he makes abbreviated mention of the slave trade responsible for the African presence in North America. From *Up from Slavery*: "In the slave quarters, and even later, I heard whispered conversations among the coloured people of the tortures which the slaves, including, no doubt, my ancestors on my mother's side, suffered in the middle passage of the slave ship while being conveyed from Africa to America. I have been unsuccessful in securing any information that would throw any accurate light upon the history of my family beyond my mother" (2). His lack of success in securing such information is to all appearances not problematic—better to know little than to know much. The only other paragraph into which we might read an (at most) attenuated consciousness of the Middle Passage reaffirms his evident conviction that the past must not distract from present ameliorative efforts. This occurs in the context of the Atlanta Exposition Speech: "A ship lost at sea for many days suddenly sighted a friendly vessel. From the mast of the unfortunate vessel was seen a signal, 'Water, water; we die of thirst!' The answer from the friendly vessel at once came back, 'Cast down your bucket where you are' " (*Up*, 219). The point of his famous analogy is that people in distress should look to the here and now: rather than cultivate historical consciousness, one must suppress traumatic memory in one's embrace of life-giving present opportunity. It is not easy to do so: the friendly vessel must repeat the advice to "cast down your bucket" several times before those aboard the lost ship understand that with minimal exertion they can help themselves to fresh water. As a trope, the ship at the mouth of the Amazon is a subliminal slaver. Whereas it is impossible in a geographic inquiry not to read Washington's errant vessel as a figure of the Middle Passage, it can hardly seem politic that the studiously inoffensive Booker T. Washington, in addressing the white cotton-planter audience, would offer an analogy in which a slave ship descends from the past of common memory. His immediate point is that black Southerners and white Southerners find themselves, after all, in the same boat. But whatever Washington consciously intended, and whatever his audience consciously heard, this ship adrift in a sea of fresh water exemplifies Washington's treatment of the past: history itself admonishes us not to let the past distract from the work of the present.[10]

Accordingly, in both *The Story of My Life and Work* and *Up from Slavery*, Washington leads his life and accomplishes his goals in the context of foreshortened history and contracted worlds. In conjuring his childhood and young manhood, the accomplished man who travels by rail recalls what it means to migrate by foot, as though to emphasize that progress is achieved by small, humble steps. Following emancipation, Washington and his siblings accompanied his mother over the mountains to join her husband in West Virginia, a trek of ten days. "Of course we had to sleep in the wagon, or what was more often true, on the ground. The children walked a great portion of the distance" (*Story*, 20). And thus his family participated in the postemancipation exodus from slavery's tainted garden. More mythic still is his pilgrimage to Hampton, a journey Washington begins as the one black passenger in a stagecoach that stops at night at an inn where he is denied food and shelter: "My first experience," Washington claims, "in finding out what the colour of my skin meant" (*Up*, 49). Continuing his journey on foot when he could not beg rides from passing teamsters, he arrives in Richmond entirely destitute: he must improvise shelter and find what work he can. Some of the most detailed and realized writing in *Up from Slavery* depicts the straitened geographies of Washington's youthful vagabondage:

> I must have walked the streets till after midnight. At last I became so exhausted that I could walk no longer. I was tired, I was hungry, I was everything but discouraged. Just about the time when I reached extreme physical exhaustion, I came upon a portion of a street where the board sidewalk was considerably elevated. I waited for a few minutes, till I was sure that no passers-by could see me, and then crept under the sidewalk and lay for the night upon the ground, with my satchel of clothing for a pillow. Nearly all night I could hear the tramp of feet over my head. (49)

Finding work at the docks, he is able to relieve an accumulated hunger and save enough money for coach fare. Finally he completes his journey to Hampton, "the promised land" (*Up*, 51), which he reaches with fifty cents in his pocket (like Benjamin Franklin, whose vagabond journey to Philadelphia anticipates Washington's to Hampton, he retains a vivid memory of pocket change at critical moments in his life). Arriving at the school without advance notice and with nothing to recommend his admission, he rapidly exhibits a work ethic and native aptness that, combined with a politic humility, lead to his brilliant success.

From his position of prestige and mobility, Washington regards these harsh erstwhile geographies with the fondness one is apt to feel for hardships overcome. Traveling on behalf of Tuskegee, he finds himself covering ground "in well-appointed steam cars" (*Story*, 21–22) that he had formerly traversed by foot. Such travel permits him to savor both the privation and the privilege that comes as the reward of privation survived. His Richmond shelter figures for him as a sentimental point of reference: years later "the coloured citizens of Richmond," he reminisces in *Up from Slavery*, "very kindly tendered me a reception, at which there must have been two thousand people present. This reception was held not far from the spot where I slept the first night I spent in that city, and I must confess that my mind was more upon the sidewalk that first gave me shelter than upon the reception, agreeable and cordial as it was" (50). His affection for the problem-posing scenes in which he meets personal challenge does not, however, cease with his arrival at Tuskegee. The following anecdote from his career as a fundraiser exemplifies his cartographies early and late:

> More than once I have found myself in some pretty tight places while collecting money in the North. The following incident I have never related but once before, for the reason that I feared that people would not believe it. One morning I found myself in Providence, Rhode Island, without a cent of money with which to buy breakfast. In crossing the street to see a lady from whom I hoped to get some money, I found a bright new twenty-five-cent piece in the middle of the streetcar track. I not only had this twenty-five cents for my breakfast, but within a few minutes I had a donation from the lady on whom I had started to call. (*Up*, 189)

Here, the phrase "tight places" serves as a resonant keynote: his spatiotemporal situation, first to last, has been a sequence of tight places from which he has had to descry or create, according to his lights, the grounds of sustainable black community life, and he has had to do so on donated money and with the fragile reprieve of a white South given to spasms of genocidal rage.

It is for this reason that the Atlanta Exposition Address, delivered a year before *Plessy v. Fergusson* (1896) codified the "separate but equal" doctrine he so presciently anticipated in his analogy of separate fingers on a common hand, marks for Washington the pinnacle of his career. In explaining the anxiety that he, a practiced speaker, experienced prior to this moment—"I felt a good deal as I suppose a man feels when he is on his way to the gallows"—he recalls what a white farmer remarked to him in somber jest: "'Washington, you have spoken before the Northern white people, the Negroes in the South, and to us country white people in the South; but in Atlanta, to-morrow, you will have before you the Northern whites, the Southern whites, and the Negroes all together. I am afraid that you have got yourself into a tight place.'"

"This farmer diagnosed the situation correctly," Washington observes, "but his frank words did not add anything to my comfort" (*Up*, 213). From that tight place, Washington narrates the sequel, printing the speech with the famous lines "In all things that are purely social we can be as separate as the fingers, yet one as the hand in all things essential to mutual progress" (*Up*, 221–22) and "The wisest among my race understand that the agitation of questions of social equality is the extremest folly" (*Up*, 224). In recollecting this, his most famous speech, he represents himself as successfully appeasing all three audiences.

When he gets down to details, however, it is more like he has pleased two of the three and displeased the third mightily. As though the truest measure of the occasion's success lies in his host's response, he reports that as soon as he spoke the last word, Governor Bullock rushed forward to shake his hand on behalf of the white South. The acclamation of the moment is only the beginning of Washington's conquest. "The papers in all parts of the United States published the address in full, and for months afterward there were complimentary editorial references to it" (*Up*, 225). In addition to quoting correspondents who wrote for the *Atlanta Constitution* and *Boston Transcript*, Washington reprints the florid report James Creelman published in the *New York World*. Complimentary this account certainly is, but one wonders what Washington thought of the intensely racialized portrait in which he appears as "a Negro Moses" with the visage of a "Sioux chief," "big feet" positioned "with the heels together and toes turned out" (*Up*, 238, 240)—a cross between noble savage and vaudeville minstrel.[11] Washington also quotes approving comments received from President Grover S. Cleveland, to whom he sent a copy of the address: this begins a relationship in which Washington figures as Cleveland's black consultant on matters relating to the "Negro Problem," a position he will also fill in the Roosevelt and Taft administrations. In a short paragraph he acknowledges that the response of black auditors and readers was less enthusiastic inasmuch as some felt "that I had been too liberal in my remarks toward the Southern whites, and that I had not spoken out strongly enough for what they termed the 'rights' of the race." Washington minimizes the sense of anger, humiliation, and betrayal his critics had only begun to express, and lightly dismisses their objections: "For a while there was a reaction, so far as a certain element of my own race was concerned, but later these reactionary ones seemed to have been won over to my way of believing and acting" (*Up*, 230). But such assurances are directed to the white audiences with whom in after years he will more easily maintain an authority than with a black intelligentsia skeptical of a leader slow to acknowledge the peonage and terror that shaped life for the mass of black people in the post-Reconstruction South. Given the record numbers of blacks lynched in the 1890s, his comment that "I felt a good deal as I suppose a man feels when he is on his way to the gallows" must have struck many readers as more than a little tone-deaf.

On the other hand, the remark might express the fears of a man who understood only too well the stage on which his life had played out. In chapter 6 of *Up from Slavery*, "Black Race and Red Race," Washington recalls his return to Hampton in 1879 as a teacher and continuing student; on arrival he finds himself assigned lodgings in a residence hall housing seventy-five Native American youths. A curious and illuminating passage occurs arising from Washington's momentary exposure to the red-white color line and his position as observer of the Native Americans' struggle to adapt to white expectations. The impositions his dormitory mates most objected to "were to have their long hair cut, to give up wearing their blankets, and to cease smoking," all of which would have counted as adjustments a person would naturally make in entering a world governed by alternative conventions. But for Washington this narrative moment becomes the occasion of a sweeping comment as to the price one pays to go among white-dominated society: "No white American ever thinks that any other race is wholly civilized until he wears the white man's clothes, eats the white man's food, speaks the white man's language, and professes the white man's religion" (*Up*, 98). At no point in *Up from Slavery* does Washington make such observations in conjunction with what has been required of Africans under enslavement, emancipation, and beyond, but in this momentary identification with and insight into the predicament of the Native American students, he speaks as one who recognizes white cultural forms as just one variety of civilized life, even as whites recognize, in their ethnocentric limitation, their own ways as the only possibility. He thus calls attention to the masquerade that has become second nature to African Americans such as himself. From his handling of a broom to his advocacy of the toothbrush, he has been playing a deep psychological game founded in his understanding of what Du Bois would term the condition of double consciousness.[12]

Washington's profile of himself as a speaker in chapter 15, "The Secret of Success in Public Speaking," immediately following the chapter devoted to the Atlanta Exposition Address, underscores the degree to which he sees himself as a performer whose success lies in speaking a language adapted to the susceptibilities of a white audience. Confessing that he is invariably nervous before addressing a gathering and often incredulous as to the value of what he may have to say, he marvels over the bond that nonetheless forms between speaker and auditors: "There is rarely such a combination of mental and physical delight in any effort as that which comes to a public speaker when he feels that he has a great audience completely within his control. There is a thread of sympathy and oneness that connects a public speaker with his audience, that is just as strong as though it was something tangible and visible." In coming around to identify what the chapter title promises—the secret of success—Washington suggests that public speaking is more than technique: "Although there are certain things, such as pauses, breathing, and pitch of voice, that are very important, none of these can take the place of *soul* in an address." But the address, in his system, is a particularly tailored self-representation: speaking, for Washington, is an exercise in secular theater, with philanthropy as the great object. "As to the kind of audience that I like best to talk to, I would put at the top of the list an organization of strong, wide-awake, business men, such, for example, as is found in Boston, New York, Chicago, and Buffalo" (*Up*, 243–45). Throughout this chapter he quotes various newspaper correspondents as to the power of his oratory and the stature of his public presence; again and again his autobiography refers readers to the accessible, objectified Booker T. Washington as though this public persona were who he is. But such serves to reinforce the distance between Washington and his print readership.

Nothing, Washington admonishes, "can take the place of *soul* in an address," but in the context of a technical discussion of how to succeed as a public speaker, he hardly suggests that he lifts the veil on his inmost spiritual identity, the core of his private personhood, or that he finds ways to reveal the invisible, suffering, but persevering life that Du Bois invokes in the title of *The Souls of Black Folk*. He cites, rather, his ability to affect conviction and sincerity, and to succeed in that task with different audiences on different occasions. For Washington, *soul* is an effect of the performance he has perfected over the course of a long career. The public speaker's *soul* resides in the audience's impression that the speaker is wholly present in the words he speaks. But Washington presents evidence in both autobiographies of his sedulous mastery of "the white man's language" and "the white man's religion": for him to recognize that such ethnocentric forms exist signals a concomitant recognition that these forms, as "white" conventions, are not quite his, however effectively he may enlist them and with whatever seeming sincerity. His public performances may convey a soulful transparency, and at times he may be as persuaded by the force of his utterance as are his white auditors. But his autobiographies provide abundant evidence that, like Benjamin Franklin, he has spent his life refining strategies of crafting a particular impression toward achieving a strategic end.

Sell-out that Du Bois and Wells-Barnett consider him to be, however, Washington ever speaks his word at the boundaries of contested territory: although he adopts a strategy of compromise, and although Tuskegee represents an appeasement of the white South's wish to curtail the citizenship of a black populace, to the degree that Tuskegee promotes literacy and portably marketable skills, it exists as a challenge to powers that would immobilize the descendants of the enslaved in rural peonage.

"We never talked about dying any more"

Six years younger than Booker T. Washington, six years older than W. E. B. Du Bois, Ida B. Wells-Barnett shared with her male contemporaries the challenge of navigating a post–Civil War America in which racial geographies were subject to abrupt and lethal vicissitude. As a woman who rose to leadership in the national antilynching campaign and as a feminist who contested black as well as white patriarchal oppression, Wells-Barnett pursued paths independent of those mapped out by Washington and Du Bois. When she sat down to write *Crusade for Justice: The Autobiography of Ida B. Wells* in 1928, three years before her death, she attested to the paradigmatic migration from rural South to urban North and bore witness to an in-the-trench activism absent from the narrative of the concession-prone Washington, if not from the memoirs of the cerebral Du Bois. In composing her autobiography, she invoked the rising generation of black youth as her primary audience, specifically ascribing the text's genesis to the inquiries of a twenty-five-year-old woman who had heard Wells-Barnett likened to Joan of Arc but knew nothing about the post–Civil War past and Wells-Barnett's role in the struggles of black people. "It is therefore for the young people who have so little of our race's history recorded that I am for the first time writing about myself," Wells-Barnett remarks. "I am all the more constrained to do this because there is such a lack of authentic race history of Reconstruction times written by the Negro himself."[13] Douglass, she observes, has written about slavery, but "the time of storm and stress" just after the war and "the wholesale murders of Negroes who tried to exercise their new-found rights as free men and citizens" (4) have not been adequately treated from a black perspective. Conspicuously, Wells-Barnett mentions neither *Life and Times of Frederick Douglass* nor *Up from Slavery* as works that address the turbulence of the postwar decades. Later Wells-Barnett does mention *The Souls of Black Folk*, but restricts her citation to the chapter in which Du Bois addresses the inadequacy of Booker T. Washington's program, a critique that meets with Wells-Barnett's fervent endorsement.

Born into slavery the year before the Emancipation Proclamation, Wells-Barnett possesses no direct memory of the condition of bondage that Washington, born in 1856, recalls in his account of early childhood. As she is careful to point out, her memory of slaveholder cruelty is secondhand, deriving from fragments of overheard conversation, as we see in her recollection of her father discussing Miss Polly, the former mistress, with her grandmother. "I'll never forget how she had you stripped and whipped the day after the old man died," her father remarks in this anecdote. "I guess it is all right for you to take care of her and forgive her for what she did to you, but she could have starved to death if I'd had my say-so." Wells-Barnett goes on to observe: "I was burning to ask what he meant, but children were seen and not heard in those days. They didn't dare break into old folks' conversation. But I have never forgotten those words. Since I have grown old enough to understand I cannot help but feel what an insight to slavery they give" (10). Nevertheless, as she describes her girlhood in Holly Springs, Mississippi, she emphasizes privilege over privation. Like Linda Brent, she is the daughter of parents who live together as a married couple. Victorian in her view of family structure, Wells-Barnett informs readers that her parents wed as slaves and again as ex-slaves, when the relationship acquired legal standing. Both parents possess artisanal status, her mother "a famous cook," her father a skilled carpenter. Having come into his rights of citizenship, moreover, her father becomes politically active and serves as a trustee of the local Freedmen's Aid College. In Wells-Barnett's depiction, her family is nuclear and self-respecting, a model of middle-class virtue. This comfortable normality comes to an end in 1878, when her parents and an infant brother die in the yellow fever epidemic that sweeps north through the lower Mississippi from New Orleans to Memphis. At age sixteen, Wells-Barnett becomes responsible for her surviving siblings.

Thereafter, she engages in a career as schoolteacher, journalist, and activist, residing first in Memphis before fleeing the South and establishing a base in Chicago. As a teacher and journalist at a time of segregated schools and a flourishing black press, she fosters literacy among the postslavery generation and produces texts for an emerging black readership, writing about current events and issues with a readiness to combat the constant stream of white derogation and disinformation.[14] Advancing rapidly along these lines, at age twenty-seven she becomes a full-time journalist and part owner of the Memphis *Free Speech*, an organ through which, at great personal peril, she makes her voice heard following the 1892 lynching of three Memphis grocery store proprietors.

From early adulthood, Wells-Barnett traveled frequently, and her memoir records little opposition to her will-to-move. As though to highlight the defiant core of a personality destined for political activism, she recounts an episode in which the twenty-one-year-old schoolteacher takes a seat in the "ladies coach" on the train from Memphis to her school in Shelby County. In response to this trespass, railroad officials physically remove Wells-Barnett and force her to ride in the smoking car. Pursuing legal redress, she hires a lawyer, who successfully argues her case against the railroad, a ruling later reversed on appeal. Wells-Barnett depicts the youthful Ida as one who knows her rights, understands legal remedy, and resists any power that would impose limits on her free movement and free expression. As a young woman in search of teaching positions, she travels as far west as California; as a reporter, she takes every advantage of her professional privilege to ride the rail system gratis. In the aftermath of the Memphis lynching, she visits Oklahoma to determine whether the recently opened territory offers suitable conditions for black emigrants. Against historical associations of the American West with exclusionary white settlement, her travel demonstrates that westward migration in pursuit of space that could support a life of self-governance had begun to appeal to black people whose post–Civil War mobility, constrained as it might be, permitted the recourse of removing as a body from sites of persecution. Wells-Barnett writes of how, after the eruption of racial violence, a sizable portion of the Memphis black community took to the road in response to advice from one of the men about to be lynched, who encouraged the people to head west not only to secure a refuge from white violence but also to punish the oppressors by withdrawing their vital contribution to the labor pool and economic life of Memphis.

The eruption of white mob violence in what had become her home city inaugurates a chain of events that confirms Wells-Barnett in her activist vocation and sets her on a course of exile. "While I was thus carrying on the work of my newspaper," she reflects, "happy in the thought that our influence was helpful and that I was doing the work that I loved and had proved that I could make a living out of it, there came the lynching in Memphis which changed the whole course of my life" (47). The triple lynching of the People's Grocery Company proprietors arises from their economic challenge to the spatial status quo. Contesting the market share of a white business class within a black residential neighborhood, the African American grocers become victims of a terror campaign in keeping with post-Reconstruction white violence against ambitious and enterprising blacks. Arming against the inevitable confrontation, they are arrested for firing upon and injuring their white attackers, and before their case can come to trial, a mob removes them from jail and puts them to death. The incident marks the beginning of Wells-Barnett's antilynching career and residence outside the South.[15] Her account of the event published in the *Free Speech* is deeply critical of the white elite's complicity in extrajudicial mob killings, but her continued residence in Memphis becomes especially untenable after she extends her analysis to a taboo topic: the allegations of rape by which lynching is commonly justified. To excite the mob to kill, she observes, one need only suggest that a black man has in some manner violated the sanctity of a white female. When Wells-Barnett suggests that sexual relations between black men and white women were at times initiated by the white women themselves, a mob destroys the newspaper office, threats are made against her life, and she is advised by friends to stay in New York, where she happens to be at the time. What she refers to as her banishment from the South would last thirty years.

In *Southern Horrors: Lynch Law in All Its Phases* (1892), Wells-Barnett documents instances of consenting relations between white women and black men that the white patriarchy insistently construes as capital rape even as it refrains from prosecuting flagrant instances of white male ravishment of black women and girls.[16] *Southern Horrors* depicts a scandalous cartography in which white women of genteel as well as impoverished class origin invite black men into their bedrooms, highlighting interracial encounters that occur every day in domestic space conventionally regarded as rigidly segregated—segregated, that is, except when the white male or female sees fit to admit the black party to the white sexual arena or abruptly intrude upon the black domicile, a pattern familiar to readers of *Incidents in the Life of a Slave Girl*. The boldness of *Southern Horrors* consists not only in Wells-Barnett's imputation of sexual desire to an idealized Southern white womanhood but also in her suggestion that white women may be interested in something other than white male partnership. In chapter 9 of *Incidents*, "Sketches of Neighboring Slaveholders," Jacobs anticipates Wells-Barnett in writing of a slaveholder's daughter who selects "one of the meanest slaves" on the plantation to be the father of the slaveholder's first grandchild.[17] Both Jacobs and Wells-Barnett thus address the sexual border crossings that eventuate in genetic mixing, brown bodies emerging from black bodies, brown bodies emerging from white. Wells-Barnett's Northern resettlement (she describes herself at the beginning of the pamphlet as writing in exile) undoubtedly contributed to the directness with which she described the white South's rampant sexual transgression. Behind Wells-Barnett's analysis of the social phenomenon of lynching is a keen recognition of the capacity of whites to deny the black subject, male or female, legal and thus spatial standing, and to claim the power to invade black habitations and seize the black body for sexual gratification or extrajudicial violence. It is thus that Wells-Barnett vigorously advocates the defense of black space:

> A Winchester rifle should have a place of honor in every black home, and it should be used for that protection which the law refuses to give. When the white man who is always the aggressor knows he runs a great risk of biting the dust every time his Afro-American victim does, he will have greater respect for Afro-American life. The more the Afro-American yields and cringes and begs, the more he has to do so, the more he is insulted, outraged and lynched.[18]

Like Douglass and Jacobs, Wells-Barnett appeals to the reader's consensus belief in the inviolability of the nuclear family home, domestic space that whites and blacks alike might agree to defend (in the phrase Malcolm X would give special currency) "by any means necessary."[19]

Wells-Barnett's abrupt displacement may appear at first to contrast with the less outwardly dramatic migration of black people from the states of the former Confederacy to the Northern industrial cities, but given the suddenness with which African Americans in the post-Reconstruction South could become victims of public or private violence, the decision to leave hardly required a clear and present danger.[20] The itinerary Wells-Barnett describes in *Crusade for Justice* conforms at once to the pattern of escape from Southern bondage familiar to readers of fugitive slave narratives and to the larger migratory trends among African Americans after the Civil War. Like Douglass and Jacobs before her, she describes the hardships of exile. As "my mind went back to the scenes of the struggle," she writes of her refugee status when it became clear that she might forfeit her life in returning to Memphis, "to the thought of the friends who were scattered throughout the country, a feeling of loneliness and homesickness for the days and the friends that were gone came over me and I felt the tears coming" (79). Her campaign in exile to publicize the outrage of lynching corresponds with the efforts of Douglass, Jacobs, and others to publicize the outrage of slavery, and her speaking tour of England and Scotland for the purpose of arousing international support resembles the travels Douglass and Jacobs undertook in their effort to recruit British public opinion and financial backing. Settling permanently in Chicago after her return to the United States, Wells-Barnett becomes active in the formation of African American women's clubs and emerges as a force in the organization of black advocacy groups at the local and national levels. The bulk of Wells-Barnett's memoir documents her continued protest against lynching as well as the multitude of discriminatory practices that separate black people from the rights of citizenship accorded them in the Reconstruction era. Although Wells-Barnett writes glowingly of the fulfillment she experienced as a mother of four children, thereby endorsing traditional models of a woman's procreative role, *Crusade for Justice* also records her advocacy of female suffrage and the resistance she faced among her male civil rights colleagues to the idea of enfranchising women.

Whereas Washington and Du Bois choose to live and work in the South, confronting the condition of black America where the concentration of former slaves is highest and conditions are most oppressive, Wells-Barnett, a refugee from those conditions, returns to the South only thirty years after the Memphis lynching. Specifically, she travels to Little Rock, Arkansas, to investigate the case of twelve black farmers condemned to death for allegedly conspiring to kill white people after the farmers themselves had been attacked for refusing to sell their cotton at a price below market value. In a signal moment, the celebrated Chicago crusader, who is able to draw on the resources of numerous black advocacy groups and who can make governor and president attend to her words, visits the men in their jail cell in the company of their wives and mothers and counsels against passivity and defeat. In response to their singing of spirituals expressive of longing for the next world, Wells-Barnett preaches a liberationist theology: "Why don't you pray to live and ask to be freed? The God you serve is the God of Paul and Silas who opened their prison gates, and if you have all the faith you say you have, you ought to believe he will open your prison doors too" (403). Through publicity generated in the Chicago *Defender* and the efforts of various activist organizations, funds are raised to hire lawyers, who press for a new trial that results in the men's acquittal. The story ends on a postscript that combines South-to-North migration with motifs of uplift: Wells-Barnett returns home one day to find an Arkansas defendant waiting for her in her parlor. "He was well dressed and had been living in Chicago for three months; he said he had been looking for me all that time" to express his gratitude (404). The ex-prisoner's trajectory mirrors her own. Throughout *Crusade for Justice*, Wells-Barnett portrays herself as one who will not submit to bounds imposed on her free expression and free movement, and it is significant that she should characterize her return to the South, which she has had good reason to avoid, as fulfilling her role as liberator. Her jailhouse visit, as she would have us understand from the words of the former prisoner, had been transformative: "We never talked about dying any more, but did as she told us, and now every last one of us is out and enjoying his freedom" (404).

Although freedom for black people begins, in Wells-Barnett's account, only when the South has been left behind, she fully understands that the North operates as well on the principle of racial apartheid. Early in her Chicago residence she witnessed the nearly complete erasure of a black presence in the exclusionary history showcased at the 1893 World's Columbian Exposition, in protest of which she authored three of the six chapters, plus preface and epilogue, of a pamphlet titled *Reasons Why the Colored American Is Not in the World's Columbian Exposition*.[21] Nor does the North provide a safe haven from white rage that vents itself in ritual lynching, examples of which include well-publicized incidents in Springfield and East Saint Louis and lesser-known atrocities such as occur when a black teenager drowns while bathing in Lake Michigan after having been set upon by a group of white boys pelting him with stones. As we have seen, in African American migration narratives, the familiar binaries slave/free and South/North are liable to collapse, with persecutions extending and freedoms denied north of the old slave South. For Wells-Barnett, however, "North" retains a relative value as a signifier of safety and freedom.

"Hear my cry, o God the reader"

On occasion, as we have seen, Booker T. Washington concedes that public performance—both oral and written—serves as the veil behind which he curates his knowledge of cruelty and privation. Such moments are fleeting: his persona ever reverts to the thesis that the history of African American grievance is best put aside as the black community sets its shoulder to the wheel of a common national purpose, contributing to the great democratic experiment even as it defers expectation of political participation and economic recompense, and even as it maintains its distance from, and invisibility to, the majority white citizenry.

By contrast, W. E. B. Du Bois begins a career of first-person testimony by proposing that literary expression can lift the veil and attenuate the color line to the degree that it makes audible "the striving in the souls of black folk."[22] If the first of what would prove to be his four exercises in memoir writing succeeds in bringing a white readership closer to an oppressed people's experience than *Up from Slavery* ever does, it is because Du Bois, unlike Washington, not only itemizes the exceptional suffering of black people in America but begins by addressing that suffering's invisibility in a post-Reconstruction nation devoted to industrial development, material acquisition, and imperial expansion. In the very first sentence of *The Souls of Black Folk* he takes the idea a step farther: white people, he propounds, can no longer afford to turn a blind eye to their black fellow citizens nor, for that matter, to the people of color with whom they increasingly share the globe. Du Bois implores his white readers to consider the advantages of reconciling with their black neighbors; he suggests, moreover, that whites may benefit from learning about the spiritual disciplines that have enabled black people to survive. White Americans, he argues, stand to gain from the richness of folkways that already pervade national life more than they generally recognize. White people hold a stake in acknowledging and understanding an African American presence that is only one face of the nonwhite world destined to become highly visible. "Herein lie buried many things which if read with patience may show the strange meaning of being black here in the dawning of the Twentieth Century," he begins prophetically. "This meaning is not without interest to you, Gentle Reader; for the problem of the Twentieth Century is the problem of the color-line" (1). Significantly, before the end of the first paragraph Du Bois has invoked a global geography in demographic flux as the necessary context of his own story and those of his people.[23]

Du Bois closes his prefatory remarks with a question aimed at testing the theory that one can speak meaningfully across the color line—that the living substrate of the black body is only an illusory barrier: "Need I add that I who speak here am bone of the bone and flesh of the flesh of them that live within the Veil?" (1).[24] Presenting what to a white audience would be the unexpected combination of educated mind and black body, the question positions the reader as one who must consent to hear across that barrier. In his mastery of a late Victorian belletristic style (as opposed to the minstrel-show plantation dialect that whites commonly associated with black speech), Du Bois linguistically diminishes the breach that makes black experience inaudible to whites. The chapters that follow will speak in the genres of narrative testimony and discursive exposition and then conclude with instructions on how to hear black experience as expressed in the spirituals or, as Du Bois calls them, "sorrow songs"—suffering and sorrow qualifying, in Du Bois's view, as universally relatable human experience. Confident that he can diminish the breach, however, he is less convinced that he can eliminate it.[25]

Mindful of misunderstandings that serve to divide educated blacks from educated and moderately sympathetic whites, Du Bois endeavors to probe that breach in the sentence that opens chapter 1, "Of Our Spiritual Strivings": "Between me and the other world there is ever an unasked question," a question that whites may not know how to phrase but that Du Bois knows how to hear: "How does it feel to be a problem?" (2). In characterizing the relationship that exists between well-meaning residents of that "other world" and individuals (like himself) prepared to testify to the spectrum of North American black experience, he recognizes that nonhostile whites bring to this relationship curiosity and compassion. As a scholar with a Harvard dissertation on the history of the slave trade and a monograph examining the urban geography of black Philadelphia, Du Bois can fashion academic commentary aimed at generalizing the issue and setting it in a world-historical context: "After the Egyptian and Indian, the Greek and Roman, the Teuton and Mongolian, the Negro is a sort of seventh son, born with a veil, and gifted with second-sight in this American world" (3).[26] But alongside his more discursive and learned discussion of black life in the decades following emancipation, the first-person attestation that Du Bois intersperses throughout *Souls* reinforces the argument that the "Negro problem" is a burden borne by individuals who are problems before they are persons. By demonstrating the ways in which a person leads the life of a problem incarnate, Du Bois seeks to build throughout *Souls* a dynamic and evolving relationship with readers, engaging whites who dwell in that remote "other world" and whose ignorance of the nation's black populace is as much a matter of institutional structure as individual prejudice, all the while serving notice that "the problem" is by no means the special province of a downtrodden minority.[27]

Du Bois further personalizes the issue in an anecdote dramatizing his first recognition of the veil that isolates him from his white fellows, dissolving what had been the illusion of his seamless integration into the juvenile society of Great Barrington, Massachusetts:

> In a wee wooden schoolhouse, something put it into the boys' and girls' heads to buy gorgeous visiting-cards—ten cents a package—and exchange. The exchange was merry, till one girl, a tall newcomer, refused my card,—refused it peremptorily, with a glance. Then it dawned upon me with a certain suddenness that I was different from the others; or like, mayhap, in heart and life and longing, but shut out from their world by a vast veil. I had therefore no desire to tear down that veil, to creep through; I held all beyond it in common contempt, and lived above it in a region of blue sky and great wandering shadows. (3)

On the surface, the color line intervenes to disrupt the children's imitation of the genteel custom of house-to-house socializing, but the anecdote also contains the specter of interracial sexuality—it is a "tall," presumably adolescent girl who rejects the overture of the black boy, and does so, Du Bois suggests, with fear and loathing. Apart from these sexual overtones, however, it is significant that Du Bois's awareness of the veil should be precipitated by an unreciprocated exchange, particularly given that he begins *Souls* (which he invites us to imagine as a kind of extended visiting card) by greeting and seeking to engage a "Gentle Reader" from whom he hopes to elicit the reciprocation of an attentive, curious, and compassionate reading—a spiritual intimacy as threatening in its own way to a system of apartheid as interracial sexual contact.[28]

This small, inconspicuous, and intensely local event, taking place in "a wee wooden schoolhouse," is part and parcel of a global predicament that, in Du Bois's prophecy, will dominate the lives of generations to follow: "the problem of the Twentieth Century is the problem of the color-line." From the modest home and schoolhouse of his New England village origins, remote from the population and cultural centers of black life in late nineteenth-century America, Du Bois would travel far. By 1903, the year that he published *The Souls of Black Folk*, at age thirty-five, he had long since left Great Barrington for college at Fisk in Nashville; after living in the South for the first time, he returned north to enter Harvard, completing a second bachelor's degree, earning a master's degree, and completing most of his work toward the doctorate before moving to Berlin for additional postgraduate study. Returning from two years' residence and travel in Europe, he completed a dissertation, which immediately appeared as his first book, *The Suppression of the Slave Trade in the United States of America, 1638–1870* (1896). With his new degree, he spent a year at Wilberforce University before residing in Philadelphia as a fellow at the University of Pennsylvania, where he conducted research toward his second book, *The Philadelphia Negro* (1899). Following eighteen months in Philadelphia, he accepted a position at Atlanta University, where he remained for the next thirteen years. Within such constraints as limit the mobility of all African Americans, his travels were generally volitional. His departure at age seventeen for Fisk with the support of local money raised to send him to a black college represented a momentary thwarting of his ambition to attend Harvard, afterward triumphantly realized, but his initial residence in the South, as he would affirm in "The Shadow of Years," the autobiographical first chapter of *Darkwater: Voices from Within the Veil* (1920), would introduce him to the black collective and prove crucial to his emotional as well as intellectual development. From 1897 to 1910 and again from 1933 to 1944, his seat of operations was Atlanta. From his New England birthplace, his travels exhibited a southern tendency, although at no point did he put down roots, as Washington did in Tuskegee. Still, for Du Bois as for Washington, the Deep South figured as the field of labor to which he was called, and given his status as one of only a handful of African American youth in Great Barrington, Fisk offered opportunities to go among "his people" after it became clear to him that in his native village he would always be a visible if not entirely unwelcome minority.

In later years Du Bois traveled extensively throughout Europe (east as well as west), Asia, and Africa. He begins the posthumously published *Autobiography* by narrating his fifteenth trip abroad: a tour of western Europe, rapidly rebuilding under the Marshall Plan, followed by excursions to the Soviet Union and the People's Republic of China. In 1961, at age ninety-three, he moved to Ghana in final flight from U.S. political and racial oppression. Throughout much of his career, Du Bois demonstrated that a black academic American traveler is as threatening in his own way to white authority as any black person thought to be out of place. Even before he sojourned in the postwar Communist bloc, the federal government deemed his travel activities sufficiently subversive to confiscate his passport, an action only reversed by order of the U.S. Supreme Court.[29] His autobiographical writings reveal that, even as a child, he formed a sense of himself as one whose identity requires an international understanding of history and geography. His family's historical isolation in rural New England, far from the currents of a black Southern population, does much to explain Du Bois's global and emphatically diasporic vision, in contrast with Washington's sense of the world as a temporally shallow sequence of "tight places," situations requiring pragmatic solutions for which historical knowledge must prove irrelevant if not counterproductive.

In *Darkwater*, *Dusk of Dawn*, and the *Autobiography*, Du Bois explains his Northern upbringing in light of a genealogy by which he identifies ancestors in the African diaspora as well as European forbears active in the slave trade and colonization. Unlike Washington, whose ancestral knowledge does not extend beyond his mother's immediate family, Du Bois is able to name his great-great-grandfather, one Tom Burghardt, brought by a Dutchman of that surname to the Hudson and Housatonic Valleys, along with his wife, Violet, a small Bantu woman whose lullaby-lament has passed from one generation to the next even as the meaning of the words has been lost. (Significantly, Du Bois places this song first in the sequence of sorrow songs that he anthologizes in *Souls*; in all four memoirs he prints the words and in two the musical score, as though to provide an indispensable sample of individual and cultural DNA.) Because his mother's family, settled in the North, was never subjected to the geographic dispersions of the Southern slave market, and because his father's family can be traced to the migration of a French Huguenot and his union with a mixed-race Bahamian, Du Bois possesses exceptional access to a genealogical past, one that predisposes him to understand the post-Reconstruction black predicament in the broad context of European colonialism.[30] Unlike Washington, the former slave who writes of having to appropriate a surname when faced with the institutional need to construct a post-Emancipation identity, Du Bois's four-part legal name documents the European interventions that situate him, as a mixed-race individual, child of free-born Northern parents, in the "wee wooden schoolhouse" where he first encounters an uncivil response to his difference.

With its subtle invocation of the Middle Passage, the second memoir's title, *Darkwater*, articulates the diasporic theme, and the volume's fast-paced narrative portion emphasizes the fluidity of black life as Du Bois has known it. The reminiscence opens on an idyllic note: "I was born by a golden river and in the shadow of two great hills, five years after the Emancipation Proclamation."[31] In this self-introductory first sentence Du Bois responds to the first sentences of *Narrative of the Life of Frederick Douglass* and *Up from Slavery* and thereby establishes a signal difference: that he was born *after* the Emancipation, an event of profound but less immediate relevance for the son of a family that has lived free in the North for generations. Two pages farther we learn that the "river of my birth was golden because of the woolen and paper waste that soiled it," a qualification that admonishes readers that we are born to a world of deceptive appearance, but even given the treacherous surfaces he has had to navigate, Du Bois recalls the days of his childhood as "very happy" (5), living alone with his mother after his father's desertion but surrounded by the large black Burghardt clan and a village community in which he feels himself to blend in, more or less, until adolescence. He experiences poverty but not pauperdom, enjoying the companionship of his white classmates, whose families never exclude him from their households. He excels in school and basks in the recognition academic success brings him, and feels at home amid the village streets and in the solitude of the encompassing countryside: "The town and its surroundings," he elaborates in *Dusk of Dawn*, "were a boy's paradise" (6). Autobiographical accounts subsequent to *The Souls of Black Folk* place much less emphasis on the schoolhouse incident as precipitating acute color consciousness and a sense of isolation; only "very gradually," he writes in *Darkwater*, "I found myself assuming quite placidly that I was different from other children" (6). Whereas a difference of physical feature establishes a foundational distinction, Du Bois's academic superiority, spurred by a need to defy expectations that persons of color must underachieve, provides a way for him to be different on his own terms. Given his scholarly promise, "Harvard was the goal of my dreams, but my white friends hesitated and my colored friends were silent." The color line once again enforces separation, this time with a sharp geographical bias. "Finally it was tactfully explained that the place for me was in the South among my people" (6).

The fifty-year-old who composed this reminiscence had long since moved beyond the young man's disappointment: in three years he would earn his Fisk bachelor's degree and then proceed to Harvard, where, in 1895, he became the first African American to earn that university's doctorate. *Darkwater* showcases the Fisk detour as the necessary first immersion in the greater black community: "After a twinge I felt a strange delight," he writes, inasmuch as he "was being sent to a far land among strangers who were regarded as (and in truth were) 'mine own people' " (6–7). In the mythic tone with which Du Bois tells his story in *Darkwater*, the Fisk episode stands at the head of what he designates as his young manhood's "Age of Miracles": the memoirist sets the vision of a Southern, black, erotically charged nation against the white, subdued, constrained New England of early youth. "Consider, for a moment," writes Du Bois, projecting the young man as a special kind of fugitive, "how miraculous it all was to a boy of seventeen, *just escaped from a narrow valley*: I willed and lo! my people came dancing about me,—riotous in color, gay in laughter, full of sympathy, need, and pleading; darkly delicious girls—'colored' girls—sat beside me and actually talked to me while I gazed in tongue-tied silence or babbled in boastful dreams" (7; emphasis added). This passage in *Darkwater* further underscores the anguish of the incident in *Souls* where an attempted exchange of cards elicits peremptory exclusion. But it also articulates a theme that recurs throughout Du Bois's oeuvre: exaltation of women and womanhood, all women who seek democratic autonomy (the Nineteenth Amendment was ratified the year *Darkwater* appeared) but long-suffering and long-surviving black women in particular. This theme achieves its culminating statement in the *Darkwater* essay "The Damnation of Women," a prescient affirmation of women's intellectual capacity as well as reproductive rights, the more remarkable in that Du Bois retained throughout his life patriarchal structures of thought and feeling. His paean to the African maternal line, which begins with the book's latinate dedication to his wife, Nina Gormer Du Bois, brings together his celebration of women and a cultural memory of the Middle Passage and, in so doing, invests the enigmatic *Darkwater* title with specific associations—waters of birth but also transatlantic ocean currents. "They came first, in earlier days," he writes in "Damnation," "like foam flashing on dark, silent waters,—bits of stern, dark womanhood here and there tossed almost carelessly aloft to the world's notice" (83).[32] The young man's arrival at Fisk facilitates a first acquaintance with a racial culture that he would ever associate with transpersonal, transhistorical maternal origins.[33]

But the South that occasioned his first discovery of a black American collective, with its erotic ambience, expressive ease, and release from the austere double consciousness that dominates minority life in Great Barrington, was not without alienating features for the descendent of Northern freeborn blacks. Before he returned north, he became acquainted with the Jim Crow car; he witnessed firsthand the grinding and seemingly irredeemable poverty of black people in the rural districts where he conducted school during summers in Tennessee. He learned to fear the explosively belligerent reflex of an embittered white population. Later, residing in Atlanta, he had to contend with the personal and institutional presence of Booker T. Washington. His Southern education, initial and continuing, was foundational to his career, but Du Bois never naturalized to the American South.

He never naturalized to the American South; neither did he entirely reconcile with his native New England of narrow valleys and elite white universities.[34] His books document continuing displacement: *Souls* is datelined Atlanta, 1903; *Darkwater*, New York, 1919. Until he settled in Ghana, two years before his death, there existed for him few paths that describe a definitively emancipatory trajectory. Moments of emancipation coincided with what for him was the achieved proximity to the black collective—that collective in festive as opposed to persecuted or carceral phase. Those scenes in which, as he says, "my people came dancing about me," recur transregionally, in keeping with the dispersal of African peoples; to the degree that they answer to Du Bois's poetic vision, they transcend geography altogether. As a student at Fisk on an all-black campus (and itinerant teacher in the Tennessee rural districts during summer recess), as a researcher in Philadelphia, as a professor at Atlanta University, and as a resident of New York City in the early years of the Harlem Renaissance, Du Bois accumulated a layered experience as participant-observer of the segregated black nation—a community outwardly entrapped in the varied apartheids of diasporic distribution, even as, for Du Bois, this nation provides release from the constraints of double consciousness, at least in theory. In the course of his career, he would write about the black collective as a social scientist and memoirist; in *Dusk of Dawn* and the *Autobiography* he would document his travels among communities of color beyond the United States. The migratory nature of his life and inquiry reflected the mobile condition of African Americans, whose narrative had at its core a series of displacements even when they found themselves immobilized in the historical present by segregation and peonage. Alongside his documentation, as historian and social scientist, of black people and places, the racial collective existed for him as a mythic nation occupying a variable geography.

The following lyric depiction of Harlem is very much in line with his rhapsodic recollection of the community he discovered as the Northern young man just arrived at Fisk:

> Again New York and Night and Harlem. A dark city of fifty thousand rises like magic from the earth. Gone is the white world, the pale lips, the lank hair; gone is the West and North—the East and South is here triumphant. The street is crowd and leisure and laughter. Everywhere black eyes, black and brown, and frizzled hair curled and sleek, and skins that riot with luscious color and deep, burning blood. Humanity is packed dense in high piles of close-knit homes that lie in layers above gray shops of food and clothes and drink, with here and there a moving-picture show. Orators declaim on the corners, lovers lark in the streets, gamblers glide by the saloons, workers lounge wearily home. Children scream and run and frolic, and all is good and human and beautiful and ugly and evil, even as Life is elsewhere. (119)

Worthy of Langston Hughes, this paragraph, from *Darkwater*, chapter 9, "Of Beauty and Death," situates the black community firmly within "the Veil," surrounded by a white Euro-American world that has ravaged communities of color throughout the globe and that Du Bois indicts forcefully in *Darkwater*, chapter 2, "The Souls of White Folk," a brief history of European colonization and the white supremacist reign over the Americas, Africa, and Asia.

In the twenty years that elapse between *Darkwater* and *Dusk of Dawn* (1940), the colonized condition of nonwhite people commanded much of Du Bois's attention. His continued pursuit of a macrocosmic understanding of the color line led him in time to adopt economic and specifically Marxist interpretations of global power asymmetries. During these decades he was intensely involved in the Pan-African Conferences and traveled to the Soviet Union, China, and West Africa. Residing in New York City until 1933, and thereafter until 1944 in Atlanta, his ever-expanding global view provided a ground against which he situated microcosmic study of regional incarnations of the diasporic African community. Du Bois the social scientist and academic activist coexisted with Du Bois the poet, who, in addition to Hegelian and Marxist paradigms, sought explanation in metaphoric expression and mythic pattern. At no point in in his long career would he exclude the evidence of his own individual experience—to such evidence he accorded, early and late, an Emersonian privilege.[35] Over time his autobiographical testimony would become less floridly expressive and more expository and analytical, but he would continue to maintain the centrality of personal testimony.

In the preface to *Dusk of Dawn* (1940), Du Bois nevertheless addresses what he sees as the qualified nature of the truth as articulated in autobiographical genres. He reflects on his recurrent activity as a memoirist and how each of his (by then) three life narratives—*The Souls of Black Folk*, *Darkwater: Voices from Within the Veil*, and *Dusk of Dawn*—develops a different perspective on what remains the "problem of the Twentieth Century." His remarks illustrate the degree to which first-person retrospection is governed by one's state at the moment of inscription, although in his case the present moment in all its flux reflects what for him are consistently changeful geographical and professional circumstances.[36] Besides identifying the life stages that each narrative was written to clarify, his preface (titled "Apology") provides evidence that, despite his ability to conduct his life among expansive horizons—the far-flung travels beginning with departure from his "narrow valley"—he, like Washington, has felt himself recurrently occupying "a tight place," the existential condition of nonwhite individuals living under a white supremacist regime. Thus: "I have essayed in a half century three sets of thought centering around the hurts and hesitancies that hem the black man in America." *Souls* he characterizes as "a cry at midnight thick within the veil, when none rightly knew the coming day." *Darkwater* expresses "an exposition and militant challenge, defiant with dogged hope." *Dusk of Dawn*, consistent with what he represents as the willful optimism of his life and work, emanates from a wish "to record dimly but consciously that subtle sense of coming day which one feels of early mornings even when mist and murk hang low." Although not written in "tears and blood," *Dusk of Dawn* reprises for Du Bois the familiar theme of a life that is significant "because it was part of a Problem; but that problem was, as I continue to think, the central problem of the greatest of the world's democracies and so the Problem of the future world."[37]

Dusk of Dawn differs from both *Souls* and *Darkwater* in its commitment to maintaining a continuous narrative thread. In *Souls*, Du Bois focuses on specific moments: the shock of his first real recognition of the color line in the village schoolhouse; the summer spent teaching in the rural district of

Alexandria, Tennessee, and his particular reminiscence of his student Josie; the death of his infant son, Burghardt. The first chapter of *Darkwater*, "The Shadow of Years," provides a compressed and lyric summary of his first five decades, from childhood in Great Barrington to his leadership of the Niagara Movement and resignation from Atlanta University. By contrast, the seventy-two-year-old Du Bois revisits his life with a determination to combine detailed narrative with close analysis that generates a more discursive treatment of a life that continues to move forward. Setting out to address the ways in which that well-traveled life illustrates the problem of the color line, he provides a much fuller picture of his formative years than he did in his previous life narratives and a more fully developed argument as to how his formation reflects large historical and national events. The chapter titles themselves suggest the broad historical inquiry that his more narrow autobiographical focus is intended to serve: "A New England Boy and Reconstruction," "Education in the Last Decades of the Nineteenth Century," "Science and Empire." These chapters depict the evolution of a youth whose social isolation fosters a richly introspective life and whose curiosity and intellectual ambition compel the traversing of geographical boundaries. They trace his acculturation to the ways of regional, national, and international academic life and his emergence as a polymath scholar and public intellectual whose inquiries recurrently lead to controversy. As Du Bois looks back on his social and political education, he correlates events taking place within his own horizon with events and trends elsewhere in an effort to understand the stages of his life macrocosmically. Accordingly, as he is born into the microcosm of Great Barrington, it is important for him to note that the Fifteenth Amendment is ratified, the Meiji emperors come to power in Japan, and the Suez Canal opens.

In equal part case study and bildungsroman, *Dusk of Dawn* conducts a sustained interrogation of its autobiographical subject, one that enlists historical context and sociological analysis in the telling of a life shaped, it would seem, for a singular destiny. Du Bois has much more to say in *Dusk of Dawn* than in his previous life writings about the social dynamics of childhood in Great Barrington and his initiation into the black collective that awaited his arrival at Fisk. He provides for the first time the portrait of a young man whose temperament retains (so he claims) much of the Dutch and English reserve of the Housatonic Valley, a detachment that would consign him to participant-observer status among black and white communities alike. His story coheres as a travel narrative in which his understanding of a given locality proceeds from his discernment of how the color line functions to position nonwhite communities in relation to whites of various classes and European ethnicities. Of particular interest is the account of his return north—from an all-black community in the segregated South to the ostensibly integrating elite Northern university where the color line all but vanishes in his relationships with mentors such as William James, George Santayana, and Albert Bushnell Hart, only to reappear in the social currents of Harvard life, from which, in any case, Du Bois preemptively absents himself. Similarly, he provides a detailed narrative of his studies in Germany and travels in Europe as well as instances of white companionship that could not have taken place in the United States. Presenting his life as an embodied and animated curriculum vitae, he recounts the process by which his quest for such knowledge as would explain the Problem (the general predicament of black people in post-Reconstruction America, the individual predicament of one W. E. B. Du Bois) leads to the study of history, philosophy, and economics at Harvard and (drawing upon all three) sociology in Berlin. As a young and ambitious scholar, he fervently believes that if the Problem can be scientifically analyzed, solutions can be formulated and applied.

Youthful ambition finds opportunity but also encounters its share of obstruction in chapter 4, "Science and Empire," which examines the recent doctoral graduate settling into his life work as he moves from a teaching position at Wilberforce to a research appointment at the University of Pennsylvania and from there to the professorship he would hold for thirteen years at Atlanta University. Situated in the South, in proximity to the largest concentration of black Americans, Du Bois is poised to assess the physical, social, and political conditions under which the survivors of slavery and their descendants lead lives that fall well short of realizing the Jeffersonian promise of American life. Engaged as a scholar of black life in an era of disenfranchisement, lynching, and general terror, he readily assumes an activist position and takes a leading role in the Niagara Movement. Building on the scientific observation and analysis he had pioneered in *The Philadelphia Negro*, Du Bois establishes the Atlanta Conferences, and he and fellow researchers lay the foundations of what they hope will be a systematic knowledge of black life in America. However, because the Atlanta University project leads to a critique of the South's abridgment of black rights and the multitude of indignities imposed by Jim Crow laws, Du Bois challenges not only the white power structure but also the hegemony of a Tuskegee that has opted for an accommodationist approach to racial uplift. In *The Souls of Black Folk* Du Bois had already challenged the doctrines of Booker T. Washington and in doing so opened a bitter quarrel. The Atlanta Conferences can only go forward if adequately funded; through the workings of the "Tuskegee machine," as Du Bois tells it, with its powerful connections to the white South and the Northern industrial empire, the conferences (and the science that would know and address the plight of black Americans) are halted. Du Bois resigns and moves to New York City to work for the NAACP. Connecting events in his life with the national and international macrocosm, Du Bois correlates what he sees as his defeat at Atlanta with the "development of larger social forces beyond personal control." He finds the "industrial imperialism" that resulted in "the expulsion of black men from American democracy" consistent with white Europe's domination over "black Africa and yellow Asia" (48). In 1940 he makes connections that in 1910 or 1920 he could not.

Dusk of Dawn's chapter 5, "The Concept of Race," marks a climactic moment in his inquiry: "I want now to turn aside from the personal annals of this biography," he writes, "to consider the conception which is after all my main subject" (49). In supposedly turning aside from the personal, he does not take leave of first-person attestation; in this extraordinary chapter, he distills a lifetime's worth of reflections about an issue he has lived and studied, studied and lived. He begins by recalling his first introduction to race as a concept, its presentation in elementary school as a geographical sorting of static types characterized pictorially: uncivilized "Indians, Negroes, and Chinese" contrasted with the refined and philanthropic European. Whereas at Fisk he is exposed to the vigorous assertion of "essential racial equality," at Harvard he confronts for the first time "scientific race dogma" linked to evolutionary theory. Still later at Harvard and again at Berlin, he is exposed to theories that redefine race as "a matter of culture and cultural history" (49) privileging Europeans and to a lesser extent Asians for the simple reason that their histories were part of a traditional curriculum. "Which was the superior race? Manifestly that which had a history, the white race" (49): so Du Bois represents the logic of white supremacy as proposed by the academic establishment. That the doctrine of white supremacy should be supported by such variant and unstable proofs suggests to Du Bois that the thesis is perpetuated by assertion rather than argument; moreover, the vast diversity of skin tone among black people as well as his own triracial genealogy demonstrates that "race lines were not fixed and fast" (51). Taking himself as the primary point of reference, he provides in this chapter a family tree that includes the European Burghardt and Du Bois lines as well as what is known of the African and what can be speculated about the probable Native American heritage. Du Bois's conception of race abandons, finally, genetics and even culture, replacing it with the historical experience of power asymmetry that produces a global kinship among those marked by "the social heritage of slavery," a kinship that "binds together not simply the children of Africa, but extends through yellow Asia and into the South Seas" (59). As Du Bois focuses on the oppression of empire, he sees kinship among any and all peoples who have been subject to colonization. Racial distinction, according to the increasingly Marxist Du Bois, is driven by greed, as he comes to realize "that the income-bearing value of race prejudice was the cause and not the result of theories of race inferiority" (65).

The autobiographical narrative is extended further in this chapter as Du Bois recalls his first arrival in Africa, yet another moment when the native of the Housatonic Valley enters into an incarnation of the black collective. The two-month visit begins on Christmas Eve, 1923. Since he has been appointed to represent President Coolidge at the inauguration of the new Liberian president, he arrives with an official duty to discharge in addition to the settling of some personal business: a resolution of the unanswered question (after Countee Cullen, whom he quotes), "What is Africa to me?" (59). In a manner reminiscent of Marlow's approach to Africa in *Heart of Darkness*, Du Bois recalls the first appearance of the Liberian coast and his nighttime landing in Monrovia under a vibrant equatorial sky. No detail of his journey by long boat to the harbor is unimportant as Du Bois recalls the song of the oarsman and the lights of the Liberian capital whose population parades in festival mode. "Christmas Eve, and Africa is singing in Monrovia" (60). For the scholar who in *The Souls of Black Folk* had written of the sorrow songs as the fullest expression of African soul in response to its American experience, and for whom the black collective has existed preeminently as a mystic and musical experience, it is significant that in the Christmas Eve singing he hears a "rhythm I heard first in Tennessee forty years ago: the air is raised and carried by men's strong voices, while floating above in obbligato, come the high mellow voices of women" (60). The poetry of Du Bois's recollection of this visit, however, is mostly expended in his description of first contact.

Thereafter, the narration provides a fairly conventional travelogue in which Du Bois records his observation of people and places (including a visit to a forest replete with leopards and monkeys), dress and manners, and the mark of colonization and global economics as evinced in the defunct sugar plantations. It provides as well an account of the inauguration ceremony in which he formally participates. His presence as a foreigner is particularly evident in his observation of how marginalized Liberia remains with respect to global flows: "Communication as represented by human contact, movement of goods, dissemination of knowledge," which Westerners "have in such crushing abundance that they have mastered us and defeated their real good." But whereas "African life with its isolation has deeper knowledge of human souls," and whereas Du Bois sees much to praise in the good manners and sexual modesty of the Liberian people, he does not finally celebrate the African scene as a reclaimable utopian origin. There is the barrier of his modern Western sensibility: "Shall we all take to the Big Bush? No. I prefer New York" (65). Whereas Du Bois finds a place in this chapter to quote once again the syllables of his great-great-grandmother's melody, his connection to Africa remains abstract: the continent in which, six generations ago, the larger portion of his ancestry resided.

Chapter 5 concludes not so much with a final clarification of "the concept of race" as with a depiction of how it feels to live that concept, to be a member of a community of color in the modern world—in the New York that Du Bois prefers to an irretrievable Africa. The paragraph merits quotation at length: it is Du Bois's restatement, at age seventy-two, of what it means to speak and write from within the veil—or, in this alternate figure, cave, but in any case from a retreat that, as the first sentence suggests, he may be reluctant to abandon after all:

> It is difficult to let others see the full psychological meaning of caste segregation. It is as though one, looking out from a dark cave in a

> side of an impending mountain, sees the world passing and speaks to it; speaks courteously and persuasively, showing them how these entombed souls are hindered in their natural movement, expression, and development; and how their loosening from prison would be a matter not simply of courtesy, sympathy, and help to them, but aid to all the world. One talks on evenly and logically in this way, but notices that the passing throng does not even turn its head, or if it does, glances curiously and walks on. It gradually penetrates the minds of the prisoners that the people passing do not hear; that some thick sheet of invisible but horribly tangible plate glass is between them and the world. They get excited; they talk louder; they gesticulate. Some of the passing world stop in curiosity; these gesticulations seem so pointless; they laugh and pass on. They still either do not hear at all, or hear but dimly, and even what they hear, they do not understand. Then the people within may become hysterical. They may scream and hurl themselves against the barriers, hardly realizing in their bewilderment that they are screaming in a vacuum unheard and that their antics may actually seem funny to those outside looking in. They may even, here and there, break through in blood and disfigurement, and find themselves faced by a horrified, implacable, and quite overwhelming mob of people frightened for their own very existence. (66)

The cave, like the veil, exists as a cardinal metaphor in the Western philosophical and spiritual tradition, both serving as figures of separation from enlightenment and salvation.[38] Du Bois's allegory of the cave sealed in plate glass lends a particularly urban, capitalist, carceral, and dystopian note to his characterization of a predicament that he had previously imagined through the image of a veil that might one day be raised if not rent. It expresses his increasing doubt as to the reconciliation of African America with the white majority nation. Occurring in the same chapter in which he identifies a preference for New York over the African bush, it also expresses what in 1940 is his profound ambivalence of placement.

One phrase is particularly striking: "The passing throng does not even turn its head." Du Bois's conceit of separation, proceeding from his deep and complicated sense of isolation, is all the more noteworthy given the massive bibliography he has compiled by his early seventies. Throughout his career, in contrast with the majority of black authors, Du Bois had access to mainstream venues of publication.[39] With regard to the autobiographical writings alone, early essays appeared in such widely distributed periodicals as the *Atlantic Monthly* and *The Dial*. *The Souls of Black Folk* was published by A. C. McClurg, the firm that sponsored the late nineteenth-century revival of *The Dial*, while *Darkwater* and *Dusk of Dawn* were published by Harcourt Brace, the American imprint of works by Virginia Woolf and T. S. Eliot, among others.[40] As the editor of *Horizon*, *The Crisis*, *Phylon*, and even *Brownie's*

Book (the NAACP-sponsored magazine for children), Du Bois exerted direct power over the productive capacity of the print medium in a democratic society. Notwithstanding these opportunities to connect with a broad range of readerships, the veil lifting he imagined *Souls* might accomplish remained an unachieved goal even after he had published nearly twenty volumes comprising a range of academic and literary genres. When he speaks, in 1940, of that "thick sheet of invisible but horribly tangible plate glass" that comes between his people and the world, he describes a barrier that his relentless effort to publicize the travails of African America has done seemingly little to reduce. Du Bois's allegory of a people entombed in a cave conflicts with the optimism offered in the "Apology" that serves as preface to *Dusk of Dawn*, an optimism also expressed by the book's title with its cautious intimation of a new day. By contrast, in *The Autobiography of W. E. B. Du Bois: A Soliloquy on Viewing My Life from the Last Decade of Its First Century*, published by the leftist International Publishers in an edition prepared by Herbert Aptheker four years after Du Bois's death, we hear an author who has severely pared his hopes for his native country. We see a Du Bois whose legal status in the United States has been and is likely once again to be that of a near fugitive. Moreover, the fact that, before he died, Du Bois became a citizen of Ghana emphasizes the uncertain and outbound itinerary that the *Autobiography* implicitly describes.

"I found new friends and lived in a wider world than ever before"

The *Autobiography* marks a turbulent epoch in Du Bois's already well-advanced life. Much of it retraces familiar ground: whole passages narrating boyhood, education, and his early career derive verbatim from *Dusk of Dawn*. The *Autobiography*'s distinction consists in its dramatic framing of the indefatigable scholar amid the public and private trauma of the postwar years, which Du Bois, the near-centurion, refers to in the subtitle as "the last decade" of his "first century." In the aftermath of World War II, the increasingly Marxist inquirer and activist attracted the attention of the U.S. State and Justice Departments by participating in conferences of international groups suspected of Soviet sponsorship, such as the Council of African Affairs and Defenders of Peace. His travels to Moscow, Paris, and Stockholm as a peace promoter and his presentation to the United Nations of an NAACP petition appealing for international recognition of his country's discrimination against black Americans branded Du Bois an enemy of the state. Accordingly, in 1951 the Justice Department indicted Du Bois for failing to register as a foreign agent on the supposition that his role with the Peace Information Center, an organization that promulgated data regarding nuclear disarmament, disseminating such allegedly communist-inspired documents as the Stockholm Peace Appeal, meant that he took marching orders from the Soviet Union.[41]

Acquitted of all charges after a five-day trial, Du Bois still left the courtroom as a citizen whose passport had been confiscated and whose movements and communications would henceforth be closely monitored.[42] Although *Dusk of Dawn* tells the life story of one who has been thwarted and stultified at critical junctures by institutions and organizations (the Tuskegee machine, the NCAAP, and even Atlanta University) led by small-minded rivals, the *Autobiography* unfolds as a self-vindication in response to the felt humiliation of being publicly accused and tried as a traitor—the complaint of one who, in the midst of his suffering, has been abandoned if not betrayed by friends, colleagues, indeed a whole nation, from whom he had a right to expect material and moral support.

The *Autobiography* opens on a note of triumphant release. Chapter 1, "My 15th Trip Abroad," initiates a five-chapter sequence recounting the excursion he is able to take after the U.S. Supreme Court, in *Kent v. Dulles* (1958), ruled that the State Department had acted unconstitutionally in denying passports to U.S. citizens over its disapproval of professed political beliefs, a violation of First Amendment protections of the right to free speech. Restored to the international mobility to which he has been accustomed for most of his adult life, Du Bois and his second wife, Shirley Graham, embark on a journey that will take them first to western Europe before steering a course due east across the Iron Curtain. He meets with Khrushchev in Moscow and Mao in Beijing. In his account of these travels, he decries what he characterizes as the resurgence in the West of an industrial-imperialist ruling class under the political leadership and with the financial support of the United States, and exalts what he depicts as the classless societies emerging in Czechoslovakia, Poland, East Germany, the Soviet Union, and China. Contrary to the experience of most leftist American intellectuals who had turned to the Soviet Union between the World Wars for inspiration and instruction, the Stalinist purges do not dampen Du Bois's enthusiasm for the Soviet experiment, and his inspection of life in the People's Republic of China is similarly uncritical.[43] In the concluding lines of his travelogue through the Communist world, Du Bois exhibits a desperate need to believe he has toured a veritable utopia: "Fifteen times I have crossed the Atlantic and once the Pacific. I have seen the world. But never so vast and glorious a miracle as China."[44]

Between parts 1 and 2, Du Bois inserts "Interlude: Communism," his candid profession of faith. "I believe in communism," he declares, by which he means "a planned way of life in the production of wealth and work designed for building a state whose object is the highest welfare of its people and not merely the profit of a part." In keeping with his increasing conceptualization of race as a function of colonial economic models, he observes that political rule falls to "those who control wealth and who by that power buy or coerce public opinion" (35). In this oddly placed prolegomenon to what he fully expects to be the final narration of his life story, he positions himself firmly as outsider.

Outsider status per se is hardly new: from his first self-characterization in the "Forethought" of *Souls* as one who resides behind a veil to his allegory of the cave sealed behind plate glass in *Dusk of Dawn*, he has consistently spoken as one excluded, and his sense of occupying a separate world persists even when he commands institutional support and the resources of print culture. Part 2 of the *Autobiography* reprises the story of the black rural New Englander who, defying constraints of the color line, succeeds in achieving an education reserved for a white elite, secures positions of prominence, and moves through global space as though no barriers could possibly hinder a geographic mobility compelled by a wide-ranging scholarly inquiry and multifarious political engagement. At the center of the narrative is Du Bois's ambition to produce and archive a body of knowledge concerning the condition of black people in America that would lead to strategic interventions on their behalf; as one who always viewed African American experience in an international context, he has consistently conceived the black American as a subset of the world's colonized peoples and increasingly understands colonization in the light of dialectical materialism. The *Autobiography* extends the narrative of exclusion to which he had assigned an economic logic in *Dusk of Dawn*. On the black side of geographies marked by the American color line, Du Bois finds himself isolated as a result of internecine struggles within the NAACP and Atlanta University that pertain to his supposedly radical persuasions. Racial apartheid is no longer the chief isolating factor.

The sense of liberation conveyed in part 1, as Du Bois narrates his fifteenth trip abroad, is fleeting. And although, in part 2, he takes due satisfaction in his extraordinary achievements, he concludes by emphasizing that his highest aims have miscarried, the casualty of personalities but also of trends that pervade the public and private spheres on either side of the color line. "It is the tragedy of the day," writes Du Bois with reference to his fallings out with Atlanta University and the NAACP, "that the democracy of which we prate so glibly is being murdered in the house of its friends, and in everyday life far more than in broad governmental decisions" (216).[45] Part 3 follows with four chapters whose titles articulate idealism subject to persecution: "Work for Peace," "An Indicted Criminal," "The Trial," and "My Tenth Decade." These chapters project a state of reduction that no subsequent mobility can recuperate. Acquitted of all charges, he remains an enemy of the state, a martyr to his convictions, a virtual criminal in those spaces where he formerly made his home. "The secret police swarmed in my neighborhood asking about my visitors; whether I entertained and whom." His wonted access to an American readership is blocked: "My manuscripts and those of Shirley Graham were refused publication by reputable commercial publishers." He depicts himself as a pariah within his own community, prevented from publishing in black newspapers, speaking on black campuses, or appearing at events sponsored by the NAACP: "From being a person whom every Negro in the nation knew by name at least and hastened always to entertain or praise, churches and

Negro conferences refused to mention my past or present existence." White people "now ignored me or deliberately distorted my work." The isolation within his native land could not be more complete. "In fine," writes Du Bois, "I was rejected of men, refused the right to travel abroad and classed as 'controversial figure' even after being acquitted of guilt by a Federal court of law" (255).

Du Bois expresses his fear of exclusion and erasure from the American black collective in the starkest terms: "The colored children ceased to hear my name." Such in his view was the consequence of an African American community assimilating to capitalist practices. "The color line," as a result of such developments, "was beginning to break" but at the expense of a democracy with power to resist asymmetries of wealth. As a professed communist, Du Bois could not accept dissolution of the black-white color line on those terms. At the same time, in the state of exile he had embraced even before his resettlement in Ghana, he situated himself imaginatively amid the international community of the colonized and exploited emerging from capitalist domination—a collective that transcends any definition of race which is not first and foremost economic. "I found new friends and lived in a wider world than ever before—a world with no color line" (255). The *Autobiography* does not end before Du Bois provides an account of the celebration held on the occasion of his ninetieth birthday, an event that draws two thousand well wishers, thus demonstrating that his post-trial ignominy is not quite so dire as he reported earlier. And in the "Postlude" he affirms that the United States "is still a land of magnificent possibilities" (273) even as it prepares for a Third World War. "Hell lies about us in our Age" (275), Du Bois observes on the penultimate page, inverting the line from Wordsworth's "Intimations Ode," which must have spoken deeply to him at one point in his life.[46] The solution in his view is clear: the world must adopt socialism, and for that ideal he will strive. But he is under few illusions that his country provides ground on which one may labor effectively toward that goal.

Chapter 5

✦

Notes from Underground

Richard Wright, Ralph Ellison, James Baldwin, Malcolm X

W. E. B. Du Bois's remarkable longevity spans the Reconstruction and civil rights eras. Born a half decade after Emancipation, he lived to see his career's final phase shaped by the politics of the Cold War. He stands, therefore, as predecessor and contemporary to a generation born after the turn of the twentieth century. Unlike Booker T. Washington and (to a lesser degree) Ida B. Wells-Barnett, Du Bois witnessed the failure of uplift expectations as, decade by decade, the African American community, professional elite and underclass commons, led the life of a nation apart, consigned to institutional separation and material inequality, the casualty of a white regime of racial marking, the blanket "Negro" descriptor.[1] Exceptional in his social and geographic mobility, even so distinguished a personage as Du Bois was hardly exempt from the macro- and microcosmic constraints of segregation, his veil and cave metaphors expressing his naturalization to an apartheid policed by subtle cue as much as by crude enforcement. Although Du Bois seldom testifies to the violence of that enforcement in the ways that Richard Wright, Ralph Ellison, James Baldwin, and Malcolm X do, the restlessness that marks his career anticipates the unsettled condition of the younger generations of men who, like Du Bois, work out an understanding of themselves as black Americans at a hard-won distance from their geographic origins.

Wright, Ellison, Baldwin, and Malcolm X attest on occasion to the pleasures of voluntary travel, but the *flight* motif occupies a central place in the work of all four, and the history of African American displacement (the South-to-North mass migration but also the mythic Middle Passage) informs their representations of twentieth-century black mobility. Each embraces a degree of expatriation: whereas Wright and Baldwin become permanent residents of France, the New York City of Ellison and Malcolm X is a world apart from the rural, white supremacist South and Midwest of their respective origins. Wright in *Black Boy* (1945) and Ellison in *Invisible Man* (1952) generate texts that clearly reprise the paradigm of the (male) slave narrative as established by Douglass, in which the first-person narrator recounts his flight from South to North but depicts, more emphatically, an internal emancipation from a condition of ignorance and intimidation to a state of recognition and defiance, a transformation that culminates in the literary performance of the life story. *Black Boy* qualifies as autobiography, whereas *Invisible Man* is overtly fictive, however much it may parallel Ellison's own migratory and self-educative history.[2] For the purposes of this study, however, the genre distinction makes little difference, since both make use of a narrative structure built around an I-centered testimonial personhood, a position that preexists specific witness. (In chapter 6, we again explore I-centered testimonial personhood, this time in the fiction of Toni Morrison and Octavia Butler.) Although *The Autobiography of Malcolm X* revises the South-to-North plot as it locates the sites of early-life oppression in Nebraska and Michigan, it embeds Malcolm's path within those of his Grenada-born mother and Georgia-born father.[3] Like Wells-Barnett, moreover, Malcolm demonstrates that the rural Midwest is not substantially different from the rural South as a locus of racial terrorism.

As writers-in-exile, each of the four articulates a particular relationship between his life's itinerary and the testimony made possible by the geographic, cognitive, and affective distance that itinerary allows him to achieve; this chapter examines the specific trajectories that accrue to their respective literary performances. But with all four it is also necessary to speak of "destination" with reference to the different order of proximity they are able to achieve with their readerships as compared with even the well-published authors of previous generations (Washington, Wells-Barnett, and Du Bois, but also Charles W. Chesnutt, James Weldon Johnson, and Paul Laurence Dunbar).[4] Their success in securing access to major commercial publishers occurs during a period of expanding general readership, and their consequent arrival as national literary figures established their presence on both sides of the color line.[5] Harper Brothers, Random House, Knopf—the houses that published the first books of Wright, Ellison, and Baldwin—marketed their products to an expanding midcentury "mainstream" audience: a readership dominated by middle-class whites consuming black literature in suburban and academic settings. Grove, publisher of *The Autobiography of Malcolm X*, targeted a more left-leaning avant-garde urban audience, but its readership would massively include children of the white postwar suburbs encountering Grove titles on the liberal arts syllabus.[6] From midcentury on, general and academic readerships exhibited an increasing receptivity to black literary expression, an interest confirmed by the Book-of-the-Month Club's 1940 promotion of *Native Son*, the first best-selling title by an African American author.[7] The life one leads as a literary presence—and with all four, such presence rose to the level of celebrity—does not transcend geographic location, since all writing and all reading occur in specific sites. But the author-reader transaction takes place in variable contexts, and black literature, in becoming consumable across lines of color and class and along a broad spectrum of demographic situations, instantiates geographic encounters that far exceed the author's expectation. Even the sworn expatriate leads an effectively multiple life when engaging readerships back home.

Wright, Ellison, Baldwin, and Malcolm X all develop their own ways of invoking and inscribing readers on either side of the color line as well as across regional and national borders. Such inscription is a way of configuring and occupying geographic space—and again, "space" is always a shorthand for systems of representation by which we imagine and navigate a world that can only be entered as a field of signification. All four authors cultivate geographies in which narrator and reader may achieve tentative contiguity, although here we should insist on reader*s* (plural), inasmuch as texts attesting to conflictive experience cannot help but divide readerships, even if such division is necessary to establish the clarity requisite to a possible reconciliation. Ellison's prologue and epilogue to *Invisible Man* stage such a process in the narrator's account of colliding with the tall, blue-eyed blond man, the latter perfectly unaware of the former's presence before the moment of impact, their confrontation setting off a violent contest not so much for territory as for mutual recognition of the black man's claim to what Doreen Massey terms the individual's "trajectory" through consensually imagined public space.[8] Although the tall white man attempts to preempt the black man's claim by calling Ellison's protagonist an offensive name (which readers will readily surmise even as Ellison significantly refrains from inscribing it), the Invisible Man chooses not to kill his white antagonist, which in the context of this charged narrative qualifies as a first step toward reconciliation. The narrator-protagonist's critical appropriation of the Jeffersonian vision in the epilogue completes the offer of contiguity with readers regardless of color. The nation-state, as hypothetically an inclusively inhabitable territoriality founded on what (to vary Benedict Anderson's phrase) may be termed an *imaginable* community, remains tentatively intact, and does so (as imagined communities ever do) through the ubiquity of print culture.[9] In ways that even so well-published an author as Du Bois might not have imagined, Wright, Ellison, Baldwin, and Malcolm X could aspire to new orders of omnipresence.

"I would hurl words into this darkness and wait for an echo"

With *Uncle Tom's Children* (1938) and *Native Son* (1940), both published by Harper Brothers, Richard Wright launched his career as an author who articulated twentieth-century black experience and the paths by which migrants from the cotton states sought opportunity in the North. The Mississippi Delta and Chicago's South Side figure in much of his writing as the poles of a South-to-North migratory axis; his work thus provides a generational sequel to the memoirs of Ida B. Wells-Barnett. The stories collected in *Uncle Tom's Children* portray lives constrained by the terror of Southern white supremacy, whereas *Native Son* focuses on the entrapments that await those who arrive on Chicago's South Side. Wright's full career comprises what might be described as a double flight: escape from the South to Chicago and later New York City, and then relocation from the United States to France, where he would sustain a prolific output before dying at fifty-two. Identifying Wright as "the first black writer to be put forward as a major figure in world literature," Paul Gilroy has lamented the neglect Wright's later fiction and travel narratives have suffered. To some degree that neglect has been redressed, and the burgeoning interest in travel writing has made *Pagan Spain* (1957) a focus of belated scrutiny.[10] My discussion centers on earlier works in which Wright's protagonists contend with the social entrapments of North American topographies, but Gilroy's point is well taken. By its very title, *White Man, Listen!* (1957), Wright's late collection of four essays that originated as lectures delivered before European audiences underscores the rhetorical situation we have seen from Wheatley and Equiano forward: the black author speaking self-consciously of the diasporic experience in the colonizer-oppressor's language to a largely white European readership whose listening skills are almost certainly inadequate to the task of comprehending what the speaker and his community have endured.[11] For the author of *White Man, Listen!* that community is the colonized nonwhite world much as Du Bois imagined it—specifically, Wright speaks for the African-Asian collective whose representatives convened in the Bandung Conference of 1955.[12]

White Man, Listen! reflects evolutions in Wright's career that might not have been predicted from his early writings, but the imperative mood of the later work logically extends the implicit appeal of *Native Son*. With its tripartite division—"Fear," "Flight," and "Fate"—Wright's first published novel is commonly read as a textbook example of the cautionary social tale, naturalism within a Marxist interpretive frame.[13] Bigger Thomas, the son in question, serves as an object lesson of how the harsh environments of structural racism necessarily produce the black urban criminal. In the opening pages Wright portrays the Thomas family's virtual incarceration amid the oppressive spaces of Chicago's South Side. Their day begins in the bedroom Bigger shares with his mother, sister, and brother, as well as one of their dilapidated tenement's free-range rats, the killing of which constitutes the morning's first order of business. Leaving the apartment after the inevitable quarrel with his sister and mother, Bigger drifts about the ghetto streets with his similarly idle adolescent friends. As though to underscore the boys' entrapment as well as their dreams of escape, an early scene depicts Bigger and his friend Gus observing an airplane in the act of skywriting: "I could fly one of them things if I had a chance," laments Bigger.[14] The moment compactly articulates themes of flight, authorship, and blocked aspiration.[15] Later that day, the employment agency finds work for Bigger beyond the boundaries of the South Side, but the situation affords little more than an onerous commute to a low-wage job. Leaving his vermin-infested neighborhood to work in the slumlord Henry Dalton's mansion, moreover, he enters a world of abundance in which he feels his confinement all the more, as every step he takes must conform to the script by which his white patrons define his place among them.[16]

From Bigger's perspective, the script remains dangerously inscrutable, the more so as the Daltons identify themselves as the aspiring patrons of his potential uplift. Whereas the conservative Mr. and Mrs. Dalton entertain paternalistic if rigidly hierarchical views concerning the improvability of Bigger's lot, their rebellious daughter, Mary, complicates matters by affecting to treat him as an equal. Bigger's confused geographical predicament achieves an absurdist moment when he is tasked with chauffeuring Mary and her self-styled communist boyfriend, Jan Erlone, through the streets and parklands of Chicago, an occasion the intoxicated couple seize to conduct sexual relations on the backseat, indulging in a privileged-class exhibitionism, obtruding a quintessential private-space activity on Bigger's rearview observation. Obliged that evening to carry Mary to her bedroom after she has passed out in the car, a situation in which (as Bigger is well aware) the momentary contiguity of black to white body could have lethal consequences for the black young man, Bigger smothers the girl in an effort to keep her quiet within earshot of her (significantly) blind mother. Following his panic-driven decision to dismember and burn her body in the Dalton's furnace to conceal this unintended murder, he conceives the idea of staging her absence as a case of kidnapping, and this leads to his one act of authorship: the composition of the ransom note that he signs "Red" in a clumsy attempt to pin the supposed disappearance on Jan. But the ruse collapses after a few hours when pieces of bone and a lone earring turn up in the furnace's ash pan, and in flight the literate but radically inarticulate Bigger seeks refuge in the blocks of abandoned Southside tenements. After murdering his girlfriend, Bessie, to keep her from betraying him, Bigger must reckon with the futility of attempting even to flee the neighborhood microcosm, and the tightening police cordon eventuates in his apprehension. By one path or another, the narrative argues, from birth Bigger is destined for a jail cell. Given the ludicrous circumstances into which his path leads, he secures as well a date with the electric chair. In colloquy with his communist Jewish lawyer, Mr. Max, Bigger is finally able to stammer out something of a testimony regarding his life and suffering, although nothing he can say succeeds in mitigating the profound isolation in which he has lived and now must die.

Black Boy (American Hunger), Richard Wright's account of youth and young adulthood, reprises the major themes of the first two books but develops them with the self-reflection that an articulate first-person survivor of harsh conditions brings to the testimonial occasion. *Black Boy* is first and foremost an author's bildungsroman, documenting Wright's journey against formidable discouragements to the republic of letters. In this regard it replicates Douglass's theme of extracting an education from whatever materials fall in his way and mastering those materials to the extent that he can command the resource of autobiographical narrative. Although Wright enjoys, as Douglass did not, the benefit of formal if ever disrupted schooling, he must still contend with forces that would reduce the lives of African Americans to servile reflex and mindless impoverishment and that equip white people (police but also random civilians) with a license to humiliate, maim, and kill. In counterpoint to the revolving tale of family crisis and displacement, Wright traces the evolution of a child who, by acts of attention and insatiable curiosity, gains access to a world of fascinating if often brutal sensation (blue sky, green field, and dusty road, if also burning house, public privy, and barroom) and whose solitary disposition provides psychic space for reverie and dreams of alternate worlds. Like Douglass, Wright addresses a physical hunger that is also a cognitive hunger, partial satisfaction of which transports the autodidact beyond the horizons of Southern oppression even before his actual removal to the urban North. In the prolepsis of autobiographical retrospection, Wright's literary activity is from inception a mapping of the world and his place in it.

The publication history of *Black Boy (American Hunger)* merits attention, as it exists as a metanarrative not only of Wright's flight from what he describes in part 1 as "Southern Night" and relocation amid "The Horror and the Glory" of the black urban North, but also of his engagement with the expanding cultures of American reading as those cultures evinced a broadening interest in black American experience. Having achieved celebrity with the success of *Native Son*, a triumph for which the novel's selection as a Book-of-the-Month Club option was instrumental, Wright composed his autobiographical narrative under the working title *Black Confession* and later *American Hunger*. When the club expressed interest in publishing part 1 as *Black Boy*, Wright excised the chapters recounting life in Chicago with a view to publishing them piecemeal (a long excerpt would appear as "The Man Who Went to Chicago" in the 1961 collection *Eight Men*).[17] Only with the 1991 Library of America edition were part 1 ("Southern Night") and part 2 ("The Horror and the Glory") published in conformity with Wright's original design. His willingness to accept the amputation proposed by Book-of-the-Month Club editors in exchange for high-powered promotion and distribution demonstrates Wright's understanding of midcentury marketing and his ambition to meet a white middle-class audience among the leisurely landscapes of mass literary consumption. Penetrating such readerly horizons, the author-protagonist of *Black Boy* figures perhaps as no less exotic than Bigger Thomas, the all-but-aphasic protagonist of *Native Son*, but Wright's depiction of young Richard as a child drawn to the written word establishes him as a subject with whom any readership might find common ground. The story of a reader who aspires to authorship, *Black Boy* concludes with the young man's determination to forge "a bridge of words"[18] to convey the truth of his experience to the world at large. Having identified an ambition fostered by his self-directed immersion in continental and American naturalism, he submits the present text along with those that preceded it as just such a bridge.

Wright clearly imagines his bridge as two-way: if it can situate his voice in the republic of letters, it may succeed in transporting his mass-market readership to the vertiginous and claustrophobic spaces of black poverty, or do so to the degree that literature can accomplish such displacement. The first chapter of *Black Boy* plunges the reader into the chaos and violence of Wright's early childhood, highlighting the boy's intellectual no less than emotional need against the meager sustenance his life has to offer. Introducing Richard as a four-year-old child seeking to satisfy an idle curiosity by setting fire to the living room curtains, Wright clearly prefigures the dissolution of family and household, but he also identifies the boy's inquiring intellect as a factor in his world's perpetual disruption. This is a child for whom the life of the mind counts for much, a child who experiences anguish when confronted with boredom and confinement. An example of such a response may be seen in Wright's recollection of one of the family's many removals, a journey by riverboat from Jackson to Memphis. Amid other sources of distress that plague the boy's daily life at that time, Wright cites the failure of the *Kate Adams* to meet his expectation of a "*huge* white boat floating on a *vast* body of water" (11; emphasis added) as an acutely memorable disappointment. Soon after the family has settled in Memphis, the father's desertion deepens the household's straitened condition, as the distraught mother must explain to her sons why regular meals are no longer served. Richard's first solo foray into the world has as its object the purchase of food in the father's absence; twice beaten and robbed of grocery money by neighborhood boys who form a gauntlet he must run, Richard succeeds only after his mother arms him with a big stick and locks him out of the house, forcing him to meet violence with violence. Later, inured to a recurrent visceral hunger, Richard resists abject humiliation in refusing to accept the nickel from his father the last time they meet during his childhood. To retain the dignity requisite to any chance for self-determination, the child repudiates the father.

Having presented in this first chapter a portrait of early childhood harassed by poverty and dislocation, hostage to the fortunes of short-tempered adults whose lives achieve a tentative foothold only to spiral out of control, Wright shifts to the moment twenty-five years later when he meets his father again for the first time. The cold and accusatory parent who abandoned the family and whom Richard last saw in the company of a random girlfriend is now an old man living on a Mississippi plantation, leading an existence defined by the rhythms of Southern peonage. Deferring to subsequent chapters the account of how he made his escape, Wright concludes chapter 1 with a definitive statement of how far he has come from origins that typically sentence black people to permanent entrapment, and he does so by juxtaposing his trajectory with that of his father. Whereas Richard's boyhood migration to

Memphis had initiated a sequence of relocations among increasingly cosmopolitan sites, the father's experiment in urban living does not survive its first trial. The breach between father and son is absolute. "I was overwhelmed," Wright observes, "to realize that he could never understand me or the scalding experiences that had swept me beyond his life and into an area of living that he could never know" (35). Although Wright expresses confidence that he can convey his life story to a general readership acquainted with the generic dislocations of modernity, no "bridge of words" exists to reunite father and son. Having attained perspectives shaped by naturalist fiction and Marxist analysis, Wright frames this estrangement with reference to a rural-urban binary, the racialized geographies of South and North. From the metropolitan perspective of the literary intellectual, he observes that his father's "soul was imprisoned by the slow flow of the seasons, by wind and rain and sun." Thus before he proceeds to narrate the story of his escape from the condition of the child consigned to his family's poverty and dysfunction, he affirms that such escape is a fait accompli:

> From far beyond the horizons that bound this bleak plantation there had come to me through my living the knowledge that my father was a black peasant who had gone to the city seeking life, but who had failed in the city; a black peasant whose life had been hopelessly snarled in the city, and who had at last fled the city—that same city which had lifted me in its burning arms and borne me toward alien and undreamed-of shores of knowing. (35)

To express such distance from the father is to express a greater relative proximity to the reader (any reader, on whichever side of the color line), with whom at the very least the author shares the culture of a world in which such a book can exist.

Wright's path of escape is cognitive and literary; it leads to a world in which books exist to be written as well as read, and the core narrative of *Black Boy* involves Richard's resolution to command a language by which to imagine alternate worlds—such language as Bigger Thomas catastrophically lacks. Whereas the adolescent is drawn to narrative fiction as an escape from his harsh daily life, the literary practice Wright later espouses revisits scenes of autobiographical experience from a critically distant perspective, the alternate world that exists beyond the oppressor's frame of reference. Throughout his first three books, having attained a literary and geographical position from which he exerts authorial control, Wright assesses the lexicon by which a white supremacist regime dehumanizes a black underclass.

Indeed, the story of Wright's literary career is rooted in his lexical confusion with respect to such terms as "white" and "black." The child's puzzlement regarding these signifiers (how is it that his "white" mixed-race grandmother leads the "black" life of her darker family members?) leads to a precocious recognition that literal meaning has no validity and that language conventions serve to mystify an irrational social order. Recollecting his boyhood curiosity over the use of racially charged terms, he contrasts his innocence with the incurious mind of his deeply scarred mother, for whom the existing order is a fact of life, a reality one interrogates at grave personal risk: "I had begun to notice that my mother became irritated when I questioned her about whites and blacks, and I could not quite understand it. I wanted to understand these two sets of people who lived side by side and never touched, it seemed, except in violence" (46). In the autobiographical essay "The Ethics of Living Jim Crow" (1937), Wright compiles a sequence of anecdotes that mark those boundaries, incidental contacts that culminate in verbal and physical assault and that threaten the lives of those who reject their "Jim Crow lessons." In *Black Boy*, Wright depicts a young man who has learned to accommodate a capricious white supremacist power whose absurdity he well understands. "To our minds the white folks formed a kind of superworld: what was said by them during working hours was rehashed and weighed here. . . . But under all our talk floated a latent sense of violence: the white had drawn a line over which we dared not step and we accepted that line because our bread was at stake." Yet the black community has its own citadel to protect: "Within our boundaries we, too, drew a line that included our right to bread regardless of the indignities or degradations involved in getting it" (219). Within Wright's larger trajectory, discerning the geography of day-to-day survival precedes ascertaining a geography of flight.

Even within the black community, Wright characterizes himself as self-isolating, his childhood exposure to dislocation, abandonment, and his mother's steady decline limiting his elective affinities. "A somberness of spirit that I was never to lose settled over me during the slow years of my mother's unrelieved suffering," Wright observes, "a somberness that was to make me stand apart and look upon excessive joy with suspicion, that was to make me self-conscious, that was to keep me forever on the move, as though to escape a nameless fate seeking to overtake me" (96). In his state of adolescent solitude and unsettlement, he is susceptible to any suggestion of distant horizons, and it is a measure of the power of such suggestion that the fiction supplement of a racist Chicago newspaper figures as his initiation to the world of literature. Through the crudest productions of mass print culture Wright finds his door of escape: "I became aware of the life of the modern world, of vast cities, and I was claimed by it" (123). Sensational and unenlightened as his reading may be, it instructs and provokes by virtue of the fact that it conjures the vision of other lives, other places: "The cheap pulp tales enlarged my knowledge of the world more than anything I had encountered so far. . . . [T]hey were revolutionary, my *gateway to the world*" (124; emphasis added). From pulp tale he progresses to the canon of naturalist and modernist novelists, poets, and philosophers. As with Frederick Douglass, an imaginative leave-taking precedes cartographic relocation: "My reading had created a vast sense of distance between me and the world in which I lived and tried to make a living, and that sense of distance was increasing each day" (242). Wright's testimony to the power of the written word compares with that of Douglass, but in the century that has elapsed since Douglass published his *Narrative*, new literary genres and markets have arisen. Wright's Northern fantasies are those not of the aspiring freeman but of the professional author: "I dreamed of going north and writing books, novels." He is quick to admit the fantastic nature of his ambition. "The North symbolized to me all that I had not felt and seen; it had no relation whatever to what actually existed. Yet, by imagining a place where everything was possible, I kept hope alive in me" (161). The fact that he publishes *Black Boy* having already succeeded in this aim demonstrates the material consequence of desperately preserved hope.

Wright's location vis-à-vis his 1945 mass-market readership remains ambiguous throughout *Black Boy*. As we have seen in chapter 3, Frederick Douglass and Harriet Jacobs prompt readers to speculate where and under what circumstances they compose their testimonies given their current or recent fugitive status and the understanding that, as long as slavery exists in the South, no free person of color, North or South, is entirely safe. Well before the publication of *Invisible Man*, they engaged in a species of author invisibility. Whereas Wright cannot elicit the same concern, his work stimulates readerly curiosity as to where in the North he has found refuge (if indeed he has found refuge) from persecutions that threaten his status as a person. Wright's escape from the South does not lead to permanent settlement elsewhere: he does not create a post-South center of operation, as Douglass does in Rochester and later Washington, D.C., as Ida B. Wells-Barnett does in Chicago, or as Ralph Ellison is able to do in Manhattan. Rather, like Du Bois, Wright perceives himself as a wanderer ("forever on the move") and in his wandering ultimately stateless. At one level he attributes this isolation to his having witnessed his mother's disintegration and to assuming in consequence the position of skeptical outsider within his own family: "I felt that I had been emotionally cast out of the world, had been made to live outside the normal processes of life" (195). But he also argues that this emotional condition, so extreme in his case, is the epistemological and political condition of black Americans generally, a discovery that he makes upon arriving in segregated Chicago: "When I contemplated the area of No Man's Land into which the Negro mind in America had been shunted I wondered if there had ever existed in all human history a more corroding and devastating attack upon the personalities of men than the idea of racial discrimination" (253). Positioned on the far side of his "bridge of words," Wright's midcentury reader is challenged to imagine, politically and personally, the No Man's Land from which those words emanate.

Wright's sense of having been "cast out of the world" and of residing in an inescapable "No Man's Land" achieves further articulation in "The Man Who Lived Underground," a story that channels Fyodor Dostoevsky's *Notes from Underground* while invoking the literature and history of the Underground Railroad. An allegorical supplement to *Black Boy*, the story tracks an (initially) anonymous black man in flight from the police on a subterranean journey through the sewers and cellars of the urban North. In the process of this journey the protagonist gains new perspective on the quotidian scenes and crimes of his city and critical knowledge of the world he has occupied all his life, a world that has indoctrinated him in its monetized priorities even as it has assigned him a place of servility and disesteem. In the cave to which he hauls the booty of his raid on the jewelry store safe, he comes to understand the fundamental worthlessness of what he and his fellow citizens conventionally value and the guilt they all share for perpetuating a system of mutual degradation. Emancipated from values that have never benefited him personally, he looks upon his fellow citizens with pity. Such knowledge compels him to express himself, to speak to the aboveground world as prophet and, if necessary, martyr.

Beginning with the first sentence, "I've got to hide, he told himself,"[19] the narration hovers between first and third person. In accompanying the protagonist into the municipal sewer, the reader is drawn into spaces of civic abjection and must map, with the fugitive, the system of passageways that treacherously slope to darkness and death but that also touch the foundations of social life among a maze of porous border-works. At no point in the story are we encouraged to believe that the protagonist will discover an escape route, a corridor that will lead to a place of freedom. Rather, the liberation he experiences resides in his recognition of the deluded nature of the lives he witnesses from below, delusions without which no one can survive, as he discovers when he attempts to share his illumination with the very policemen who arrested him and extracted from him a false confession. To the extent that the story is told in a first-person voice, we are privy to the protagonist's cognitive process, first, as he fights to maintain his balance in the rushing water, and then as he discovers the old disused channels and the walls that only partially separate the sewer from the living city. We share his struggle to identify everyday sounds and sights amid the strangeness of approaching a familiar world from the consciousness of death the sewer represents. And after he has brought jewels, cash, a meat cleaver, a radio, a gun, and a typewriter into his below-ground den, we witness his first literary efforts, the typing out of the first line of a story, lifted though it be from such pulp fiction as Wright consumed in his own first discovery of letters.

Just as the view from the sewer builds upon the *Black Boy* moment in which five-year-old Richard and his companions observe from below the anatomical function of men and women, black and white, and of varied class status, as they make egalitarian use of the public outhouse, so Fred Daniels's attraction to the jewelry store typewriter reflects Wright's gravitation to print expression. The fugitive who "had signed his name to a confession, a confession he had not even read" (27), now takes a first active part in the generation of text: "Spelling in a soft diffident voice, he pecked out his name on the keys: *freddaniels*. He looked at it and laughed. He would learn to type correctly one of these days." He ceases in that moment to be anonymous and creates an alter ego with a sense of futurity. "Yes," he tells himself, "he would take the typewriter too" (47). His subsequent activity at the keyboard is short lived: moving toward a more desperate and radical frame of mind than Wright achieves in *Black Boy*, a condition in which he forgets his name, having reinvented the world by means of his bricolage installation, he leaves the sewer as the word incarnate and seeks to cross from his transvalued geography of spiritual illumination to the fallen world from which the sewer offered refuge. The narration leaves no doubt that he acts from a state of spiritual sanity, however doomed he may be to failure: "When he moved again his actions were informed with precision, his muscular system reinforced with a reservoir of energy" (64). But in the aboveground world his status as an anonymous and foolish black has not changed, and upon emerging from the manhole he is greeted by a white voice alerting him to his inveterate and indeed existential transgression: "Look where you're going, nigger!" (66). He fails in his prophetic object of leading his policemen-oppressors to the site of illumination. "He was eager to show them the cave now. If he could show them what he had seen, then they would feel what he had felt, and soon everybody would be governed by the same impulse of pity" (81). His second errand into the sewer is his last, and he becomes the inevitable victim of a police shooting. When we last see him, the man whose subjectivity we as readers have shared has reverted to the category of thing: "He sighed and closed his eyes, a whirling object rushing alone in the darkness, veering, tossing, lost in the heart of the earth" (84). So much for the "bridge of words." As an allegory of African American authorship, and black expressiveness generally, "The Man Who Lived Underground" suggests there is little possibility that black artists can speak from the No Man's Land across the chasm that separates them from the majority-white nation. First published in 1942, the novella still spoke for Wright on its republication in 1961. Celebrated author notwithstanding, Wright was ever skeptical of his own success as an international literary figure.

"On the lower frequencies"

In "The Man Who Lived Underground," Ralph Ellison would find the germ of *Invisible Man*: a fugitive running for his life drops into a manhole and, after a period of acclimation, makes a home, however temporarily, in the underground bunker he has fashioned from available space and spare materials. But there is one signal difference: speaking from below ground, Ellison's protagonist is a practiced orator who signifies ebulliently in the literary genre toward which Wright's fugitive only takes the first step.[20] While the Invisible Man's career, like that of Fred Daniels, has culminated (thus far) in flight and underground concealment, his testimony anthologizes many travel stories, comprising a wide spectrum of male African American displacement narratives and tropes of mobility.[21] Isolated from the opening scene amid the internal dissentions of the black community, and destined for all of his professional-class aspirations to seek refuge from a white power structure that persists in defining him as a murderer, rapist, and thief, he does not so much diverge from a path as recognize that his ingenuous itinerary and its anticipated arrivals have been steeped all along in delusion. His good behavior has bought him nothing—at least not yet.

This paradigm is established in the overtly allegorical first chapter. The protagonist, valedictorian of his Jim Crow high school, is asked to attend an evening gathering of his Southern town's white male elite, where he is supposed to be honored for his scholastic achievements and given the opportunity to reprise his graduation speech. He arrives at the venue to find that nine of his classmates have also been invited to the event; before he is recognized for his individual merit, he must participate, as the Du Boisian "talented tenth," in a battle royal.[22] The young men are subjected to terror and humiliation, forced to witness the gyrations of a white stripper in the knowledge that they could be lynched for evincing the mere suggestion of sexual response, then blindfolded and set upon each other in a slugfest. At the conclusion of this orchestrated free-for-all, they are lured into tumbling over an electrified carpet in a scramble for worthless coins. Toward the end of the program the white city fathers, as an afterthought to the evening's real agenda, ask the protagonist to read his speech, with its heavy citation of Booker T. Washington's Atlanta Exposition Address (significantly, the young man begins by quoting the passage in which Washington invokes the image of the ship at the mouth of the Amazon River). The city fathers remain inattentive until a stray rebellious impulse induces the protagonist to speak the insurgent phrase "social equality," at which point his auditors halt the speech and interrogate the young man, reminding him that they mean "to do right" by him so long as he knows his "place at all times."[23] Having affirmed that he simply misspoke and that in fact he does know his place, the young man completes his performance to general acclaim. "He makes a good speech," the master of ceremonies declares, "and some day he'll lead his people in the proper paths" (32). Awarded the leather briefcase containing a certificate of his scholarship to the black state college, he sets off upon one such path—the black professional uplift track consistent with Tuskegee ideals.

Elated with his opportunity, he represses the suspicion that arises in a dream later that night, in which his deceased grandfather instructs him to open the briefcase and read aloud the letter he extracts from a sequence of envelopes within envelopes, each one symbolizing, as the grandfather points out, a year of delusion he is fated to endure. Rather than white affirmation of his individual merit and commendation to those who will assist his professional advancement, the protagonist discovers, and must recite to his grandfather's corrosive laughter, the following message: "'To Whom It May Concern,' I intoned. 'Keep this Nigger-Boy Running'" (33). The dream foreshadows the moment in which the young Mr. Emerson forces the protagonist to read Bledsoe's treacherous letter of introduction, but his own naive faith in "the proper paths" leads him to dismiss the disruptive recognition the dream encodes. Recognition followed by summary repression dominates this fictional bildungsroman.

The college in *Invisible Man* is a satiric rendition of Tuskegee: Southern black utopian space situated within a national geography of white economic and political domination but subject to the autocratic rule of the black college president, H. B. Bledsoe. A subaltern of the Northern industrialists who fund the college and sit on the board of trustees, Bledsoe serves as a Washington-like president, successor to a personage referred to as "the Founder," the mythic patriarch whose life story conflates heroic black escape motifs with the itinerary recounted in *Up from Slavery*. In the protagonist's erotically charged reminiscence, the campus figures as an oasis in the stricken landscape of the Black Belt, a fragrant and flowering world apart where students divide their time between love trysts and half-hearted study. The wasteland of poverty lies just beyond the border, however, as the protagonist discovers when he takes Mr. Norton, the patrician trustee, on a tour of the environing countryside, obeying once again contrarian impulses that lie just beneath his earnest resolve to keep to the path of the model striver. Against the Tuskegee formula of appealing to the white powers-that-be through a display of humble and industrious virtue, Ellison introduces the off-the-map figure of Jim Trueblood, whose real or imagined incestuous relationship with his daughter provides material for his folksy performance, designed to titillate the white patron while confirming the latter's suspicion that black people are hopelessly degenerate, a performance for which he receives the handsome reward he fully anticipates. Likewise off the official itinerary, the bar-and-brothel operating under the name Golden Day exposes Norton and the protagonist alike to black men who have attained professional status but whose education and talent have made little difference in their material condition and whose wartime sacrifices have gone unrecognized upon their return to the States. Having attained a position in which he is determined not to please, the "insane" black physician with whom Norton converses speaks truth to power in ways that the protagonist will later emulate.

Ellison's campus is conventionally understood as a satirically allegorical portrait of Tuskegee. For the most part this discussion concurs with that reading. To the extent, however, that such treatment presumes that a "real" college is mirrored in a fictional one, it benefits from critical qualification. As I have argued throughout this study, all geography proceeds from systems of signification founded in ideological and symbolic understandings of space: there are no "literal" or "value-neutral" representations of the world through which the human subject moves. The material Tuskegee that Booker

T. Washington creates exists as a black geographical entity locked in a state of tension not only with an overtly white supremacist South but also, more generally, with the racially exclusionary conception of North America articulated by Franklin, Jefferson, Cooper, and Emerson, among others. Tuskegee as an inherently symbolic place thus precedes Ellison's allusively and literarily symbolic depiction of a Tuskegee-like campus. In juxtaposing scenes of uplift pageantry with sites that testify to continuing violence, suffering, and failure, Ellison draws on a modernist meta-geography that T. S. Eliot establishes in *The Waste Land* and that F. Scott Fitzgerald naturalizes to the American scene with the Valley of Ashes in *The Great Gatsby*. It would be a mistake, however, to read *Invisible Man* as simply dismissing Tuskegee as the repressive materialization of what Du Bois calls Washington's "Atlanta Compromise" without also appreciating the degree to which Ellison understands the college as a historically significant countergeography, just as it would be a mistake to accept the protagonist's contrarian interpretation of Charles Keck's sculpture, "Lifting the Veil of Ignorance," dedicated on the Tuskegee campus in 1922, as definitive. In its catalog of black places—from "the state college for Negroes" (32) to the still-inhabited slave cabins and black saloons on its periphery, from the Jim Crow seats on the interstate bus to its Harlem destination and the latter's broad spectrum of club, church, tenement, and street life—the narrative represents a working out of cartographic possibility. It does so, moreover, from the vantage point of the protagonist's underground site, a place that remains off the map and that the author secures against the spatial domination of a white hierarchy, a loophole of retreat that affords a counterepistemology comparable to the hermeneutical position Linda Brent's garret offers her.

Satire though it may be, the Tuskegee-like campus retains the power to reprise a promised land of uplift and self-empowerment to which the Washington-like Founder stands as a Moses leading his people through the mythic geography of the black refugee. In telling the oft-repeated story in his address at the college convocation, shortly after the young man has returned with a shaken Mr. Norton from a tour of the borderlands, Homer Barbee (epic poet of black perseverance) emphasizes the degree to which flight—from bondage, lynch mobs, and degradation generally—resides in collective memory: "You recall how you plunged with the Founder, the Leader, deep into the black art of escape," he prompts his youthful audience (122).[24] The ancestral travel to which Barbee would attach the individual histories of his auditors is an elaboration of the Middle Passage, which exists for Barbee and Ellison alike as the foundational narrative of the African presence in the Americas:

> And so, my young friends, my sisters and brothers, you went with him, in and out of cabins, by night and early morning, through swamps and hills. On and on, passed from black hand to black hand and some white hands, and all the hands molding the Founder's freedom

> and our own freedom like voices shaping a deep-felt song. And you, each of you, were with him. Ah, how well you know it, for it was you who escaped to freedom. Ah, yes, and you know the story. (123)

"You know the story," he tells the audience, "and you know the song": music as a way of mapping the collective past is a recurrent theme in this novel, which begins, from the prologue, in response to the question "What did I do to be so black and blue?" Chronologically, the protagonist must outlast a series of harsh lessons before he can turn to Louis Armstrong for ironic insight into the repressed complications of his history, insight that comes to him—under the time-annulling influence of cannabis illumination—as he contemplates the spatial and specifically chthonic dimensions of the song. As we listen to the words of Barbee, we are conscious that the protagonist is about to be ostracized from the Promised Land that is the campus. In no way, however, will he be dispossessed of the genealogy and geography of flight that Barbee invokes and that Armstrong, Barbee's complement, confirms.

Sent to New York with the understanding that his exile will be temporary and that he will not only be permitted to graduate but may even be invited to remain at the college as Bledsoe's administrative assistant, the young man is relieved of these illusions when young Mr. Emerson forces him to read the letter of introduction with which he had been equipped upon expulsion. Trusting in Bledsoe's honorability, and having resisted the temptation to steam one of the seven envelopes open, he must now reckon with the depth of Bledsoe's betrayal. In the latter's phrase he has crossed into territory from which he cannot be recalled: "One for whom we held great expectations has gone grievously astray." Moreover he has been sent on a fool's errand: "I beg of you, sir," Bledsoe writes to the college's white patrons, "to help him continue in the direction of that promise which, like the horizon, recedes ever brightly and distantly beyond the hopeful traveler" (191). Abandoning expectation of aid and comfort from college-affiliated white patronage and deprived of all hope of returning to campus, he will nevertheless "continue in the direction" of illusory personal and professional advancement through his work with the Brotherhood. Caught up in his duties as public speaker and community organizer, yet never entirely assimilating to the life and culture of the Harlem streets, he must serve an apprenticeship punctuated by hazing and betrayal before he can recognize that he and his district's people are mere pawns in Brother Jack's cynical pursuit of theoretical and corporate goals. Only gradually does it dawn on him that Brotherhood ideology with its professions of equality has had anything but a purgative effect on the entrenched practices of white supremacy.

In the course of his New York residence, both before and during his Brotherhood employ, the protagonist crosses paths with a number of characters who have migrated to the city from a Southern origin no more than a generation removed from slavery. Mary, the motherly woman who provides care and housing after his release from the factory hospital, is herself a migrant who has assisted many new arrivals in their adjustment to city life. The elderly couple at whose eviction the protagonist begins his Northern career as orator are former slaves from Georgia, as we learn from the free papers the protagonist finds among the personal belongings stacked on the snowy sidewalk. Brother Tarp, a colleague in the Harlem Brotherhood office, is more fugitive than migrant in the usual sense, having fled the involuntary servitude of the chain gang: "I was down there for a long time before I come up here, and when I did come up they was after me," confides Tarp. "What I mean is, I had to escape, I had to come a-running" (386). In a fatherly gesture meant to convey the memory and evidence of an erstwhile bondage, Tarp presents the narrator with a broken link of the chain that held him prisoner. Although it ends up in the briefcase with an assortment of metonymic reminders of bondage and freedom, the protagonist flinches inwardly at the brutality of the object and must suppress an aversion in accepting it as well as the ancestral relationship Tarp bears to him. The broken link pointedly signifies paradox: connection that presumes and confirms separation. Ever in the role of the talented tenth, the protagonist prefers, generally, a more cerebral conception of the nexus between past sufferings and present struggles. In his first Brotherhood speech, he expresses his heroic if abstract notion of emancipatory history as follows: "I feel that I can see sharp and clear and far down the dim corridor of history and in it I can hear the footsteps of militant fraternity!" (346). But while he may be able to trace lines of descent by which he stands as successor to his traitorous grandfather or to Brother Tarp, "militant fraternity" dissipates in internalized violence—whether the battle royal of the opening chapter or the brawl with Ras and his followers in the last.

What puzzles the protagonist more than the varieties of black mobility, "proper paths" or treasonous indirection, is black pathlessness, or what appears to be such. Soon after the death of Brother Tod, a casualty of the regressive behavior in which a living is made by pandering to white notions of black inferiority, the protagonist observes a group of zoot-suiters at the subway station (*The Autobiography of Malcolm X*, specifically the Detroit Red incarnation, palpably overlaps with *Invisible Man* at this point)—icons of a street culture that remains unintelligible to him insofar as he cannot locate these young men in any progressive uplift sequence. "What about those fellows waiting still and silent there on the platform, so still and silent that they clash with the crowd in their very immobility; standing noisy in their very silence; harsh as a cry of terror in their quietness?" (440). Where they have come from, and where they are going, remain a mystery to the protagonist, who, in the wake of Tod's death, itself a reversal of progressive racial views, affirms with renewed fervency the uplift path and who has yet to hear the cautionary message of Louis Armstrong. Soon after Tod's impromptu funeral, the protagonist will come to a full recognition that the Brotherhood is no such path, personally or collectively. Although he participates willingly in acts of destruction that erupt the night after the funeral, and although he fulfills his role in the battle royal that Jack has staged between Brotherhood Harlemites and Ras, he is philosophically as well as temperamentally at odds with the chaos of a rioting Harlem and thus seeks the heterotopic refuge from which he delivers his testimony. Even then, he has not abandoned the concept of the path: to emerge from the chthonic depth, the professed next item on his agenda, necessitates some manner of uplift. If, in discarding his persistently earnest outlook, he opts for defensive duplicity, he will model himself after the grandfather, whom he has come to see as a subversive idealist, and reject the self-serving cynicism of Bledsoe, the professional-class subaltern to the white industrial ruling class, or Rinehart, the urban trickster whose incarnation of pimp, bookmaker, preacher, and conjure-man exploits the community's chronically unanswered needs.

The immobility in which the Invisible Man appears in the prologue and epilogue is in any case qualified. By his own account, he has sufficient access to the aboveground world to collide with the tall blond (blind) man. This collision—the result of two moving bodies attempting to occupy the same geographic space—elicits the significant exchange of words: "Perhaps because of the near darkness he saw me and called me an insulting name," which in turn incites what the protagonist represents as a violent rage consistent with white notions of black criminal tendencies, such tendencies as Bigger Thomas exemplifies: "Oh yes, I kicked him! And in my outrage I got out my knife and prepared to slit his throat, right there beneath the lamplight in the deserted street, holding him in the collar with one hand, and opening the knife with my teeth—when it occurred to me that the man had not *seen* me, actually; that he, as far as he knew, was in the midst of a walking nightmare!" (4). Up to the point at which the protagonist experiences a leap of empathy, this encounter suggests irreconcilable difference, the old Jeffersonian notion that black and white people cannot share space without one party rising up to exterminate the other. But given his sudden capacity to imagine the other from the inside out, the protagonist prefers to think of this clash as initiating a process of reconciliation. "Poor fool, poor blind fool, I thought with sincere compassion, mugged by an invisible man!" (5). The protagonist frames the incident as the genesis of the narrative to follow, in which compassion will vie with lingering outrage: "*He* bumped me, *he* insulted me" (14). But the attempt to explain is manifestly directed aboveground and across as well as within the color line. In remarking that "I don't live in Harlem but in a border area" (5), the protagonist reaffirms his residence in an interconnected world.

By the time the narrator has told the story of how he came to be so black and blue, he has clarified for his own purposes the logic by which such reconciliation must go forward: a radical interpretation of the "principle" of equality in diversity on which the country had (arguably) been founded. The "treachery" of the grandfather is none other than an appropriation of the core Jeffersonian tenet that David Walker, reading Jefferson against Jefferson, seized upon in his own brief moment of treason and would-be insurrection. The epilogue thus projects the protagonist's re-emergence in a shared public space governed by consensus, a geography that can accommodate all who agree on the meaning of the nation's founding principle. The proposition is not without problems. "Diversity," observes Barbara Foley, "the demographic ideal now enshrined by 'affirming the principle,' converts the American dilemma, that is, its past and present practice of racism, into the basis of American exceptionalism, indeed national redemption." Accordingly, "the Negro stands forth as a metonymy of the nation as a whole, what Ellison would later call the contribution of the 'harsh discipline' of African American experience to the 'American heritage.' "[25] Ellison's utopian conclusion begs the question of how, in a country still two years away from the *Brown v. Board of Education* ruling, might the segregated nations-within converge: does this novel propose that the process begins with such testimony as its narrator has compiled?[26] Such acts of witness certainly aspire to citizenly participation, but the novel's specifically political valence remains ambiguous at best. Aesthetically, Ellison has drawn on the resource of modernist and existentialist expression to situate this testimony among a cosmopolitan, multinational, multiethnic readership.[27] The novel's learned allusiveness to an American and European literary heritage petitions the reader to shelve the book among the canonical works of the Western tradition as the latter was academically determined in the Cold War era.[28] On the wide-ranging lower frequencies, Ellison might imagine diverse reading publics, but it takes a well-schooled reader to appreciate this book's frame of reference.[29]

A crossover success, *Invisible Man* garnered the 1953 National Book Award for fiction, emerging victorious from a field that included Steinbeck's *East of Eden* and Hemingway's *The Old Man and the Sea*. Arnold Rampersad deems Ellison "lucky in having three young progressive Jewish writers as a majority on the panel," two of whom—Saul Bellow and Alfred Kazin—qualified as friends.[30] The politics of the National Book Award would nevertheless remain cautious and conservative. Despite the steady emergence of African American writers in the postwar era and equally steady expansion of their readerships, thirty years would pass before another African American author would win this award in any category: Alice Walker for *The Color Purple*.

"Here in this wilderness of North America"

In the blush of conversion to Elijah Muhammad's interpretation of Islam, Malcolm X wrote the mayor of Boston, the governor of Massachusetts, and the president of the United States, Harry S. Truman, proclaiming the truth that had illuminated his inner man while incarcerated in a Concord, Massachusetts, prison. Transferred from the cell block of Concord to the more communal structure of the experimental Norfolk Prison Colony, he had begun a self-directed education in the prison library, working through whole shelves of history, philosophy, and sociology, recovering in the process an ability to write syntactically sound sentences in a legible hand. As he recounts this moment in the *Autobiography*, chapter 11 ("Saved"), he had taken his first decisive steps toward spiritual and intellectual rehabilitation. Already in possession of what he regarded as the critical explanation of his miserable condition, an explanation to which his voluminous reading all seemed to lend support, he was eager to share his newfound enlightenment with the white authorities for whom such insight must serve as an indictment. "I hand-scratched to them how the white man's society was responsible for the black man's condition in this wilderness of North America."[31] The locational phrase—"this wilderness of North America"—derives from Allah's supposed message to Wallace D. Fard, conveyed to Elijah Muhammad when Fard commanded him to awaken and unite the "Lost-Found Nation of Islam" (164) in the wilderness to which the slave trade had abducted America's "so-called Negroes." Malcolm chooses the verb "hand-scratched" to emphasize his naive enthusiasm and the crudeness of means by which he would publish the truth that has transformed his world, speaking that truth to white people whose attention could hardly be diverted by a letter with a penitentiary's return address.[32] But the geographical understanding of the black person's place in the New World that accompanies Elijah Muhammad's teaching is the foundation on which Malcolm builds what will become a much more nuanced understanding of his historical and contemporary situation.

"Wilderness" figures as a key term in the Nation of Islam's message to black Americans as well as that message's transformative effect on Malcolm X. Its usage reflects the appropriation of what in origin is a profoundly Eurocentric word, applied by English settlers to a landmass without clear boundaries, natural or political. That landmass abounded in danger but also potentiality for Europeans who presumed that such territory was theirs for the planting of Christian communities. As a heuristic in the education of Malcolm X, "wilderness of North America" invokes a historical context that predates the United States as nation-state and that highlights the slave trade and Middle Passage as the foundational history of the New World. In the long view of Elijah Muhammad's Afrocentrist perspective, the "Lost-Found Nation of Islam" is the legitimate and recuperative community for African Americans, whose U.S. citizenship is and always has been illusory. Except for the phrasing's overtly scriptural overtones, the "Lost-Found Nation" is consistent with the Garveyite nationalism that Malcolm's father advocated and to which Malcolm was exposed in early childhood. Even after he leaves the Nation of Islam, the vision of African America as a nation determined and constrained by its Middle Passage entry informs not only the liberating message he would convey to black people but also the jeremiad he preaches to the white heirs of Europe's violence against Africa: "Any intelligent, honest, objective person cannot fail to realize that this white man's slave trade, and his subsequent devilish actions, are directly *responsible* for not only the *presence* of this black man in America, but also for the *condition* in which we find this black man here" (271). Such pronouncements emphasize the degree to which black people have been forcibly displaced from one continent to another, only to occupy North American space under more or less brutally carceral conditions.

In the broader context of the *Autobiography*, "wilderness" encourages us to examine Malcolm's rural origins, the childhood that preceded his hustler's acculturation to Roxbury and Harlem and his canonized role as spokesperson for the black urban North. With chapter 1, "Nightmare," the action begins in what most readers would register as the nation's pastoral hinterland (Nebraska), where events that might appear more stereotypically "southern" (especially in 1965, when the book first appeared) than "western" play out: "When my mother was pregnant with me, she told me later, a party of hooded Ku Klux Klan riders galloped up to our home in Omaha, Nebraska, one night. Surrounding the house, brandishing their shotguns and rifles, they shouted for my father to come out" (1). Malcolm's father, the Reverend Earl Little, had made himself persona non grata for preaching the doctrine of Marcus Garvey and its defiance of white institutional dominance of black people. When Malcolm's mother explains that he is not at home, the Klansmen order the family to vacate before galloping "around the house, shattering every window pane with their gun butts" (1). The *Autobiography* thus opens with the Littles being driven from the land.

As a follower of Garvey, Malcolm's father concedes that North America is not the appointed place for people of African descent. "He believed, as did Marcus Garvey, that freedom, independence and self-respect could never be achieved by the Negro in America, and that therefore the Negro should leave America to the white man and return to his African land of origin" (2). At the same time Malcolm writes that, in moving to the countryside outside of Lansing, Michigan, "my father wanted to find a place where he could raise our own food and perhaps build a business" inasmuch as "Garvey stressed becoming independent of the white man" (3). Realistically, one might sooner achieve a life of independence within hostile American territory than fulfill the mythic aspiration of a return to Africa. During the period of the family's comparatively self-subsistent existence in rural Michigan, the child Malcolm receives permission to cultivate his own "little plot" (8), and his memory of this activity provides a glimpse into his personality on the rare occasion in which he is not subject to some present or imminent harassment. Prior to his hajj and the experience, in Mecca, of oneness with fellow Muslims, Allah, and the creation, his recollection of tending his garden in the solitude of the land counts as the one moment in the *Autobiography* when he depicts himself as at home, terrestrially and cosmically: "Sometimes when I had everything straight and clean for my things to grow, I would lie down on my back between two rows, and I would gaze up in the blue sky at the clouds moving and think all kinds of things" (9). In *Black Boy (American Hunger)*, a narrative similarly scant of childhood joys, Wright likewise associates peace and contentment with solitary moments in garden settings—as though to emphasize the innocence poor black children manage to preserve despite their exposure to violence and privation.[33]

Following the murder of his father, Malcolm loses the occasion of any such pastoral tropes. With the household's economic collapse and the psychological decline of his mother, the Littles become wards of the state, and the white welfare workers invade and take over—"the state white people always in our house" (162)—placing the mother in the state mental hospital (another instance of the carceral theme) and assigning the children to various foster homes. By the time Malcolm has reached adolescence, he has experienced bereavement and dispossession; the popularity he enjoys among white classmates (chap. 2, "Mascot") only temporarily masks his relegation to underclass standing. The narrator's depiction of his trip to Boston to visit his half sister, Ella, provides an opportunity for the adult to limn the alien status to which the young man had become accustomed: "From my seat in—you guessed it—the back of the bus, I gawked out of the window at white man's America rolling past for what seemed a month, but must have been only a day and a half" (35–36). The phrasing reflects the adult's (if not the youth's) sense of having only marginal space on public transportation and none at all in the America the vehicle traverses—a continental expanse magnified by the excruciatingly slow passage of time, during which he must keep to his assigned place.

After he has moved to the East Coast, first to Boston, later to New York City, Malcolm's occupation of space falls into several genres. As a resident, he lives in established African American neighborhoods (Roxbury, Harlem) where he rents and does not own. As a participant in legitimate economies, he works menial jobs in confined local venues (shining shoes in the Rose State Ballroom men's room, serving ice cream behind a drugstore counter, waiting tables at Small's Paradise) as well as cramped mobile sites (dining cars on the New York, New Haven, and Hartford Railroad and Seaboard Route). As a participant in criminal economies, he delivers reefers to uptown and downtown locations as well as to points in distant cities he is able to reach on his railroad pass; he leads johns to uptown prostitution houses and burgles the homes of the well-to-do. Space by day presents barriers and constraints that space by night does not: in his hustling days Malcolm is far more mobile after dark. Criminal activity requires specialized mapping procedures, and the *Autobiography* addresses in detail how Malcolm and his accomplices understood the spaces they were to enter as thieves. On the basis of his experience as one who stood outside of houses in the night weighing the risks of entry, he even advises readers wishing to discourage burglary while they sleep "to leave a bathroom light on all night" (147). Finally, as one who participates in social rituals, Malcolm occupies space as a lindy-hopper in the spatiotemporality of live dance music.

It is as a thief, finally, that he enters the criminal justice system, having sought the repair of a watch that the jeweler identifies as stolen, and is sent to the penitentiary with a sentence whose harshness reflects, in his telling, the fact that young white middle-class women served as his gang's accomplices.[34] In addition to documenting the three prisons he inhabits during the seven years he serves of his ten-year sentence—Charlestown State, where he is placed in solitary, Concord, where he first receives tidings of Islam, and Norfolk—he presents himself more categorically as having occupied "the white man's prison" (167), a condition in which Elijah Muhammad, himself an ex-convict, speaks to him, and to which all black people might attest inasmuch as their life in the wilderness of North America is led under one or another form of incarceration. The centrality of the carceral metaphor emerges in chapter 17, "Mecca," which recounts the hajj Malcolm undertakes after breaking free of the confinements and hypocrisies the Nation of Islam had come to represent. Embracing a mobility that has as its object an immersion in the nonwhite postcolonial world, Malcolm finds himself in a Muslim community that transcends the color lines that seem so absolute in North America. Joining an international body of pilgrims in Cairo on the last layover before the final flight to Mecca, Malcolm is transformed by a spectacle of inclusion: "Throngs of people, obviously Muslims from everywhere, bound on the pilgrimage, were hugging and embracing. They were of all complexions, the whole atmosphere was of warmth and friendliness. The feeling hit me that there wasn't really any color problem here. *The effect was as though I had just stepped out of prison*" (328; emphasis added). In an epistle sent to assistants at his independent mosque, he lays out the changes he has undergone as a result of the interethnic fellowship to which his pilgrimage has introduced him. Signing the letter El-Hajj Malik El-Shabazz, he directs that his statement be released to the press, for at this point in his meteoric career he commands readership among whites at every point on the political spectrum as well as a black community caught up in what Malcolm has brought to the civil rights movement: a voice—urban, Northern, and militant—contrasting with that of Martin Luther King Jr.

Through Alex Haley's service as amanuensis, Malcolm X enters into the as-told-to project with the knowledge that he speaks to large readerships on either side of the color line—those (blacks, whites) who support his role in articulating American racial injustice as well as those (blacks, whites) who regard his activities as divisive and demagogic.[35] Previous to their collaboration in fashioning the *Autobiography*, as Haley documents in the book's epilogue, he had consulted Malcolm X in preparing an article on the Nation of Islam for *Reader's Digest* and had conversed with him at length, tape recorder running, to produce the *Playboy* interview.[36] Exerting the fascination of the charismatic iconoclast, speaking for urban African America and presenting a contrast to the Southern Christian pacifism of Martin Luther King Jr. Malcolm X had become a high-profile media figure by the time he and Haley began their collaboration, the 1959 Mike Wallace–Louis Lomax television documentary *The Hate That Hate Produced* having projected Elijah Muhammad's gifted protégé into white middle-class living rooms. In the *Autobiography*, Malcolm would express his astonishment over the evidence of white admiration, even adulation, of his public persona. Following his rupture with the Nation of Islam and experience of colorblind fellowship during his hajj, he would express a tentative openness to white American support but remain wary of convergence—no map for him even came close to reconciling white and black geographies. The death he predicts in chapter 1 will indeed prevent him from beholding the fruits of his collaboration with Haley; to a readership that possesses the *Autobiography* as a posthumous text, his assassination in the Audubon Ballroom finalizes his inaccessibility. Through Haley, Malcolm X speaks consciously to a broad, international, multiethnic audience and does so with the uncanny recognition that by the time of the book's launch, his words set down in the Grove Press first edition might well be those of a voice from beyond the grave.

"Letter from a region in my mind"

Nine months older than Malcolm X and a half generation younger than Wright and Ellison, James Baldwin differs from all three in that his life begins in the urban North. Although he characterizes the Harlem of his childhood as a Southern city populated by adults who, like his mother and stepfather, arrived in the first Great Migration, Baldwin's own escape paths do not fit a South-to-North or rural-to-urban narrative. Citing what he calls Wright's "odyssey" (the trajectories of Ellison and Malcolm X fit the same epic template), Baldwin reflects, "I have not, in my own flesh, traveled, and paid the price of such a journey, from the Deep South to Chicago to New York to Paris."[37] He makes this concession in 1961, a moment when the civil rights movement was directing national attention to a stridently white supremacist South. Although Baldwin's cartography cannot be framed in hard departures and definitive arrivals, he has much to say about his own journey and the costs incurred to stay or to leave. Flight, from Harlem to Greenwich Village or from the United States to Europe, is a recurrent theme in much of his memoir writing, but a Harlem remembered and a Harlem revisited likewise recurrently engross his attention.[38] His several accounts of sojourning in Europe culminate in the recognition that the black American expatriate is never free of a troubled heritage and that character (white or black) formed on American soil cannot assimilate to Europe or Africa. Saint-Paul-de-Vence may have become his permanent residence and the site of his last days, but as distant as southern France is from Harlem, Baldwin would describe himself in the late essay "The Price of the Ticket" (1985) as "mysteriously shipwrecked forever, in the Great New World" (842).

Baldwin's inability to reconcile himself with a conflicted national identity that he nonetheless cannot jettison is a dominant theme of his travel writing. Any idea that he could shed that identity along with the daily aggravation of residing in his white supremacist homophobic homeland is the first casualty of his life abroad. As he explains in the introduction to *Nobody Knows My Name: More Notes of a Native Son*, a volume that enacts a symbolic homecoming, geographical flight prompted recognition of what it would be impossible for him to flee. "In America, the color of my skin had stood between myself and me; in Europe, that barrier was down." Self-confrontation in the international context leads him to see himself as one irreversibly formed by American conditions: the problem of having been shaped by the vectors of a structural oppression "was not solved because I had removed myself from the social forces which menaced me—anyway, these forces had become interior, and I had dragged them across the ocean with me" (135). In comparing his odyssey with Richard Wright's, Baldwin portrays himself as one who calls the bluff of any notion that flight offers genuine liberation. In the younger man's assessment, Wright "was fond of referring to Paris as the 'city of refuge'—which it certainly was, God knows, for the likes of us. But it was not a city of refuge for the French, still less for anyone belonging to France; and it would not have been a city of refuge for us if we had not been armed with American passports. It did not seem worthwhile to have fled the native fantasy only to embrace a foreign one" (249). Although he gravitates to Paris like many Americans under the spell of an interwar expatriate mythology, Baldwin's experience of French urban poverty strips romance from the bohemian adventure. The account of his five-day incarceration, "Equal in Paris," collected in *Notes of a Native Son*, stands in stark opposition to the Paris of Hemingway. But Baldwin's critique of Wright's attachment to Paris is less important for demystifying the City of Lights than for its categorical dismissal of geographical refuge.

Baldwin consistently argues that flight, South-to-North or U.S.-to-Europe, does little to effect deliverance. He establishes this thesis early in his career with the title essay of *Notes of a Native Son* in the person of his embittered and self-isolating stepfather, whose migration from New Orleans to Harlem has substituted one life of poverty for another and, in so doing, hardened a chronic resentment. In the same essay Baldwin depicts his own initiation into what, in "Stranger in the Village," he terms "the rage of the disesteemed" (121) while working in a defense plant in Belle Mead, New Jersey, his first encounter with overtly Jim Crow forms of discrimination. Rage induces him to seek such confrontations as the episode that unfolds in the whites-only restaurant in Trenton, where he seats himself knowing full well he will be refused service but is perilously unable to predict the violence of his response. After heaving a water glass at the hapless waitress who acts as the minion of a discriminatory policy, for the first time in his experience as a young black man he literally has to run for his life.[39] The incident in turn prompts his recognition that "my life, my *real* life, was in danger, and not from anything other people might do but from the hatred I carried in my own heart" (72). This leads to the further perception that the Harlem to which he returns is a hive of hatred and anger, erupting in such futile albeit necessary expressions as the 1943 riot (a point of overlap between *Notes of a Native Son* and *Invisible Man*), the collective and public event to which Baldwin juxtaposes his stepfather's and his own private agony. Suppressing his inner Bigger Thomas, the Baldwin of "Notes of a Native Son" brings his raging core into a state of truce with insufferable conditions.[40] This essay serves as a prelude to Baldwin's flight to Europe, but he brings to the retrospection that "Notes" represents the knowledge that life outside the United States provides only a distant perspective on the immutable nature of a conflicted identity, confirming the degree to which his American formation is the burden he takes with him everywhere. This knowledge shadows the narrative in which he buries his stepfather and begins his lifelong exile from the Harlem homescape—a homescape to which he nevertheless returns again and again.

No specifically geographical refuge exists for the black American, who cannot evade a conflict-born identity: this is the special argument of "Stranger in the Village," an essay that also argues—importantly—that no refuge exists for white Americans who wish to pretend that they do not have a historically compelling relationship with their black fellow Americans. For Baldwin, situated amid Switzerland's "absolutely alabaster landscape" (138), the village in question, Loèche-les-Bains, not only figures as the farthest point attainable from his native Harlem but also as the inmost circle of the folk culture from which a European, white supremacist, colonizing civilization emanates. So far is this village from the interethnic contact zones and so novel is the phenomenon of black humanity to the village's isolated residents that Baldwin declares them innocent of ill will when they palpate his skin and hair or when the children cry out "Neger" at his approach. No possible refuge exists for him here, but neither can Baldwin look upon Africa as offering sanctuary from the formative agony of the American experience. From the polar vantage of the Swiss village, then, Baldwin articulates his black American birthright. Speaking as one whose pursuit of genealogical origins is "abruptly arrested by the signature on the bill of sale which served as the entrance paper for his ancestor" (125), he specifies that birthright in "Princes and Powers" (1957), an essay that first appears in *Encounter* and later in *Nobody Knows My Name*:

> We had been born in a society, which, in a way quite inconceivable for Africans, and no longer real for Europeans, was open, and, in a sense which has nothing to do with justice or injustice, was free. It was a society, in short, in which nothing was fixed and we had therefore been born to a greater number of possibilities, wretched as these possibilities seemed at the instant of our birth. Moreover, the land of

> our father's exile had been made, by that travail, our home. . . . [N] othing, in any case, could take away our title to the land which we, too, had purchased with our blood. (147)

"Stranger in the Village" serves as the foundation for such pronouncements in the way that it stages the author's out-of-place ontology; for if he is unable to look upon Africa as affording anything like home—indeed he is agonizingly more at home in Loèche-les-Bains, at the center of a Europe whose colonial interventions have fashioned his destiny as an author of English prose—he is equally unable to see in the United States a future that will not continue to extract the blood of natives like himself who already hold title to the land. "Stranger" concludes with the affirmation that white and black people, while anything but reconciled to one another, have entered a historical process by which the common identity that differentiates Americans from their African and European forebears will continue to evolve for good or for ill. Just as the African homeland is inaccessible to African Americans except as a fantasy of origin, so Baldwin affirms that "no road whatever" can return European Americans "back to the simplicity of this European village where white men still have the luxury of looking on me as a stranger"—for in the intimacy of a historically violent relationship, "I am not," he asserts, "really, a stranger any longer for any American alive" (129).

Baldwin's "not really a stranger" foregrounds issues of proximity, author to reader, and although the European-sojourning Harlem native has set himself at a distance from U.S. readerships regardless of color, the essay so pointedly identifies differences between white Europeans and white Americans that his "any American alive" has special application to those who trace an exclusively European descent. As does *Invisible Man* and *Playing in the Dark*, "Stranger in the Village" posits an intimacy between black and white Americans beneath a veneer of strangeness and separation, invoking a history that has fashioned Americans as a united and conflictive people whose identity is exactly constituted by the other's "human weight and complexity" (127), a condition citizens deny at their peril. Incalculably remote but insistently near, Baldwin speaks in this essay on the lower frequencies, which, hugging the earth, travel the greatest distance. He would speak on those frequencies throughout his career.

Nobody Knows My Name (1961) incorporates two essays that extend the European travelogue ("The Meaning of What It Means to Be an American" and the aforementioned "Princes and Powers," his account of the 1956 Conference of Negro-African Writers and Artists held at the Sorbonne). Beginning, however, with "Fifth Avenue, Uptown: A Letter from Harlem," Baldwin enacts a symbolic homecoming to neighborhood and national origins, a return that includes, in "Nobody Knows My Name: A Letter from the South," an account of his first trip below the Mason-Dixon Line. In the first of these essays, "Fifth Avenue, Uptown," Baldwin surveys the microlocality of childhood, a neighborhood "bounded by Lenox Avenue on the west, the Harlem River on the east, 135th Street on the north, and 130th Street on the south. We never lived beyond these boundaries; this is where we grew up" (170). What principally attracts his attention in this essay, besides the grocery store that remains in business and the shoe-repair proprietor who has stood for decades in the same shop window, are the projects—Riverton Homes in particular—built by the state and private interests as an answer to the housing needs of the poor but which dramatize the spectacle of a people immobilized in poverty. The projects' residents, having moved en masse from the South, ancestrally if not in person, "do not escape Jim Crow: they merely encounter another, not-less-deadly variety" (177). This observation resonates further as Baldwin reports from the "Old Country" that is the South. The Northern-born descendant assumes "a position similar to that of the son of the Italian emigrant who finds himself in Italy, near the village where his father first saw the light of day. Both are in countries they have never seen, but which they cannot fail to recognize" (197). Bringing to this sojourn an ever-brooding historical awareness and a sharp analytical eye, Baldwin reads the Southern land- and cityscape in the light of his memories of a Harlem populated by émigrés facing alternate forms of structural white oppression.

Baldwin's "letter from Harlem" and "letter from the South" position him as roving correspondent, a role he maintained throughout his career in his nonfiction prose. From the moment he leaves Harlem for Greenwich Village, he assumes the guise of one constantly on the move. Although New York would serve as the node through which his writings were dispatched to a large educated readership, he would never identify a fixed abode that might constitute the symbolic antithesis of the site of original bondage—no "free North" marked his successful flight from a "slave South." "Down at the Cross," the second essay collected in *The Fire Next Time*, bears the subtitle "Letter from a Region in My Mind," and that region substitutes for anything like a geographical placement with a postal address. Harlem, to be sure, remains the lodestar to which his imagination constantly turns, and never so intensely as it does in *The Fire Next Time*, but the intimacy of deep memory is a function of his remote post-Harlem location, and when he writes of the old 131st Street block in *Nobody Knows My Name*, he does so as something of a tourist. Rejecting Paris as refuge except in fantasy, he establishes the closest thing to a permanent residence in the south of France, meanwhile affirming the inalienable relationship of African Americans to European Americans as well as to the continent on which the national mixed-race destiny is to be settled. Thus he speaks, in "Princes and Powers," of "our title to the land which we, too, had purchased with our blood" (147), a phrase that finds an echo in everyone from David Walker, Martin Delany, and Frederick Douglass to W. E. B. Du Bois, James Weldon Johnson, Malcolm X, and Toni Morrison.[41] In "The Price of the Ticket" (1985) he could reaffirm, further, that "Europe has never been, and cannot be, a useful or valid touchstone for the American experience because America is not, and never can be, white" (836). But the United States nevertheless does not yet afford the conditions of what to Baldwin is a sustainable residence, and in that same essay, written in France, he declares, "My diaspora continues, the end is not in sight" (841). Diaspora for Baldwin is double, North America figuring as a secondary originary scene.

Migratory and exilic as Baldwin may be, he would command powerful access to major American publishing channels from the beginning of his career forward. He could write with confidence that his testimonial letters would not fail to arrive even if they should be met with various forms of incomprehension. Knopf and Beacon published his first books, and Dial Press published those that followed. He would place essays in such widely distributed periodicals as the *Partisan Review*, *Harper's Magazine*, *Esquire*, the *New York Times Magazine*, the *Saturday Review*, the *New Yorker*, and *Playboy*. Through these outlets his work reached a white educated demographic; whereas he never lacked an African American readership, the prestige of his literary placements might well suggest a degree of co-optation, the result of his recognition as *the* black public intellectual at a time when one such personage fulfilled the needs of white American media culture.[42] Baldwin pressed back against any suggestion that he was the mouthpiece of a liberal but moneyed establishment—a power structure that, even in its most enlightened and egalitarian representatives, luxuriated in hereditary white privilege—and no doubt the mobile epistolary position he assumes in his essays about race in America preserves a distance between that uncompromised "region" in his mind and the readerships served by an elite mainstream publishing apparatus. By that means he would seem to insist that the map on which he would meet his white fellow Americans remains to be drawn.

Chapter 6

✦

Next Worlds

Toni Morrison and Octavia Butler

Born a half-generation and continent apart, Toni Morrison and Octavia Butler achieved celebrity as contributors to a literary flourishing that dates from the waning years of the civil rights era. Coinciding with the emergence of the Black Power, Black Arts, and Black Studies movements, narratives of this period frequently offer long, layered, cartographic views of black experience in the New World.[1] The historical sweep of works such as Margaret Walker's *Jubilee* (1966), Ernest J. Gaines's *The Autobiography of Miss Jane Pittman* (1971), Gayl Jones's *Corregidora* (1975), Alex Haley's *Roots* (1976), Ishmael Reed's *Flight to Canada* (1976), David Bradley's *The Chaneysville Incident* (1981), August Wilson's *The Pittsburgh Cycle* (1982–2005), Sherley Anne Williams's *Dessa Rose* (1986), and Charles Johnson's *Middle Passage* (1990) prompts examination of the paths by which generations of black people, bond and free, have migrated across the face of North America, and the countergeographies with which they have met entrapment, exclusion, and the threat of extermination. *Kindred* (1979) and *Beloved* (1987), two works discussed at length in the following pages, figure prominently among the list of titles that collectively define the neo-slave narrative—a genre that, as Colson Whitehead's *The Underground Railroad* (2016) demonstrates, retains its relevance well into the twenty-first century. But neo-slave motifs are not limited to narratives that invoke the past in the manner of historical fiction. Whether Morrison retells the story of Margaret Garner, revisits slave life in the Hudson Valley, or explores the homecoming of a Korean War veteran, she foregrounds *displacement* as a feature of slavery and its enduring heritage in all of her work. Similarly, Butler understands enslavement as the repressed but unforgotten past that destabilizes the present and shapes a future in which multiethnic demographic convergence generates fresh color lines—a future, moreover, in which political, social, and environmental convulsions produce new imperatives of flight.

Taking as its focus selected works of Morrison and Butler, this chapter explores two distinct orientations toward African American history and geography. For Morrison, the trans-Appalachian interior figures as natal terrain. Although she sets *Jazz* in Harlem, *Paradise* in Oklahoma, and *God Help the Child* in California, her work foundationally probes the slave heritage as it informs unincorporated black communities scattered among the semirural, semiurban landscapes that tumble between the Ohio River and southern shores of the Great Lakes, conjuring the oral histories of microlocalities that do not appear on white official maps.[2] With the Bottom of fictional Medallion, Ohio (*Sula*), Not Doctor Street, Southside, and Blood Bank of an anonymous Michigan city (*Song of Solomon*), or rural Bluestone Road on the periphery of Cincinnati (*Beloved*), Morrison articulates African American sites that remain largely invisible to white surveillance and that provide robust if vulnerable opportunities of refuge, habitation, and community.[3] For her part, Butler reanimates the slave past and visualizes a slave future from a West Coast perspective. Multiethnic Los Angeles and a predominantly white Pacific Northwest serve as backdrops for what she imagines as a continuous evolution of American identities, even as vestiges of white supremacist ideology vengefully persist. In contrast with Wright, Ellison, Malcolm X, and Baldwin, Morrison and Butler address the theme of black displacement with pointed reference to female experience—specifically, the complications that pregnancy and motherhood impose on the fugitive condition. Both authors differentiate a comparatively light-footed male nomadism from a typically burdened female embarkation, and both create female characters who seek necessary stasis. Yet each develops memorable protagonists (Pilate Dead, Sethe Garner, Dana Franklin, Lauren Oya Olamina, and Asha Vere) whose identities emerge as resourceful at-risk travelers.[4]

This chapter's title, "Next Worlds," reflects the spectral and prophetic geographies to which Morrison and Butler draw our attention: for Morrison, the ghost dimensions or death spaces that environ, haunt, taunt, and support the living; for Butler, the topographies of a slave past but also those of a catastrophic future in which the will to survive compels the search for extraterrestrial escape routes. "Next" in this context is at once a temporal and spatial concept. It is fitting that this study concludes with Morrison's contemporary meditations on the Middle Passage and Butler's enlistment of the slave-narrative past to write the history of the future.

"Picking around the edges of the world"

Beloved (1987) famously transports the reader to the postslavery past in the decade following Emancipation. *Song of Solomon* (1977), by contrast, conjures that past as it appears to characters caught up in the turbulence of the mid-twentieth century. The earlier novel develops a retrospective survey of the geographies of flight, reclaiming a heritage from the amnesiac present of black urban-industrial Michigan in the late 1950s and early 1960s. Beginning with a portrait of the feckless Milkman Dead and his dysfunctional, dismembered family, the novel traces his bloodline's migratory path back to the black Virginia village that exists not only as a site of family provenance but as the New World nexus point with the mythic African origin. Drawing upon traditions of the Flying Africans, who, at the signal of a male magician-elder, ascend and fly home to Africa from the fields where they have been set to labor, Morrison undertakes a fresh elaboration of the slave-narrative motif in which "flight" stands in predicate relationship to the verbs "flee" and "fly," bracketing the diegesis between the suicidal leap of the insurance agent, Robert Smith, in the opening chapter and Milkman's liberating if fatal plunge in the novel's final scene.[5] As Milkman shakes off the lassitude of a privileged middle-class life to embark on a reverse genealogical journey, he reconstructs the escape routes trod by his father and aunt and discovers the experiment in land ownership that forms a triumphant if short-lived chapter of his family's history.

Published ten years after the 1967 Detroit riot, *Song of Solomon* at once reexamines the recent (1960s) past and the sedimentary heritage of Reconstruction, post-Reconstruction, and twentieth-century South-to-North migration.[6] Unlike the works discussed thus far in *Geographies of Flight*, this novel's testimony emanates from a third-person selectively omniscient narrative voice, but by dating Robert Smith's leap February 18, 1931, her own birthday, Morrison signals an autobiographical investment in the saga she will unfold. Milkman, born February 19, figures as the author's exact contemporary if not imaginary fraternal twin. His odyssey to rural Pennsylvania and Virginia takes place in fall 1963, after the September 15th Birmingham church bombing but before the assassination of John F. Kennedy. Guitar, Milkman's politically astute friend and older brother surrogate, characterizes the then situation of black America as one of virtual statelessness: "Where's the money, the state, the country to finance our justice," he asks with general reference to the history of white violence and, more specifically, to the targeting of the Sixteenth Street Baptist Church and his commitment to exact symmetrical retribution in the random slaughter of four white girls. On the question of black testimonial personhood—a matter, as we have seen, always at issue when African American authors in any genre write in anticipation of a readership across the color line—Guitar echoes a grievance Equiano had expressed two centuries earlier: "There are places right now where a Negro still can't testify against a white man. Where the judge, the jury, the court, are legally bound to ignore anything a Negro has to say."[7] Milkman recoils from the spectacle of Guitar's militant extremism, but although the novel implicitly condemns his solutions, it leaves intact the credibility of his analysis. It thus speaks for those whom, in 1977 as in earlier decades, the state can officially ignore.

As for Milkman, civil rights agitation and Black Power insurgency exist at the edge of his self-absorbed world. His position as the son of the city's leading slumlord insulates him from anything like political engagement. Through much of *Song of Solomon* he presents a case of arrested development, but from the long view we can see that a subliminal need to conduct and resolve four generations of family business impedes his potential as activist. Abstracted as Milkman mostly remains, however, he, along with Morrison's readership, will be exposed to a historico-political education.

For the reader, that education begins with the opening paragraph, where we learn not only about Robert Smith's proposed flight from the whites-only Mercy Hospital to the far side of Lake Superior but also of the black community's ongoing contest with white city fathers over occupation and designation of shared urban space. Robert Smith's gesture invokes both the legend of the Flying Africans and historical flights to Canada, the culmination of a fugitive's successful Underground Railroad passage. The apologetic tone with which he declares his intention to attempt the feat—"Please forgive me. I loved you all" (3)—makes clear that his statement also functions as the suicide note of one who has lived under several conditions of exile and as a veteran, we later learn, of the secret guerilla war to which Guitar will be recruited. As an agent of the North Carolina Mutual Life Insurance Company, Robert Smith has professional but presumably also personal ties to the South, as do his clients living in the segregated city's black Southside. The first paragraph foregrounds the Southern origin of the city's black residents in accounting for how "Mains Avenue" became "Doctor Street" and subsequently "Not Doctor Street." Accordingly, after Milkman's grandfather, the first black physician, moves to a house on Mains Avenue, he is followed by other upwardly mobile black families, and the destination becomes known as "Doctor Street" among the local black community and the Southern relatives of intracity migrants. Thus "envelopes from Louisiana, Virginia, Alabama, and Georgia began to arrive addressed to people at house numbers on Doctor Street" (4). When white officials declare that Mains Avenue is "not Doctor Street," the black community reappropriates Mains Avenue by capitalizing the "n" in "not." In contrarian spirit, black residents likewise rename Mercy Hospital "No Mercy Hospital." The novel's opening paragraphs suggest that the black community succeeds incrementally in expanding its range over time: just as Milkman's grandfather is a "first" in breaching the barrier to black residence on Mains Avenue, so Milkman is a "first" inasmuch as his birth takes place in the hitherto exclusively white-serving hospital, a consequence of his mother's labor being brought on by the traumatic spectacle of Robert Smith's plunge. But separate and unequal persists as the regime under which the action will go forward.

Although Milkman is born by accident in Mercy Hospital, it is ironically apt that he enters the world at a site where blacks have hitherto been excluded. The grandson of Dr. Foster, local exemplar of black professional success, and son of Macon Dead, owner of a large swath of Southside real estate, he is destined to enjoy a geographic mobility that reflects his family's upward trend, a trajectory that functions to repress lessons in aggravated geography that form whole chapters of family history. His father, the would-be agent of that history's erasure, serves also as its first medium when, in an uncharacteristically reminiscent moment touched off by a dinner-table quarrel over Milkman's visit to Aunt Pilate's house (an alternate source of heritage information), he relates the story of Lincoln's Paradise, the farm created by Milkman's freedman grandfather, and his murder at the hands of white people who wanted his land. "Your father was a slave?" the twelve-year-old Milkman asks his father. "What kind of foolish question is that?" Macon replies, although the question itself is indicative of the distance Macon would insert between present and past. "Course he was. Who hadn't been in 1869?" (53). Having indulged in a brief backward glance in which he reveals the degree to which his life has been shaped by traumatic dispossession, Milkman's father encourages his son to regard the past as irrelevant to the present business of wealth accumulation: "Own things," he tells Milkman. "And let the things you own own other things" (55). The son thus absorbs an ethos that emphasizes liquidity, mobility, and leverage. Growing up on Mains Avenue, Milkman travels back and forth between his privileged residence and the business and pleasures of Southside; he can spend part of the day slumming and another participating in the social life of Honoré Island, a resort community for black professionals who, like his father, can afford the status marker of a vacation home. Later, when Milkman travels to Pennsylvania and Virginia in search of a mysterious patrimony, he commands the means to travel by airplane and bus, and he can even purchase a secondhand car as the need arises.

As his father's employee tasked with door-to-door rent collections, the young adult has business reasons for spending much of his time in the Southside, but as a child and adolescent he is drawn as an outsider to the district's street life, folk culture, and promise of forbidden pleasure. Guitar, a Southerner by birth, serves as his guide to pool hall, bar, and barbershop; he introduces him, moreover, to Milkman's own unapologetically Southern family, the matriarchal household of Macon's estranged sister, Pilate, whose granddaughter, Hagar, Milkman's first cousin twice removed, becomes an early and long-standing sexual partner. Milkman reciprocates Guitar's invitations by introducing him to the Honoré set, but Guitar is too hostile to the idea of a black bourgeoisie to feel at home in an upscale setting. If Macon Dead's business practices are any measure, the bourgeoisie's wealth derives from the exploitation of the black underclass. "He behaves like a white man," Guitar observes of Macon (223), for as a child he had watched his grandmother fail to convince the landlord not to evict her and her grandchildren from one of his properties, yet another instance in a life of forced displacement.[8]

Whereas Milkman's comparatively free range makes him oblivious to zones and borderlines, Guitar's experience of wide space and cartographic constraint fosters critical consciousness with respect to mobility and privilege. As the two friends enter manhood, Guitar exposes Milkman to his ever more frequent moments of ideological reflection: "There are things that interest me," he remarks to the younger man in one of several philosophical dialogues, "that don't interest you," and the subsequent exchange comes down to the question of placement—geographic and social:

> "How you know they don't interest me?"
> "I know you. Been knowing you. You got your high-tone friends and your picnics on Honoré Island and you can afford to spend fifty percent of your brainpower thinking about a piece of ass. You got that red-headed bitch and you got a Southside bitch and no telling what in between."
> "I don't believe it. After all these years you putting me down because of where I live?"
> "Not where you live—where you hang out. You don't live nowhere. Not Not Doctor Street *or* Southside." (103)

Unmindfully mobile in his pleasure-seeking ways, Milkman has no place that is specifically his. In the vast underprivileged stretches of black America, he is a tourist, indifferent to the particularities of place. By contrast, Guitar, whose tally of displacements includes South-to-North migration and summer trips to visit still-in-the-South family as well as Northern evictions, has a very clear sense of where he lives and with whom. His extensive travels have provided him with oppositional perspectives regarding what differentiates place from place. In a subsequent conversation with his younger friend, after noting the historical and sociopolitical nature of any proper geographical understanding, he deconstructs the North/South binary. "Goddam, Milk, I do believe my whole life's geography. . . . For example, I live in the North now. So the first question come to mind is North of what? Why, north of the South. So North exists because South does. But does that mean North is different from South? No way! South is just south of North" (114). Southside, as a Northern black ghetto populated by Southern migrants subject to arbitrary arrest and interrogation, corroborates Guitar's observation. When white police stop the two men after they pilfer the skeleton from Pilate's house, Milkman experiences what it means to be racially profiled and must explain to his father that his supposed status as Macon Dead's son would not have spared him the ordeal.

Whether Milkman will acquire a place to live in the course of the novel remains an open question: when we last see him, he is in motion as a flying, falling body. But long before he embarks on the quest for gold that culminates with his arrival in Shalimar, Virginia, the ancestral Southern seat, he first entertains sensations of placement in the visit to Aunt Pilate's Southside home that occasions the quarrel at the conclusion of which Macon tells Milkman about the lost family farm. In contrast with his grandfather's Not Doctor Street residence, a large house in which family members lead silent, repressed, isolated lives, Pilate's cramped domestic interior enforces human connection, and the space rings with laughter and song. His initial visit is a revelation: "Milkman was five feet seven then but it was the first time in his life that he remembered being completely happy" (47). Lacking electricity and indoor plumbing, Pilate's household operates according to a Southern rural subsistence economy in the midst of the Great Lakes conurbation.[9] Morrison thus presents another side of the black South, one that emphasizes female resourcefulness in the absence of men. Pilate, whose few essential belongings include a geography textbook, exemplifies in her own right a readiness to migrate, although she equally exhibits the power to create a home in the place where she chooses to rest. Drawn north by a desire to reunite with Macon and his household, "for the child, Hagar, needed family" (151), Pilate meets with her brother's outright repudiation. The businessman is embarrassed by her country ways; he suspects, moreover, that she has lost, squandered, or otherwise mishandled the bags of gold she refused to help remove from the cave and that he has come to regard, along with Lincoln's Heaven, as the lost patrilineal inheritance. By insisting that the twelve-year-old Milkman steer clear of Pilate, Macon concedes her power to seduce the boy to a view of the world antithetical to his doctrine of black capitalism. "Pilate can't teach you a thing you can use in this world," Macon observes while enjoining his son to "own things." "Maybe the next, but not this one" (55). However, it is not so much a "next" world as the anterior one that Pilate represents, an ancestral past and future placement that claims Milkman's fascination.[10]

This anterior world is one of suspended but retrievable connections. Having grown up in a rigidly patriarchal home where his mother and sisters press through routines of sterile activity (the cutting and stitching of the velvet red rose petals) but otherwise languish in solitude, Milkman is drawn to Pilate's house by intimations of a vibrant African American collective. Readers are provided a glimpse of this world when Pilate sings "Sugarman" in the novel's opening scene, a prelude to Robert Smith's plunge and Milkman's birth, but the latter's initiation coincides with his first visit to Darling Street, when Pilate draws Reba and Hagar into three-part harmony to console Hagar's chronic emotional hunger. In Pilate's house Milkman becomes acquainted with kinship as ongoing performance, as opposed to the history of family loss that he receives from a father who looks for compensation in male individualist pursuit of wealth. Moreover, in Pilate's house he senses the possibility of bonds he cannot experience in the male fellowship of the Southside community, among whom, as Macon Dead's son, he is ever the class alien. In Shalimar, Milkman will learn to hear Pilate's song as key to his genealogy and transindividual identity, but in the meantime the allure of black collective life takes exploitable and expendable form as Hagar's sexual accessibility. In Darling Street as in Southside generally, the son of privilege behaves as a tourist for whom connections remain superficial. In keeping with his father's predatory ethos, he will commit crimes against Pilate's household: the theft (with Guitar) of the green tarpaulin on Macon's mistaken suggestion that it contains the lost gold, but, more seriously, his abandonment of Hagar, whose emotional needs he refuses to acknowledge let alone fill, and who, lovesick, succumbs to the neglect with which the Dead men habitually treat the Dead women. Returning from Shalimar, however, Milkman is equipped at long last to recognize his errors and to atone for them.

The transformation that allows Milkman to seek atonement and deep connection with the anterior world Pilate represents comes about in the course of an extended itinerary that begins with his departure to Pennsylvania and ends with his return from Virginia, only to be followed by a second, final journey back to Shalimar in the company of Pilate and her father's skeletal remains.[11] Ostensibly, he undertakes the first leg of his journey motivated by customarily self-centered needs: if he can locate the cave in Danville, Pennsylvania, and recover the gold Macon insists must still be there, he can fashion a life independent of his father's business and apart from the home on Not Doctor Street where his mother and sisters steadily deliquesce. Dreams of treasure nourish his fantasy of escape from a life of privileged bondage, and on the airplane to Pittsburgh he experiences a predictable euphoria of flight. His encounter with the magical Circe in the dilapidated house of the white family responsible for the death of Macon Dead I, where Macon II and Pilate briefly hid (under conditions reminiscent of those chronicled by Linda Brent) before embarking on their own fugitive careers, signals an immersion in the ancestral narrative from which there can be no turning back—his odyssey has begun in earnest. The cave, predictably, yields no gold, and his beige suit and Florsheim shoes are ruined by the city man's inability to reckon with the deep foliage, rushing water, and rocky terrain he must cross in order to search it, but in conversation with Reverend Cooper and his cronies the night before he undertakes this trek he has learned about his heroic grandfather and the heroic figure his own father cut as a young man, and so patrimony as memory has already begun to replace patrimony as capital wealth.

Given the geographical themes of *Song of Solomon*, the lost farm epitomizes the predicament of black place and displacement. In the epic recollection of the older men, Lincoln's Paradise comes alive for Milkman not only as the birthright he has lost as his grandfather's descendent, but as the rightful inheritance of a black collective relegated to segregated parcels of a North America conceived from colonial times as the domain of an exclusionarily white nation. The freedmen living in Montour County regarded the farm as a real and symbolic countergeographical claim, a material refutation of the idea that black people must lead the lives of aliens and fugitives in the New World. Lincoln's Paradise accordingly

> spoke to them like a sermon. . . . "See? See what you can do? Never mind you can't tell one letter from another, never mind you born a slave. . . . Stop picking around the edges of the world. Take advantage, and if you can't take advantage, take disadvantage. We live here.

> On this planet, in this nation, in this country right here. *No*where else! We got a home in this rock, don't you see! Nobody starving in my home; nobody crying in my home, and if I got a home you got one too! Grab it. Grab this land! Take it, hold it, my brothers, make it, my brothers, shake it, squeeze it, turn it, twist it, beat it, kick it, kiss it, whip it, stomp it, dig it, plow it, seed it, reap it, rent it, buy it, sell it, own it, build it, multiply it, and pass it on—can you hear me? Pass it on!" (235)

But the fact that it was stolen before it could be passed on, that Macon Dead I figures as a martyr to black North American settlement, that his son and daughter became fugitives and refugees navigating segregated rural and urban space, and that his grandson, although leading a comparatively comfortable existence, lives "nowhere" that he can call home, speaks to the elusiveness of black placement not only in the decades following the Civil War but well into the twentieth century.

Satisfied that the cave holds no bags of gold, Milkman continues southward to Shalimar, Virginia, still thinking that he might discover how Pilate disposed of them. However, a rapid succession of events that begins with the town's young blades testing his citified virility but then proceeds to the older men initiating a humbled but increasingly self-confident Milkman into the brotherhood of the hunt distracts him from his original pursuit as he finds traces of his ancestry in the living memory of village residents as well as in the vertical topography of its environs ("Solomon's Leap," "Rynah's Gulch"). As he hears the variation of Pilate's "Sugarman" sung by children playing a timeless ring game and decodes the verses in light of information he has gleaned from Mrs. Byrd and the older men, he pieces together the genealogy and map of displacements that explain his own quasi-fugitive condition, and the task that remains is to return to Michigan to inform Pilate of the song's meaning and, after atoning (as he can) for Hagar's death, to bring his aunt to Shalimar, where the bones may be properly interred on the heights from which her grandfather's spirit might be thought to have leaped—like Sugarman, like Solomon—into flight. To do so restores a dignity lost when Macon Dead I, perched on his fence guarding his property, is shot five feet into the air before dropping to an agonized earthbound death.

But if Milkman has given up all thought of recovering the gold, Guitar has not, and fixated on revenge as a member of the Days, he has counted on exchanging gold for dynamite. *Song of Solomon*'s final scene stages the clash of the itineraries of these two brother figures as Guitar, convinced that Milkman has betrayed him, lies in wait to assassinate his friend. However, by instead assassinating Pilate, who has no interest in worldly truck and who embodies a collective ancestry that had fostered Guitar himself in his youth, he demonstrates the aberrant character of his political response. Milkman's fatal leap into the arms of his murderous friend proposes that both are at an impasse, coming as they do from widely different directions.[12] Interestingly, the one fugitive in the novel who does find a home is Corinthians, who, having left the house on Not Doctor Street, moves in with Henry Porter, former tenant of Macon Dead and retired member of the Days. Given the fate of Robert Smith and Guitar Bains, and given the sustainable existence that Corinthians and Henry might well enjoy, this minor detail is conspicuous among so many itineraries that come to a dramatic dead end.[13]

"My plan was to take us all to the other side"

In her preface to the 2004 Vintage edition, Toni Morrison describes what she wished to accomplish by *Beloved*'s vertiginous opening lines: "I wanted the reader to be kidnapped, thrown ruthlessly into an alien environment as the first step into a shared experience with the book's population—just as the characters were snatched from one place to another, from any place to any other, without preparation or defense."[14] "Alien environment" will become broadly inclusive of the territory readers traverse in the company of those characters, but the immediate reference is 124, the house on Bluestone Road, a nondescript frame structure rising from an open field, "just another weathered house needing repair" (311) except for the fact that it is haunted.[15] Morrison begins each of the novel's three parts by escorting the reader up to and then across its threshold: "124 was spiteful" (3), "124 was loud" (199), "124 was quiet" (281). Given that the house serves not only as the point of arrival and departure in a material world subject to the uncertain geographies of slave and free state but also as an interchange between past and present, domain of the dead and sphere of the living—a world, in sum, that knows neither spatial nor temporal boundaries—the "environment" Morrison cites extends in all directions, even within the strict borders of the house and its outbuildings. As a matter of author/reader cartography, Morrison wishes to "kidnap" and plunge the reader into what she is able to reconstruct of slave and ex-slave subjectivity: a complex of memory/(re)memory, defense mechanism, and affective response, mind embedded in the scarred and violated body. That subjectivity pertains to Sethe, Denver, Beloved, Paul D, Ella, and Stamp Paid (among others) individually, but it transcends any one personality to comprise all who lived in bondage under conditions of perpetual transfer or abduction and whose lives and deaths have been lost beyond anyone's capacity to remember—a subjectivity whose passage to oblivion Morrison invokes when she inscribes the book to "Sixty Million and more."[16]

Beloved is a novel of multiple story lines, but its central narrative concerns Sethe's escape from Sweet Home; her solo trek among the bluffs and bottoms of the Ohio River, during which she gives birth to her second daughter, Denver, with the assistance of the runaway white girl; her arrival with the new baby in Cincinnati; and her twenty-eight-day residence at 124, the house her mother-in-law, Baby Suggs, occupies courtesy of white abolitionists, before Schoolteacher and his accomplices track Sethe to the house and attempt to return mother and children to bondage. The slave catchers' arrival sets Sethe off on a second and drastic bid to escape by murdering her children and taking her own life, a plan she is prevented from implementing but only after she has succeeded in killing her eighteen-month-old daughter. Eighteen years later that daughter materializes as the young woman she might have become had she lived. The euphoria occasioned by Beloved's return momentarily masks what develops into an impossible encounter with "the black and angry dead" (234). Denver's escape from her psychically imploding household, Sethe's deliverance from the ghost's vengeful clutch, and her reunion with Paul D, whose arrival at the beginning of the novel with the promise of a life's renewal sets in motion this grievous and ever incomplete reckoning with the past, complete the trajectory.

Morrison situates Sethe's flight—her successful passage from Kentucky to Ohio, and her unsuccessful passage from 124 "to the other side" (240)—against the macrocosmic displacement of a black community caught up in imperiled fugitive transit:

> The War had been over four or five years then, but nobody white or black seemed to know it. Odd clusters and strays of Negroes wandered the back roads and cowpaths from Schenectady to Jackson. Dazed but insistent, they searched each other out for word of a cousin, an aunt, a friend who once said, "Call on me. Anytime you get near Chicago, just call on me." Some of them were running from family that could not support them, some to family; some were running from dead crops, dead kin, life threats, and took-over land. Boys younger than Buglar and Howard; configurations and blends of families of women and children, while elsewhere, solitary, hunted and hunting for, were men, men, men. Forbidden public transportation, chased by debt and filthy "talking sheets," they followed secondary routes, scanned the horizon for signs and counted heavily on each other. Silent, except for social courtesies, when they met one another they neither described nor asked about the sorrow that drove them from one place to another. The whites didn't bear speaking on. Everybody knew. (63)

Having come to the end of her fugitive career, and having seen her two sons, Buglar and Howard, survivors of the attempt to pass "to the other side," disappear into this flux, Sethe constitutes a stationary point among this incessant movement as the novel opens. "I will never run from another thing on this earth" (18), she declares to Paul D soon after he appears at 124. The narrative action begins with his arrival: his own itinerary has taken him from the Ohio Valley south to Georgia and then north to Delaware and New York

State before he heads west in search of Sethe. Having reunited with his friend from Sweet Home, Paul D is ready to suspend his travels.

Against the fluid panoramas of Sethe's South-to-North flight and the macrocosmic cartography of a black population uprooted, displaced, and exposed to random white violence, Morrison develops the microcosm of 124 Bluestone Road: house, privy, cold house, woodshed, field, woods, and the stream behind them, the clearing where Baby Suggs preached, as well as the riverfront, industrial peripheries, and residential streets of Cincinnati, where black people work and walk mindful of block-by-block color zones. Small as it is, the interior of 124 has a complicated geography of its own. Prominent features include the one door that opens on the front porch, kitchen, keeping room, white staircase, and two upstairs bedrooms. Each site has a history. A given space is never empty but bears the impress of every person that has occupied that space and every event that has transpired therein. Sethe explains her intuition of the dense residuum of inhabited space in the following conversation with Denver:

> "Some things you forget. Other things you never do. . . . Places, places are still there. If a house burns down, it's gone, but the place—the picture of it—stays, and not just in my rememory, but out there, in the world. What I remember is a picture floating around out there outside my head. I mean, even if I don't think it, even if I die, the picture of what I did, or knew, or saw is still out there. Right in the place where it happened."
>
> "Can other people see it?" asked Denver.
>
> "Oh, yes. Oh, yes, yes, yes. Someday you be walking down the road and you hear something or see something going on. So clear. And you think it's you thinking it up. A thought picture. But no. It's when you bump into a rememory that belongs to somebody else. Where I was before I came here, that place is real. It's never going away." (43)

For Sethe, the ghost of past life informs the structure and texture of the present. In this belief she is not alone: everyone in the postslave community understands that "nothing ever dies" (44). This conversation reflects the storytelling by which the characters, together and apart, map the worlds of a shared and private past and define the space of present occupancy. When Paul D arrives at 124, he supplements what Sethe already knows about the thwarted escape from Sweet Home in what he is able to reveal about the death of Sixo and collapse of Halle, details that recall the plantation microcosm and the fugitive corridors in and about it. Denver's self-identity is founded in Sethe's account of her birth, the origin story to which Sethe's flight, for Denver's purposes, exists as subplot.

The arrival of Beloved imports an additional, spectral cartography to the macro- and microlocalities through which Morrison's characters move, although such cartography is consistent with Sethe's experience of inhabited space and her contention that "nothing ever dies." When Sethe, Denver, and Paul D return from the carnival, Beloved awaits on the butternut tree stump in front of 124 wearing a dress and straw hat. But she enters the reader's awareness with the enigmatic line that begins the chapter segment: "A fully dressed woman walked out of the water," an event that is the more enigmatic in that "nobody saw her emerge or came accidently by" (60). The reader is thus positioned to witness the onset of Beloved's magical visitation, to mark the interchange between material and immaterial world, and to recognize from her first appearance the unnatural status of her personhood.[17] Still, even after we have fully surmised that this is the ghost incarnate of Denver's dead sister whom Paul D had driven out the evening of his arrival, the corridors through which she has passed remain deeply mysterious if compellingly relevant to the family circle and the larger black community, who never question the existence of the ghost dimensions that environ the waking world of hard and fast bodily form. Responding to Denver's questions, Beloved maps as she can where she has been and the reason she has made her way to 124:

> Denver scooted a little closer. "What's it like over there, where you were before? Can you tell me?"
>
> "Dark," said Beloved. "I'm small in that place. I'm like this here." She raised her head off the bed, lay down on her side and curled up."
>
> Denver covered her lips with her fingers. "Were you cold?"
>
> Beloved curled tighter and shook her head. "Hot. Nothing to breathe down there and no room to move in."
>
> "You see anybody?"
>
> "Heaps. A lot of people is down there. Some is dead."
>
> "You see Jesus? Baby Suggs?"
>
> "I don't know. I don't know the names." She sat up.
>
> "Tell me, how did you get here?"
>
> "I wait; then I get on the bridge. I stay there in the dark, in the daytime, in the dark, in the daytime. It was a long time."
>
> "All this time you were on a bridge?"
>
> "No. After. When I got out."
>
> "What did you come back for?"
>
> Beloved smiled. "To see her face."
>
> "Ma'am's? Sethe?"
>
> "Yes, Sethe." (88)

Throughout this conversation Morrison interweaves the theme of bodily proximity: Denver's impulse to scoot closer, the bodies heaped together dead and alive in the dark, hot, cramped place of the "over there," where Beloved was "before," one of numerous slave-hull invocations that occur in the novel, and Beloved's determination to see Sethe's face, an effort to recover the mother-infant gaze that precedes the infant's individuation and departure into a world of peril and death. The unstable verb tenses in which Beloved speaks indicate that her journey is not a linear series of spaces she occupies and then vacates. Rather she is in all of these places, and nowhere definitively, at all times, leading an existence that is out of time and that endlessly reenacts the Middle Passage from which return to the mother's or father's living face is never a sustainable possibility. As Beloved remarks in her extended soliloquy, the unpunctuated sentences reinforcing the idea that she does not live among the coordinates of ordinary human space and time, "There will never be a time when I am not crouching and watching others who are crouching too" (248).

Beloved's occupancy of 124 threatens to remove the site from a world in which lifelines may be tenuous but are nevertheless open. Paul D's arrival and prompt exorcism of the baby ghost may excite the false hope that the household can be retrieved from the isolation in which Sethe leads a meager day-to-day existence and an adolescent Denver, outgrowing the tight confines of 124 but hesitant to step beyond the porch, languishes in autoerotic fantasy. But Paul D cannot put matters to rights simply by assuming the role of husband and father: he cannot reconfigure the household as man, woman, and child, the adult couple actively and heteronormally if not procreatively sexual, and seeking under the new male headship reintegration with the postslave community (as is suggested by the threesome's attendance at the carnival), or at least not yet. He must come to terms with Sethe's post–Sweet Home history and Denver's unappeased hunger. When the baby ghost returns as Beloved, her first order of business is to drive Paul D out of the house and to reassert the configuration of the former threesome, this time in restored if ever-scarred flesh. But given Sethe's irreversible act of bloodletting, and given the vengeance the ghost cannot help but exact, there can be no return to the premurder status of mother and infant. Crouching and watching the others who are likewise crouching, as Beloved remarks, is the permanent state. As for Denver, the younger sister is less a sister than competitor for the mother's undivided attention. As the baby's unbounded rage spends itself within the confines of 124, the rapture of Sethe's and Denver's apparent reunion with the lost daughter and sibling rapidly evolves into a state of severed lifelines and deepening entropy.

In the bliss of the miraculous reunion, Sethe celebrates her reclusion from the world and in doing so outlines the stark geography she has come to inhabit. "Paul D convinced me there was a world out there and that I could live in it," she reflects. "Should have known better. *Did* know better. Whatever is going on outside my door ain't for me. The world is in this room. This here's all there is and all there needs to be" (215). "I was right all along: there is no world outside my door" (217). Although Denver at first shares the euphoria of her sister's return, Beloved's rebuffs and single-minded focus on Sethe further isolate Denver in her agoraphobia. Whereas Sethe is content to withdraw into the closed circle of 124, absenting herself from the external world even at the price of starvation, Denver's paralysis is produced by terror that lies both outside and inside the house. She is ever mindful of her mother's capacity to kill: "Maybe there is something else terrible enough to make her do it again," she remarks during her own soliloquy. "I need to know what that thing may be, but I don't want to. Whatever it is, it comes from outside this house, outside the yard, and it can come right on in the yard if it wants to. So I never leave this house and I watch over the yard, so it can't happen again and my mother won't have to kill me too" (242). Sethe's storytelling has mapped the world beyond the house as one of absolute danger, and Denver's apprehension of space must thus contend with a traumatic epistemology, her mother's but also her own. Against the necessity of stepping off the porch to avert the starvation that has settled over the household, Denver hesitates. "Out there where there were places in which things so bad had happened that when you went near them it would happen again. . . . How would she know these places?" (287). Prompted by her memory of a conversation with Baby Suggs, who had assured her that "there was no defense" but that one has to proceed against all odds, Denver acts finally on her grandmother's defiant injunction: "Know it, and go on out the yard. Go on" (288). Denver's successful flight from 124 reconnects the household to the world that must sustain it: it leads to the community's support in the manner of food donations as well as its convergence to perform the rite of exorcism by which Beloved, the insupportable phantasm of the collective past, is driven from the premises, so that at least tentative boundaries are reestablished between the living and the dead.

The catharsis with which Sethe is rescued from Beloved's malevolent and predatory visitation does not, however, resolve the problem of living with the ghosts of the slave past. Nor does it discharge the obligation to mourn a multitude who exceed the capacity of living memory and who experienced a magnitude of horror that overwhelms the capacity of the living to imagine, let alone document. Still, the novel concludes with Denver's reintegration into the black community and what appears to be the strong likelihood of a viable, self-supporting, and sexually mature life. It concludes as well with Paul D's return to 124, having reconciled himself to Sethe's portion of what he understands as the collective past. Against the nightmare landscapes that recur micro- and macrocosmically throughout *Beloved*, Morrison presents Paul D as imagining a North America that reserves some possibility of black inhabitation, some measure of adequate and lovely hospitality:

> In all those escapes he could not help being astonished by the beauty of this land that was not his. He hid in its breast, fingered its earth for food, clung to its banks to lap water and tried not to love it. On nights when the sky was personal, weak with the weight of its own stars, he made himself not love it. Its graveyards and low-lying rivers.

> Or just a house—solitary under a chinaberry tree; maybe a mule tethered and the light hitting its hide just so. Anything could stir him and he tried hard not to love it. (316)

Given the displacement, abduction, dispossession, and terror that mark what Morrison presents as African American experience in North America, her celebration of the possibility of black countergeographies, whether they take the form of Lincoln's Heaven or Paul D's vision of "just a house," adequate shelter at the end of a long and circuitous road, is all the more conspicuous. In such a recuperative light, Morrison at the novel's end asks the reader to reimagine 124 as a sustainably inhabitable space in which Paul D's love of place and person redeems what remains an abundant possibility of life.[18]

"My left arm"

In Sethe, Morrison seeks to recover the inner life of a Margaret Garner whose subjectivity is excluded from historical accounts of escape, recapture, and infanticide. If the task of *Beloved*'s opening paragraph is to abduct a twentieth-century readership "ruthlessly into an alien environment"—the long ago and far away that shapes Sethe, Denver, Paul D, and the larger postslave community—Morrison's goal is to naturalize her audience to the affective economies of loss, grief, and survival, or what contemporary inference can make of those economies from imaginative consultation of the archive. In *Kindred*, by contrast, Butler arranges for her protagonist, a contemporary African American woman, to be kidnapped into the alien environment of the antebellum Maryland Eastern Shore, although readers cannot help but be dragged along with her and take part in her horrifying acculturation to the slave past. The novel implicitly poses the question: What would it be like for those who live at a century's remove from the era of chattel slavery to contend with the realities of bondage? Will not an articulate, independent-minded, twentieth-century black woman exert a commanding resistance to the slave regime and its strategies to assimilate her to its order? What happens when that woman perceives how deeply she owes her genealogical existence to the condition of bondage from which black Americans seek recovery as late as 1976, the nation's bicentennial year, contemporary embarkation point for the novel's time travel? Even more to the point: On those occasions in which Dana Franklin is summoned to rescue Rufus Weylin from a life-threatening situation, and thus determine whether her predatory slave master–progenitor lives or dies, must she secure his survival in order to preserve her line of descent? Must she choose to live on the condition that she exist as his direct descendent? Would it not be better to cut the rapist's career short? Would it not be best that she never exist at all?[19]

Such questions have little relevance to Dana before her first fugue-like episode. A post–civil rights era middle-class black woman, she is situated as far from the scenes of slavery, Reconstruction, and post-Reconstruction as she possibly could be without taking leave of North America entirely. A legatee of the second Great Migration, she resides in Southern California rather than in one of the more typical destinations—Chicago, Detroit, Cleveland, Buffalo, or New York City—associated with Southern exodus, and unlike a number of Morrison's characters who live in the North but have enduring connections with Southern relatives and places, her only links are the vague knowledge that her grandparents worked the cane fields in Louisiana and a memory of the family Bible in which the genealogy of a remote Maryland-residing ancestry had been set down. As a child of the Los Angeles black community, moreover, Dana has separated herself from that community's conservative religious tradition in abandoning the Baptist church and has rejected its pragmatic middle-class ambitions in pursuing a literary vocation. She takes further leave by marrying a white fellow writer, in response to which her uncle disowns her. She thereafter maintains only tenuous contact with a cousin skeptical of her choice of a mate. Within the geography of the Los Angeles basin, she rents an apartment on Crenshaw Boulevard (somewhere, presumably, in the Leimert Park to Mid-City corridor) before migrating (in 1976) to a predominantly white Altadena to share an apartment with Kevin. Having set Dana at such spatiotemporal removes from the sites of slavery and separated her from a black community in which a memory of those sites persists, the novel proceeds to demonstrate that neither time nor space affords protection when the past asserts its claim on the present. For no apparent reason, boundaries collapse—between past and present, West Coast and East Coast, black bodies and white bodies.[20]

When, in response to Rufus's first summons, Dana finds herself in antebellum Maryland, she registers the scene to which she is transported only as a microlocality outside of all spatiotemporal frames of reference. "Suddenly, I was outdoors kneeling on the ground beneath trees. I was in a green place. I was at the edge of a woods. Before me was a wide tranquil river, and near the middle of that river was a child, splashing, screaming . . . drowning!"[21] Dana retrieves and revives a half-asphyxiated five-year-old Rufus, only to find herself attacked by his mother and threatened by his rifle-toting father, whose menacing aspect sends her hurtling back through time. Only after she has returned to Altadena does she recall that Rufus's belligerent mother "had spoken with an accent—a southern accent" (16), her first clue as to where the scene is located. Much more than by topographical feature, Dana, in voyaging to the Eastern Shore a first and then a second time, identifies place by linguistic cues, indices of a cultural geography, and no cue more obvious than the word that preeminently invokes the regime of the slave South. In the second chapter, after meeting the emergency Rufus has created by setting his bedroom curtains on fire, Dana engages the boy, now eight, in conversation.

And in no time at all Rufus, whose accent is "unmistakably southern" (21), refers to her as a "nigger," terminology by which he innocently differentiates black from white. Having processed the import of his language, Dana extracts from the boy information regarding their location "across the bay" from "Baltimore City" (26–27) as well as the date: 1815. In response to this astonishing intelligence, Dana is oddly *not* incredulous, as though 150 years and the breadth of a continent are powerless to thwart a Sophoclean return to the site of ancestral enslavement: "I sat still, breathed deeply, calming myself, believing him. I did believe him. I wasn't even as surprised as I should have been. I had already accepted the fact that I had moved through time. Now I knew I was farther from home than I had thought. And now I knew why Rufus's father used his whip on 'niggers' as well as horses" (27). Drawing on what she recalls of the genealogy inscribed in the family Bible, Dana matches names with place and grapples with the recognition that Rufus, her great-great-great-grandfather, is white. She understands that he will father a daughter, Hagar, her great-great-grandmother-to-be, with the freeborn Alice who lives in the neighborhood.

Dana's initiation into life as a fugitive begins shortly thereafter, when she perceives that her status as the magically appearing intruder in the boy's bedroom might bring her a second time into ugly confrontation with Tom Weylin. Equipped with Rufus's vague directions, she makes her way along the edge of the nighttime woods and fields toward the cabin where Alice lives with her parents, dodging, in the process, dogs and patrollers. Although complete strangers, Alice's family are her ancestors, and as a marked wayfarer on hostile ground, Dana must turn to black folk for shelter and knowledge. Already casting herself in the role of runaway, she hopes to learn from Alice's mother "the quickest, safest way North" (39). When the patrollers arrive at the cabin ahead of her, the absolute defenselessness of the black body engrosses her attention. Keeping her distance, she watches as the patrollers break through the door and terrorize the family, subjecting Alice's father to the whip before returning him to the Weylin plantation, which he has left without permission to visit his freeborn wife, and then beating and harassing Alice's mother. This, Dana claims, is her first experience of close proximity to human brutality, although as a postwar black Los Angelina (the Watts riots took place in 1965, when she would have been fifteen) she has to have some idea, however repressed, of violent confrontation: "I had seen people beaten on television and in the movies. I had seen the too-red blood substitute streaked across their backs and heard their well-rehearsed screams. But I hadn't lain nearby and smelled their sweat or heard them pleading and praying, shamed before their families and themselves" (36). Dana's turn awaits: after the incident seemingly has concluded and she has helped mother and daughter recover from the assault, she too is manhandled when she goes outside to retrieve a blanket, and the episode ends when she becomes convinced that the patroller, whom she has just attacked with a heavy branch, will now respond with lethal force, as fear of imminent death triggers the mechanism that returns her to the apartment in Altadena. From this second insertion in antebellum Maryland, she escapes through time rather than across space, but anticipating now further adventures as Rufus's guardian, she prepares for the probability that she will be summoned again. In doing so she can expect that, as a black woman in the slave South, she will be subject to all manner of violation and that she will need to seek refuge in the North.

Her preparation includes practical measures such as packing a canvas bag with toiletries, medicine, clothes, and a history book, as well as secreting a knife on her person. Once she has accepted what she cannot explain—that she is caught up in a series of visits to the antebellum Maryland of her black and white ancestors—she marshals her psychological resources as a well-informed, outspoken, free-standing citizen whose understanding of nineteenth-century history and an evolving regional and national geography affords a degree of mastery over wayward and unpredictable spatiotemporal displacement. Occupying, during her residence on the Weylin plantation, uncertain terrain between slave and free, and enjoying privileged if revocable liberties of movement among the color-delineated zones of house, kitchen, quarters, yard, and field, she succeeds at first in maintaining a cognitive aloofness even as she becomes increasingly aware of the real dangers of her position. As she will learn repeatedly, those dangers are brutally physical, but they are also psychological, as when she and Kevin, in chapter 3, "The Fall," witness the slave children imitate the ritual of the auction block. In recoil from that spectacle, she remarks to Kevin, "Most of the time, I'm still an observer. It's protection. It's nineteen seventy-six shielding and cushioning eighteen nineteen for me. But now and then, like with the kids' game, I can't maintain the distance. I'm drawn all the way into eighteen nineteen, and I don't know what to do" (101). But 1976 proves to be even less of a shield than she can yet know. Because Kevin has accompanied her in this third episode, the result of an attempt to hold her in place during the onset of time-travel vertigo, they have been forced into the masquerade of master and slave, and although Kevin abhors slavery and in his protracted nineteenth-century sojourn will actively assist fugitives, the power asymmetry of their necessary role-playing upsets the balance they have succeeded (more or less) in striking as a twentieth-century mixed-race couple. To be sure, that balance was already tenuous, as Kevin, whose enlightened views inevitably coexist with lingering white and male supremacist reflexes, had assumed early in the marriage that Dana would serve as his typist and general factotum. But upon returning to Altadena they will have much more work to do.

Events progressively erode the distance Dana strives to maintain. We see this erosion particularly toward the end of chapter 3, when Tom Weylin catches Dana in the cookhouse teaching Nigel to read. "I never saw where the whip came from," she writes of the attack from nowhere, "never even saw the first blow coming" (107). This rite of passage, which figures in the slave narrative tradition as the preeminent mode by which white master inscribes subjection on the black body, causes Dana to fear for her life, and soon afterward she finds herself (without Kevin) lying face down in her Altadena apartment. Because her perception of existential threat has up to now reliably activated retrieval, it would seem that a check has been set in place to prevent her from losing her twentieth-century identity. Yet, eight days later, when she is once again summoned to antebellum Maryland to intervene in a fight between Rufus and Isaac, she discovers herself acclimated to this new and fearsome normality. As the still resourceful woman of 1976, she is able to dissuade Isaac from delivering a deathblow to the prostrate Rufus, to encourage Isaac and Alice to make haste in their flight, and to convince Rufus not to report Isaac as the source of his injuries. Only after swearing Rufus not to betray Isaac does Dana agree to begin the long walk to the Weylin residence to recruit assistance. As she comes in sight of the house, however, the emissary from 1976 passes a new increment in acculturation: "I was startled to catch myself saying wearily, 'Home at last' " (126). Later, in chapter 5, "The Storm," after she has reckoned with the possibility that as a black sojourner in the slave South she enjoys no protection against being sold and has faced the fear that she may permanently lose contact with Kevin, she will remember the occasion as a threshold-crossing moment: "I could recall feeling relief at seeing the house, feeling that I had come home. And having to stop and correct myself, remind myself that I was in an alien, dangerous place" (190). Although fully cognizant of her status as one radically out of place, she steadily naturalizes to the condition of slavery.

Alien and dangerous as the Eastern Shore is to Dana, in many respects it is familiar to her and to her readership. A writer by profession, Dana is an accomplished reader, and her testimony builds consciously on a slave narrative tradition in which Frederick Douglass centrally figures. For Dana as for her readers, Douglass's cartography of scenes from childhood and youth has made the antebellum Eastern Shore one of the best-known corridors in the literary atlas of North American slavery. In chapter 4, "The Fight," Dana takes stock of what the citizen of 1976 would know as the region's heroic history: "There were two important slave children right here in Maryland. The older one, living here in Talbot County, would be called Frederick Douglass after a name change or two. The second, growing up a few miles south in Dorchester County was Harriet Ross, eventually to be Harriet Tubman" (140). Their stories, along with that of Nat Turner, are included in the history book Dana has packed in her canvas bag. Fearing that Rufus's perusal might lead to a preemptive erasure of these exemplary lives, she decides to place the book in the fire as Rufus, who has only read a little way into the narrative of emancipation, has urged her to do. In all three of his autobiographies, Douglass emphasizes the practical difficulties of escaping from the Eastern Shore and his supreme good fortune, after the abortive attempt to escape via the Chesapeake Bay, to have been sent back to Baltimore, from where he would succeed in departing by rail. No longer in possession of a map, which Rufus feeds to the flames that consume the book, Dana will nevertheless attempt the overland flight that Douglass deemed too dangerous. She undertakes this escape in response to learning that Rufus has failed to send the letters she has written to Kevin notifying him of her reappearance at the Weylin plantation. Recaptured before she can even reach Easton, Dana is whipped a second time, and amid the flurry of blows, her mind channels the famous line from Douglass's *Narrative*, "You have seen how a man was made a slave; you shall see how a slave was made a man":[22]

> I moved, twisted myself somehow, from my stomach onto my side. I tried to get away from my thoughts, but they still came.
>
> See how easily slaves are made? They said. (177)

To know antebellum Maryland from the historical perspective of 1976 does not prevent Dana from living the trauma of one embedded among spaces organized to propagate slave subjectivity. At this point in *Kindred*, 1976 offers no shield at all. Even after she and Kevin have succeeded in making it back together to Altadena, reverse culture shock disrupts resumption of their life as a couple. "I felt as though I were losing my place here in my own time," she reflects (191), and much of her difficulty derives from a husband who to his horror finds that he has absorbed Weylin speech patterns and attitudes.

In chapter 5, "The Storm," the narrative moves toward fulfillment of what Dana conceives as her obligations to the Weylin heritage.[23] Alice gives birth to Hagar, which renders Rufus dispensable as a genetic link. As importantly, however, Rufus's increasingly erratic behavior begins to shatter the emotional bond by which he and Dana have become mutually attached, beginning with his first intrusion into her life as a five-year-old near-drowning victim. Rufus destroys what little is left of mutual trust when he sends Dana to the fields to labor under the whip of the overseer, Fowler, and does so out of the spiteful fiction that Dana had allowed the ailing Tom Weylin to die. Although Rufus promptly recalls her from that ignominious site of the slave past, his cruelties to Alice steadily accumulate, and his decision to sell a man whom he suspects of making advances to Dana confirms her suspicion that Rufus's possessiveness of both Alice and herself knows no bounds. Retreating to the attic sleeping quarters in the Weylin residence, she cuts her wrists as a way to return to Altadena. Once there, she readies herself for what she knows must be the fatally climactic episode. Given that Hagar has been born, she is at liberty, should circumstance dictate, to be the agent of her forefather's death.

Prompted by an intuition that Rufus's genuine if distorted love for her must culminate in his attempt to possess her sexually, Dana prepares for what is to be the final excursion by once again packing a knife. In chapter 6, "The Rope," Dana arrives to discover that Alice has put an end to her life of unrelieved torment, which has included Rufus's dissolution of her marriage to Isaac, his repeated rapes, and his endless psychological assaults, the last of which is his false claim to have sold their children. Dana's physical resemblance to Alice—the sisterhood of distant grandchild to grandmother—is a theme Butler has developed throughout, so it is inevitable that a Rufus bereaved of Alice, and who has declared the women to be two halves of a whole, will cast this preternaturally appearing woman who has served in the capacity of maternal guardian, older sister, and platonic friend into the role of sexual partner, the defining patriarchal gesture toward those he intends to dominate. In his move to establish this relationship with Dana, Rufus seeks her out in the attic sleeping quarters, a zone in which she preserves the advantage of ready access to the knife. It is there that he would seduce or, failing that, rape Dana, and it is from that attic that Dana, having stabbed Rufus twice, returns to Altadena through the apartment's wall, her left arm in the grip of the dying ancestor.

Late in the series of excursions, Dana reflects, "Once—God knows how long ago—I had worried that I was keeping too much distance between myself and this alien time. Now, there was no distance at all" (220). The "no distance at all" assumes vivid incarnation in her passage from the Maryland attic to the California living room, in the course of which, as Dana writes in the prologue's opening line, "I lost an arm on my last trip home" (9). The physical mutilation eliminates the possibility that Dana can return to a purely cerebral relationship with the slave past. Still, the epilogue reestablishes some distance in recounting the trip Dana and Kevin undertake to a twentieth-century Eastern Shore, to an Easton of gas stations, fast-food restaurants, and integrated schools, and to the site of the Weylin plantation, now occupied by a cornfield. As they discover from documents at the Maryland Historical Society, the fire (set presumably by Nigel) that destroyed the house had erased all evidence that Rufus's death is attributable to anything but fire. The past, as *Kindred* concludes, is in its place, at least in the story's terminal "now." The narrative's last words, however, concern the testimony that Dana, as writer, is destined to bear, and by foregrounding her reasonable hesitation to tell what likely will be interpreted as a chronicle of psychotic episodes, Butler prompts readers to consider once again the violence with which the historical past inhabits the present. "If we told anyone else about this," Dana remarks to Kevin, "anyone at all, they wouldn't think we were so sane." In speaking the novel's concluding lines, Kevin opts for simple affirmations: "'We are,' he said. 'And now that the boy is dead, we have some chance of staying that way'" (264). Presuming upon the readership's willing suspension of disbelief, Butler's wager has been that we will associate true insanity with the white supremacy that overwhelms Rufus's native decency and capacity for kindness. But Rufus is but one ancestor, and *Kindred* leaves open the probability that many such boys persist in an unresolved anterior time and that they exert from the shadows a disruptive influence over the contemporary moment, notwithstanding that moment's spatiotemporal distance from the sites of bygone enslavement. Kevin's ready absorption of the Southern master's affect and gesture on top of his contemporary white person's unconscious supremacist ontology confirms that Rufus perniciously persists.

Indeed, Kevin's inability to appreciate the continuing threat the slave past poses to people of color confirms his role as the well-meaning white person whose understanding of black experience extends only so far. With reference to her final fatal encounter with Rufus, Dana asserts, "Kevin would never know what those last moments had been like" (263). As witness to and participant in Dana's trials, Kevin plays the role of white corroborator, as Garrison and Phillips did with Douglass, and as Child and Post did with Jacobs. Butler thus inscribes within the text the distance between a black female and a white male reading of the experience, a distance that cannot be bridged even within the intimate space of a marriage.

"If everyone could feel everyone else's pain"

In *Kindred*, Los Angeles exemplifies contemporary metropolitan America—so removed in time and space from the rural slave past and so caught up in continuous self-reinvention as to make amnesia an existential condition, notwithstanding the "slave market" to which Dana willingly subjects herself as a temporary worker, supporting by day her nocturnal endeavors as a novelist. In *Parable of the Sower*, Butler returns to the urban oasis Edward Soja has called a "shattered metro-sea of fragmented yet homogenized communities"[24] but shifts to a hypothetical future of civic dysfunction in which everything that breaks stays broken. Routine circulation within the basin has come to a halt, and isolated communities hunker down behind insecure walls. Steady erosion of the commonwealth model and contraction of basic services produce a society that cannot guarantee police and fire protection, much less foster foundational literacy skills. Under the duress of a changing climate and consolidation of authoritarian rule, American society is dominated by those who have amassed great wealth and who have positioned themselves to exploit and enslave its more vulnerable citizens. Amid these dystopian conditions, *Parable* introduces us to Lauren Oya Olamina, a black, middle-class teenager who leads a comparatively protected life within her neighborhood's enclosure but whose peculiar disability—hyperempathy syndrome—causes her to experience the symptoms of bodies experiencing states of pleasure and pain, although in her world pain is the far more common sensation. Lauren's first-person testimony records, among other trials, her response to the hordes of street people leading horrific lives in the full light of day. The novel's insistent visualization of social abjection—a homeless populace whose bodies exhibit mutilated limbs and festering wounds—challenges readers to reimagine and remap their own relation to bodies that suffer under regimes of domination and exploitation, disparities of power and privilege with which any reader possessing leisure (space, time) to read and reflect is, as the narrative urges one to recognize, structurally complicit.

In this first installment of the projected *Parable* trilogy, Butler visualizes the American spatial past and present in the light of a dire speculative future. She does so by setting several familiar geographic tropes in dynamic narrative relation: the gated suburban community; the impoverished crime-ridden city core whose blight metastasizes through a vast conurbation; the South-to-North paths of escape associated with the slave narrative tradition; the pastoral destination associated with Old to New World exodus, and the agrarian utopia suggested by the novel's title. Plantation, prison, and company town likewise figure within the narrative's frame of reference. California—signifier of twentieth-century ideals of opulent progressivism but also a historic zone of multiethnic inequality to which Latinos, Asians, and African Americans from the second Great Migration bear ample witness—underlies the topography and tropology of this futuristic novel's mise-en-scène. In addition to invoking the mobile demographics of North American history, these tropes, as Butler deploys them in *Sower*, mark the production and unequal distribution of social misery. A privatized economy in deep recession has rendered Greater Los Angeles a patchwork of fortressed affluence and effluvial poverty; the walled neighborhood in which the story begins exists as a remnant of middle-class life where residents now devote their time to cultivating an insular subsistence while training as a defense corps against the misery beyond the perimeter. Such misery takes the form of open depredation: poor people attacking one another for food, money, drugs, and sex. One drug in particular, pyro, induces an orgasmic ecstasy in response to the spectacle of burning things—houses, trees, bodies. Pyro addiction, a startling vision of orgiastic social entropy, is clearly a way for the world to end—the perfect convergence of Eros and Thanatos.

The novel is a compilation of Lauren Olamina's journal entries from July 20, 2024, to October 10, 2027. The oldest child in a blended Hispanic and African American family presided over by her Baptist minister father, the neighborhood's de facto leader, Lauren appears in her journals as a confiding and ingenuous if critically minded narrator. We first meet her as an anxious fifteen-year-old who secretly prepares to migrate north in flight from a region where life has become climatologically unsustainable. In the novel's first paragraphs she introduces herself by recounting a vivid recurrent dream: alone in her suburban bedroom, she has begun to teach herself to fly and has just mastered elementary levitation. Defying gravity but still unsure of how to direct her movements, she seeks egress from her suburban house, which she suddenly realizes is engulfed in flames. In view of the projected culmination of the never-to-be-completed *Parable* trilogy—departure from earth into outer space—Butler thus opens her narrative by referencing the familiar trope of Africans taking flight.

In preparing for departure, Lauren immerses herself in survivalist literature, collects archaic maps of the California highway system, and gathers a variety of seed. At the same time, she undergoes a deconversion from the Protestant faith of her father, developing in its stead a new belief system, Earthseed, built on the principles that God is change and humans are destined to colonize the universe ("The destiny of Earthseed is to take root among the stars")—yet another variation of a familiar geographic trope, that of a people setting off on errands of conquest and settlement. In addition to chronicling the descent of her world into chaos, the journal provides space for setting down the New Age verse aphorisms that will constitute Earthseed scripture. Embracing change as a cosmic principle, Lauren is still caught off guard by how rapidly her home and community life dissolve: following a series of incidents in which the neighborhood wall fails to keep back intruders, a younger brother ventures outside, becomes first a lone predator and then gang member, and finally is tortured to death by persons unknown. Soon afterward, Lauren's father disappears outside the wall. A short time later, pyro addicts breach the wall and slaughter, among a majority of her neighbors, Lauren's stepmother and all but one of her remaining brothers. Meeting up with two neighborhood survivors, one black and one white, Lauren leads the way north on a perilous trek, assembling a mixed-race band along the way, refugees from debt slavery, sex slavery, and general destitution, and eventually reaching a patch of land in Humboldt County owned by a group member, Taylor Franklin Bankole, a retired physician said to resemble Frederick Douglass, with whom Lauren has fallen in love despite a thirty-year age difference. There, the company—some converts to Lauren's gospel, others (including Bankole) not—begin to build the Earthseed community.

In the course of the narrative Lauren transforms from suburban teenager to charismatic prophet, wily defender of her people, pathfinder amid burning landscapes and predatory hordes. In making this transition, she labors under a secret burden: she is afflicted with congenital "hyperempathy syndrome," a consequence of her birth mother's addiction to a drug called Paracetco. Hyperempathy, also known as "sharing," causes her to experience the sensorium of others to the point of absorption in the other's physical symptoms. "The sharing," Lauren explains early in the narrative, "isn't real. . . . It's delusional. Even I admit that."[25] A strictly neurochemical response to the suffering or ecstatic bodies with which she comes in contact, and not in itself an empathetic engagement with the affected subjectivities of her fellow creatures, the predicament of immersion in another's sensorium gives rise to obvious socioethical considerations. While this "disease" positions her literally to feel the pain of others irrespective of class, gender, ethnicity, and even species (early in the novel she agonizes over an injured dog and decides she must shoot it), and thus potentially to "sympathize" in the conventional and actionable sense of the term, it also makes her vulnerable to the immobilizing effects of pain experienced by friend and foe alike. If hyperempathy induces her at times to perform the office of Good Samaritan, at other times she must kill to release herself from the paralysis of the other's affliction.

Lauren thus focalizes the theme of another's suffering and the space that does or does not exempt one from the sufferer's fate. Such space that does or does not so exempt correlates with social geographies that in *Sower* are in a state of flux. Early journal entries reflect her protected status as one who lives behind a wall: as she documents her limited exposure to the severely impoverished people who inhabit the environing streets and fields, she is keen to maintain a differentiation between herself and them. For individuals like herself, housed and fed, such people represent a clear and present threat: "Most of the street poor," she observes, "are dangerous. They're desperate or crazy or both. That's enough to make anyone dangerous" (10). This last clause concedes a thread of commonality—a "but for the grace of God go I." But as a sharer she is zealous to preserve boundaries. In an early episode, her father leads a group of teenagers on an excursion to the barricaded church where they are to be baptized. As no one can afford fossil-fueled transport, they travel by bicycle, and this puts Lauren in potentially devastating visual contact with the abject denizens of the streets. Although she averts her eyes, she knows full well their sorry condition: "They cut off each other's ears, arms, legs. . . . They carry untreated diseases and festering wounds. They have no money to spend on water to wash with so even the unwounded have sores. They don't get enough to eat so they're malnourished—or they eat bad food and poison themselves. As I rode, I tried not to look around at them, but I couldn't help seeing—collecting—some of their general misery" (10–11). Before arriving at the church, her eye lights on several individual sufferers, including a naked prepubescent girl who has been raped—a recurrent figure on Lauren's radar.

The sack of her neighborhood presses Lauren into the ranks of the homeless and initiates her necessary conversion of hyperempathy to an instrument of survival. In escaping from her sundered enclave, involuntary sharing nearly costs Lauren her life, as she must navigate a scene of carnage reminiscent of a captivity narrative's opening tableau. Her first homicide takes place amid this chaos, as a pyro addict tackles her in an attempted rape. Having just plucked a firearm from the hand of a deceased neighbor, she is prepared for self-defense: "I fired the gun in reflexive terror, and took the terrible impact in my own stomach. . . . I shot him again, terrified that his pain would immobilize me when he did feel it. . . . When I could move again, I pushed his body off me" (154). In the refuge of darkness beyond the broken wall, she begins to reckon with her new status: "*I* am one of the street poor, now," she reflects. "Not as poor as some, but homeless, alone, full of books and ignorant of reality. Unless I meet someone from the neighborhood, there's no one I can afford to trust" (156). Almost providentially, she connects the next day with two acquaintances with whom she joins to form a core survival unit: Zahra Moss, a petite, street-raised African American woman whom one of Lauren's neighbors bought from Zahra's mother, and Harry Balter, a large-framed and physically courageous young white. Like Lauren, Zahra and Harry have been traumatized by the catastrophe that has overtaken their neighborhood. In this instance Lauren's sharing brings some relief. "Their misery eases my own," she observes (167), distracting her mind from her singular loss and establishing a bond across race (with Harry) and class (with Zahra). The misery of others will function throughout the narrative as a dilution of the private sorrow that threatens her with paralysis. Book-learned and street-naive as Lauren may be, she recognizes that the three will survive to the extent that they succeed in becoming "a pack" (182) for defensive if not overtly predatory purposes.

Zahra, whose early education as a street person serves the group well as they adapt to life among a homeless multitude for whom survival preempts ethics, admonishes her fellow travelers that mixed-race couples on the road "catch hell" (171), but it will be by virtue of this multiethnic group's ability to attract a similarly mixed company that they achieve comparative safety in numbers. Lauren functions as gatekeeper, and her preference privileges family groups, single parents with children, women whose victimhood is clearly legible, and in the case of Bankole, an older, patriarchal man of professional standing. Although in the first days of their trek Lauren demonstrates a capacity to kill quickly and without remorse as a way of avoiding the prostration of her hyperempathetic response, she also exhibits conventional sympathy for those whose vulnerability acts as a magnet for predators. It is thus that she makes overtures to migrants whose names (like her own) often encode their ethnicity: Travis, Natividad, Dominic, Bankole, Allie, Jill, Justin. Consistent with Butler's implicit argument that catastrophic demographics promote a human leveling (we are all on this planet together), Lauren's journal documents a striking breakdown of ethnic boundaries. Zahra and Harry become lovers careless of birth control, and the offspring they produce will conform to an established trend. Well into the journey Lauren adopts what she describes as "the most racially mixed" (287) individuals that she has hitherto met—a woman with a black mother and Japanese father, and her daughter, fathered by the woman's deceased Mexican husband. Through this woman's advocacy, a black Latino and his daughter also join the group. While Lauren travels with her stockpile of seeds, her gathered company bears a diverse gene pool, one that prompts readers to envision a posterity of blurred color lines.

The trek northward that Butler imagines in *Parable of the Sower* introduces a new and striking variation on the geographies of flight surveyed up to now, for instead of the woodland path, open field, cave, swamp, ditch, indoor passageway, cellar, attic, water crossing, and urban alley associated with the slave and neo-slave narrative traditions, that geography consists of what to contemporary readers is the familiar infrastructure of an automobile-dependent West Coast: Los Angeles freeways, interstate corridors, state highways threading a system of parks and reservoirs, all in disrepair if not ruin. Except for the large armored trucks that ply the nighttime roads, the traffic along these corridors is pedestrian, in desperate migration from the harsh, dry climate and social anarchy of Southern California to a Northwest that holds some promise of ecological and economic sustainability. Dystopian narratives typically take a known contemporary world and, by presenting it in ruins, defamiliarize it, adumbrating thereby the catastrophe that lurks in all stable-seeming systems.[26] Butler's innovation consists in her repurposing the landscapes of apocalyptic dystopian vision in accord with the fugitive slave narrative tradition and the dystopias that pertain to that tradition's scenes of persecution. Slavery, Butler proclaims, is not confined to the past: let us see how it might unfold in a near-future world.

The thirteen individuals who make it all the way to Humboldt County survive a broad spectrum of misery, everything from hunger, homelessness, wildfire, injury, and disease to rape, incest, debt slavery, sex slavery, in addition to countless bereavements and the uncertainty of whether a loved one is dead or alive. Further bereavement awaits at their pastoral destination: instead of the idyllic farm worked by Bankole's sister and her family, the company comes upon burned buildings and his relatives' unburied bones. Still, as the future husband of the community's now eighteen-year-old leader, Bankole enters into a hopeful configuration with Lauren, who, sharer though she may be, has never experienced the extreme abjection of the rape and incest victims among their company. *Sower* ends with the founding of the pilot Earthseed village, Acorn, and the first group activity is a funeral during which individuals name the dead and plant trees. Given the thematic pairing of male and female, the bodies of Butler's sufferers propose a regenerative communal social possibility even as they bear in injury and traumatic memory the inscription of late-most capitalism.[27] *Parable of the Talents*, the sequel to *Parable of the Sower*, illustrates how rapidly a near-utopian community like Acorn can be invaded and subjected to the state of exception from which it emerged, but in the Gospel according to Lauren, the survivors who lay Acorn's foundations persist as a viable hypothesis.[28]

As a meditation on present and future misery, *Sower* draws on the slave narrative past while suggesting that the condition of slavery extends to anyone not a member of the moneyed elite. Although white people retain certain relative advantages, abuse is more a function of one's class position than one's ethnicity. Lauren, again, is a decidedly privileged witness. The African American daughter of professional parents (her father and stepmother both hold doctorates), she embodies transitional social categories: whereas she figures as a quasi-autonomous subject, she does so mindful of past ancestral enslavement and a future in which she might well be reduced to a chattel state (as will happen in *Talents*). Literacy has been her birthright: "full of books," she has never thought twice about using words to command attention. The inscribed relationship of narrator to reader is crucial to any testament of suffering, and it is therefore instructive to contrast Lauren's manner of addressing a readership with that of a historical witness to the misery of enslavement, such as Harriet Jacobs in *Incidents in the Life of a Slave Girl*. That narrative, as we have seen, also constructs a female protagonist as heroic action figure. As Linda Brent recounting "A Perilous Passage in the Slave Girl's Life," Jacobs alternates between apology and defiance: her misery, she presumes, is beyond the conceptual powers of her white, Northern, middle-class readership. Although in her preface to *Incidents*, Lydia Maria Child works to establish a common ground of sisterhood between Northern female readers and women held in bondage throughout the South (and does so surely with the understanding that white privileged women were themselves not immune from physical and sexual abuse), Jacobs writes of her misery from the position that no one who has not lived her life can conceive of her degradation or understand the situational necessity of entering into a liaison with one man to forestall the advances of another.

By contrast, Lauren speaks to her readership in the confiding voice of young adult fiction. Even when, as a survivalist, she depicts herself engaged in "the ordinary, unspeakable things that we did now to live" (312), like shooting or knifing a would-be assailant or stripping the clothes off the corpses they come upon, her narrative invites the reader's willing identification with her predicament and the choices she makes. At no point does she proclaim her misery to be beyond the cognitive or emotional grasp of her reader. On the other hand, some of the misery experienced by her fellow travelers exceeds her own cognitive capacity, even with hyperempathy to instruct her in the pain of others. The journals cultivate the reader as confidant(e) entrusted with the confessions of a young woman who, unlike Linda Brent, has spent most of her life amid the relative if incarcerating safeguards of middle-class life. She herself figures as a reader and invites her readers to identify with her as one who similarly is "full of books" (156). Having never personally been reduced to chattel status or subjected to routinized sexual violence, she does not speak the language of shame that Linda Brent cannot avoid. This is not to say that Lauren is without shame: her syndrome, treated as a family secret inasmuch as it derives from her deceased mother's addiction, is the "truth" about her that she must confess to her fellow travelers. Yet one might argue that, to her reader-confidant(e), she becomes the more approachable because afflicted with a "syndrome" that marks her as someone paying a price for living in an era of chemical addiction. Hyperempathy furthermore serves Butler's audience as a metaphor of the immersions that occur when we read of the pleasure and pain of others. We meet the world through protocols of necessary delusion.[29]

That Lauren's response to another's misery is "delusional," even as it replicates within her sensorium the extremes of the other's pain, brings us back to the question of what it means—from positions of comparative privilege and self-control—to form a relationship with the world's suffering, and because we always encounter Lauren as one who writes, we may suspect that she herself never speaks as one abjected—not, at least, in the sense Julia Kristeva gives to the word.[30] Moreover, in the course of her journey Lauren learns the limits of what "sharing" can contribute to one's response to another's suffering. "If hyperempathy syndrome were a more common complaint," she speculates soon after the recovery of her brother's mutilated body, but before she herself has ventured into the world beyond the neighborhood wall, "people couldn't do such things. They could kill if they had to, and bear the pain of it or be destroyed by it. But if everyone could feel everyone else's pain, who would torture?" (115). Toward the end of the journey, however, her opinion has evolved. "I've read about the syndrome," observes Bankole. "I remember thinking that it might not be so bad a thing if most people had to endure all the pain they caused." To this Lauren replies, "Bad idea. . . . Bad, bad idea. Self-defense shouldn't have to be an agony or a killing or both" (277–78).[31] Implicit in Lauren's response is that hyperempathy is simply sensation, not empathy in a conventional sense, certainly not conscience, and that only those disinclined to torture in the first place could learn from becoming sharers—but then, what exactly would they learn? She has become, as a result of experience, a pragmatist skeptical of the moral lesson of pain. We learn, sadly, very little from our delusional immersion in the suffering of others. What we know of misery is that it propagates, that it cannot be walled off or otherwise geographically contained, and that it threatens civil life. It requires what must seem to be utopian solutions. But individuals survive in proportion as they maintain an affective distance from the other's suffering, or so Lauren's example proposes.

To the degree that Lauren figures as reader-surrogate and her hyperempathy serves as the reader's portal to the (delusive) contemplation of the other's bodily sufferings, we are brought back to the ethical dilemma that Saidiya Hartman frames in the introduction to *Scenes of Subjection*. Hartman directs her interrogation to testimonies of past sufferings, but we need only make slight adjustments to apply her questions to the premonition of what will happen based on what unfolds in the present moment: "Are we witnesses who confirm the truth of what happened in the face of the world-destroying capacities of pain, the distortions of torture, the sheer unrepresentability of terror, and the repression of the dominant accounts? Or are we voyeurs fascinated with and repelled by exhibitions of terror and sufferance?" And if the latter, we might insert, does our voyeurism serve only to anesthetize our sensibilities? "What," Hartman asks, "does the exposure of the violated body yield?" In Butler's dark Afro-futurism it is clearly meant to yield admonition: this suffering could be so commonplace as to become unremarkable and, inconceivably but really all too conceivably, tolerable. "At issue here," continues Hartman, "is the precariousness of empathy and the uncertain line between witness and spectator," particularly in the face of "the tortured body or endless recitations of the ghastly and the terrible. In light of this, how does one give expression to these outrages without exacerbating the indifference to suffering that is the consequence of the benumbing spectacle or contend with the narcissistic identification that obliterates the other or the prurience that too often is the response to such displays?"[32] Or how, in view of Lauren's strong survival imperative, does one avoid apprehending the pain of others as the confirmation if not congratulation that one has survived against all odds?

The journals of Lauren Oya Olamina neither identify an audience nor envision the circumstances in which they might be read by anyone other than herself. In this regard they support the fiction that we are reading the testimony of an American adolescent, self-absorbed as is typical of the age, bright and precocious as the individual may be. Does the fifteen-year-old who inaugurates the journal-writing process imagine people like herself (female, teenage, middle-class, of no particular ethnicity necessarily) as the hypothetical readership? Would this be why the narrative often reads as though marketed to a young adult audience? The destiny of *Parable of the Sower* as testimony is to some extent addressed in the sequel, *Parable of the Talents*, in which Lauren's daughter sorts and publishes her mother's writings along with those of her father, Bankole, presenting those writings with commentary that constitutes testimony of her own.

"My ancestors in this hemisphere were, by law, chattel slaves"

Readers of the sequel, *Parable of the Talents*, learn how briefly the pilot Earthseed settlement, Acorn, succeeds in reinventing the social order. Five years from inception, its population has increased from thirteen to fifty-nine, and the experiment in homesteading has advanced to the point where it meets the community's basic needs. Lauren and company have attended to the sick and injured, farmed the land, traded in local markets, provided refuge to the dispossessed, and established an educational program for children and adults. Buildings have been erected and systems implemented for the community's defense. Such measures prove no match, however, for the armed crusaders of Christian America (CA), the vengeful followers of Andrew Steele Jarrett, a former U.S. senator from Texas who campaigns successfully for the presidency on the promise to "make America great again."[33] Although Acorn is protected in the early years by its remote Humboldt County location, its reputation as the center of a pagan cult attracts the notice of CA militants, who besiege Acorn with armored vehicles. The strike force attacks the colony and kills numerous residents, including Zahra and Bankole, before enslaving the adult survivors and relocating the children in CA orphanages and foster homes. After seventeen months of concentration-camp hardship, Earthseed adults along with other prisoners (assorted "criminals" incarcerated on site) are able to remove the punitive electronic collars they have been forced to wear when heavy rains produce a landslide that disrupts the network's mainframe. The captives stage a murderous revolt, set fire to Camp Christian, as Acorn has been renamed, and disperse in all directions.

Bankole and Lauren's infant daughter, Larkin, is among the children removed from Acorn. Placed with a black conservative Christian couple, she grows to adulthood as Asha Vere Alexander. Her adoptive parents instruct the child in the fundamentalist tenets of Christian America, but the foster mother, whose biological daughter died just prior to Asha Vere's arrival and who persistently regards the newcomer as heathen offspring, withholds affection, while the foster father molests her throughout girlhood. Subsequent events put Lauren's daughter in contact with her biological family. After she has left the Alexander household, Asha Vere by chance encounters Marcos Duran, the young, charismatic preacher who has acquired celebrity in CA circles and who happens to be her Uncle Marc, whom Lauren years before redeemed from slavery and resettled in Acorn. Once Marc recovers from the physical damage of his captive years, his Christian convictions prompt him to flee in horror at his sister's pagan theology. Knowing that Christian America's militant wing had occupied Acorn and relocated the children, Marc had been aware that his niece was settled in the CA foster system. Following the meeting in which they recognize the familial relation, Asha Vere and Marc bond, and although Marc has the power to reunite Lauren and her daughter, he chooses instead to tell Asha Vere that her mother is dead. A decade passes: Asha Vere and Marc have established a household; she has entered adulthood, earned a master's degree and a doctorate, and become a software designer. Running across excerpts from *The Books of the Living* online, Asha Vere learns that Lauren has not died—she has, in fact, reestablished Earthseed in the waning years of Christian America's power and influence, and become a wealthy and prominent spiritual leader.

Estranged from her parents at two months and never able to shake the conviction that Lauren in any case would have abandoned her in favor of Earthseed, Asha Vere appears in *Parable of the Talents* as her mother's posthumous editor, framing lengthy selections of Lauren's journals with the narrative of her own troubled and neglected childhood and interspersing short selections from the writings of Bankole, the Earthseed skeptic, and Marc, the Christian believer and keeper of his father's faith. From her daughter's perspective, the heroic Lauren Olamina, who successfully leads an ethnically diverse band of refugees in their exodus from Southern to Northern California, who founds an intentional community, who survives its destruction and the loss of her family, and who reconstitutes Earthseed as a rich and politically influential organization with communities throughout the United States, Canada, Mexico, and Brazil, is a ruthless and egocentric personality driven by the impossible and preposterous vision first articulated in *Parable of the Sower*: "The Destiny of Earthseed is to take root among the stars" (77). Asha Vere's intervention in her mother's first-person testimony at times seems to lift Lauren's trajectory out of the slave narrative paradigm and to reinsert it into that of the corporate success story. Such reinterpretation is to some extent justified: the turn in Earthseed fortunes occurs when Lauren, accompanied by a new and savvy convert, Belen Ross, arrives in Portland, Oregon, and begins to proselytize a different demographic: white progressive professionals, who take an interest in Lauren's verse and assist her in publishing *The Books of the Living* online—where Asha Vere eventually encounters her mother's writings. The Olamina her daughter learns about, the Olamina she suspects may be her mother, is a formidable figure, the CEO, as it were, of more than the average religious organization:

> Granted, Earthseed was an unusual cult. It financed scientific exploration and inquiry, and technological creativity. It set up grade schools and eventually colleges, and offered full scholarships to poor but gifted students. (379)

> It owned land, schools, farms, factories, stores, banks, several whole towns. And it seemed to own a lot of well-known people—lawyers, physicians, journalists, scientists, politicians, even members of Congress. (380)

In Asha Vere's account of their long-deferred reunion, mother and daughter briefly converse at a posh Earthseed-owned property in the Adirondacks. Lauren figures as a fifty-eight-year-old female executive whose overtures the thirty-four-year-old daughter adamantly resists.

Had Butler completed *Parable of the Trickster*, the third novel in the projected trilogy, readers would have a better idea of the planetary exodus the author had in mind, for in that installment the Destiny was to be put to its next-world test. Whatever brief may be assembled with reference to her inadequate motherhood and love of power, Lauren exists as the Moses to an interstellar occupation of the Promised Land. In the journal excerpt dated July 20, 2090, with which the daughter concludes the compilation of her mother's writing and which the reader understands to be the Earthseed matriarch's final entry, Lauren watches the first shuttles depart with their store of seed, tools, libraries, and frozen embryos. The shuttles are to link up with the starship *Christopher Columbus*, a name that meets with Olamina's disapproval even as she dismisses the idea that this vessel will replicate the devastation wreaked in consequence of its namesake's voyages.[34] In this Olamina may be deceiving herself (Asha Vere repeatedly suggests that her mother is blinded by the power she wields), but Butler's vision of cosmic diaspora represents at least a partial transcendence of race and racialized geographies, as does Earthseed's earthbound multiethnic community with its vast holdings of American hemispheric real estate. Viewed cynically, Earthseed's success would seem to indicate that for all the chaos and disintegration besetting the United States, wealth exists in the late twenty-first century to accumulate so long as a charismatic personality also exists to deliver a compelling message.[35] Yet it is well to recall that Butler's *Parable* series begins, in *Sower*, at a hypothetical point in American society where middle-class egalitarianism is no longer viable and enslavement awaits anyone unwilling to adopt extreme measures to preserve a degree of self-determination. It is thus that *Sower* and *Talents* together propose fresh installments in the slave narrative tradition, the trek from Southern to Northern California reprising the familiar escape cartography while established tropes reappear in *Talents* in the Maroon settlement from which the utopian Acorn arises as well as in the site of horrors into which Acorn is transformed: a Camp Christian that is equal parts plantation and concentration camp. As they recall geographies of race rooted in a persistent heritage of slavery, these narratives document evolving demographics in which color lines become increasingly multiple and, in their multiplicity, blurred.

The rich and powerful Lauren Olamina of Asha Vere's third-person narration may bear little outward resemblance to the heroic figure gathering her people on the perilous trek northward from Southern California, the teenage visionary dispossessed of such meager protection as had exempted her and her distressed community from utter destitution. But as a wealthy, formidable, and dangerous black woman, Lauren remains true to the vision of her adolescence. However ruthlessly, and with whatever megalomaniacal intensities, she has devoted her life to imagining the cosmos as the rightful domain of a multitude whose earth history has been that of coerced displacement and geographical marginalization. "My ancestors in this hemisphere were, by law, chattel slaves," she observes soon after the Earthseed community has overwhelmed its Christian America captors to embark on yet another diaspora up and down the Pacific coast. Contemplating, in the light of a seventeen-month captivity, her remote slave heritage and what she computes as the ten generations of ancestral bondage, Lauren concedes that she "can't begin to imagine" the effects of such prolonged trauma: "How did they survive it all and keep their humanity?" (270). Asha Vere's critique of her mother calls into question whether Lauren's survival has indeed come at the expense of her humanity. But from what readers are given to know about her long-term management of hyperempathy syndrome, they have come to understand that she has had to find ways to detach body and mind from the full devastating impact of sharing her neighbor's suffering. Perhaps, then, it should not surprise us that accumulation of wealth and power has become Lauren's method of hardening the borders between herself and the world's unbounded pain. In the long view, moreover, the human and material resources Earthseed has amassed set the stage for the planetary exodus that Lauren observes in her final entry. This multiethnic egress, we are encouraged to hope, channels the wisdom garnered over many generations from the African diaspora to which Lauren traces her origins.

In Lauren's determination to see Earthseed take root among the stars, we may see an analogy to Butler's determination to occupy a literary genre in which intergalactic space has always been the major theme, a genre and associated literary cartography that from inception have been dominated by white authors and white readers.[36] Butler's work preserves a memory of gender and color lines even as she demonstrates their failure to serve as a bar—to female authors discouraged from entering a world of technological speculation and to authors of color discouraged from entering a world of scientific and speculative epistemology. The cartographies in which Butler meets her readers project a world where color lines are recognized as posing the danger of mutual destruction, where survival is understood as collective, and where *kindred* reigns as the central trope.

Epilogue

✦

Color outside the Lines

The successor to the first African American to occupy the White House would be a Caucasian businessman of seventy, a real estate "mogul" who began his career by excluding a black applicant from a Queens apartment complex for which he and his father served as gatekeepers.[1] From the niche in public consciousness he had carved out as a reality television personality, he inaugurated his campaign by voicing concerns that the black sitting president was not who he said he was, recirculating rumors of his crypto-Kenyan origins and continuing crypto-Muslim practice, questioning his qualification to hold the office to which he had been twice elected, and insinuating that his status as a natural-born citizen could only be established by presentation of a birth certificate, and then only if the certificate's authenticity should be verified. Americans acquainted with Jim Crow efforts to require of black voters impossible proofs of enfranchisement might see in the antics of the businessman-turned-politician a similar ploy to impugn the black president's birthright. With talk of a Mexican border wall, Muslim ban, and mass deportations, Barack Obama's successor shoved his way into national attention as but the latest defender of the principle of white North American space, the stentorian voice of a "silent majority" suspicious of color and difference.[2]

That the forty-fifth president should be an elderly white with a record of racist and sexist behavior is not quite the pure anomaly self-respecting Americans might wish to see it as. Any thought that Obama's accession had signaled a watershed in race relations, much less the attainment of a color-blind society, had been challenged in his election's immediate aftermath by vows of a congressional Republican leadership to oppose categorically the president-elect's initiatives and to do everything in its power to limit his mandate to four miserable years. Republicans might plausibly claim that impassioned opposition to this president was "not about race," that the visceral vehemence of their response to his election reflected only the scale of their defeat, and that defiance was simply the natural reflex of a party that had lost the White House and now held minority positions in House and Senate. But that the response was very much "about race" is supported by the party's patent enlistment of what might be termed white heritage resentment, a potent resource among its portfolio of affects, the legacy of Richard Nixon's "Southern Strategy" to recruit Wallace Democrats away from the party that had championed the Civil Rights Acts of 1964 and 1968. Working more or less subliminally, focusing on policy issues (affirmative action, universal health care, and judicial reform) in which Democrats could be depicted as unduly privileging African Americans, the G.O.P. did not hesitate to harness racial animosity in the campaign leading up to the 2010 midterm elections.

Republican midterm election success reflected the slow and uneven progress of economic recovery as well as the mobilization of traditional conservative resistance to federal rule (especially as exemplified by the Affordable Care Act), but the emotion that drove Republican insurgents is more directly attributable to the successful depiction of Obama as a foreign and dangerous Other, the opposition's semistealth method of assailing him for being black. This line of attack was spearheaded by the Tea Party Movement, an assemblage of middle- and working-class whites, many of whom had lost jobs and savings during the 2008 recession and who saw little prospect of recuperation under an administration perceived as intent on revitalizing the legacies of the civil rights era.[3] The movement built on red-state populism but was largely underwritten by industries that chafed at the regulatory prospects of a green-friendly administration.[4] The rise of the Tea Party caught progressives off guard; it constituted a stinging rebuke to those who had read Obama's arrival as a genuinely millennial moment. Fueled by the steroid of right-wing talk radio and cable news, Obama's opponents laid bare the virulent persistence of antiblack sentiment (a revelation much less astonishing to African Americans than to their progressive fellow citizens) as the forty-fourth president became the target of an animus fixated on his other-than-whiteness. The deeply personal nature of the attacks could not be explained solely with reference to the policies his administration advocated and the legislation it sought to enact. For in many regards Obama was a traditional centrist; from the left came charges of betrayal and perpetuation of a neoliberal agenda.[5] The global appeal of this president whose full name, as his critics pointed out, invoked the nation's bitterest enemies (Saddam Hussein, Osama bin Laden), his rejection of an "America First" approach to international problems, and his skeptical interpretation of the doctrine of American exceptionalism evinced a statesman hesitant to perform the rites of national idolatry. In a country of historically anti-intellectual tendencies and suspicion of technocratic elites, a professorial-mannered black president with an exotic name was destined to provoke negative reaction.

Well-meaning Americans appalled by the degree to which color prejudice and xenophobia pervaded the language of the Obama opposition, alarmed by the shootings of unarmed black men, and dismayed by the June 2015 massacre of the Charleston Mother Emanuel African Methodist Episcopal (AME) Church parishioners were in for even greater shocks as the 2016 presidential campaign revealed the full electoral force of populist racial resentment.

Against a cable news feed in which angry black people protested against police and vigilante shootings, Latinx "illegals" scattered amid the moon glow of night-vision surveillance, and Middle Eastern visages wheeled into view as operatives of thwarted or successful terrorist plots, candidate Trump challenged his supporters to "take back our country," a provocation that would achieve lethal culmination with the August 12, 2017, Unite the Right rally in Charlottesville, Virginia. Throughout his campaign he would demonstrate that it was only too possible to engage in hateful rhetoric and, far from consigning his campaign to instant and ignominious failure (the prediction of Republicans and Democrats alike), meet with rousing success. In attacking whole communities of color, he presented himself as defying the canons of "political correctness," parading an unapologetic racism as though to do so reclaimed a First Amendment birthright. His bigotries revealed a mind attached to rigidly partitioned cartographies: Muslims belong in Muslim nations, Mexicans are "illegal" when not in Mexico, and African Americans naturally congregate in crime-ridden "inner cities," dystopian spaces reflective of the economic misrule of the sitting president as well as the flawed character of the residents themselves. By this logic, black citizens (for, unlike the others, they were indeed citizens and could not be dismissed as foreigners) qualified as criminals or victims: in either case something had to be done to or for them. While assuring black and white voters alike that he would solve the problem of "the inner city," the candidate pledged unqualified support to those who patrolled the urban war zone. In keeping with his white conservative base, the candidate exhibited a furious unconcern when it came to police shootings of unarmed black residents.

The new president's geography broke down into static containment units and ethnically inflected zones. Concerned with hard borders, his chief priority was to wall off an imaginary southern frontier where jihadists and drug dealers darkly foregathered amid caravans of indigents from "shithole countries."[6] Elsewhere on his map, removed from the worlds of the black and brown but vulnerable to infiltration, stretched the small towns and rust belt cities where financially distressed middle-class whites awaited the return of factory, mining, and shopkeeping jobs. The executive suburb represented another realm entirely, as did the hotel, casino, resort, and golf course where a white, elite, mobile demographic, served by a largely immigrant underclass (not excluding the very "illegals" against whom the candidate directed his rants), combined business with pleasure. The Trump empire itself stood first in this world of mobility and privilege. Ever fond of the grandiose adjective, the real estate magnate pointedly decreed that his hotels incorporate "international" into their titles and his golf links bear the epithet "national" or "international" depending on whether they were located in the United States or abroad. Devoid of any but evocative significance, such qualifiers ministered to corporate fantasy as they flattered the clientele's cosmopolitan self-regard. While wishing to invoke such larger contexts, Trump looked upon his properties as island domains detached from the world, if not contemptuous of specific localities with which the sites existed in contiguity.[7] Eager to develop property anywhere in the world where money could be made, he had litigated aggressively against local economic and environmental resistance. A longtime participant in multinational capitalism, as candidate and president he nonetheless expressed strong isolationist "America First" tendencies. His advocacy of asymmetrical trade agreements demonstrated an adversarial and unnuanced approach to international business, and his rejection of climate science and his decision to withdraw from the Paris Accords dramatized a refusal to comprehend the borderless nature of global ecology. His outlook communicated a determination to deny the world's interconnectivity. He worked from a map of isolated sites that exist in a condition of depleted relationality.[8]

The election of a man whose cartography is founded on principles of segregation and the reflex denial of interrelationship, site to site, person to person, except where relation facilitates accumulation of wealth, could only exacerbate the bitter historical divisions in American society. How, one asks, could a candidate who embodies such retrograde attitudes propel himself into the White House? Does the Trump victory confirm the immutability of racial animosity, or, as has been more persuasively argued, does it express white reaction to signal evolutions in American demographics, specifically the U.S. Census Bureau projections that, by 2043, white people will have lost majority status?[9] Tea Party demonization of Barack Obama and the rise of white nationalist groups suggest that the imminent minoritization of European Americans does in fact terrify those who trace U.S. institutions to ancient Greece and Reformation England.[10] In Carol Anderson's analysis, the steady entrance of black people into high-profile professional and public life incited during the Obama years a "white rage" that has flared periodically since Reconstruction.[11] Toni Morrison would see the election of Trump as a sign of how deeply inscribed white supremacist attitudes remain at the nation's cognitive and emotional core. "Unlike any nation in Europe," she writes, "the United States holds whiteness as the unifying force. Here, for many people, the definition of 'Americanness' is color." For those attached to such definitions, a two-term black president initiated a crisis of faith that has yet to run its course: "White people's conviction of their natural superiority is being lost. Rapidly lost. There are 'people of color' everywhere, threatening to erase this long-understood definition of America. And what then? Another black President? A predominantly black Senate? Three black Supreme Court Justices?" In Morrison's assessment, the election of Trump figures as a moment of collective white panic:

> On Election Day, how eagerly so many white voters—both the poorly educated and the well educated—embraced the shame and fear sowed by Donald Trump. The candidate whose company has been

> sued by the Justice Department for not renting apartments to black people. The candidate who questioned whether Barack Obama was born in the United States, and who seemed to condone the beating of a Black Lives Matter protester at a campaign rally. The candidate who kept black workers off the floors of his casinos. The candidate who is beloved by David Duke and endorsed by the Ku Klux Klan.[12]

Written in the week following the November 8, 2016, election, these observations are full of the anguish that overtook an electorate disappointed that a second consecutive "first"—the election of a female president—did not occur, an electorate that might more readily have accepted defeat under circumstances that did not involve a candidate whose ethics, intellect, and temperament so obviously disqualified him for high office. Implicit in Morrison's itemization of Trump's affront to nonwhite voters is the question: Haven't we progressed as a multiracial society beyond the point where such undiluted and unapologetic racism is tolerable? Is fear that potent? Is shame itself powerless to recall the country to its egalitarian ideals?

People of color, as Morrison observes, are everywhere, but that has hardly dissolved the separate geographies by which whites and nonwhites navigate American space. One might well begin with what to a U.S. majority are the invisible geographies of the national prisons, in which African Americans, Latinos, and Native Americans form a grossly disproportionate percentage relative to the population outside. Michelle Alexander's landmark study, *The New Jim Crow: Mass Incarceration in the Age of Colorblindness* (2012), documents the degree to which the Clinton-era phase of the "war on drugs" initiated during the first Reagan administration consigned hundreds of thousands of nonviolent black offenders to long prison terms from which white offenders were systematically exempt. As the title of this book published two years into the Obama era suggests, policy decisions have lasting effects, and institutional structures can remain untouched by signal turns in a nation's politics. Alexander documents the dramatic rise, compared with other advanced industrial nations, of the U.S. prison census in the 1980s, but a key part of her argument addresses the degree to which mass incarceration spreads well beyond the prison wall, not only in the vast numbers of released convicts who remain "under correctional control" and, depending on the state in which they reside, stripped of their rights as citizens, but also in the "stigma of criminality" that pertains to anyone who happens to be young, black and male.[13] "Because black youth are viewed as criminals," Alexander observes, "they face severe employment discrimination and are also 'pushed out' of schools through racially based school discipline policies." Moreover, "the first police stop, interrogation, search, or arrest" exists in black communities as a rite of passage.[14]

People of color may be everywhere, but there is little safety in numbers. The deaths of Trayvon Martin (2012) and Michael Brown (2014), among many others, have directed attention to the intensity with which black men, particularly young black men, find themselves everywhere under scrutiny and, with disturbing and seemingly self-propagating regularity, on the receiving end of police or civilian bullets. White apologists of such surveillance are quick to point out that young black men are much more frequently the victims of other young black men than of police personnel or vigilantes, but black-on-black violence stems from complex causes associated with poverty and isolation and is further evidence that black and white worlds remain materially distinct. Police or vigilante shootings, particularly when the shooter is white and acts as the commissioned or self-appointed agent of law enforcement, confirm the persistence with which young (and not so young) black men, and occasionally women, embody to large portions of American society a predisposition to lawless behavior, if not a clear and present threat. Such incidents take place in black neighborhoods, mixed neighborhoods, white neighborhoods, and the public space of arterial borderlands. In response, groups such as Black Lives Matter (BLM) have launched demonstrations that conspicuously involve countergeographical direct action. The occupation of designated "whites only" space as well as public buildings and outdoor venues has long been associated with civil rights protest, but BLM blockage of interstate highways—significant from a historical perspective given the role the routing of such highways has played in the destruction and isolation of black urban neighborhoods[15]—makes an especially forceful argument that everything must stop until justice has been served. BLM has enjoyed support among some white progressive groups, who accept the disruption of business as usual as a necessary cost of the effort to compel a society to change. But the inability or refusal of large segments of the white community to comprehend the BLM message is evident from the adversarial rejoinders, "*All* Lives Matter," "*Blue* Lives Matter," and "*White* Lives Matter"—responses that indicate a failure to register the lack of symmetry people of color experience in the United States with respect to institutional recognition of their basic humanity. Black testimony, in short, must still speak from a world of sociogeographic difference, a world distant and different from that structured by historical white privilege.

Black testimony speaks from narrative spaces that, absent such testimony, remain invisible to the worlds of white privilege. "Even as a child," writes Saidya Hartman, retracing the map of sociogeographic difference in *Lose Your Mother: A Journey along the Atlantic Slave Route* (2007), "I knew that a wrong turn off the highway, a whistle, or a walk on the wrong side of town could cost you your life if you were black."[16] A half century and more after the 1963 March on Washington, nonwhites enter public and private spaces as suspected intruders except when "at home" in the designated ghetto or barrio or on the reservation, zones that in turn provide little refuge from institutional violence. In the letter to his son that he published as *Between the World and Me* (2015), Ta-Nehisi Coates frames the constrained geography of his childhood and adolescence as follows: "I knew that West Baltimore, where I lived; that the north side of Philadelphia, where my cousins lived; that the South Side of Chicago, where friends of my father lived, comprised a world apart. Somewhere out there beyond the firmament, past the asteroid belt, there were other worlds where children did not regularly fear for their bodies. I knew this because there was a large television resting in my living room."[17] Hartman and Coates highlight remarkable continuities in the spatial regimes of America before and after the civil rights era, continuities evinced (among other proofs) by the advice-book institution known as *The Negro-Motorist's Green Book* and its recent sardonic successor. Victor Hugo Green published this directory of services and homestays open to black patronage annually from 1936 to 1967. A survival guide for black people taking to American highways, the *Green Book* constituted a specialized application of long-standing proactive geographical epistemologies.[18] That it ceased publication in 1967 may reflect changes spurred by the Civil Rights Act of 1964, but long after the disappearance of the more obvious Jim Crow exclusions with their overt "whites only" and "colored" designations, black countergeographical mapping of the world remains in force. In 2017, Jan Miles would publish *The Post-Racial Negro Green Book*, a cartography not of services but of incidents: micro- and macroaggressions directed against black people between 2013 and 2016.[19]

People of color are everywhere, but many still go home to neighborhoods in which the heritage of segregation (and therefore of slavery) materially persists. In 2017, against the shallow memory of an American public which prefers to believe that 1960s civil rights legislation leveled the playing fields of national life, legal scholar Richard Rothstein published *The Color of Law: A Forgotten History of How Our Government Segregated America*. "Forgotten" as this history may be, it has never settled entirely into the oblivion of the national past, living on in the memory of those who have been victims of the segregation he describes. However, by exposing the extent to which the Federal Housing Administration, the Home Owners' Loan Corporation, the Veterans' Administration, and other governmental entities colluded with the real estate and insurance industries to deny African American access to housing markets, confining people of color to neighborhoods isolated from educational and economic opportunity, Rothstein has sought to "arouse in Americans an understanding of how we created a system of unconstitutional, state-sponsored, de jure segregation, and a sense of outrage about it."[20] He does so at a time when such outrage is particularly needful. Aside from documenting the extent of federal, state, and local governmental involvement in establishing conditions of separation and inequality, and doing so in defiance of U.S. constitutional guarantees of equal treatment under the law, Rothstein demonstrates that past actions commonly viewed as unconstitutional live on in the present and continue to generate a devastatingly unequal society.[21]

The Color of Law appears at a time when public awareness of the differential geographies of black and white worlds, already prompted by a recognition of the very different roles police play in white and nonwhite neighborhoods, has also been reinforced by the Flint, Michigan, water crisis, an instance of administrative negligence that contributes a memorable chapter to the larger narrative of lead poisoning (ubiquitous wherever poor residents inhabit old and badly maintained housing) and the exposure of low-income populations to environmental hazards, pathogens, and cataclysms (such as Hurricanes Katrina, Sandy, Harvey, Irma, and Maria) more generally. As ocean levels rise and storms of all categories become more frequent and slow-moving, large coastal communities of color occupy a geography susceptible to Katrina-like devastations and, with those devastations, the further laying bare of long-standing institutional environmental injustice.

Police and white civilian shootings of unarmed black people are not new, nor is the disproportionate exposure of underprivileged populations to industrial toxins and storm surges. Novelty does lie in the power of contemporary media to generate spikes in public awareness, though it is incautious to generalize to what effect. But what happens (or does not happen) when such spikes coincide with the ascendency of an administration unlikely to interrogate local police practice, an administration determined to relax environmental regulation, an administration committed to weakening the enforcement of civil rights legislation, an administration skilled in the art of disinformation? People of color are everywhere, and white people are a minority already in California and New York City. But numbers in themselves do not alter structures of power and are less likely to do so when democratic processes are subverted—as they are when supermajorities in statehouses gerrymander the lines of legislative districts, or when opportunities to engage in the electoral process are restricted by laws that narrow the window of participation. Politicians in states north and south have discovered that by contracting the time frame in which voting is permissible, by strategically locating polling stations at a distance from where poor people live, and by introducing burdensome protocols of identification, they may diminish participation among those whose work schedules, immobility, and lack of specific documentation discourage a trip to the polls.[22] The second decade of the twenty-first century will be remembered as a time when the voting rights of low-income Americans and nonwhite communities in particular came under persistent and coordinated attack.

I set out in this book to examine the geographies of flight in the slave narrative tradition as well as in those narratives that, from the nineteenth to the twentieth century, and from the twentieth to the twenty-first, descend from that tradition and the social conditions that fostered it. Recurrently I have focused on first-person testimony that foregrounds the cartographic discrepancy between (black) author and (generally white) reader and on issues in play when the fugitive speaks from a world of persecution to auditors in a more or less "free" world. In the prologue I had included among my core questions whether these texts enforce an unbridgeable distance even as they compel us to imagine a counter-nation of resettlement and reconciliation. Unsurprisingly, this study concludes without definitive answers.

Throughout, I have examined the way these texts mark geographies that counter the traditionally dominant national geography, the North America of open horizons, free movement, and inhabitable space, a conception inherently if often invisibly white supremacist. Escape, never a matter of arriving free and clear in a land of equal treatment regardless of color and class, becomes ever more complicated over time, as slavery is abolished but the institutions and cultural practices that instantiate discrimination persist. As we have seen, moreover, *flight* in the overt sense of escaping from bondage and crossing the border from slave to free state is in many respects the least part of an emancipatory narrative. Typically, emancipation entails an internal liberation by which the enslaved subject prepares to undertake a perilous overland or overwater journey and, having embarked on that journey and attained the sought-after destination, awakens to the sobering recognition that the free state, once achieved, offers only qualified release from the condition of bondage. By the time Du Bois writes of his travels, the flight motif has shed much of its South/North territorial associations, articulating rather a struggle with constraints imposed by legal, social, and psychological conditions. The written testimony itself becomes the principal enactment of flight. Wright, in *Black Boy (American Hunger)*, reprises the territorial arc, but in *Native Son* and "The Man Who Lived Underground" (among other works) identifies flight as a futile response to the existential condition of being black anywhere and under any circumstance in America. Ellison, Malcolm X, Baldwin, Morrison, and Butler likewise draw on territorial associations but are more generally concerned with predicaments for which flight offers only temporary or doubtful resolution. From an expatriate perspective, Baldwin and, later, Coates, articulate a condition of black life in urban America from which no escape offers that is not attributable to random individual good fortune. It is not that opportunities for African Americans to advance from conditions of poverty and underprivilege into the professional classes do not exist in the twenty-first century, for clearly they do. But antiblack cultural currents persist, and the odds of an African American not at some point leading a coercively segregated life remain astonishingly low. In addition, according to statistics compiled by the Sentencing Project, the odds of a black male leading an incarcerated life remain staggeringly high—one chance in three for those born in 2001 and after.[23]

Nonetheless, the contemporary imagination of the slave past continues to deploy territorial tropes. In extending the neo-slave narrative tradition, filmmakers and authors have affirmed that, just as we are not yet ready to move on from the vivid contemplation of the cruelties and degradations of slavery, so too do we still wish to conjure geographical paths of escape, perhaps precisely because issues of race are ubiquitous and existential and do not admit of resolutions implemented by strategic and liberating displacement.

Steve McQueen's 2013 adaptation of Solomon Northup's *Twelve Years a Slave* presents upstate New York as a site where a free black citizen of merit can establish a comfortable, self-supporting life—if anything, the film suggests, ease prompts Solomon to let down his guard sufficiently to fall into the hands of abductors. Northern whites are presented as white supremacist but mildly so: befriended in Louisiana by an iterant Canadian tradesman who assists Solomon in posting a letter to his powerful Northern patron, after twelve years the black freeman is rescued through the intervention of benevolent whites. The South, by contrast, is hell. Adhering closely to the 1848 text, the film makes frequent use of long camera shots to portray the corporal, sexual, and psychological abuse of the enslaved. While the narrative returns full circle in Solomon's reunion with a family that has survived in his absence, just as memorable, as the film concludes, are the scenes in which Solomon bids adieu to his companions in bondage, for whom no liberating white patron will ever materialize. Colson Whitehead's *The Underground Railroad* (2016) takes the trope of "underground" and renders it literal by developing a narrative in which two fugitives, Cora and Caesar, escape by means of a rail network constructed beneath the slave South. Whitehead thus creates a new trope that builds on traditional metaphors of mask, veil, and invisibility, all of which point to the life beneath the surface. Invoking the myth of Persephone (Kore) and its seasonal death and rebirth associations, the novel combines a subterranean journey in which Cora figures as one who enters and reemerges from the underworld with the trope of South-to-North escape and, at the very end, East-to-West release. Without specifying a destination, the novel suggests that, after all, North America might yet prove hospitable to the black survivor.

Less optimistic still is Jordan Peele's *Get Out!* (2017), a variation on *Guess Who's Coming to Dinner* (1967) in which protagonist Chris Washington, the black boyfriend of an upper-class white girl, Rose Armitage, is held captive by her parents, members of the liberal elite and constituents of the Obama coalition, whose practice of body-snatching African Americans is as insidious as any other attempt to subjugate black people to a white territorial totalitarian regime. Beginning with the abduction of Andre Hayworth in a leafy white suburban neighborhood and concluding with Chris's rescue—engineered, ironically enough, by his friend, the TSA/Homeland Security officer Rod Williams—the film portrays the existential threat that affluent white spaces pose to blacks, irrespective of how fully they have achieved middle-class law-abiding professional status. *Get Out*'s argument is clear and persuasive: Caucasian patronage of nonwhite progress has always been and must ever be problematic. Even as the film emphasizes escape from the seductions of co-optation and captivity, the question of where to find refuge remains unaddressed.

As the Obama era transitions to the age of Trump, such fables of race in America speak to deeply ingrained conflicts that do not admit of ready settlement. How can they, in a nation haunted by the Tulsa Race Massacre, the murder of Emmett Till, the bombing deaths of Addie Mae Collins, Carol Denise McNair, Carole Robertson, and Cynthia Wesley, and the premature, frequently violent demise of so many others, not to mention the lengthening roster of black and brown victims of legally sanctioned deadly force? Still, as testimonies of black experience that engage readers and viewers on both sides of the color line, as well as readers and viewers through whom the color line (or color lines) pass and in whom those same lines blur, contemporary as well as historical narratives of bondage and liberation prompt us to reimagine the world in which we are party to such dramas. They compel us to meditate on the relationalities that, as Massey argues, constitute our sense of place and form the cartographies of coexistence. Donald Trump is not wrong to presume that, even in a world where people of color are everywhere, citizens inhabit distinct zones. Where he errs is in assuming that such divisions are part of the order of things and that flux does not operate to dissolve such lines. "Though they seem to invoke an origin in a historical past with which they continue to correspond," observes Stuart Hall regarding the cultural identities that set citizens at odds, how we identify ourselves entails "using the resources of history, language and culture in the process of becoming rather than being: not 'who we are' or 'where we came from,' so much as what we might become, how we have been represented and how that bears on how we might represent ourselves." And as Hall further underscores, "identities are therefore constituted within, not outside representation," an observation that leads to the recognition that we can exert power over that identity, over its always politicized performance.[24] Dismayed by renewed spectacles of racial animosity, discouraged that the heritage of slavery, hiding in plain sight, continues to inform the American present, we should not lose sight of the certainty that, in the mixed-race demographic of the near future, people of color will be everywhere and even more so.

Will demographic transformation progressively mitigate our geographic separations? How will demands for recognition and justice—for neglect and injustice are not likely to disappear—be heard and across what gulfs? Will the polarizations of the Trump years produce a salutary catharsis? What color lines will pervade a society in which color (as the U.S. Census assures us, and as Octavia Butler, among others, envisions) must fall outside the accustomed lines? One may and probably should resist viewing the ephemeral rise of a septuagenarian white racist as wholly negating the real and enduring if limited significance of the twice-elected Barack Obama. Beyond the retrograde moment in which we pose such questions, we have every reason to seek hopeful if yet-to-be-elucidated prospects.

ACKNOWLEDGMENTS

Geographies of Flight emerged from my many years of reading and teaching American literature of the color line. It came together conceptually, however, through my deepening engagement with Octavia Butler's *Parable* series and her prognostication of a future America that must—if it is to survive—evolve beyond its white nationalist foundational idea. For this catalyzing encounter with Butler's work I'm indebted to Véronique Bragard, who asked me to pick up a copy of *Parable of the Sower* for one of her doctoral students at Université catholique de Louvain, my academic home as a 2008–9 Fulbright Scholar. Reading *Sower* on the flight to Brussels, I was struck by Butler's defamiliarization of every conceivable American geographical trope—and so this inquiry commenced. In addition to Véronique I also thank my other great UCL colleague, Guido Latré, an authority on everyone from William Tyndale to Toni Morrison, for prompting me to explain (beginning in fall 2008 when Barack Obama became president-elect) the astonishing swings and counter-swings of U.S. electoral politics and the forces that drive the American culture wars. Another UCL friend, Matthieu Sergier, now of the Université Saint-Louis, Brussels, has been a wonderful partner in animated conversation on topics ranging from the literatures of autobiographical witness to issues of immigration and environmental justice.

Other European colleagues with whom I have discussed this project and who have invited me to present work in progress include Christoph Ribbat and Miriam Strube, Universität Paderborn, gracious hosts during my 2012 DAAD Guest Professorship, as well as Annick De Houwer and Ilka Saal, Universität Erfurt, who know how to press their American friend for ever clearer explanations.

Closer to home, Arthur Redding, York University (Toronto), has read and critiqued every chapter with habitual generosity and enthusiasm. Joanne Jacobson, Yeshiva University, and John Orr, University of Portland, have listened to me talk out ideas and made excellent suggestions. Robert W. Decker, Princeton University, has been a frequent interlocutor particularly with regard to common questions we share as scholars of the African diaspora.

Numerous past and present colleagues at Oklahoma State University have contributed to the intellectual atmosphere that has fostered my work: Linda Austin, Andrew Belton, Brewster Fitz, Ritch Frohock, Bob Graalman, Elizabeth Grubgeld, Kate Hallemeier, Lisa Hollenbach, Edward Jones, Linda Leavell, Carol Mason, Robert Mayer, Jeff Menne, Carol Moder, Tim Murphy,

Dennis Preston, Amilcar Shabazz, Lindsey Smith, Stacy Takacs, Graig Uhlin, Martin Wallen, Jeffrey Walker, and Ed Walkiewicz. My department head, An Cheng, has provided both moral and material encouragement. My two most recent doctoral students, Michelle Dostal and Jason Tillis, have enriched my thinking with their own related inquiries. Michelle assisted magnificently with documentation and proofreading—I cannot overstate my gratitude for her expertise and care. Over the years my students have consistently exemplified scholarly engagements that are also social engagements, and those who have contributed to the quality of departmental life make a long list. But a short list would include Jean Alger, Chris Black, LuElla D'Amico, Leah Palmer, Oliver Spivey, and Jared Young. An academic department is a high-maintenance concern: were it not for the patience, generosity, and infinite resourcefulness of Clarissa Bonner, Robert Estes, JuDean Howerton, Brenda Maxwell, and Charissa Prchal, there would not be a department to support our endeavors.

Although this will date me, I must acknowledge the continuing intellectual and spiritual sustenance I derive from the two late scholars who served as my mentors: Sherman Paul, my dissertation director at the University of Iowa, and J. C. Levenson, University of Virginia, a champion of my early scholarship on Henry Adams. Mentored in their turn by two extraordinarily expansive thinkers, F. O. Matthiessen and Perry Miller, Sherman and Jack modeled the kind of transhistorical, comprehensive, and socially driven inquiry I have tried to emulate in this book. My concerns may differ from theirs, but from both I learned that in exploring the past one works to define the possibilities of the present and that, for critically minded citizens, there are compelling reasons to do so. My longstanding gratitude further extends to Susan Belasco, Linck Johnson, and John Carlos Rowe for many acts of generosity over the years.

The staff at Northwestern University Press has been supportive and helpful at every stage of this book's composition and production. I begin by thanking Gianna Francesca Mosser, former editor-in-chief, for reaching out to me on the basis of my presentation on Octavia Butler at the 2015 American Studies Association meeting and who believed from day one that my paper presaged a monograph. With Gianna's departure for Vanderbilt University Press, Trevor Perri has been unfailingly helpful is escorting the book through the review process. I thank Maia Rigas for seeing the project through production, Elizabeth Berg for copyediting the manuscript, and Anne Tappen Strother for strategizing its launch. *Geographies of Flight* has benefited enormously from the suggestions and support of the manuscript's anonymous readers, and I am deeply grateful for their thorough and critical perusals. I thank Marianne Jankowski for the book's beautiful cover, based on a painting by Alma Thomas, reproduced courtesy of the Smithsonian American Art Museum: many thanks to Richard Sorensen for facilitating permissions. For pointing me in the direction of Thomas's work, I thank Kimia R. Shahi,

Princeton University, who unites a broad and loving knowledge of American art with a joyously sharing disposition.

Finally, I thank my family: Elizabeth Grubgeld, with whom I've discussed nearly all of the texts I address in this book for many, many years; Edward, Jessica, and Henry Decker; Robert Decker and Kimia Shahi; Tom and Barbara Decker (steadfast residents of Rochester, New York, my highly instructive city of origin); Katie and Mike Caster; and James and Maria Decker. Thank you for understanding and supporting my commitment to this project. I know that you share my sense of the urgency with which *Geographies of Flight* was written.

NOTES

Prologue

1. The present study aligns with recent scholarship that clusters under the rubric "spatial turn" and interrogates the ways in which the lived and imagined geographies of North America (North, South, West, urban, rural, wild, etc.) proceed from ideas that intervene in accordance with ideological design: Martin Brückner, *The Geographic Revolution in Early America: Maps, Literacy, and National Identity* (Chapel Hill: University of North Carolina Press, 2006); Anne Baker, *Heartless Immensities: Literature, Culture, and Geography in Antebellum America* (Ann Arbor: University of Michigan Press, 2006); Edlie L. Wong, *Neither Fugitive nor Free: Atlantic Slavery, Freedom Suits, and the Legal Culture of Travel* (New York: New York University Press, 2009); Robert T. Tally Jr., *Melville, Mapping, and Globalization: Literary Cartography in the American Baroque Writer* (London: Bloomsbury, 2009) and *Spatiality* (London: Routledge, 2013); Hsuan L. Hsu, *Geography and the Production of Space in Nineteenth-Century American Literature* (New York: Cambridge University Press, 2010); Thadious M. Davis, *Southscapes: Geographies of Race, Region, and Literature* (Chapel Hill: University of North Carolina Press, 2011); Martha Schoolman, *Abolitionist Geographies* (Minneapolis: University of Minnesota Press, 2014); Herman Beavers, *Geography and the Political Imaginary in the Novels of Toni Morrison* (London: Palgrave Macmillan, 2018). Martin Brückner and Hsuan L. Hsu, eds., *American Literary Geographies* (Newark: University of Delaware Press, 2007), includes the section "The Spaces of Social Death," featuring the following essays: Anna Brickhouse, "Manzano, Madden, 'El Negro Mártir,' and the Revisionist Geographies of Abolitionism" (209–35); Ian Finseth, "Geographic Consciousness in the American Slave Narrative" (236–58); and Martha Schoolman, "White Flight: Maroon Communities and the Geography of Antislavery in Higginson and Stowe" (259–78).

2. The terms "flight" and "fugitive" ("fugitivity") invoke in recent scholarship not only the regimes under which enslaved subjects acquire a qualified freedom of movement, resettlement, and intellection, but also the means by which Afro-diasporic peoples have successfully occupied geographical, epistemological, and social space in defiance of a capriciously repressive white purview. Some titles of note: Michael A. Chaney, *Fugitive Visions: Slave Image and Black Identity in Antebellum Narrative* (Bloomington: Indiana University Press, 2008); Michelle D. Commander, *Afro-Atlantic Flight: Speculative Returns and the Black Fantastic* (Durham, N.C.: Duke University Press, 2017); and Britt Rusert, *Fugitive Science: Empiricism and Freedom in Early African American Culture* (New York: New York University Press, 2017). My extension of "flight" to the inscribed articulation of distances achieved is compatible with Commander's application of

the term to speculative fictions by which diasporic peoples seek to possess the sustaining narratives of an ancestral land, and with Rusert's history of African American efforts to counter such antebellum "race science" as would represent Africans as the inferior production of polygenetic evolution.

3. Deriving principally from Frantz Fanon's and Orlando Patterson's observations concerning the ontological condition of colonized and diasporic Africans, Afro-pessimism pertains to the logic by which historical oppressions and the trauma they inflict propagate conditions of present and future replication. In framing the binary Black/Human, Frank B. Wilderson formulates perhaps the starkest expression of the Afro-pessimist position. For a comprehensive and nuanced treatment of the term, see Jared Sexton, "Afro-Pessimism: The Unclear Word," in "Black Holes: Afro-Pessimism, Blackness and the Discourses of Modernity," ed. Dalton Anthony Jones, special issue, *Rhizomes* 29 (2016), https://doi.org/10.20415/rhiz/029.

4. Olaudah Equiano uses this phrase to describe the euphoria of his postslavery status after he has purchased himself from Robert King. Equiano, *The Interesting Narrative and Other Writings*, ed. Vincent Carretta (New York: Penguin Books, 1995), 138.

5. Glissant cautions against "a return to the longing for origins, to some immutable state of Being." Édouard Glissant, *Caribbean Discourse: Selected Essays*, trans. J. Michael Dash (Charlottesville: University Press of Virginia, 1989), 26. What follows is a fuller version of the statement as it appears in his *Le discours antillais*: "Il faut revenir au lieu. Le Détour n'est ruse profitable que si le Retour le féconde: non pas retour au rêve d'origine, a l'Un immobile de l'Être, mais retour au point d'intrication, dont on s'était détourné par force; c'est là qu'il faut à la fin mettre en oeuvre les composantes de la Relation, ou périr." Glissant, *Le disours antillais* (1981; repr., Paris: Éditions Gallimard, 1997), 56–57.

6. As William L. Andrews has shown, black antebellum autobiography typically labors against the white reader's suspicion of the author's ability to participate in literary culture and, begrudging that ability, the capacity for telling the truth. But even in the absence of a structural skepticism, the fugitive's acknowledgment of the inadequacy of language to articulate the slave experience contributes to the impression such autobiography conveys that much remains unsaid—and that, relative to a white if not a black readership, the fugitive's story pertains to other and distant worlds. See Andrews, *To Tell a Free Story: The First Century of Afro-American Autobiography, 1760–1865* (Urbana: University of Illinois Press, 1986), 1–3, 10–11. Such barriers extend far beyond the era of slavery, as W. E. B. Du Bois makes clear in the "Forethought" to *The Souls of Black Folk* (see chap. 4 above) and as James Weldon Johnson demonstrates in *The Autobiography of an Ex-Colored Man*. Johnson's protagonist—an expert in passing undetected from black zones to white—defines the situation as follows: "It is a difficult thing for a white man to learn what a colored man really thinks; because, generally, with the latter an additional and different light must be brought to bear on what he thinks; and his thoughts are often influenced by considerations so delicate and subtle that it would be impossible for him to confess or explain them to one of the opposite race." Johnson, *The Autobiography of an Ex-Colored Man*, ed. Jacqueline Goldsby (New York: Norton, 2015), 13.

7. Foucault, following Lefebvre, does much to spatialize a temporally dominated Marxian legacy, but his short essay, "Des espaces autres" ("Of Other Spaces"), is his most influential contribution to cultural geography. Michel Foucault, "Of Other Spaces," trans. Jay Miskowiec, *Diacritics* 16, no. 1 (1986): 22–27, https://doi.org/10.2307/464648. On Foucault as a spatial thinker, see Edward Soja, *Postmodern Geographies: The Reassertion of Space in Critical Social Theory* (London: Verso, 1989), 16–21.

8. Jeannine Marie DeLombard, *Slavery on Trial: Law, Abolitionism, and Print Culture* (Chapel Hill: University of North Carolina Press, 2007), 137.

9. James Baldwin, "Stranger in the Village," in *Collected Essays: Notes of a Native Son, Nobody Knows My Name, The Fire Next Time, No Name in the Street, The Devil Finds Work, Other Essays*, ed. Toni Morrison (New York: Library of America, 1998), 127.

10. My use of the terms "travel" and "dwelling" and understanding of human mobility generally are indebted to James Clifford, who, in "Traveling Cultures," urges that "specific dynamics of dwelling/traveling be understood comparatively." Clifford, *Routes: Travel and Translation in the Late Twentieth Century* (Cambridge, Mass.: Harvard University Press, 1997), 23.

11. David Harvey, *The Condition of Postmodernity: An Enquiry into the Origins of Cultural Change* (Oxford: Blackwell, 1989), 216.

12. Doreen Massey, *For Space* (London: Sage, 2005), 28.

13. Henri Lefebvre, *The Production of Space*, trans. Donald Nicholson-Smith (London: Blackwell, 1991), 143.

14. On the transported African slave's status as a "genealogical isolate," see Orlando Patterson, *Slavery and Social Death: A Comparative Study* (Cambridge, Mass.: Harvard University Press, 1982), 5–8. For definitions and a focused discussion of the slave's "social death," see Patterson, *Slavery*, 38–46.

15. Frank B. Wilderson, *Red, White and Black: Cinema and the Structure of U.S. Antagonisms* (Durham, N.C.: Duke University Press, 2010), 9.

16. With respect to the changeable character of humanly produced space, Edward Soja observes that spatiality "is never either inert or immutable. The geography and history of capitalism intersect in a complex social process which creates a constantly evolving historical sequence of spatialities, a spatio-temporal structuration of social life which gives form to and situates not only the grand movements of societal development but also the recursive practices of day-to-day activity—even in the least capitalist of contemporary societies." What Soja terms "actual human geography" remains "a competitive arena for struggles over social production and reproduction, for social practices aimed either at the maintenance and reinforcement of existing spatiality or at significant restructuring and/or radical transformation." Soja, *Postmodern Geographies*, 127, 130.

17. Katherine McKittrick, *Demonic Grounds: Black Women and the Cartographies of Struggle* (Minneapolis: University of Minnesota Press, 2006), xxvii.

18. In her introduction, titled "The Middle Passage Never Guessed Its End," Keizer affirms that "black identity in the Americas, from slavery to the present, has never been a fixed essence, either biological or cultural, but instead consistently marked by fragmentation and differentiation." Recognition of such multiplicity compels "a rethinking of the unitary black subject that white-supremacist and black-nationalist ideologies find necessary for their mobilization in the present."

Arlene Keizer, *Black Subjects: Identity Formation in the Contemporary Narrative of Slavery* (Ithaca, N.Y.: Cornell University Press, 2004), 11. Wright's interrogation of the epistemologies associated with the Middle Passage contributes valuably to such rethinking. Toward distinct but complementary ends, Keizer and Wright both enlist (and revise) an Althusserian model of *interpellation* in exploring the formation of African diasporic subjectivities and the complicated and conflictive "hailings" that generate black identities.

19. Katherine McKittrick, "Freedom Is a Secret: The Future Usability of the Underground," in *Black Geographies and the Politics of Place*, ed. Katherine McKittrick and Clyde Woods (Toronto: Between the Lines Press, 2007), 102.

20. McKittrick, "Freedom Is a Secret," 103.

21. Against a theme of black trauma that can never be unheard (Aunt Hester's shriek) or unseen (Emmett Till's mutilated body), Fred Moten's lyric and improvisatory monograph *In the Break: The Aesthetics of the Black Radical Tradition* extends Ellison's subterranean excursions into (and under) the Western philosophical heritage, although with a far more radical undermining than is realized by *Invisible Man*. Moten, *In The Break: The Asthetics of the Black Radical Tradition* (Minneapolis: University of Minnesota Press, 2003).

22. Here I would also cite Barbara Foley's *Wrestling with the Left: The Making of Ralph Ellison's Invisible Man* as a text that closely examines Ellison's inscribed reader against the readerships that have historically engaged with this book. Foley, *Wrestling with the Left: The Making of Ralph Ellison's Invisible Man* (Durham, N.C.: Duke University Press, 2010).

23. Hartman is particularly skeptical of the slave narrative's proposition that testimony of the fugitive or former slave to abuses suffered and survived identifies the author as a human equal while motivating the reader to take action against a regime that oppresses those who exist as brothers and sisters (fellow humans, according to Acts 17:26, "of one blood"). What, Hartman rightly asks, is our identity and function as readers of these texts? "Are we witnesses who confirm the truth of what happened in the face of the world-destroying capacities of pain, the distortions of torture, the sheer unrepresentability of terror, and the repression of the dominant accounts? Or are we voyeurs fascinated with and repelled by exhibitions of terror and sufferance? What does the exposure of the violated body yield? Proof of black sentience or the inhumanity of the 'peculiar institution'? Or does the pain of the other merely provide us with the opportunity for self-reflection? At issue here is the precariousness of empathy and the uncertain line between witness and spectator. . . . [H]ow does one give expression to these outrages without exacerbating the indifference to suffering that is the consequence of the benumbing spectacle or contend with the narcissistic identification that obliterates the other or the prurience that too often is the response to such displays?" Saidiya V. Hartman, *Scenes of Subjection: Terror, Slavery, and Self-Making in Nineteenth-Century America* (New York: Oxford University Press, 1997), 3–4. In chapter 6, I invoke Hartman's questions in addressing *Parable of the Sower* and Lauren Olamina's hyperempathy syndrome. Richard Iton extends this discussion with reference to the exponential increase, during the last decades of the twentieth century, in "the visual accessibility of black life": "the heightened visibility of raced subjects in the post–civil rights era—in which Emmett Till becomes Rodney King becomes 50 Cent and Michael Jackson becomes Michael

Jackson—arguably plays a confirming role and provides a rationale, as minstrelsy did in the nineteenth century, for the dismissal of the possibility of black humanity." Iton, *In Search of the Black Fantastic: Politics and Popular Culture in the Post–Civil Rights Era* (New York: Oxford University Press, 2008), 107, 108–9.

24. The distinction between historical author and textual narrator is clear in certain instances: Harriet Jacobs and Linda Brent, Ralph Ellison and his anonymous protagonist. It is less clear in our encounters with Phillis Wheatley, Olaudah Equiano, David Walker, Frederick Douglass, Booker T. Washington, W. E. B. Du Bois, Ida B. Wells-Barnett, Richard Wright, Malcolm X, James Baldwin, and many others. While it is important to maintain this distinction in our discussions of slave narratives and their progeny, we must also recognize a special category of surrogacy that binds the performative "I" to the social and political conditions of the historical author whose testimonial personhood has been voided (constitutionally or unconstitutionally) by a white supremacist regime that defines the nonwhite as unlettered and voiceless.

25. For David Walker, a coastal Carolinian who has migrated to Boston, the disconnection is decidedly spatial, as he directs the *Appeal* to an enslaved and largely unlettered audience in the South. See chap. 3, 69–74. For Ida B. Wells-Barnett, it is generational, as she finds herself among Northern black young people who have never been in the South and for whom slavery has largely ceased to exist as a living family memory. Chicagoan as she has become, she occupies a geography shaped by a traumatically migratory experience. See chap. 4, 122–28.

26. Stuart Hall, "Cultural Identity and Diaspora," in *Identity: Community, Culture, Difference*, ed. Jonathan Rutherford (London: Lawrence and Wishart, 1993), 222. Any legatee of the past is necessarily a legatee of the slave past, and one's complicity and/or victimhood can only enter into an approximate correlation with one's contemporary ethnic identity. What Fredric Jameson calls "the massive Being of capital" exists as the living and replicating materialization of that past; this past-becoming-present offers at best unstable positions from which to view, analyze, and atone. As Jameson remarks, "Distance in general (including 'critical distance' in particular) has very precisely been abolished in the new space of postmodernism. We are submerged in its henceforth filled and suffused volumes to the point where our now postmodern bodies are bereft of special coordinates and practically (let alone theoretically) incapable of distantiation." Jameson, *Postmodernism; or, The Cultural Logic of Late Capitalism* (Durham, N.C.: Duke University Press, 1991), 48–49. I concur generally with this observation, although I would also propose that our "postmodern bodies" retain and replicate what we understand as historical markings and that the instability of perspective hardly absolves us of the responsibility to articulate such coordinates as appear to guide our interventions.

27. The history of African American publication has become a vibrant research subset of the larger, archive-centered study of print cultures generally. Accordingly, *Geographies of Flight* has benefited from collective efforts represented by *The Black Press: New Literary and Historical Essays*, ed. Todd Vogel (New Brunswick, N.J.: Rutgers University Press, 2001); *A History of the Book in America*, 5 vols., ed. David D. Hall et al. (Chapel Hill: University of North Carolina Press, 2000–2010); and *Early African American Print Culture*, ed. Lara Langer Cohen

and Jordan Alexander Stein (Philadelphia: University of Pennsylvania Press, 2012). As subsequent discussion will show, my study is specifically indebted to the work of Eric Gardner, Joseph Rezek, Jeannine Marie DeLombard, Joanna Brooks, Robert S. Levine, Elizabeth McHenry, Edlie L. Wong, James P. Danky, and Janice Radway, as well as John Ernest, who provides a superb overview of the antebellum black press in *Liberation Historiography: African American Writers and the Challenge of History, 1794–1861* (Chapel Hill: University of North Carolina Press, 2004), chap. 5, "'Our Warfare Lies in the Field of Thought': The African American Press and the Work of History," 277–329.

28. James Clifford, *The Predicament of Culture: Twentieth-Century Ethnography, Literature, and Art* (Cambridge, Mass.: Harvard University Press, 1988), 15–16.

29. W. E. B. Du Bois, *Dusk of Dawn: An Essay Toward an Autobiography of a Race Concept*, ed. Henry Louis Gates Jr. and K. Anthony Appiah (New York: Oxford University Press, 2007), 59.

30. W. E. B. Du Bois, *The Souls of Black Folk*, ed. Henry Louis Gates Jr. and Arnold Rampersad (New York: Oxford University Press, 2007), 1.

Chapter 1

1. Glissant, *Caribbean Discourse*, 38. In the original, this sentence appears as "L'océan de traite fut notre nouveau pays." Glissant, however, consulted closely with J. Michael Dash as the latter prepared his English translation of *Le discours antillais* and must have been aware of the nuances that attach to "New World."

2. Mary Louise Pratt, *Imperial Eyes: Travel Writing and Transculturation*, 2nd ed. (New York: Routledge, 2007), 15.

3. In "Extermination and Democracy: O'Sullivan, the *Democratic Review*, and Empire, 1837–1840," Robert J. Scholnick explores the aggressively exclusionary ideology of the *Democratic Review* (which included among its contributors James Fenimore Cooper, Nathaniel Hawthorne, Henry David Thoreau, and Walt Whitman) and addresses "Manifest Destiny" as shorthand for an Anglo-Saxon occupation of North America that built upon long-standing settler doctrines bridging, to some extent, the proslavery and antislavery divide. Scholnick, "Extermination and Democracy: O'Sullivan, the *Democratic Review*, and Empire, 1837–1840," *American Periodicals* 15, no. 2 (2005): 123–41, https://doi.org/10.1353/amp.2005.0020.

4. Benjamin Franklin, *The Autobiography of Benjamin Franklin and Other Writings*, ed. Ormond Seavey (New York: Oxford University Press, 1993), 254, 256, 260, 125.

5. For an excellent account of the supposedly "vanishing" but persistently "reappearing" Indian, see Phillip J. Deloria, *Indians in Unexpected Places* (Lawrence: University Press of Kansas, 2004).

6. Robert Beverley, *The History and Present State of Virginia, in Four Parts* (London: R. Parker, 1705), vols. 2–3.

7. Thomas Jefferson, *Notes on the State of Virginia*, ed. William Peden (Chapel Hill: University of North Carolina Press, 1955), 96.

8. Once a just inventory of Native American aptitudes has been completed, Jefferson speculates, "we shall probably find that they are formed in mind as well as in body, on the same module with the 'Homo sapiens Europæus.'" Jefferson,

Notes, 62. European—and specifically English—colonization of North America presented one of the first grand-scale occasions for the exercise of what Foucault calls "bio-power" through the colonial and early national elite's hierarchical privileging of an Anglo-Saxon Protestant demographic over other ethnic communities. See Michel Foucault, *The History of Sexuality*, vol. 1, *An Introduction*, trans. Robert Hurley (New York: Vintage Books, 1990), 135–50. Even within his own household, Jefferson's proposed regulation of the body politic hardly achieved the exclusions he expressed as desirable, but seeds of policies that would restrict immigration in view of an idealized white nation can certainly be seen in *Notes*.

9. Jefferson, *Notes*, 138.

10. As primary author of the Declaration of Independence (with its statement of universal manhood equality) and *Notes on the State of Virginia* (with the defamation of black people in query 14), Jefferson figures early and late as a point of reference in African American writing. In answering Jefferson, black authors from David Walker to Ralph Ellison wrestle with Enlightenment thought as a set of doctrines that simultaneously empower and disempower subjects who are neither white nor male. "Unlike almost every other literary tradition," observes Henry Louis Gates Jr., "the Afro-American literary tradition was generated as a response to eighteenth and nineteenth-century allegations that persons of African descent did not, and could not, create literature. Philosophers and literary critics, such as Hume, Kant, Jefferson, and Hegel, seemed to decide that the absence or presence of a written literature was the signal measure of the potential, innate humanity of a race." Gates, *Figures in Black: Literary Theory and the Black Tradition* (New York: Oxford University Press, 1987), 25. In *Fugitive Science: Empiricism and Freedom in Early African American Culture*, Britt Rusert reviews African American political and literary response to Jefferson and, in chapter 1, "The Banneker Age: Black Afterlives of Early National Science," demonstrates the ways in which "*Notes* also served as the 'founding text' for a vibrant genealogy of black scientific discourse in the United States, which, like the political history of early African American literature, sought to wrench science and philosophy from white supremacists and slavery apologists in order to 'represent the race' on different terms." Rusert, *Fugitive Science*, 33.

11. David Walker, *David Walker's Appeal, in Four Articles; Together with a Preamble, to the Coloured Citizens of the World, But in Particular, and Very Expressly, to Those of the United States of America*, ed. Sean Wilentz (New York: Hill and Wang, 1995), 13, 14–15.

12. See Robert S. Levine, "Circulating the Nation: David Walker, the Missouri Compromise, and the Rise of the Black Press," in Vogel, *The Black Press*, 21. In *Forgotten Readers: Recovering the Lost Histories of African American Literary Societies* (Durham, N.C.: Duke University Press, 2002), Elizabeth McHenry argues that Walker conceived the *Appeal* as a political intervention at once practical and philosophical: "Walker believed that the disparity between the condition of people of African descent in the United States and the 'inalienable rights' and republican principles laid out in the Declaration of Independence could be a rallying point for black Americans seeking to be recognized and treated as citizens. That he turned to strategies similar to those used by colonists such as Thomas Paine, whose own pamphlet *Common Sense*, published in 1776, had

helped propel the colonies toward independence from England cannot be underestimated." McHenry, *Forgotten Readers*, 27.

13. Jefferson, *Notes*, 138, 163.

14. Jefferson, *Notes*, 84, 85.

15. James Fenimore Cooper, *The Prairie*, in *The Leather-Stocking Tales*, ed. Blake Nevius, vol. 1 (New York: Library of America, 1985), 887.

16. I explore Cooper's narrative ethnic cleansing at length in Decker, "'Surely Cora Was Not Forgotten': Remembering Africa in the Leather-Stocking Tales," in *Reading Cooper, Teaching Cooper*, ed. Jeffrey Walker (New York: AMS Press 2007), 201–221.

17. See Benedict Anderson, *Imagined Communities: Reflections on the Origin and Spread of Nationalism* (London: Verso, 1983), 37–46.

18. Ralph Waldo Emerson, *English Traits*, in *Essays and Lectures*, ed. Joel Porte (New York: Library of America, 1983), 785.

19. Emerson, *English Traits*, 794.

20. In chapters 11, 12, and 13 of *The History of White People*, Nell Irvin Painter parses *English Traits* as the often self-contradictory pastiche of mid-nineteenth-century Anglo-American white supremacist theorizing. "As author of *English Traits* and a font of themes usually located much later in the nineteenth century," writes Painter, "Emerson qualifies as a full contributor to white race theory." Painter, *The History of White People* (New York: W. W. Norton, 2010), 183.

21. Emerson, *English Traits*, 792.

22. Emerson, *English Traits*, 792. "The Poet," in *Essays and Lectures*, 457.

23. Emerson's sentence is consistent with the logic of contrastive racial identity formation that Toni Morrison highlights when she speaks of the "Africanist presence" as "the vehicle by which the [white] American self knows itself as not enslaved, but free; not repulsive, but desirable; not helpless, but licensed and powerful; not history-less, but historical; not damned, but innocent; not a blind accident of evolution, but a progressive fulfillment of destiny." Morrison, *Playing in the Dark: Whiteness and the Literary Imagination* (Cambridge, Mass.: Harvard University Press, 1992), 52.

24. Henry David Thoreau, "Walking," in *Collected Essays and Poems*, ed. Elizabeth Hall Witherell (New York: Library of America, 2001), 234, 238.

25. Margaret Fuller, *Summer on the Lakes, in 1843*, ed. Susan Belasco Smith (Urbana: University of Illinois Press, 1991), 22, 29.

26. Walt Whitman, *Poetry and Prose*, ed. Justin Kaplan (New York: Library of America, 1997), 232, 197, 225, 268, 270.

27. Whitman, *Poetry and Prose*, 113. This passage was deleted, however, from the 1881–82 *Leaves of Grass*.

28. Whitman, *Poetry and Prose*, 256.

29. Walt Whitman, "*Daily Eagle*, September 1, 1847," in *The Gathering of the Forces*, ed. Cleveland Rodgers and John Black, vol. 1 (New York: Putnam, 1920), 208–9.

30. Walt Whitman, "*Daily Times*, May 6, 1858," quoted in Robert S. Levine, introduction and notes to *Clotel; or, The President's Daughter; A Narrative of Slave Life in the United States*, by William Wells Brown (Boston: Bedford/St. Martin's, 2000), 418, 419.

31. Horace Traubel, *With Walt Whitman in Camden*, vol. 2 (New York: Rowman and Littlefield, 1915), 283.

32. For nuanced appraisals of the black presence (and absence) in Whitman's poetry, see Martin Klammer, *Whitman, Slavery, and the Emergence of Leaves of Grass* (University Park: Pennsylvania State University Press, 1995); and Ivy G. Wilson, "Black and Tan Fantasy: Walt Whitman, African Americans, and Sounding the Nation," in *Specters of Democracy: Blackness and the Aesthetics of Politics in the Antebellum U.S.* (New York: Oxford University Press, 2011), 80–99; as well as the essays collected in Wilson, ed., *Whitman Noir: Black America and the Good Gray Poet* (Iowa City: University of Iowa Press, 2014).

33. On African American participation in the World's Columbian Exposition, see Christopher Robert Reed, *All the World Is Here! The Black Presence at White City* (Bloomington: Indiana University Press, 2000); and Reed, "The Black Presence at 'White City': African and African American Participation at the World's Columbian Exposition, Chicago, May 1, 1893–October 31, 1893," in the Paul V. Galvin Library Digital History Collection, Illinois Institute of Technology, http://columbus.iit.edu/reed2.html.

34. Frederick Jackson Turner, "The Significance of the Frontier in American History," in *The Frontier in American History* (New York: Henry Holt, 1921), 1, 24.

35. Henry Adams, *Democracy, Esther, Mont Saint Michel and Chartres, The Education of Henry Adams, Poems*, ed. Ernest Samuels and Jayne N. Samuels (New York: Library of America, 1983), 937. For an assessment of Adams's implicitly white supremacist neglect of Frederick Douglass, his fellow education-as-autobiography memoirist, see William Merrill Decker, "Autobiography, Education: Henry Adams and the Definition of a Genre," *A/B: Auto/Biography Studies* 33, no 1 (2018): 47–63, https://www.tandfonline.com/doi/abs/10.1080/08989575.2018.1389838?journalCode=raut20.

36. As much as he is remembered for his accomplishments as a geologist and his friendships with Henry Adams and John Hay, Clarence King appears in the historical record as one who masqueraded as the black West Indian James Todd, common-law husband of Ada Copeland who, after the Emancipation, migrated from Georgia to New York City. Residing in a modest but well-appointed home in Flushing, Queens, the couple had five children. See Martha A. Sandweiss, *Passing Strange: A Gilded Age Tale of Love and Deception across the Color Line* (New York: Penguin, 2009).

37. Deep into the twentieth century, well past *Brown v. the Board of Education of Topeka* (1954), American literary scholarship perpetuated the association of Anglo Americans and particularly the New England Protestant heritage with a continental national destiny. In his landmark *American Renaissance: Art and Expression in the Age of Emerson and Whitman* (1941), a work that historicizes and celebrates a particular half-decade of literary creativity (1850–55) as the seminal integration of democratic ideals and highly innovative literary expression, F. O. Matthiessen identifies the Emersonian notion of an open universe as the foundational concept behind the grand liberationist national narrative. Alongside his title page Matthiessen places a daguerreotype of David McKay, the inventive New England shipbuilder whose engineering prowess did much to enhance the refinement of the clipper ship. "McKay's portrait makes the most fitting frontispiece," explains Matthiessen, "since it reveals the type of character

with which the writers of the age were most concerned, the common man in his heroic stature, or as Whitman called the new type, 'Man in the Open Air.' " Matthiessen, *American Renaissance: Art and Expression in the Age of Emerson and Whitman* (New York: Oxford University Press, 1941), xxvi. Matthiessen nowhere discusses the clipper ship as an instrument of white spatial hegemonies that also involved transport of slaves and other trafficked nonwhite labor. Even more strikingly, he nowhere mentions Frederick Douglass (who contemplates clipper ships on the Chesapeake Bay in a famous passage of his 1845 *Narrative*) in this 678-page monumental study despite the fact that *My Bondage and My Freedom* appeared in 1855, a publication date Douglass shares with Whitman's first edition of *Leaves of Grass*. Matthiessen's student, the poet Charles Olson, would similarly emphasize the Melvillean theme of the common (and implicitly white) man under democratic and geographically expansive conditions rising to unprecedented heroic (albeit tragic) stature. In *Call Me Ishmael* (1947), a book that derived from his Matthiessen-directed doctoral dissertation, Olson restates the spatial thesis that has undergirded Anglo-Saxon occupation of the New World from the colonial era forward: "I take SPACE to be the central fact of man born in America." Writing in the wake of the U.S.-led Allied victories over Germany and Japan and during the escalating geopolitical rivalry between the United States and the Soviet Union, Olson's scholarship reaffirms old imperial suppositions: "I am interested in a Melville who was long-eyed enough to understand the Pacific as a part of our geography, another West, prefigured in the Plains, antithetical." Olson, *Call Me Ishmael* (New York: Grove Press, 1947), 11, 12–13. Olson's concern with space-to-be-occupied builds on the heritage of free (white) space; such reasserted prerogatives would inform his theory of Projectivist verse. With respect to black countergeographies, however, it is worth noting that Amiri Baraka, whose poetic practice is indebted to Olson's Projectivist theories, would soon challenge the white spatial imaginary as he in turn enters into an American literary geographic dialectic by developing a poetic cartography of urban midcentury America and the Middle Passage that shadows it.

38. Willa Cather, *My Ántonia* (Boston: Houghton Mifflin, 1918), 1, 88, 119.

39. On the African American presence in the West, see Monroe Lee Billington and Roger D. Hardaway, *African Americans on the Western Frontier* (Boulder: University Press of Colorado, 1998); and Quintard Taylor, *In Search of the Racial Frontier: African Americans in the American West, 1528–1990* (New York: W. W. Norton, 1998). In *Exodusters: Black Migration to Kansas after Reconstruction*, Nell Irvin Painter documents one experiment in which a black community attempts to seize the promise of the American West. Painter, *Exodusters: Black Migration to Kansas after Reconstruction* (New York: Knopf, 1976). Eric Gardner calls attention to a commonly overlooked African American West Coast presence by examining a vigorous mid-nineteenth-century newspaper and periodical production. See "Early African American Print Culture and the American West," in *Early African American Print Culture*, edited by Lara Langer Cohen and Jordan Alexander Stein (Philadelphia: University of Pennsylvania Press, 2012), 75–89.

40. Black people in the American West would continue to incarnate an intriguing if problematic proposition. In *Dessa Rose* (1986), author Sherley Anne Williams, born in Bakerfield, California, depicts a community of fugitive slaves who imagine the West as a promised land only to find, in traveling from Alabama to Council

Bluffs, that there too white supremacist restrictions await. In Colson Whitehead's *The Underground Railroad* (2016), we last see the major protagonist, Cora, on a wagon heading west across the unsettled continent, her fate far from certain.

41. Henry Louis Gates Jr., *The Signifying Monkey: A Theory of African American Literary Criticism* (New York: Oxford University Press, 1988), 121.

42. Agoraphobia etymologically means fear (phobia) of the public square (agora), metonymically public marketplace.

43. Houston A. Baker Jr., "Autobiographical Acts and the Voice of the Southern Slave," in *The Slave's Narrative*, ed. Charles T. Davis and Henry Louis Gates Jr. (New York: Oxford University Press, 1985), 244, 245.

44. *The Dred Scott Decision: Opinion of Chief Justice Taney: A Machine Readable Transcript*, Library of Congress, https://cdn.loc.gov/service/ll/llst/022/022.pdf, 4, 6, 14.

45. Wong, *Neither Fugitive nor Free*, 240, 241.

46. For a detailed account of the political currents to which *Blake* responds, as well as Delany's ever-evolving position with respect to black emancipation and deliverance, see Robert S. Levine, *Martin Delany, Frederick Douglass, and the Politics of Representative Identity* (Chapel Hill: University of North Carolina Press, 1997), 177–80.

47. In *Fugitive Science: Empiricism and Freedom in Early African American Culture*, Britt Rusert notes how Delany's narrative "tracks the artful and nearly supernatural movements of the fugitive protagonist. . . . In *Blake*, speculative science transforms the archetypal fugitive slave narrative into speculative fiction." Rusert, *Fugitive Science*, 164.

48. Martin R. Delany, *Blake; or, The Huts of America*, ed. Floyd J. Miller (Boston: Beacon Press, 1970), 85, 101, 112.

49. Appearing serially in the *Anglo-African Magazine* in 1859 and the *Weekly Anglo-African* in 1861 and 1862, *Blake* did not appear in book form until 1970. It is difficult to gauge the power of the text in its initial appearances. In *Abolitionist Geographies*, Martha Schoolman emphasizes "the very ambiguity of *Blake's* historical moment" through a close examination of the distinct serial publications of *Blake*, the first, fractional serialization appearing just as the antebellum period was about to conclude and the full version after the war has begun in earnest. If, as Schoolman urges, we consider *Blake* as a bid to intervene in the strategic mapmaking of the era, the first appearance lends itself to an abolitionist scheme of effecting liberation at the various scales of slave-power instantiation, whereas "the *Blake* of the early Civil War years" arguably participates "in the geographic reorientation that a war would undoubtedly bring." Schoolman, *Abolitionist Geographies*, 15, 11–12.

50. For further discussion of the recurrent and passionate African American claim to the North American continent, see chap. 3, pp. 72–73.

51. Delany, *Blake*, 287.

52. As Vlach observes, "The slaves' agenda is the hidden dimension of a southern plantation." John Michael Vlach, *Back of the Big House: The Architecture of Plantation Slavery* (Chapel Hill: University of North Carolina Press, 1993), 16. In the two sections of chapter 1, "The Plantation Landscape" (1–17), he contrasts "The Planter's Landscape" with "The African American Plantation Landscape." Subsequent chapters examine specific sites of contested plantation geography. In

Closer to Freedom: Enslaved Women and Everyday Resistance in the Plantation South (Chapel Hill: University of North Carolina Press, 2004), Stephanie M. H. Camp likewise explores covert methods by which enslaved people constructed what she calls (after Edward Said) a "rival geography" within a spatial order comprising variable and typically gendered "geographies of containment."

53. Advocates of the newly emancipated black populace were certainly aware of the correlation between viable citizenship and land ownership, and the Freedman's Bureau fostered such ownership as part of an initiative to integrate that populace into a postslavery, postwar economy. With the elimination in 1876 of federal programs to support this process, opportunities for black ownership of Southern lands diminished precipitously. Claude F. Oubre's study concludes with the following observation: "The tragedy of Reconstruction is the failure of the black masses to acquire land, since without the economic security provided by land ownership the freedmen were soon deprived of the political and civil rights which they had won." Oubre, *Forty Acres and a Mule: The Freedmen's Bureau and Black Land Ownership* (Baton Rouge: Louisiana State University Press, 1978), 197.

54. Griggs shares with David Walker and Martin Delany a vision of black recuperation along patriarchal lines, in which fatherhood and territoriality serve as benchmarks of nationalist empowerment. As Kevin K. Gaines demonstrates, projection of an ultra-masculine hero has a long-standing association with the revolt-narrative tradition and resonated deeply among Griggs's turn-of-the-century contemporaries. See Gaines, *Uplifting the Race: Black Leadership, Politics, and Culture in the Twentieth Century* (Chapel Hill: University of North Carolina Press, 1996), 114–15.

55. In *The Souls of Black Folk*, W. E. B. Du Bois offers the classic contemporary perspective on the failure of Reconstruction-era initiatives to lift the newly emancipated populace to a condition of sustainable citizenship in the newly reconstituted United States. In "From Freedom to Slavery," chapter 1 of *Uplifting the Race* (19–46), Gaines provides a useful synopsis of the reversals black people experienced in the post-Reconstruction period.

56. Camp, *Closer to Freedom*, 141.

57. Toni Morrison, *Beloved* (1987; repr., New York: Vintage Books, 2004), 323.

58. M. NourbeSe Philip, *Zong!* (Middleton, Conn.: Wesleyan University Press, 2008), 190.

59. Glissant, *Caribbean Discourse*, 9.

60. Hortense J. Spillers, "Mama's Baby, Papa's Maybe: An American Grammar Book," in *Black, White, and in Color: Essays on American Literature and Culture* (Chicago: University of Chicago Press, 2003), 214–15.

61. Saidiya V. Hartman, *Lose Your Mother: A Journey along the Atlantic Slave Route* (New York: Farrar, Straus and Giroux, 2007), 68.

62. Melvin Dixon, *Ride Out the Wilderness: Geography and Identity in Afro-American Literature* (Urbana: University of Illinois Press, 1987), 2–3.

63. Davis, *Southscapes*, 19.

64. H. Bruce Franklin, *Prison Literature in America: The Victim as Criminal and Artist* (New York: Oxford University Press, 1989); and Michael Bennett, "Anti-Pastoralism, Frederick Douglass, and the Nature of Slavery," in *Beyond*

Nature Writing: Expanding the Boundaries of Ecocriticism, ed. Karla Armbruster and Kathleen Wallace (Charlottesville: University of Virginia Press, 2001), 195–210. For treatment of the swamp in the African American tradition and of the Maroon communities that occupied the Southern wetlands, see William Tynes Cowan, *The Slave in the Swamp: Disrupting the Plantation Narrative* (New York: Routledge, 2005); on the topic of garden scenes, see chapter 5, n. 33. In *Black Faces, White Spaces: Reimagining the Relationship of African Americans to the Great Outdoors* (Chapel Hill: University of North Carolina Press, 2014), Carolyn Finney reviews the historical association of nature with white adventure and advocacy and examines an increasing black participation in outdoor recreation and environmental activism.

65. Madhu Dubey, *Signs and Cities: Black Literary Postmodernism* (Chicago: University of Chicago Press, 2003); and Charles Scruggs, *Sweet Home: Invisible Cities in the Afro-American Novel* (Baltimore: Johns Hopkins University Press, 1993).

66. Barack Obama's second inaugural address can be found here: https://obamawhitehouse.archives.gov/the-press-office/2013/01/21/inaugural-address-president-barack-obama.

Chapter 2

1. Around the trope of the Talking Book, which he identifies as "the ur-trope of the Anglo-African tradition" in mediating the transition from oral to written cultures, Henry Louis Gates Jr. clusters Gronniosaw, Marrant, Jea, Cugoano, and Equiano. "The trope of the Talking Book became the first repeated and revised trope of the tradition, the first trope to be Signified upon." Gates, *Signifying Monkey*, 143, 144.

2. Although Selina Hastings has been the subject of popular church-sponsored biography, scholarly treatment of her life and activities can be found in Thomas S. Kidd, *George Whitefield: America's Spiritual Founding Father* (New Haven, Conn.: Yale University Press, 2014). Geordan Hammond addresses pro- and antislavery currents within the Anglo-American Methodist community in *John Wesley in America: Restoring Primitive Christianity* (Oxford: Oxford University Press, 2014).

3. Phillis Wheatley, *Complete Writings*, ed. Vincent Carretta (New York: Penguin, 2001), 153. Subsequent references in chapter 2 to this edition appear parenthetically in the text.

4. A long-lasting effect of Jefferson's observations, according to Henry Louis Gates Jr. has been to establish the derogatory perception of her intellectual capacity as a metonym of black intellectual capacity in general. Gates, *Figures in Black*, 73–74. As John Sekora has shown, the antislavery promoters of written slave testimony perpetuated the view of black writers as incapable of high literary achievement. Among other sponsors, Sekora quotes Lydia Maria Child, who in *An Appeal in Favor of That Class of Americans Called Africans* (1836) writes, "I am well aware that most of the negro authors are remarkable principally because they are negroes. With considerable talent, they generally evince bad taste." Sekora, "Black Message/White Envelope: Genre, Authenticity, and Authority in the Antebellum Slave Narrative," *Callaloo: A Journal of African Diaspora Arts and Letters* 32 (Summer 1987): 506, https://doi.org/10.2307/2930465.

5. Jefferson, *Notes*, 140–41.

6. See John B. Boles, *Jefferson: Architect of American Liberty* (New York: Basic Books, 2017), 481–82.

7. The neoclassical conventionality of Wheatley's poetic medium has been recognized in recent decades as affording the poet a wider range of ironic and subversive expression than commentators were willing to register through much of the twentieth century. Writing in the 1980s, Henry Louis Gates Jr. observes that "Phillis Wheatley has for far too long suffered from the spurious attacks of black and white critics alike for being the original *rara avis* of a school of so-called mockingbird poets, whose use and imitation of received European and American literary conventions has been regarded, simply put, as a corruption itself of a 'purer' black expression, privileged somehow in black artistic forms such as the blues, Signifyin(g), the spirituals, and the Afro-American dance." Gates, *Figures in Black*, 43–44.

8. For a probing and detailed account of the 1772 Mansfield ruling (*England, the King v. James Somerset*) and the rights enslaved persons could claim on British soil in the decades before the abolition of the slave trade and (later) slavery throughout the British Empire, see Wong, *Neither Fugitive nor Free*, chap. 1.

9. See Vincent Carretta, *Equiano, the African: Biography of a Self-Made Man* (Athens: University of Georgia Press, 2005). While reserving judgment as to Equiano's birthplace, Carretta builds a convincing argument that Equiano was born in what is now South Carolina. I have relied on this meticulously researched biography in my analysis of how Equiano converts the materials of a black Atlantic life into a narrative fashioned for a late eighteenth-century white British audience.

10. Michelle Wright argues that, given what we now know to be our inconclusive knowledge (but when was our knowledge ever really conclusive?) of the historic Equiano's trajectory, he must exist, like a subatomic particle to the epistemologically challenged human observer, "in several 'places at once,' because it is possible that Equiano existed in any and all those places." M. Wright, *Physics of Blackness: Beyond the Middle Passage Epistemology* (Minneapolis: University of Minnesota Press, 2015), 24.

11. The phrase recurs several times, but see especially Paul Gilroy, *The Black Atlantic: Modernity and Double Consciousness* (Cambridge, Mass.: Harvard University Press, 1993), 57. As an example of black diasporan "expressive culture" that stands in contrast to the diction of Wheatley and Equiano (and many an African American and Afro-Britton to follow), one might cite what the Barbadian poet Edward Kamau Brathwaite identifies as "nation language." Brathwaite describes "nation language" as "influenced very strongly by the African model, the African aspect of our New World/Caribbean heritage. English it may be in terms of some of its lexical features. But in its contours, its rhythm and timbre, its sound explosions, it is not English, even though the words, as you hear them, might be English to a greater or lesser degree." Brathwaite, *History of the Voice: The Development of Nation Language in Anglophone Caribbean Poetry* (London: New Beacon Books, 1984), 13.

12. In reference to Equiano but with broad application to other eighteenth-century African Anglophone authors, Ronald A. T. Judy remarks, "The humanization in writing achieved in the slave narrative required the conversion of the incomprehensible African into the comprehensible Negro." The process

entails an "emancipating death": "In writing the death of the African body, Equiano gains voice and emerges from the abject muteness of objectivity into productive subjectivity." Such productivity, however, comes at grave ontological expense—nothing less than "the interdiction of the African." Judy, *(Dis)Forming the American Canon* (Minneapolis: University of Minnesota Press, 1993), 92, 88–89.

13. For a detailed tracing of Wheatley's paths to publication, see Vincent Carretta, *Phillis Wheatley: Biography of a Genius in Bondage* (Athens: University of Georgia Press, 2011). Life history information in my discussion of Wheatley derives from this excellent biography.

14. For an illuminating discussion of what it meant for Wheatley to publish her poems in book form—as opposed to the more ephemeral formats of newspaper and broadside—see Joseph Rezek, "The Print Atlantic: Phillis Wheatley, Ignatius Sancho, and the Cultural Significance of the Book," in *Early African American Print Culture*, edited by Lara Langer Cohen and Jordan Alexander Stein (Philadelphia: University of Pennsylvania Press, 2012), 19–39. Highlighting the prestige book publication materially signified, Rezek addresses the ways in which, at the time of its publication, *Poems on Various Subjects, Religious and Moral* alternately constituted representative evidence of black aptitude, humanity, and equality with whites or confirmation (as with Jefferson) of fundamental inferiority.

15. On the evolution of Anglo-American women's authorial cultures, see David D. Hall, "Readers and Writers in Early New England," in *A History of the Book in America*, vol. 1, *The Colonial Book in the Atlantic World*, ed. Hugh Armory and David D. Hall (Chapel Hill: University of North Carolina Press, 2007), 117–51; and David S. Shields, "Eighteenth-Century Literary Culture," in Armory and Hall, *A History of the Book*, 1:434–76.

16. In "Writing 'Race' and the Difference It Makes" (*Critical Inquiry* 12, no. 1 [Autumn 1985]: 1–20, https://doi.org/10.1086/448318) and several subsequent publications, Henry Louis Gates Jr. asks contemporary readers to visualize Wheatley's "examination" by these eighteen white patriarchs as a nightmare conflation of academic and judicial interrogation, trial by racism and misogyny. In doing so, according to Joanna Brooks, Gates enlists readers in the creation of a wholly apocryphal biographical moment that diverts attention from an alternate and equally pernicious frame of gendered power relations: what Brooks presents as Wheatley's necessary cultivation of white slavery-complicit female readers and endurance of "the crippling dynamic of white female sentimentality" (21) to which she had to reconcile herself in exerting the agency requisite to becoming a published Afro-British poet. Brooks, "Our Phillis, Ourselves," *American Literature* 82, no. 1 (2010): 1–28, https://doi.org/10.1215/00029831-2009-067.

17. As Joseph Rezek observes, such was the objection of Ignatius Sancho. Writing to Jabez Fisher, a Philadelphia Quaker, "Sancho criticizes the eminent Boston individuals who are listed in the famous 'attestation' that was printed in Wheatley's volume and guaranteed the authenticity of her poems. He finds it appalling that none of them freed her from slavery: '[t]he list of splendid—titled—learned names, in confirmation of her being the real authoress.—alas! shews how very poor the acquisition of wealth and knowledge are—without generosity—feeling—and humanity.' " Rezek, "The Print Atlantic," 21.

18. Carretta, *Phillis Wheatley*, 10.

19. "Egyptian gloom" invokes a spiritual bondage analogous to the Israelites' bondage under Pharaoh; strategically the poet chooses only later to emphasize that a person of color speaks these words.

20. "When one remembers that as secretary of state for the colonies and president of the Board of Trade and Foreign Plantations between 1772 and 1775 the earl of Dartmouth became engaged in the British policy of inciting American slaves to revolt against their patriot masters," observes Betsy Erkkila, "the poet's 'hope' of freedom for 'her race' takes on a particularly insurrectionary cast." Erkkila, "Phillis Wheatley and the Black American Revolution," in *A Mixed Race: Ethnicity in Early America*, ed. Frank Shuffleton (New York: Oxford University Press, 1993), 234.

21. For a discussion of the three published versions of the poem with special attention to the transformations this verse paragraph underwent as it was revised for publication in *Poems on Various Subjects, Religious and Moral*, see Rezek, "The Print Atlantic," 33–38.

22. See Carretta, *Phillis Wheatley*, 160–64.

23. Equiano, *The Interesting Narrative*, 7. Subsequent references in chapter 2 to this edition appear parenthetically in the text.

24. Carretta provides a detailed edition-by-edition analysis of the subscriber lists. See Carretta, *Equiano, the African*, 354, 361.

25. "I am not, really, a stranger any longer for any American alive," Baldwin writes in the concluding paragraph of "Stranger in the Village." Baldwin, *Collected Essays*, 129.

26. Equiano himself footnotes Benezet. On other sources that find their way into Equiano's supposed eyewitness account, see Carretta, *Equiano, the African*, 313.

27. Edmund Burke, *Selected Letters of Edmund Burke*, ed. Harvey C. Mansfield Jr. (Chicago: University of Chicago Press, 2000), 102.

28. For an excellent account of eighteenth-century stadialism as a European concept of human social evolution, see George Dekker, *The American Historical Romance* (New York: Cambridge University Press, 1987), chap. 3.

29. Just as the dread of cannibalism recurs in the literature of European exploration, fiction and nonfiction, so too does it figure as a fear among the newly enslaved. See Hartman, *Lose Your Mother*, 65, 112–13.

30. On Equiano's "veritable descent into the loss of communicative force," see Spillers, "Mama's Baby, Papa's Maybe," 209–10.

31. Equiano's deployment of the trope of the Talking Book occurs in this context. As Henry Louis Gates Jr. remarks, by portraying his encounter with a watch, a portrait, and a book, Equiano is able to suggest the boy's process of assimilation to European objects and practices. "His ability to show his readers his own naiveté, rather than merely to tell us about it or to claim it, and to make this earlier self the focus of his readers' sympathy and amusement, are extraordinarily effective rhetorical strategies that serve to heighten our identification with the openly honest subject whose perceptions these were and who has remembered them for us to share." Gates, *Signifying Monkey*, 169. Although Gates made these observations before evidence of Equiano's possible South Carolina birth materialized, commonplace European objects associated with systems of representation would in any case have challenged the interpretive skills of the child Equiano would have been irrespective of birthplace.

32. In *Slavery on Trial*, 75–78, Jeannine Marie DeLombard discusses the shifting principles by which Africans and their descendants were denied rights of testimony under Anglo-American law. As DeLombard notes throughout her study, a flourishing print culture provided discursive space for black as well as white testimony as to the fundamental illegalities of slavery.

33. For a detailed exposition of these two complicated episodes of failed reengagement, see Carretta, *Equiano, the African*, 196–99, 224–35.

34. Carretta, *Equiano, the African*, 353.

35. Quoted in Carretta, *Equiano, the African*, 331–33.

Chapter 3

1. Edgar J. McManus, *Black Bondage in the North* (Syracuse, N.Y.: Syracuse University Press, 1973), 180–83.

2. As Christopher Malone shows, some states (such as Pennsylvania) extended and later withdrew the franchise from free blacks or imposed restrictive property qualifications. In declaring black people noncitizens, the 1857 Dred Scott decision undercut all basis in the United States for affording African Americans rights of citizenship. See Malone, *Between Freedom and Bondage: Race, Party, and Voting Rights in the Antebellum North* (New York: Routledge, 2008), esp. chap. 3.

3. Observes Eugene Genovese. "The estimate by W. E. B. Du Bois that, despite prohibitions and negative public opinion, about 5% of the slaves had learned to read by 1860 is entirely plausible and may even be too low. Undoubtedly, most of the literate slaves lived in the towns and cities or had worked in them for some time. . . . The least advance in literacy in the countryside undoubtedly occurred on the large plantations of the Black Belt, for both law and a hostile public opinion operated there with the greatest force and effectiveness. Yet, literate slaves appeared everywhere, no matter how unfavorable the atmosphere." Genovese, *Roll, Jordan, Roll: The World the Slaves Made* (New York: Pantheon, 1974), 563. Elizabeth McHenry cites predecessors such as Jupiter Hammon as providing an example of literate black people reading aloud to the illiterate (or less literate) and situates Walker's dissemination of his pamphlet in the larger context of the black community's effort to foster literacy and claims to citizenship: "Walker intended the *Appeal* to bridge the gap between the literate and the illiterate"; "Reading the Appeal aloud, Walker insisted, was part of a larger responsibility to be fulfilled by his educated black audience." *Forgotten Readers*, 34, 35.

4. Walker, *David Walker's Appeal*, 29. Subsequent references in chapter 3 to this edition appear parenthetically in the text.

5. The contexts of Walker's largely undocumented life are admirably explored in Peter P. Hinks, *To Awaken My Afflicted Brethren: David Walker and the Problem of Antebellum Slave Resistance* (University Park: Pennsylvania State University Press, 1997). I have relied on this work in my discussion of the itinerary that culminates in the *Appeal*.

6. "In an Atlantic world where freedom had become increasingly territorialized," observes Edlie L. Wong with reference to this passage, "Walker seizes on travel as an ironic test of the individual freedoms purportedly secured in the federal compact. His series of conditional 'ifs' reveal personal liberty to be both racially particularized and geographically bounded." Wong, *Neither Fugitive nor Free*, 183.

7. "Servants, obey your masters" is the theme of the Reverend Snyder's proslavery sermon in William Wells Brown's *Clotel, or The President's Daughter*, chap. 6. In *Uncle Tom's Cabin*, chap. 33, Simon Legree quotes the scripture to Tom, who has refused to whip his fellow slave, Cassy.

8. Jefferson, *Notes*, 163.

9. Du Bois, *The Souls of Black Folk*, 128. In 1913, James Weldon Johnson would reassert this claim in "Fifty Years," a poem written in commemoration of the Emancipation:

> This land is ours by right of birth,
> This land is ours by right of toil;
> We helped to turn its virgin earth,
> Our sweat is in its fruitful soil.

In the same spirit he would conclude "Lift Every Voice and Sing" as follows:

> True to our God,
> True to our native land.

Johnson, *Complete Poems*, ed. Sondra Kathryn Wilson (New York: Penguin, 2000), 119, 110. Toni Morrison would enlarge on this theme in *Song of Solomon*. See chap. 6, 184–85.

10. As McHenry observes, "Walker's *Appeal* was able to address not only his principal audience, the public constituted by the black community, free or slave. To the extent that whites noticed Walker's text and took action to suppress it, he engaged the national public as well." McHenry, *Forgotten Readers*, 30. On Walker's engagement of both white and black publics across a spectrum of literacy practices, see *Forgotten Readers*, 24–42. Robert S. Levine invokes Jürgen Habermas's notion of the public sphere in assessing Walker's contribution to an emerging black newspaper and pamphlet culture that sought participation "in a national conversation" irrespective of color lines. See Levine, "Circulating the Nation," 29.

11. In an essay that seeks to restore black gallows literature to the genealogy of an African American literary canon, Jeannine Marie DeLombard observes that even "the most virtuous black writers found incrimination closely correlated to print publicity." See "Apprehending Early African American Literary History," in *Early African American Print Culture*, edited by Lara Langer Cohen and Jordan Alexander Stein (Philadelphia: University of Pennsylvania Press, 2012), 98.

12. "The 1845 *Narrative*," writes William L. Andrews, "for all its impressiveness as an autonomous autobiographical act, should not be read without acknowledging, as Robert Stepto was the first to do, the subtle 'tension' between Garrison's preface, which takes credit for inspiring Douglass in the antislavery cause, and Douglass's own text, which seeks to flesh out a portrait of its author as something much more than an abolitionist mouthpiece." Andrews, *To Tell a Free Story*, 217. My reading emphasizes that tension, given what I view as the striking discrepancy between Garrison's third-person characterization of Douglass and Douglass's assertive first-person performance. With reference to the formally authenticating function of Garrison's introduction and Phillips's letter, Stepto phrases it well: "Douglass's tale dominates the narrative because it alone authenticates the narrative." Robert B. Stepto, *From Behind the Veil: A Study*

of Afro-American Narrative (Urbana: University of Illinois Press, 1979), 17. In "Black Message/White Envelope," John Sekora likewise addresses the white supremacist constraints under which Douglass composed the 1845 *Narrative*. Disputing the idea that Douglass's association with the Massachusetts Anti-Slavery Society hampered his free expressiveness, Robert S. Levine argues that his apprenticeship among white abolitionists was instrumental to Douglass's literary development. "Although it is tempting to view Douglass as an outlier, rebel, or critic of the man he was working for, and thus as an independent black writer and speaker who had no need for the support of a white antislavery leader and his abolitionist organization, there are good reasons to regard the *Narrative* as the result of a productive collaboration between Douglass and the Garrisonians." Levine, *The Lives of Frederick Douglass* (Cambridge, Mass.: Harvard University Press, 2016), 35. On Douglass's ultimate rejection of Garrisonian moral suasionism, see David W. Blight, *Frederick Douglass: Prophet of Freedom* (New York: Simon and Schuster, 2018), esp. 304–5.

13. "White antislavery history," John Ernest observes, "always reveals its investment in a systematic order that rests on the foundation of white supremacy, and it was this historical framework that defined the contours of African American biography and autobiography before the Civil War." Ernest, *Liberation Historiography*, 184.

14. Frederick Douglass, *Autobiographies: Narrative of the Life of Frederick Douglass, An American Slave, Written by Himself; My Bondage and My Freedom; Life and Times of Frederick Douglass*, ed. Henry Louis Gates Jr. (New York: Library of America, 1984), 3. Subsequent references in chapter 3 to this edition appear parenthetically in the text.

15. Douglass is hardly alone among fugitive slave narrators in his ironic engagement of autobiographical convention. On William Wells Brown's caustic account of his biracial parentage, see Andrews, *To Tell a Free Story*, 27–28.

16. The fondness is not Douglass's alone. Gates identifies the chiasmus as "perhaps the most commonly used rhetorical figure in the slave narratives and throughout subsequent black literature." Gates, *Signifying Monkey*, 140.

17. Of this phrase James Olney observes, "It is a very significant and immensely effective reminder" for Douglass "to refer to the writing instrument as a way of realizing the distance between the literate, articulate writer and the illiterate, inarticulate subject of the writing." Olney, "'I Was Born': Slave Narratives, Their Status as Autobiography and as Literature," in *The Slave's Narrative*, ed. Charles T. Davis and Henry Louis Gates Jr. (New York: Oxford University Press, 1985), 158.

18. The concluding paragraphs of *Narrative of the Life of Frederick Douglass*, chapter 1, have become the site of a contemporary reckoning with the persistence of the historical trauma and sadistic pleasure-generating spectacle by which black flesh is devalued, desecrated, and destroyed. "I have chosen not to reproduce Douglass's account of the beating of Aunt Hester," writes Saidiya V. Hartman, "in order to call attention to the ease with which such scenes are usually reiterated, the casualness with which they are circulated, and the consequences of this routine display of the slave's ravaged body. Rather than inciting indignation, too often they immure us to pain by virtue of their familiarity—the oft-repeated or restored character of these accounts and our distance from them are signaled

by the theatrical language usually resorted to in describing these instances—and especially because they reinforce the spectacular character of black suffering." Hartman, *Scenes of Subjection*, 3. In responding to Hartman's choice not to reproduce this scene, Fred Moten is drawn to "consider the phonic materiality of such propriative exertion" as Aunt Hester's scream embodies. Hartman's "decision not to reproduce the account of Aunt Hester's beating is, in some sense, illusory," Moten observes. "First, it is reproduced in her reference to and refusal of it; second, the beating is reproduced in every scene of subjection the book goes on to read—in both the ritual performances combining terror and enjoyment in slavery and the fashionings and assertions of citizenship and 'free' subjectivity after emancipation." Moten, *In the Break*, 1, 4. This scene is also the entry point for Christina Sharpe in the introduction to *Monstrous Intimacies: Making Post-Slavery Subjects* (Durham, N.C.: Duke University Press, 2010). Michelle D. Commander draws instructive parallels between the child Frederick's observation of Captain Anthony whipping Aunt Hester and Dana Franklin's initiatory witnessing of the patrollers beating Alice's father in *Kindred*. See Commander, *Afro-Atlantic Flight*, 41.

19. Gilroy, *The Black Atlantic*, 13.

20. The passage is repeated with only minor variations (chiefly punctuation). See *Autobiographies: Narrative of the Life of Frederick Douglass, An American Slave, Written by Himself; My Bondage and My Freedom; Life and Times of Frederick Douglass*, 311 (*My Bondage and My Freedom*) and 610 (*Life and Times*).

21. Douglass was by no means a passive participant in the fashioning of his photographic likeness. As John Stauffer, Zoe Trodd, and Celeste-Marie Bernier demonstrate, he was far ahead of his time in recognizing the power of the strategically rendered and disseminated image. See Stauffer, Trodd, and Bernier, *Picturing Frederick Douglass: An Illustrated Biography of the Nineteenth Century's Most Photographed American* (New York: Liveright, 2015). Against the stock iconography of the fugitive slave (such figures as commonly appear in handbills aimed at retrieving runaways), Michael A. Chaney discusses Douglass's frontispiece portraits and their representation of a man who, once an item of property himself, has attained a self-possession signified by the dress and posture of middle-class Victorian masculinity. See Chaney, *Fugitive Visions*, 26–35.

22. Recent scholarship has sought to restore to James McCune Smith's stature as an immensely accomplished nineteenth-century American. In *The Black Hearts of Men: Radical Abolitionists and the Transformation of Race* (Cambridge, Mass.: Harvard University Press, 2001), John Stauffer recovers his importance as an antebellum political figure. In *Fugitive Science* (51–60), Britt Rusert addresses his significance as scientific inquirer.

23. William S. McFeely probes the complexity of Douglass's quasi-familial relationships with the Aulds in *Frederick Douglass* (New York: W. W. Norton, 1991). As McFeely demonstrates, each member of this family—Thomas, Lucretia, Hugh, Sophia, and Tommy—played a significant role in Douglass's emotional and intellectual development, and the clan remained a point of reference from childhood to old age. But see note 24.

24. Celeste-Marie Bernier, "'Frederick Douglass, the Freeman' and 'Frederick Bailey, the Slave': Private versus Public Acts of Letter-Writing in Frederick

Douglass's Pre-Civil-War Correspondence," in *The Edinburgh Companion to Nineteenth-Century American Letters and Letter-Writing*, ed. Celeste-Marie Bernier, Judie Newman, and Matthew Pethers (Edinburgh: Edinburgh University Press, 2016), 369. In what is to date the fullest consideration of Douglass's engagement of epistolary genres and the ways in which that engagement shaped his understanding of "the ability of language to capture the physical and psychological realities of enslavement" (372), Bernier situates "Letter to His Old Master" in the context of the "Dear Master" subgenre (letters from escapees addressed to former masters as published in abolition periodicals).

25. William S. McFeely reviews possibilities of contact between Thomas Auld and Harriet Bailey during the months Douglass would have been conceived. McFeely, *Frederick Douglass*, 13–14. Robert S. Levine counters that Auld "was not a blood relative," assigning Douglass's probable paternity to Aaron Anthony. Levine, *The Lives of Frederick Douglass*, 243. David W. Blight concurs with McFeely and Levine that the question of paternity remains open but does not dismiss the possibility that Douglass and Amanda Auld Sears might be half siblings. Blight, *Frederick Douglass*, 13–16, 485. For Douglass, in any event, the matter was never resolved, and the suspicion of a white father forever remained a suspicion.

26. Robert S. Levine cautions against accepting the face-value truth of the late-life reconciliation of Douglass and Thomas Auld, despite Douglass's genuine bond with his daughter, Amanda. See Levine, *The Lives of Frederick Douglass*, chap. 5, "Thomas Auld and the Reunion Narrative." David W. Blight speculates that Douglass's account "revealed a deep yearning to heal his own soul, to find a purging of his scarred memory, to forgive in a way that helped *him* to finally declare publicly his survival and triumph." Blight, *Frederick Douglass*, 594.

27. Kevin K. Gaines addresses the tendency, beginning in the nineteenth century, of leaders such as Martin Delany, Alexander Crummell, and Frederick Douglass to equate "black progress and humanity with territorial nation building, civilization, and patriarchal authority." For aspiring blacks, "the family, and patriarchal gender relations, became crucial signifiers of respectability." Gaines, *Uplifting the Race*, 5–6.

28. In *Kindred*, Octavia Butler engages this issue directly as she takes up the question of how a black person reconciles herself with a violent white paternal ancestry. See chap. 6, pp. 192–99.

29. As a young man "in Boston and New York," Malcolm X writes, "I was among the millions of Negroes who were insane enough to feel that it was some kind of status symbol to be light-complexioned—that one was actually fortunate to be born thus. But, still later, I learned to hate every drop of that white rapist's blood that is in me." Malcolm X and Alex Haley, *The Autobiography of Malcolm X* (New York: Ballantine Books, 1999), 2–3.

30. Harriet A. Jacobs, *Incidents in the Life of a Slave Girl*, ed. Jean Fagan Yellin (Cambridge, Mass.: Harvard University Press, 1987), 201. Subsequent references in chapter 3 to this edition appear parenthetically in the text.

31. But the shield of protection to which Jacobs alludes hardly means that her readership was unacquainted with the psychic and physical sexual violence that took place within the white Jacksonian and Victorian era middle-class home. See Carroll Smith-Rosenberg, *Disorderly Conduct: Visions of Gender in Victorian*

America (New York: Oxford University Press, 1985). From the often invasive medical surveillance of a woman's reproductive career to the marital rape that took place behind the veneer of respectability, the patriarchal abuse that found extreme expression in the slave master's exploitation of female (and male) slaves was not unfamiliar to Jacobs's readers. Her seventeen years in the North and acquaintance with feminists such as Child and Post must have made her aware of the less than utopian lives of her inscribed female readers. William L. Andrews observes that some of the Northern white women to whom Jacobs would be directing her appeal had begun to see their own condition reflected in those of slave women. "For two decades Angelina Grimké had been referring to politically silent women in the free states as 'the white slaves of the North': by 1857 Elizabeth Cady Stanton had denounced the unequal status of the wife in marriage as 'nothing more or less than legal prostitution.'" But as Andrews notes, the structural gulf between Jacobs and even her most sympathetic or similarly injured white readers could hardly disappear. "Servants were social auxiliaries; they could not be heroines or pretend to lecture middle-class women on their moral duties." Andrews, *To Tell a Free Story*, 247–48.

32. Although Jacobs likely began *Incidents* while residing in Rochester, New York, with Isaac and Amy Post, she completed and revised it after rejoining the household of author and editor Nathaniel Parker Willis, the fictionalized Mr. Bruce, whose position on slavery was equivocal. Of Jacobs's literary practice after her return to New York City, Jean Fagan Yellin observes, "For years while living under Willis's roof she wrote secretly and at night." Yellin, preface and introduction to *Incidents in the Life of a Slave Girl*, by Harriet A. Jacobs, ed. Jean Fagan Yellin (Cambridge, Mass.: Harvard University Press, 1987), xviii. Yellin provides a detailed account of the difficulties Jacobs encountered negotiating a publishing contract and seeing the book through press (xix–xxv). Frances Smith Foster characterizes Jacobs's residence in the Willis household as follows: "The Willis home was a gathering place of the New York literati and while she probably did not participate in the salon conversations, as a silent servant Jacobs had ample opportunity to absorb the critical questions and details of literary production. Jacobs was familiar with the white literary establishment, and she moved in the circles of the best abolitionist writers." Foster, *Written by Herself: Literary Production by African American Women, 1746–1892* (Bloomington: Indiana University Press, 1993), 101.

33. In "Slavery's Pleasant Homes: A Faithful Sketch," published in the 1843 *Liberty Bell*, Lydia Maria Child establishes the white Marion and brown Rosa in a foster sister relationship while white Frederic and brown George are half brothers. In "Of the Coming of John," chapter 13 of *The Souls of Black Folk*, Du Bois develops the motif in ways that emphasize contrast over propinquity.

34. See Yellin, preface and introduction, xxii.

35. Much of the commentary on *Incidents* concerns how we should read Linda reading her anticipated audience. Thus Saidiya V. Hartman: "The narrator's appeal situates the reader in the position of the slave girl and implores the implied reader not to judge from the virtuous perspective of those whose homes are protected by law. . . . The inescapability of this violated condition provides the narrator with the license to speak the indelicate, within defined limits, and, at the same time, forestalls the condemnation of white Northern women. The

narrative creates a dynamic vortex that engulfs the reader and vividly displays the relentless forces of sexual undoing; even the most obdurate reader cannot resist such entreaties." Indeed, Linda Brent's "'Now' reflects the urgency of the effort to keep the reader's empathy and refers to the relationship between narrative and reader, at a place where narrative control is in jeopardy. It signals an endangered moment of negotiation between reader and narrator. . . . The reader, overwhelmed by the pain, shame, sorrow, pleas, and guilt, falls prey to the narrator's eloquent words just as Linda fell prey to Sands." Hartman, *Scenes of Subjection*, 106. See also Robyn R. Warhol, "'Reader, Can You Imagine? No, You Cannot': The Narratee as Other in Harriet Jacobs's Text," *Narrative* 3, no. 1 (1995): 57–72, https://www.jstor.org/stable/20107043?seq=1.

36. Hartman addresses the question of whether the enslaved subject can be said to choose under such conditions as define Linda's options when she elects to enter a relationship with Mr. Sands. Hartman, *Scenes of Subjection*, 102, 105.

37. Hartman, *Scenes of Subjection*, 107.

38. One might almost speak of the garret residence as "the Linda Brent trope," the physically agonizing and debilitating confinement for which a cultivation of psychic and cognitive space provides some compensation. Upon arrival in North Carolina, Cora, the female protagonist of Colson Whitehead's *The Underground Railroad* (2016), finds refuge in the stifling attic of her abolitionist hosts, where she spends her time pouring over the Bible and almanac in her effort to learn to read. Like Linda, Cora peers out at a perilous world from a hidden aperture. Unlike Linda, she is ultimately discovered and subjected to the slave catcher's chain.

39. McKittrick, *Demonic Grounds*, 40.

40. For an excellent account of Jacobs's epistolary practice, not only as Linda Brent operating from the Edenton garret but as the abolitionist author of public letters, see Elizabeth Hewitt, *Correspondence and American Literature, 1770–1865* (Cambridge University Press, 2004), chap. 4, "Jacobs's Letters from Nowhere."

41. McKittrick, *Demonic Grounds*, 42.

42. Jean Rhys's *Wide Sargasso Sea* (1966) helps us recognize that, as a "white creole," the scandal-stigmatized Antoinette Bertha Mason Rochester acquires in England a non-white status.

43. In the preface to her 1987 edition, Yellin writes of how, when first reading *Incidents* in the early 1970s, she "dismissed it as a false slave narrative" in keeping with "received opinion." In her introduction, she examines why the book had been considered fiction through much of its first century, in addition to adducing recently discovered evidence that definitively correlates events in the narrative with those of Jacobs's life. Yellin, preface and introduction, vii, xxix–xxx.

Chapter 4

1. In *White Rage: The Unspoken Truth of Our Racial Divide* (New York: Bloomsbury Press, 2016), 30–38, Carol Anderson showcases the sophistry with which state and federal courts, including the U.S. Supreme Court, muddied and negated the evident clarity of the Thirteenth, Fourteenth, and Fifteenth Amendments.

2. With respect to Du Bois specifically, Hazel V. Carby observes that "the narrative structure and genealogy of race, nation, and manhood to be found in *The Souls of Black Folk* imagines its community by reversing the direction of the

archetypal journey" of the slave narrative as it had evolved from the eighteenth century forward. Carby, *Race Men* (Cambridge, Mass.: Harvard University Press, 1998), 16. For a groundbreaking account of twentieth-century "black counter-migration" (142) to an ancestral South, see Farah Jasmine Griffin, "*Who Set You Flowin'?" The African-American Migration Narrative* (New York: Oxford University Press, 1995), esp. chap. 4, "To Where from Here: The Final Vision of the Migration Narrative," 142–83. The topic receives comprehensive treatment in Davis, *Southscapes*.

3. Booker T. Washington, *Up from Slavery: An Autobiography* (Garden City, N.Y.: Doubleday and Page, 1925), 16, 17.

4. Gaines, *Uplifting the Race*, 251.

5. See Robert J. Norrell, *Up from History: The Life of Booker T. Washington* (Cambridge, Mass.: Harvard University Press, 2009), 216. See also Charlotte D. Fitzgerald, "*The Story of My Life and Work*: Booker T. Washington's Other Autobiography," *Black Scholar* 21, no. 4 (2001): 35, https://doi.org/10.1080/00064246.1991.11412979.

6. Booker T. Washington, *The Story of My Life and Work* (Toronto: J. L. Nichols, 1901), 18–19. Subsequent references in chapter 4 to this edition appear parenthetically as *Story* in the text.

7. See Gates, *Signifying Monkey*, particularly 70–96.

8. Washington, *Up from Slavery*, 1. Subsequent references in chapter 4 to this edition appear parenthetically as *Up* in the text.

9. For an account of white supremacists who could not accept Washington at all, see Norrell, *Up from History*, 43–60.

10. For a consideration of "the rhetorical and affective roles that global figurations play" in Washington's "advocacy of the New South," see Hsu, *Geography and the Production of Space*, 184–91.

11. Robert Stepto identifies Washington's quotation of Creelman and others as authenticating documents that contribute to the self-authentication that is his ultimate strategy, achieved "at what seems to be, morally and aesthetically, a very high price." Stepto, *From Behind the Veil*, 43.

12. As Stepto observes, *Up from Slavery* presents "a rather extraordinary portrait of a single life within what Du Bois called the deeper recesses beyond the Veil." Stepto, *From Behind the Veil*, 35.

13. Ida B. Wells, *Crusade for Justice: The Autobiography of Ida B. Wells*, ed. Alfreda M. Duster (Chicago: University of Chicago Press, 1970), 4. Subsequent references in chapter 4 to this edition appear parenthetically in the text.

14. For a superbly researched portrait of the determination with which recently liberated African Americans sought to become literate citizens, see Christopher Hager, *Word by Word: Emancipation and the Act of Writing* (Cambridge, Mass.: Harvard University Press, 2013).

15. For an excellent recent account of the "lynching at the Curve" and Wells-Barnett's antilynching activism, see Jacqueline Goldsby, "Writing 'Dynamitically': Ida B. Wells," in *A Spectacular Secret: Lynching in American Life and Literature* (Chicago: University of Chicago Press, 2006), 43–104.

16. For a discussion of Ida B. Wells-Barnett in the context of other late nineteenth-century African American women writers and her unusual willingness to engage in the literary frontal assault, see Foster, *Written by Herself*, 179–83.

17. Jacobs, *Incidents in the Life of a Slave Girl*, 52.

18. Ida B. Wells, *Southern Horrors and Other Writings: The Anti-Lynching Campaign of Ida B. Wells, 1892–1900*, ed. Jacqueline Jones Royster (Boston: Bedford Books, 1997), 70. This passage occurs in chapter 6, "Self Help." The focus on the Winchester rifle draws attention to the Second Amendment rights African Americans have had reason to claim as United States citizens, as well as the white contestation of that specific right. No discussion of spatial politics in the United States is complete without some acknowledgment of the part firearms—and the amendment that protects citizens who wish to own them—have played in establishing and maintaining the cartographical integrity of privately held space. Indeed, what might be described as the country's gun pathology (with protections extended to citizens who wish to own semiautomatic military-grade firearms) reflects the ideals of militant privatization with which settler communities have historically occupied North American space.

19. The phrase has come to be associated with Malcolm X, who repeats it nine times in the June 28, 1964, speech delivered at the inaugural meeting of the Organization of Afro-American Unity, in which he implores African Americans to claim equality and justice and defend family and property against white aggression.

20. The urgency of South-to-North migration is evident in Wells-Barnett's account of N. S. Taylor's need to escape following his election as president of the national Equal Rights League: "On his return to his home in Greenville, Mississippi, his life was threatened by white citizens who resented the fact that he had accepted the presidency of an organization whose outstanding business was to denounce lynching, peonage, and disfranchisement. They proceeded to show that resentment, whereupon Mr. Taylor shook the dust of Greenville off his feet and came to Chicago." Wells, *Crusade for Justice*, 397.

21. The other chapters were authored by Frederick Douglass, I. Garland Penn, and F. L. Barnett, whom she would later marry. For a comprehensive picture of African American participation in the World's Columbian Exposition, see Reed, *"All the World Is Here!"* For an account of Douglass's support and mentorship of Wells-Barnett and their intergenerational collaboration, see Blight, *Frederick Douglass*, 733–39.

22. Du Bois, *The Souls of Black Folk*, 7. Subsequent references in chapter 4 to this edition appear parenthetically in the text.

23. Brent Hayes Edwards usefully reminds us that "The problem of the Twentieth Century is the problem of the color-line" first occurs in "To the Nations of the World," a speech he delivered at the 1900 Pan-American Conference held in London and that "the phrase emphatically frames the 'color line' not in the U.S. debates and civil rights struggles that are commonly taken to be its arena, but in the much broader sphere of 'modern civilization' as a whole." Edwards, *The Practice of Diaspora: Literature, Translation, and the Rise of Black Internationalism* (Cambridge, Mass.: Harvard University Press, 2003), 1–2.

24. See Brent Hayes Edwards's illuminating discussion of the "Forethought" to *The Souls of Black Folk*, in which Du Bois manages the "shifting, carefully calibrated points of entry to an 'inside' marked as 'Negro'—in a manner that stands in for social and epistemological access to the multiple layers and 'deeper recesses' of the 'world in which ten thousand thousand Americans live and strive.'" With reference to what readers have come to look upon as Du Bois's signature trope,

the *veil* that at once admits and forbids access to that world, Edwards cites precedent in the work of Olaudah Equiano, Mary Prince, Frederick Douglass, and Harriet Jacobs as well as recurrence in the work of Toni Morrison. Edwards, *The Practice of Diaspora*, 39.

25. Ron Eyerman proposes that "Du Bois' chosen audience is white, his former teachers and colleagues at Harvard and elsewhere, his fellow progressives and other members of the political and cultural establishment." Eyerman, *Cultural Trauma: Slavery and the Formation of African American Identity* (New York: Cambridge University Press, 2001), 66. But it is important also to note that Du Bois sought to create a model of black people speaking to white, and in this regard his performance appeals directly to the dignity of the book's black readership. As Eyerman points out, the invocation of a black audience is particularly felt in Du Bois's chapter critiquing Booker T. Washington (67–68).

26. Paul Gilroy identifies this passage as a particularly Hegelian moment, one that specifically reflects Du Bois's early Germanicist study in Berlin. Gilroy, *The Black Atlantic*, 134.

27. The white educated general readership Du Bois aims to reach is also in these same years the target audience of Thomas Dixon Jr. whose first installment in his fervently white supremacist Reconstruction Trilogy—*The Leopard's Spots* (1902), *The Clansman* (1905), and *The Traitor: A Story of the Fall of the Invisible Empire* (1907)—appeared the year before *The Souls of Black Folk*. In *The Story of American Freedom* (New York: W.W. Norton: 1998), 131-37, Eric Foner contextualizes such crosscurrents amid the "resurgence" in North and South of "Anglo-Saxonism" (131).

28. In *The Autobiography of an Ex-Colored Man*, James Weldon Johnson may be thought to rewrite this scene in the final chapter, when his protagonist's white beloved, upon being informed of his African ancestry, rejects his profession of love: "Under the strange light in her eyes I felt that I was growing black and thick-featured and crimp-haired." Johnson, *The Autobiography of an Ex-Colored Man*, 106. Her rejection, however, is only temporary: the lovers wed across the color line, and two children are born of their union. Still, the white woman's death upon the second child's birth contributes a note of ambiguity to the racial reconciliation the marriage might seem to represent.

29. *Kent v. Dulles* (1958).

30. Gilroy identifies *The Souls of Black Folk* as "the first place where a diasporic, global perspective on the politics of racism and its overcoming interrupted the smooth flow of African-American exceptionalisms." David Walker, if not Martin Delany, comes very close to assuming that perspective ahead of Du Bois. With regard to the vision of the black community that develops in *The Souls of Black Folk*, Gilroy adds, "Du Bois's nationalist impulses coexisted in that book with their transcendence." Gilroy, *The Black Atlantic*, 120–21.

31. W. E. B. Du Bois, *Darkwater: Voices from Within the Veil*, ed. Henry Louis Gates Jr. and Evelyn Brooks Higginbotham (New York: Oxford University Press, 2007), 3. Subsequent references in chapter 4 to this edition appear parenthetically in the text.

32. In her introduction to the *Darkwater* edition that appears in the Oxford W. E. B. Du Bois, Evelyn Brooks Higginbotham identifies "the woman angle" and this passage specifically as "the key to the book's title." Higginbotham,

introduction to *Darkwater: Voices from Within the Veil*, by W. E. B. Du Bois, ed. Henry Louis Gates Jr. and Evelyn Brooks Higginbotham (New York: Oxford University Press, 2007), xxxiii.

33. Gilroy notes Du Bois's tendency to figure the black collective as feminine and the dissonance this creates with his more patriarchal if not misogynist tendencies. "The idealized figuration of racial culture and community through the bodies of black women in Du Bois's nonfiction has to contend with the rather less celebratory images of African-American womanhood that appeared in his novels. The ambiguities which spring up around his presentation of racial culture, kinship, nationality, and community in gendered form are a big problem lying dormant in the critical writing about his work." Gilroy, *The Black Atlantic*, 136.

34. Great Barrington, his Uncle James Burghardt's permanent home, continued to serve as Du Bois's home base to the extent he could be said to have one. It is there that both of his children were born and where he would choose to bury his son, Burghardt, who died in Atlanta. In the aftermath of the 1906 Atlanta riot, Du Bois sent Nina and Yolande to live in Great Barrington.

35. I refer here to the Emerson of "Self-Reliance" and *Essays: First Series* (1840) generally, who repeatedly emphasizes the individual ego as the center and arbiter of cognition and moral adjudication.

36. Those circumstances replicate, in Gilroy's words, "the history of the black Atlantic, where movement, relocation, displacement, and restlessness are the norms rather than the exceptions." Gilroy, *The Black Atlantic*, 133.

37. Du Bois, *Dusk of Dawn*, xxxiii. Subsequent references in chapter 4 to this edition appear parenthetically in the text.

38. Although "veil" occurs in the King James Bible only seven times, those occurrences invariably signal a revelatory moment. In Matthew 27:51, Mark 15:28, and Luke 23:45, "the veil of the temple" is reported to be "rent" at the moment of Jesus's death. In Paul's Epistle to the Hebrews, reference is made to the veil of the tabernacle (9:3) but also, in 10:20, the person of Jesus as a veil: "A new and living way, which he hath consecrated for us, through the veil, that is to say, his flesh." Plato's "Allegory of the Cave" (*Republic*, VII, 514 a, 2 to 517 a, 7) counts as the ur-recognition in Western thought of the inadequacy of human epistemology and representation. In the chained condition of the cave dwellers, the allegory harbors a political subtext that clearly resonated with Du Bois.

39. In "Reading, Writing, and Resisting: African American Print Culture," James P. Danky discusses the African American community's rapid embrace of print culture in the decades following emancipation, beginning with mastery of print technology as taught in trades-oriented black colleges to the ubiquitous appearance of black newspapers and black-produced books directed to a newly literate mass readership. But such activity, Danky demonstrates, was largely contained within the black community before the decline of the black independent press in the postwar years. See Danky, "Reading, Writing, and Resisting: African American Print Culture," in *A History of the Book in America*, vol. 4, *Print in Motion: The Expansion of Publishing and Reading in the United States, 1880–1940*, ed. Carl F. Kaestle and Janice A. Radway (Chapel Hill: University of North Carolina Press, 2009), 339–58.

40. A. C. McClurg of Chicago was one of several significant emerging publishing houses that challenged the hegemony of an Anglophile U.S. publishing

industry centered in Boston, a development that began at the turn of the century and gained traction after World War I, when New York City became the industry's new center. *Darkwater* was one of the first publications of Harcourt, Brace, and Howe, which in 1920 had just been formed by former editors at Henry Holt, of which Joel Spingarn was a partner. See George Hutchinson, *The Harlem Renaissance in Black and White* (Cambridge, Mass.: Harvard University Press, 1995), 114, 345–46, 372–78; see also David Levering Lewis, *W. E. B. Du Bois: The Fight for Equality and the American Century, 1919–1963* (New York: Henry Holt, 2000), 11. As Lewis's biography demonstrates, through most of his life Du Bois seldom lacked for editors eager to publish his work.

41. For a detailed account of the U.S. Justice Department's persecution of the aged Du Bois and the NCAAP's abandonment of the organization's cofounder, see Carol Anderson, *Eyes off the Prize: The United Nations and the African American Struggle for Human Rights, 1944–1955* (New York: Oxford University Press, 2003), 171–74.

42. Through its issuance of passports, the U.S. State Department's role in regulating the mobility of black citizens and adjudicating their possession of citizen rights has a long history. See Wong, *Neither Fugitive nor Free*, 240–62.

43. David Levering Lewis helps us understand why Du Bois, at age ninety-two, beleaguered politically within and without his circle of erstwhile friends and allies, might have allowed himself to be seduced by the Soviet and Chinese socialist states. See Lewis, *W. E. B. Du Bois*, 556–64. "As they moved about Beijing in their ceremonial cocoon," Lewis writes, "Du Bois and Graham Du Bois knew absolutely nothing of the catastrophe inflicted upon the Chinese people by their omnipotent ruler" (563).

44. W. E. B. Du Bois, *The Autobiography of W. E. B. Du Bois: A Soliloquy on Viewing My Life from the Last Decade of Its First Century*, ed. Henry Louis Gates Jr. and Werner Sollors (New York: Oxford University Press, 2007), 31. Subsequent references in chapter 4 to this edition appear parenthetically in the text.

45. Richard Iton provides a wide-angle account of the pressures dividing the Cold War–era black community over the question of whether African Americans should remain loyal to the United States on the basis of its professed if grossly unrealized ideals and thus refrain from indicting the United States on the international stage. Repressive instruments, such as the 1950s era House Un-American Activities Committee, served indeed to vitiate the potential for vigorous protest, not to mention radical politics. In Iton's narrative, Paul Robeson (who, like DuBois, had to surrender his passport) emerges as the central figure in reference to whom Harry Belafonte, Sidney Poitier, Ossie Davis, and others calibrated their response to the domestic issues of the time. Iton, *In Search of the Black Fantastic*, chap. 2.

46. "The shades of the prison-house closed round about us all," Du Bois had written in chapter 1 of *The Souls of Black Folk*: "Walls strait and stubborn to the whitest, but relentlessly narrow, tall, and unscalable to sons of night who must plod darkly on in resignation, or beat unavailing palms against the stone, or steadily, half hopelessly, watch the streak of blue above" (3).

Chapter 5

1. Richard Wright speaks of this descriptor in "The Psychological Reactions of Oppressed Peoples," the first of four essays collected in *White Man, Listen!*

(1957), where he examines the "negative loyalty" of American blacks whose desire to embrace an American identity is ever subject to such markings as white people impose. R. Wright, *White Man, Listen!* (New York: HarperPerennial, 1995), 17.

2. Arnold Rampersad discusses the ways in which *Invisible Man* draws upon Ellison's life story while venturing into realms of overt allegory. See Rampersad, *Ralph Ellison: A Biography* (New York: Knopf, 2007), 225–26, 236.

3. Given Malcolm's landlocked continental origins, it may be easy to lose sight of the fact that, as Richard Iton points out, he qualifies as a second-generation Caribbean writer, whose mother was born in Grenada and whose Georgia-born father endowed him with a fierce Garveyite legacy. Iton, *In Search of the Black Fantastic*, 219.

4. Chronologically, Langston Hughes (1902–1967) and Arna Bontemps (1902–1973) are generationally proximate to Richard Wright (1908–1960), and Hughes in particular commanded an audience that comprised white as well as black readerships. But neither achieved the best-selling success and currency of Wright, Ellison, Malcolm X, and Baldwin. Zora Neal Hurston (1891–1960), another generationally proximate major author, but a casualty of male-dominated literary politics that relegated her to comparative obscurity during the last two decades of her life, would achieve celebrity only after Alice Walker saw to the 1973 reprinting of *Their Eyes Were Watching God*, originally published by J. B. Lippincott in 1937 to mixed reviews. In admirable detail, George Hutchinson documents the ways in which Harlem Renaissance authors benefited from the early twentieth-century revolt against the cultures of Anglophile gentility led by Van Wyck Brooks, Randoph Bourne, and Waldo Frank, among others, and the culture of progressive magazines and emerging publishing houses (Knopf, Liveright and Boni, Harcourt Brace, Random House, and Viking) open to New Negro writing. Whereas even the best-known Harlem Renaissance authors never came close to achieving the sales records of Richard Wright, their inclusion in the publishing programs of the New York City–based houses certainly prepared the way for the midcentury celebrity of the four authors this chapter examines. See Hutchinson, *The Harlem Renaissance*, 125–135, 342–386.

5. The literary careers of Wright, Ellison, Baldwin, and Malcolm X, like that of Du Bois, were exceptional in that they began outside the self-contained sphere of literary activity that James P. Danky describes in "Reading, Writing, and Resisting: African American Print Culture." But postwar expansion in mainstream cultures of leisure and academic reading (driven by the rising New York publishing houses) are instrumental to the celebrity this chapter's four authors were able to attain compared with what for Du Bois remained a modest portion of readership and fame as well as what held through much of his life as a primary orientation to a black readership, an orientation reinforced by his longtime (1910–33) editorship of *The Crisis*.

6. As an outlet for authors committed to literary experimentation, sexual expressiveness, and oppositional left-oriented politics, the Greenwich Village–based Grove Press flourished under the direction of Barney Rosset as an independent publishing house that promoted titles mainstream publishers were likely to reject as indecent or dangerously radical. With respect to writing that addresses color-line issues, Grove published English translations of Frantz Fanon's *Black Skin, White Masks* and *The Wretched of the Earth* as well as early work of Amiri

Baraka (still signing himself LeRoi Jones) in addition to *The Autobiography of Malcolm X*. For a discussion of Grove Press in the context of independent postwar publishing, see David D. Hall, "Cultures of Letters, Cultures of Criticism," in *A History of the Book in America*, vol. 5, *The Enduring Book: Print Culture in Postwar America*, ed. David Paul Nord, Joan Shelley Rubin, and Michael Schudson (Chapel Hill: University of North Carolina Press, 2009), 224. See also Loren Glass, *Counterculture Colophon: Grove Press, Evergreen Review, and the Incorporation of the Avant-Garde* (Stanford, Calif.: Stanford University Press, 2013).

7. For an account of Richard Wright's negotiations with the Book-of-the-Month Club and the revisions he consented to make for *Native Son* to be selected as the first featured title by an African American, see Janice A. Radway, *A Feeling for Books: The Book-of-the-Month Club, Literary Taste, and Middle-Class Desire* (Chapel Hill: University of North Carolina Press, 1997), 286–87. In exchange for the club's promotion of the book among a middle-class white audience, Wright was willing to withdraw passages depicting Bigger and Jack masturbating in the movie theater while contemplating newsreel scenes of Mary Dalton frolicking on a Florida beach. Although Wright's compliance with such requests would appear to contradict what he identifies in "Blueprint for Negro Writing" as the black author's priority to address "the Negro himself, his needs, his sufferings, aspirations," his willingness to edit secured the novel's club adoption and led to its best-seller status. R. Wright, "Blueprint for Negro Writing," in *Within the Circle: An Anthology of African American Literary Criticism from the Harlem Renaissance to the Present*, ed. Angelyn Mitchell (Durham, N.C.: Duke University Press, 1995), 98. "After being selected by the club in 1940," writes Radway, "*Native Son* sold 215,000 copies within three weeks" (287). Four years later, when the club proposed also to adopt what would appear as *Black Boy* on condition that it be cut in half, Wright, as Radway demonstrates, again proved agreeable. In doing so he evinced his desire for literary celebrity and an understanding of its power. On Wright's aggravated negotiations with the Book-of-the-Month Club's white editorial board, see also Hazel Rowley, *Richard Wright: The Life and Times* (New York: Henry Holt, 2001), 179–85, 286–93, and Davis, *Southscapes*, 149–53.

8. For Massey, the concept of "trajectory" is helpful here in that it (1) prompts us to situate the mobile human subject within a spatial field constituted by the subject's narrative understanding of the world, while it (2) reminds us that any such itinerary exists amid a multiplicity of trajectories and attendant narratives that may or may not emanate from a common historical master narrative. See Massey, *For Space*, 10–11, 113. In the collision Ellison's protagonist describes, there is at once an element of happenstance—in keeping with what Massey identifies as "the chance of space" (116)—but also destiny, as the chance urban encounter with a mutually affirmed alterity devolves into an altercation within an all-too-familiar frame of reference—the national narrative of unresolved black/white enmity.

9. In the decades during which all four authors discussed in this chapter engaged the mass and diverse readerships of the mid-twentieth century, one may begin to speak of the ubiquity of electronic media as radio and television increasingly became a presence in American homes at every economic level—harbingers of the interactive medium that is the internet, an innovation that has fostered a multiplicity of imaginable and contested communities.

10. Gilroy, *The Black Atlantic*, 146. In "Richard Wright's *Pagan Spain*," M. Lynn Weiss begins the process of contextualizing this travelogue in relation to the modernist romance of Spain instigated by Stein and Hemingway, an approach that Wright implicitly critiques. See Weiss, "*Para Usted*: Richard Wright's *Pagan Spain*," in *The Black Columbiad: Defining Moments in African American Literature and Culture*, ed. Werner Sollors and Maria Diedrich (Cambridge, Mass.: Harvard University Press, 1994), 212–25; see also Virginia Whatley Smith, *Richard Wright's Travel Writing: New Reflections* (Jackson: University Press of Mississippi, 2001).

11. Wright contemplates not so much his own historical situation as an English speaker as the intervention of European languages in the experience and meaning-making of the colonial subaltern—the elite class of African and Asian current and former colonies educated in Europe who find themselves in the position of having "no vocabulary of history" that derives from their native culture. R. Wright, *White Man, Listen!*, 36. In "Men without Language" and "The Zone of Silence," two sections of "The Psychological Reaction of Oppressed People," Wright explores a predicament that Frantz Fanon treats in *Black Skin, White Masks* (1952) and James Baldwin addresses in "Stranger in the Village" (1953). Famously, the predicament would figure as the point of departure for Gayatri Chakravorty Spivak in "Can the Subaltern Speak?" (in *Marxism and the Interpretation of Culture*, ed. Cary Nelson and Lawrence Grossberg [Basingstoke: Macmillan, 1988], 271–313) and a topic of extensive theorization for Homi K. Bhabha in *The Location of Culture* (London: Routledge, 1994).

12. Wright records his reflections as participant-observer in *The Color Curtain: A Report on the Bandung Conference* (1956). In view of what Harper Brothers considered the meager interest a mainstream American readership would take in this geographically remote convergence of African and Asian intellectuals, Wright's long-standing publisher declined the manuscript, although the niche-genre-oriented World Publishing Company picked it up immediately. See Rowley, *Richard Wright*, 468. The University Press of Mississippi republished the book in 1995.

13. In *The Emergence of Richard Wright*, Keneth Kinnamon writes of "the determinism of Wright's naturalistic and Marxist vision." Kinnamon, *The Emergence of Richard Wright: A Study in Literature and Society* (Urbana: University of Illinois Press, 1972), 127. At the start of his career as a publishing author, James Baldwin critiques *Native Son* for this determinism—"its insistence" that Bigger's fulfillment of categorical expectations "alone . . . is real and . . . cannot be transcended." James Baldwin, "Everybody's Protest Novel," in *Collected Essays*, 18.

14. Richard Wright, *Early Works: Lawd Today!, Uncle Tom's Children, Native Son*, ed. Arnold Rampersad (New York: Library of America, 1991), 460.

15. In "On Knowing Our Place," Houston A. Baker Jr. discusses this scene as exemplifying black urban placelessness. "Under the displacing impress of authority even what one calls and, perhaps, feels is one's *own place* is, from the perspective of human agency, *placeless*." Baker, "On Knowing Our Place," in *Richard Wright: Critical Perspectives Past and Present*, ed. Henry Louis Gates Jr. and K. A. Appiah (New York: Amistad Press, 1993), 201. Baker connects this moment in *Black Boy* with a scene in *Invisible Man* in which a low-flying aircraft passes above the protagonist while he is conversing with Ras the Exhorter.

16. The contrastive geographies Wright establishes between the Thomas and Dalton households are mirrored by those Ann Petry establishes in *The Street*, where the small house in Jamaica, Queens, and, later, the claustrophobic walkup on 116th Street, Harlem, contrast with the Chandler household in Lyme, Connecticut. "From the time she was born," the narrator observes of the protagonist, Lutie Johnson, "she had been hemmed into an ever-narrowing space, until now she was very nearly walled in and the wall had been built up brick by brick by eager white hands." Another passage depicts the small boy Bub's terror of confined interior space. Lutie, his mother, requires that he sleep in the dark to economize electricity consumption. Just as she leaves to work at the nightclub, she switches the light off: "Instantly the living room was plunged into darkness. He opened his eyes wide in an effort to see something other than this swift blackness. The corners of the room were there, he knew, but he couldn't see them. It made him feel as though he were left hanging in space and that he couldn't know how much space there was other than that his body occupied." Ann Lane Petry, *The Street* (Boston: Houghton Mifflin, 1946), 323–24, 215. Perhaps Ralph Ellison has this passage in mind when his protagonist in *Invisible Man* boasts of the 1,369 bulbs that light his retreat, illumination that not only defines inhabitable space but also combats the existential dysmorphia to which he, like Bub, is prey.

17. See Radway, *A Feeling for Books*, 286. For a more detailed treatment of *Black Boy*'s derivation from the *American Hunger* project, see Janice Thaddeus, "The Metamorphosis of *Black Boy*," in *Richard Wright: Critical Perspectives Past and Present*, ed. Henry Louis Gates Jr. and K. A. Appiah (New York: Amistad Press, 1993), 272–84.

18. Richard Wright, *Later Works: Black Boy (American Hunger), The Outsider*, ed. Arnold Rampersad (New York: Library of America, 1991), 365. Subsequent references in chapter 5 to this edition appear parenthetically in the text.

19. Richard Wright, *Eight Men: Stories by Richard Wright* (New York: Harper Collins, 1996), 19. Subsequent references in chapter 5 to this edition appear parenthetically in the text.

20. In considering the parallels between Fred Daniels and the Invisible Man, Arnold Rampersad sees more similarity than difference. The allegories both authors construct permit "no wholesome resolution of their heroes' dilemmas of identity and consciousness. Instead, they left these heroes isolated in a hole or a room, bound for an early death in Wright's case, in a limbo of uncertainty about the future in Ellison's." Rampersad, *Ralph Ellison*, 246. But a major difference lies in the fact that Ellison's protagonist writes and completes his testimony and that the latter will secure variable if uncertain predication among a broad, intergenerational, racially diverse, and politically polarized readership.

21. Henry Louis Gates Jr. offers Ellison's variations on Wright's themes as an object lesson of the *signifying/Signifyin(g)* he identifies as the core dynamic of African American literary traditions. See Gates, *Signifying Monkey*, 120–21.

22. Although associated with W. E. B. Du Bois, the phrase "Talented Tenth" was coined by the white philanthropist Henry Lyman Morehouse. See Janice A. Radway, "Learned and Literary Print Cultures in an Age of Professionalization and Diversification," in *A History of the Book in America*, vol. 4, *Print in Motion: The Expansion of Publishing and Reading in the United States, 1880–1940*, ed.

Carl F. Kaestle and Janice A. Radway (Chapel Hill: University of North Carolina Press, 2009), 227. See also Eyerman, *Cultural Trauma*, 28.

23. Ralph Ellison, *Invisible Man* (New York: Vintage, 1952), 31. (Subsequent references in chapter 5 to this edition appear parenthetically in the text.) The phrase alludes to Washington's affirmation that "the wisest among my race understand that the agitation of questions of social equality is the extremest folly." Washington, *Up from Slavery*, 224.

24. In his "Working Notes for *Invisible Man*" in *The Collected Essays of Ralph Ellison*, Ellison writes the following about a tradition that sustains its heirs even as it burdens them with impossible and delusionary expectations: "Invisible man [sic] has dedicated himself to a false dream but one that has been presented couched in the form of the great rituals of human hope, such as Barbee with a semifolk evocation of the Founder—mocked by time and reality in the very process—attempts to manipulate in his address to the student body. It is this hope which gives Invisible Man's quest any semblance of dignity." Ellison, "Working Notes for *Invisible Man*," in *The Collected Essays of Ralph Ellison*, ed. John F. Callahan (New York: Modern Library, 2003), 344–45.

25. Foley, *Wrestling with the Left*, 341. Foley elaborates further: "A nonblack (especially white) reader, uncertain about the degree of his or her identification with the novel's protagonist but certain about the dangers posed by communists and communism, can thus request entry into the text's charmed circle of initiates and reply affirmatively to the narrator's closing invitation. . . . In order to secure and invoke the universals necessary for successful artistic communication, Ellison has sutured the disparate elements in his audience by expelling from the tribe those members who can be 'othered' as un-American" (346).

26. In "The Function of Black Literature at the Present Time" (1970), Addison Gayle Jr., a major voice of the Black Arts movement and theorist, with Amiri Baraka, Hoyt W. Fuller, Maulana Karenga, and others, of a black nationalist aesthetic, expresses his skepticism as follows: "A man without a distinctive identity, he is all things to all men, and after the excursion through the black world, he retreats to his dungeon to await the coming millennium, when race will have become irrelevant." Gayle Jr., *The Addison Gayle Jr. Reader*, ed. Nathaniel Norment Jr. (Urbana: University of Illinois Press, 2009), 153. As Arthur F. Redding argues, although the protagonist "promises an end to his hibernation," to the degree that "Ellison never dramatizes the possibility" of emerging except insofar as the narration itself engages a readership in a gesture toward political reconciliation, such "promise rings hollow." Redding, *Turncoats, Traitors, and Fellow Travelers: Culture and Politics of the Early Cold War* (Oxford: University Press of Mississippi, 2008), 68. For an entirely different perspective on the heterotopia Ellison's protagonist inhabits, see Katherine McKittrick, "Freedom Is a Secret: The Future Usability of the Underground," in McKittrick and Woods, *Black Geographies and the Politics of Place*.

27. Redding assesses the impasse of the novel's epilogue as follows: "By the end of the novel, the narrator has become battered and disillusioned with all varieties of political action, and finds freedom rather in an expansive and refined critical consciousness, a classic move in American existential texts of the period. A universal and humanist poetic freedom—forging a form of utterance and expression adequate to one's condition—comes to supplant political freedom, establishing

one's very right to voice within a discriminatory social terrain. Collectivism is abandoned, and the epilogue celebrates difference, diversity, spontaneity, and the uniquely American possibilities of individual self-styling, even if this endorsement of plurality is both a decidedly male privilege and is rendered as a fantasy of impotence." Redding, *Turncoats, Traitors, and Fellow Travelers*, 67.

28. Alan Nadel remains an invaluable guide to Ellison's more and less visible interaction with the (white) American canon as well as with the modernist models (Joyce, Eliot) from which he learned to weave a densely allusive web. See Nadel, *Invisible Criticism: Ralph Ellison and the American Canon* (Iowa City: University of Iowa Press, 1988).

29. In "The Function of Black Literature at the Present Time" (1970), Gayle explicitly rejects Ellison's example: "The Black writer at the present time must forgo the assimilationist tradition and redirect his art to the strivings within the race—those strivings that have become so pronounced, here, in the latter half of the twentieth century. To do so, he must write for and speak to the majority of Black people; not to a sophisticated elite fashioned out of the programmed computers of America's largest universities." Gayle, *The Addison Gayle Jr. Reader*, 155.

30. Rampersad, *Ralph Ellison*, 269.

31. Malcolm X and Haley, *Autobiography*, 174. Subsequent references in chapter 5 to this edition appear parenthetically in the text.

32. For an account of Malcolm X's considerable epistolary activity while incarcerated at Norfolk Prison Colony, see Manning Marable, *Malcolm X: A Life of Reinvention* (New York: Viking, 2011), 90–99.

33. "Each event spoke with a cryptic tongue": so Wright begins a Whitmanesque catalog of joys salvaged retrospectively from a brutal childhood, among which figure the following items:

> There was the delight I caught in seeing long straight rows of red and green vegetables stretching away in the sun to the bright horizon.
>
> There was the faint, cool kiss of sensuality when dew came on to my cheeks and shins as I ran down the wet green garden paths in the early morning. (R. Wright, *Later Works*, 9)

In describing his world of early childhood, the protagonist of James Weldon Johnson's *The Autobiography of an Ex-Colored Man* also makes use of the garden trope: "Back from the house a vegetable garden ran, perhaps, seventy-five or one hundred feet; but to my childish fancy it was an endless territory. I can still recall the thrill of joy, excitement and wonder it gave me to go on an exploring expedition through it, to find the blackberries, both ripe and green, that grew along the edge of the fence." Johnson, *The Autobiography of an Ex-Colored Man*, 6. More recently, in *Belonging: A Culture of Place* (New York: Routledge, 2009), bell hooks extends this theme in writing about her childhood in rural Kentucky. See especially "Habits of the Heart," 215–23.

34. Manning Marable fleshes out what in contrast to the autobiographical narrative appears to be a rather anxious and amateurish criminal career. See Marable, *Malcolm X*, 39–69.

35. In "Dreams of a Native Son," Addison Gayle posits Malcolm X as the prophet of antiassimilation: "Malcolm forced us to look at that with which we would integrate, to examine the history of those with whom we would assimilate,

and to carefully observe this 'burning house,' which we sought so ardently, vigorously, and persistently to enter." Gayle, *The Addison Gayle Jr. Reader*, 66. For Gayle, Malcolm's testimony and the activist literature of those for whom he served as martyred older brother contrast with the self-consciously literary productions of Ellison and Baldwin, conceived in conformity with a white modernist aesthetic.

36. *Playboy* interview, May 1963.

37. Baldwin, *Collected Essays*, 257. Subsequent references in chapter 5 to this edition appear parenthetically in the text.

38. Baldwin's abiding relationship to Harlem and major figures associated therewith is the focus of Herb Boyd, *Baldwin's Harlem: A Biography of James Baldwin* (New York: Atria, 2008). In reassessing Baldwin's outbound arc, Boyd usefully addresses the sexual incentives of the young man's initial flight from Harlem to Greenwich Village.

39. David Leeming provides detail and context to this pivotal life moment in *James Baldwin: A Biography* (New York: Alfred A. Knopf, 1994), 38–41.

40. With reference to Bigger as a persistent if commonly repressed component of black male personality, Baldwin writes, "There is, I should think, no Negro living in America who has not felt, briefly or for long periods, with anguish sharp or dull, in varying degrees and to varying effect, simple, naked, and unanswerable hatred; who has not wanted to smash any white face he may encounter in a day, to violate, out of motives of the cruelest vengeance, their women, to break the bodies of all white people and bring them low, as low as that dust into which he himself has been and is being trampled; no Negro, finally, who has not had to make his own precarious adjustment to the 'nigger' who surrounds him and to the 'nigger' in himself." Baldwin, *Collected Essays*, 29.

41. See chap. 3, n. 5.

42. In "Cultural Nationalism: The Black Novelist in America," Addison Gayle Jr. concedes that Baldwin, in contrast with Ellison, "wavers between the philosophy of assimilationism and that of nationalism." Gayle, *The Addison Gayle Jr. Reader*, 96.

Chapter 6

1. Bernard W. Bell was perhaps the first scholar to bestow a categorical rubric on texts that may be considered "neoslave," a term he is credited with coining. See Bell, *The Afro-American Novel and Its Tradition* (Amherst: University of Massachusetts Press, 1989). In *Neo-Slave Narratives: Studies in the Social Logic of a Literary Form*, Ashraf H. A. Rushdy devotes his first two chapters to correlating the proliferation of such narratives with the cultural transitions of the late 1960s (the New Left and Black Power movements in particular) and the emergence, inside and outside the academy, of new historiographies of the slave past. For his purposes, Rushdy develops a fairly narrow definition of "neo-slave narrative"; interestingly, he brings William Styron's *Confessions of Nat Turner* into his discussion of four principal texts: *Flight to Canada*, *Dessa Rose*, *Oxherding Tale*, and *Middle Passage*. See Rushdy, *Neo-Slave Narratives: Studies in the Social Logic of a Literary Form* (New York: Oxford University Press, 1999). Elizabeth

Beaulieu focuses on the genre as particularly suited to the exploration of female subjectivities under slavery in *Black Women and the American Neo-Slave Narrative* (Westport, Conn.: Greenwood, 1999). As an alternative to "neo-slave," Arlene R. Keizer usefully proposes "contemporary narratives of slavery" as a term more answerable to the diversity of texts that address the African diaspora as generative of contemporary identities and that sets African American works in the wider Afro-Caribbean and Afro-British Anglophone context. She suggests, moreover, that such narratives "take shape" in the late sixties and early seventies "at precisely the moment that the last of those who had experienced New World slavery firsthand passed away." Keizer, *Black Subjects*, 3, 5. On the neo-slave narrative moment and its indictment, in late twentieth-century America, of "rational, scientific, and enlightened Euro-American thought," see Gilroy, *The Black Atlantic*, 219–23.

2. *The Bluest Eye*, *Sula*, *Song of Solomon*, and *Beloved* map a region that stretches from northern Kentucky to Detroit and Windsor and from the Virginia highlands to Pittsburgh. In novels appearing after *Beloved*, Morrison compiles a literary atlas that comprehends the North American continent, Sea Islands and Hudson Valley to Southern and Northern California.

3. For a comprehensive examination of geographical themes in Morrison's fiction and the challenges to "place-making" her characters face, see Beavers, *Geography and the Political Imaginary*.

4. The list could easily extend to books not discussed in this chapter, e.g., Morrison, Sula Peace, *Sula*; Grace (Gigi) Gibson, *Paradise*; Butler, Anyanwu, *Wild Seed*; Shori Matthews, *Fledgling*.

5. Contemporary readers are most likely to know the oral tale through John Bennett's transcription of Caesar Grant's relation of it, first published in *Doctor to the Dead: Grotesque Legends and Folk Tales of Old Charleston* (1946) and later reprinted in Langston Hughes and Arna Bontemps, *Book of Negro Folklore* (1958) and Henry Louis Gates Jr. and Nellie Y. McKay, *The Norton Anthology of African American Literature* (1st edition, 1997). La Vinia Delois Jennings explores the multiple sources (including oral transcriptions compiled in the 1930s under sponsorship of the Federal Writers' Project) upon which Morrison draws in her retelling of the story in *Toni Morrison and the Idea of Africa* (New York: Cambridge University Press, 2008), 114–20.

6. By not naming the city Detroit—or, for that matter, Warren, Pontiac, or Flint—Morrison is able to create an urban site that combines features of the Motor City with those of Chicago (Southside) and any number of industrial cities (Rochester, Buffalo, Cleveland, Toledo, and so forth) that figured as Underground Railroad terminals and later as First Great Migration destinations, where black people found themselves confined to old residential districts formerly occupied by late nineteenth-century European immigrants. Isabel Wilkerson's compilation of narratives in *The Warmth of Other Suns: The Epic Story of America's Great Migration* (New York: Random House, 2010) provides valuable context for all of the works discussed in chapters 5 and 6.

7. Toni Morrison, *Song of Solomon* (New York: Knopf, 1977), 160. Subsequent references in chapter 6 to this edition appear parenthetically in the text.

8. Lucille P. Fultz cites Macon's eviction of the Bains family as one of numerous instances of "black-on-black 'crimes of the heart'" that recur throughout

Morrison's work and that replicate and internalize power asymmetries that subsist between white and black people, contributing to the fissures that pervade the black community. Fultz, *Toni Morrison: Playing with Difference* (Urbana: University of Illinois Press, 2003), 108–9. One could make a case that one of the more serious "crimes of the heart" in *Song of Solomon* is Milkman's longtime exploitation of Hagar. Farah Jasmine Griffin identifies this exploitation as part of a larger pattern by which manhood (defined implicitly by some combination of social, psychological, and geographical mobility) "is achieved by sacrificing women." Griffin, *"Who Set You Flowin'?,"* 177. However, in Paul D (*Beloved*) Morrison will present an alternative model.

9. On Morrison's invocation of a "southern folk aesthetic" in her characterization of Pilate's household in the urban North as well as in her depiction of Shalimar as a black rural town that does not appear on Milkman's Texaco map, see Dubey, *Signs and Cities*, 158–70.

10. On Pilate Dead as Milkman's link to a genealogical past that preserves a subliminal memory of Africa, see Jennings, *Toni Morrison and the Idea of Africa*, 106–14.

11. It is noteworthy that Danville, Pennsylvania, and Montour County are "real places" in the sense that they can be found on the map and that the topography as described in *Song of Solomon* corresponds to this region north of the Susquehanna River, whereas Shalimar, Virginia, wholly exists in a mirror world. The novel's geography is ever spectral but never far removed from the world of consensual cartographies.

12. The leap, in this reading, represents a literal displacement, the antithesis of which is Lincoln's Paradise, the partially realized dream of possession. In "Formalism Comes to Harlem," Hortense J. Spillers observes that "Morrison applies the flying metaphor and its complementary ideas to a problem: What gestures would make possible the total freedom of movement? The meeting place of opposites—control and surrender—identifies the figurative space which the novel would make manifest." Spillers, "Formalism Comes to Harlem," in *Black, White, and in Color: Essays on American Literature and Culture* (Chicago: University of Chicago Press, 2003), 87. But the mythic gesture (absolute self-possession in the absolute if momentary freedom of movement) constitutes a problematic compensation for the repeated dispossession and marginalization the novel depicts.

13. Such domestic arrangements as we may imagine First Corinthians fashioning with the retired Henry Porter exemplify the home-making Morrison's characters occasionally achieve after leading lives of unsettlement and displacement. Still, as Doreen Massey observes, "Toni Morrison's writing, especially in *Beloved*, undermines for ever any notion that everyone once had a place called home which they could look back on, a place not only where they belonged but which belonged to them, and where they could afford to locate their identities." Massey, *Space, Place, and Gender* (Minneapolis: University of Minnesota Press, 1994), 166.

14. Morrison, *Beloved*, xviii. Subsequent references in chapter 6 to this edition appear parenthetically in the text.

15. Herman Beavers identifies what he calls "the recurring trope of the *two-story house*," a site that reappears throughout Morrison's oeuvre "where the occlusion of history and the wholesale erasure of black subjects can only be

countermanded by the establishment of counter-publics that privilege collaborative forms of narration that penetrate silence and counteract the effects of tight space." Beavers, *Geography and the Political Imaginary*, 6.

16. Arlene R. Keizer treats *Beloved* as a prime example of the effort of contemporary black authors to postulate the bygone but genealogically significant slave/postslave subjectivity and to place that subjectivity in relation to the "subjugated system of West African beliefs and practices" (23) that preserves models of sustaining community. Keizer, *Black Subjects*, 23.

17. "Beloved," A. Timothy Spaulding observes, "exists in a state of perpetual liminality, caught between slavery and the present moment of social (and narrative) reconstruction, between the spirit and material world, between the real and the imaginary. As such, she risks losing stable form and content for herself, the characters in the novel, and perhaps even the reader. . . . As symbol or sign of the 'sixty million or more' lost in the Middle Passage, Beloved cannot hope to maintain singularity or coherence." Spaulding, *Re-Forming the Past: History, the Fantastic, and the Postmodern Slave Narrative* (Columbus: Ohio State University Press, 2005), 70.

18. A measure of how this novel set in the historical past speaks to its contemporary (late eighties, early nineties) moment may be found in *Race Matters*, chapter 1, "Nihilism in Black America," where Cornel West cites the loving relationships depicted in *Beloved* as exemplary of a "love ethic" that must form the center of a necessary "politics of conversion." West, *Race Matters* (Boston: Beacon Press, 1993), 19. For a fuller account of the contemporary response to *Beloved*, see Keith Byerman, *Remembering the Past in Contemporary African American Fiction* (Chapel Hill: University of North Carolina Press, 2005), 36.

19. Michelle Wright puts Dana's predicament into a sobering context. Contemplation of her guardian relationship to Rufus "leaves a question for Dana—to what degree is she a coconspirator in rape and other forms of brutalization?—a question that is easily extended to almost all individuals on this planet by moving far back enough on a family tree." Given the sexual violence that accompanies war and conquest, moreover, "one would be hard put to find anyone, even the descendants of royalty (or perhaps, considering all the forced marriages, them *least* of all), whose entire family tree is free of involuntary procreation." M. Wright, *The Physics of Blackness*, 85.

20. But the slave past is only deceptively remote. Consistent with her exposure of Middle Passage epistemologies and challenge of the simplistic linearity such epistemologies presume, Michelle Wright suggests that we read the crisis that sets off Dana's time travel as her present circumstances rather than unresolved issues associated with the slave past. Dana, she observes, "speaks an ambivalent foreshadowing of her violent travel back to slavery in her introductory descriptions of her courtship and marriage to her white husband, Kevin. Dana describes the employment agency where they meet as a 'slave market' and not much later relates Kevin's intense anger over her continuing refusal to type his manuscripts for him—even though, she notes, they are both professional writers." M. Wright, *Physics of Blackness*, 84.

21. Octavia Butler, *Kindred* (Boston: Beacon Press, 1979), 13. Subsequent references in chapter 6 to this edition appear parenthetically in the text.

22. Douglass, *Autobiographies*, 60.

23. Again, preservation of the aggravated genealogy responsible for her existence puts Dana on increasingly treacherous ground as the narrative unfolds. "Although Butler represents Dana more as an agent than as a victim who merely endures suffering," observes Bernard W. Bell, "Dana's political accommodationism with slavery and moral complicity in the sexual violation of her great-grandmother are disturbing imaginative truths about the legacy of American racism and slavery." Bell, *The Contemporary African American Novel* (Amherst: University of Massachusetts Press, 2004), 347.

24. Soja, *Postmodern Geographies*, 244.

25. Octavia Butler, *Parable of the Sower* (New York: Grand Central Publishing, 1993), 11. Subsequent references in chapter 6 to this edition appear parenthetically in the text.

26. "The power of Butler's novel," observes Madhu Dubey, "inheres in the fact that its dystopian urban future is so closely extrapolated from current trends that it creates a shock of familiarity rather than estrangement." Dubey, *Signs and Cities*, 57.

27. What Lauren Berlant has called the "cruel optimism" of attachments to compromised future possibility sustains Olamina as she opposes the Earthseed vision to the abjection that rapidly consumes her world. Berlant, *Cruel Optimism* (Durham, N.C.: Duke University Press, 2011), 24–25.

28. The vision of a dysfunctional, anarchic, and fragmenting United States in the *Parable* series is one in which due process has no meaning and "government" proceeds in turn from an exercise of feeble and robust executive powers. "The state of exception," writes Giorgio Agamben in clarification of the term as framed by Carl Schmitt, "is not a dictatorship but a space devoid of law, a zone of anomie in which all legal determinations—and above all the very distinction between public and private—are deactivated." Agamben, *State of Exception*, trans. Kevin Attell (Chicago: University of Chicago Press, 2005), 50. Earthseed cannot hope to reverse such a state; at best it simulates a primitive democracy dominated by the powerful personality of its founder, Olamina.

29. Rebecca Wanzo ("Apocalyptic Empathy: A Parable of Postmodern Sentimentality," Obsidian III: Literature in the African Diaspora 6/7, no. 2/1 [2005–6]: 72–86), https://openscholarship.wustl.edu/wgss/32/, examines Butler's hyperempathy trope in the context of protocols of reading in the sentimental tradition exemplified by such works as *Uncle Tom's Cabin* that seek to mobilize an individual's sympathetic response and (in consequence) political action but from a position of privilege established by the very social and racial hierarchies the literary gesture purports to critique. "On trial throughout the texts," Wanzo observes, "is not only feeling in itself but 'right feeling' and of its makeup" (77). Wanzo also relates the *Parable* series' phantom text, *Earthseed: The Books of the Living*, to modes of feeling characterizing New Age literature (79–85) and notes that, whereas New Age genres emphasize the atomized individual sensorium, Olamina's writings are directed toward affects that heal the individual in a community context, as evidenced in the social reading of her verse.

30. Kristeva's association of abjection with the mother's body is especially relevant to the daughter/mother animosities at play in the *Parable* series. See Julia Kristeva, *Powers of Horror: An Essay on Abjection*, trans. Leon S. Roudiez (New York: Columbia University Press, 1982), 10, 12–15, 55–56, 101–3. Just

as Lauren abjects her mother, the source of her hyperempathy, so too does she actively abject those whose suffering exceeds her own capacity to sustain the neurochemical response. Asha Vere, who can never overcome the conviction that her mother abandoned her, in turn abjects Lauren.

31. Hee-Jung Serenity Joo contextualizes Olamina's hyperempathy as follows: "In traditional science fiction, the trope of empathy is commonly used to distinguish humans from robots, androids, cyborgs, and other non- or less-human entities." But having striven and survived against a spectrum of entirely human depravity, Olamina's "insistence that empathy is a 'bad, bad idea' provides a science fiction critique of liberal humanism. If empathy has replaced intelligence as the marker that distinguishes humans from non-humans in contemporary science fiction, Butler rejects a simplistic celebration of emotions and affect that merely reifies the category 'human.' Rather, Butler deploys empathy to further question the contours of humanity, particularly in terms of race and exploitation." Joo, "Old and New Slavery, Old and New Racisms: Strategies of Science Fiction in Octavia Butler's Parables Series," *Extrapolation* 52, no. 3 (2011): 288, 290, http://scifilit.pbworks.com/w/file/fetch/62674673/old%20and%20new%20slavery%20-%20joo.pdf.

32. Hartman, *Scenes of Subjection*, 3–4.

33. Octavia Butler, *Parable of the Talents* (New York: Grand Central Publishing, 2000), 20. Subsequent references in chap. 6 to this edition appear parenthetically in the text. "Let's Make America Great Again" figured as the leading slogan of Ronald Reagan's 1980 presidential campaign, whereas the shortened "Make America Great Again" would serve as the mantra of Donald Trump's 2016 campaign and subsequent presidency. In both instances, the message, couched in nostalgia for a time that never was, targeted a xenophobic white demographic anxious about the putatively illegitimate presence of people of color.

34. "I object to the name," Olamina remarks. "This ship is not about a shortcut to riches and empire. It's not about snatching up slaves and gold and presenting them to some European monarch. But one can't win every battle. One must know which battles to fight. The name is nothing." Butler, *Parable of the Talents*, 406. Readers, however, may be less convinced of the benign nature of the starship's agenda.

35. Given its ethnically "rainbow" demographic and its South American colonies, Earthseed inevitably recalls Jim Jones's disastrous People's Temple of the Disciples of Christ. Given its accumulation of wealth, it also invokes the Church of Scientology.

36. As she makes clear in such interviews as that conducted by Charles H. Rowell in 1997, Butler chose to become a science fiction writer even though she was highly conscious of her anomalous status as one who entered a field dominated by white men. The notable exception to this rule was Samuel R. Delany, with whom she briefly studied. She settled on her genre of choice, moreover, just as Ursula K. Le Guin and other female science fiction authors were beginning to emerge and, with Butler herself, proceed to challenge the idea that science fiction was restricted to male practitioners, perspectives, and themes. Through the early part of her career, she was isolated from fellow science fiction writers, preponderantly male and white, as well as from other African American writers, who did not know that she was black. See Charles H. Rowell and Octavia E. Butler, "An Interview with Octavia E. Butler," *Callaloo: A Journal of African Diaspora*

Arts and Letters 20, no. 1 (Winter 1997): 47–66, https://www.jstor.org/stable/3299291. For a useful survey of participation on the part of nonwhite authors in what through much of the twentieth century remained a predominantly white literary practice, see Elisabeth Anne Leonard, "Race and Ethnicity in Science Fiction," in *The Cambridge Companion to Science Fiction*, ed. Edward James and Farah Mendlesohn (Cambridge: Cambridge University Press, 2003), 253–63.

Epilogue

1. Donald Trump's well-documented participation in the discriminatory real estate practices of his father, Fred C. Trump, is recounted in Jonathan Mahler and Steve Eder, "'No Vacancies' for Blacks: How Donald Trump Got His Start, and Was First Accused of Bias," *New York Times*, August 27, 2016. See also Michael Kranish, "FBI Releases File on 1970s Trump Housing Discrimination Case," *Washington Post*, February 15, 2017.

2. Trump recycled this phrase in a speech he delivered in Phoenix, Arizona, on July 11, 2015, at the conclusion of which he declared: "The silent majority is back, and we're going to take our country back." Nicolas Fandos, "Donald Trump Defiantly Rallies a New 'Silent Majority' in a Visit to Arizona," *New York Times*, July 11, 2015. In Nixon's time as in Trump's, however, the phrase mystifies which constituencies have actually had to overcome conspiracies to silence their political voice, and which have not. As this study has shown, African diaspora testimony has struggled repeatedly against those powers that would suppress what it has to say, beginning with the slave regime's denial of black people's status as legal witnesses on their own or others' behalf.

3. Andrew J. Perrin, Steven J. Tepper, Neal Caren, and Sally Morris ("Political and Cultural Dimensions of Tea Party Support, 2009–2012," *Sociological Quarterly* 55, no. 4 (2014), https://doi.org/10.1111/tsq.12069) provide a granular analysis of the demographics of the Tea Party Movement and its nativist and racist tendencies. "The idea that Obama represented the changing face of America—a face exotic and foreign to many Americans—was evident by the fact that as many as 18 percent of Americans (and 34 percent of conservative Republicans) thought that Obama was a Muslim [Luis Lugo et al., "Growing Number of Americans Say Obama Is a Muslim"] Pew Research Center, "Religion & Public Life," August 18, 2010, https://www.pewforum.org/2010/08/18/growing-number-of-americans-say-obama-is-a-muslim/. And, with the Birther movement in full force, many doubted Obama's citizenship. Finally, vice presidential candidate Sarah Palin's contrast of Obama and his supporters to 'real Americans' served to reinforce the perception among many conservatives that the Democratic candidate was 'not like us.' Based on the demographics of the electorate as well as the discourse and rhetoric from both campaigns and the press, Obama's election signaled a significant cultural transformation" (631). They also note that "in October 2010, the National Association for the Advancement of Colored People, in coordination with the Institute for Research and Education on Human Rights, released a report contending that the Tea Party not only was giving a platform to 'well-known anti-Semites and white supremacists,' but attracting white nationalist organizations seeking new recruits from within the ranks of TPM members. Our larger point is not whether or not the TPM was explicitly racist or xenophobic, but rather that its 'nativist' cultural disposition

shows up in varied accounts where movement participants express concern about the country's changing demographics" (643).

4. See Jane Mayer, "Covert Operations: The Billionaire Brothers Who Are Waging a War against Obama," *New Yorker*, October 30, 2010; and Jeff Nesbit, "The Secret Origins of the Tea Party: How Big Oil and Big Tobacco Partnered with the Koch Brothers to Take Over the GOP," *Time*, April 5, 2016.

5. The most prominent and vocal critic was Cornel West, who from early in the administration characterized Obama as a self-serving sellout. See Thomas Frank, "Cornel West: 'He Posed as a Progressive and Turned Out to Be a Counterfeit. We Ended Up with a Wall Street Presidency, a Drone Presidency,' " *Salon*, August 24, 2014. See also West, foreword to *The New Jim Crow: Mass Incarceration in the Age of Colorblindness*, by Michelle Alexander (New York: New Press, 2010), ix–xi. Frank B. Wilderson III is if possible even more trenchant in his dismissal of the Obama promise: "Neoliberalism with a Black face is neither the index of a revolutionary advance nor the end of anti-Blackness as a constituent element of U.S. antagonisms. If anything, the election of Obama enables a plethora of shaming discourses in response to revolutionary politics and 'legitimates' widespread disavowal of any notion that the United States itself, and not merely its policies and practices, is unethical." He continues, "In other words, the election of a Black president aside, police brutality, mass incarceration, segregated and substandard schools and housing, astronomical rates of HIV infection, and the threat of being turned away en masse at the polls still constitute the lived experience of Black life." Wilderson, *Red, White and Black*, 4–5, 10.

6. Trump's utterance of this phrase in a January 11, 2018, Oval Office meeting has been widely documented. See, for example, Josh Dawsey, "Trump Attacks Protections for Immigrants from 'Shithole Countries' in Oval Office Meeting," *Washington Post*, January 11, 2018.

7. For a history of Trump's conflicts with his Aberdeenshire and Ayrshire neighbors, see Severin Carrell, "Donald Trump Faces a Wall of Opposition as He Returns to Scotland," *The Guardian*, June 23, 2016. In Country Clare, Ireland, Trump has faced similar opposition over plans to construct a sea wall. See Griff Witte, "Trump Tried and Failed to Build a Wall in Ireland: That Could Mean Big Trouble for Europe," *Washington Post*, February 6, 2017.

8. My use of the word "relationality" is indebted to Massey. See Massey, *For Space*, 184.

9. "The U.S. is projected to become a majority-minority nation for the first time in 2043. While the non-Hispanic white population will remain the largest single group, no group will make up a majority." U.S. Census Bureau, "U.S. Census Bureau Projections Show a Slower Growing, Older, More Diverse Nation a Half Century from Now," press release, December 12, 2012, https://www.census.gov/newsroom/releases/archives/population/cb12–243.html.

10. For a widely cited 2014 study that directly addresses this question, see Maureen A. Craig and Jennifer A. Richeson, "On the Precipice of a 'Majority-Minority' America: Perceived Status Threat from the Racial Demographic Shift Affects White Americans' Political Ideology," *Psychological Science* 25, no. 6 (2014): 1189–97, https://doi.org/10.1177/0956797614527113.

11. See *White Rage: The Unspoken Truth of Our Racial Divide*, esp. chap. 5, "How to Unelect a Black President" (138–60), in which Carol Anderson

documents how white rage fueled state-level efforts to suppress the black vote, encouraged personally disrespectful behavior toward Barack and Michelle Obama, and culminated in a young white supremacist's murder of nine parishioners at Mother Emanuel AME Church in Charleston, South Carolina.

12. Toni Morrison, "Mourning for Whiteness," *New Yorker*, November 21, 2016, 54.

13. Michelle Alexander, *The New Jim Crow: Mass Incarceration in the Age of Colorblindness* (New York: New Press, 2010), 101. For a breakdown of state-by-state abridgment of felon rights, see the following page at the National Conference of State Legislatures website: http://www.ncsl.org/research/elections-and-campaigns/felon-voting-rights.aspx.

14. Alexander, *The New Jim Crow*, 199. "I was stopped three times in my first ten days in Princeton for driving too slowly on a residential street with a speed limit of twenty-five miles per hour," writes Cornel West. "And my son, Clifton, already has similar memories at the tender age of fifteen." West, *Race Matters*, x.

15. See Richard Rothstein, *The Color of Law: A Forgotten History of How Our Government Segregated America* (New York: Liveright, 2017), 127–31. Anyone familiar with the paths interstate highways take through the heart of American cities might surmise as much.

16. Hartman, *Lose Your Mother*, 132.

17. Ta-Nehisi Coates, *Between the World and Me* (New York: Spiegel and Grau, 2015), 20.

18. Valuable discussions of *The Green Book* include Cotton Seiler, "'So That We as a Race Might Have Something Authentic to Travel By': African American Automobility and Cold-War Liberalism," *American Quarterly* 58, no. 4 (2006): 1091–117, https://www.jstor.org/stable/40068407; and Michael Ra-Shon Hall, "The Negro Traveller's Guide to a Jim Crow South: Negotiating Racialized Landscapes in United States Cultural History, 1936–1967," *Postcolonial Studies* 17, no. 3 (2014): 307–19, https://doi.org/10.1080/13688790.2014.987898. Relevant to the memory of how African Americans have had to negotiate American public space is Calvin Alexander Ramsey and Gwen Strauss's children's book, *Ruth and the Green Book*, illustrations by Floyd Cooper (Minneapolis: Carolrhoda Books, 2010). The film *Green Book* won 2018 Best Picture at the ninety-first AMPAS Academy Awards. Depicting pianist Don Shirley's road tour through the Midwest and South in the company of his Italian American chauffer and bodyguard, Frank Anthony "Tony Lip" Vallelonga, the film foregrounds (among other themes) a white man's education with respect to the dangerous geographies black people navigated in 1960s America. A Trump era exercise in nostalgia for a time of unlikely encounters and epiphanies, *Green Book* presents a curious fable of racial reconciliation.

19. Jan Miles, *The Post-Racial Negro Green Book* (New Orleans: Brown Bird Books, 2017).

20. Rothstein, *The Color of Law*, 238.

21. In conjunction with Rothstein's study, one can explore redlining in selected cities at the online archive: Robert K. Nelson et al., "Mapping Inequality: Redlining in New Deal America," *American Panorama*, ed. Robert K. Nelson and Edward L. Ayers, https://dsl.richmond.edu/panorama/redlining/#loc=11/40.7902/-73.9589&opacity=0.8&sort=98,197&area=D7&city=bronx-ny&text=bibliograph.

22. The Brennan Center for Justice (New York University School of Law) monitors efforts to restrict as well as to expand voting rights. Legislation aimed at establishing how citizens must document their right to vote as well as when and where they may cast their ballots is complicated and contested. For a state-by-state overview of recent voting rights legislation, see https://www.brennancenter.org.

23. See the website for the Sentencing Project, https://www.sentencingproject.org. In *The New Jim Crow: Mass Incarceration in the Age of Colorbindness* (2012), Michelle Alexander documents the (to whites) generally invisible topography of black incarceration as a legacy that the Obama administration could only begin to mitigate.

24. Stuart Hall, "Introduction: Who Needs Identity?" in *Questions of Cultural Identity*, ed. Stuart Hall and Paul du Gay (London: Sage, 1996), 4.

BIBLIOGRAPHY

Adams, Henry. *Democracy, Esther, Mont Saint Michel and Chartres, The Education of Henry Adams, Poems*. Edited by Ernest Samuels and Jayne N. Samuels. New York: Library of America, 1983.

Agamben, Giorgio. *State of Exception*. Translated by Kevin Attell. Chicago: University of Chicago Press, 2005.

Alexander, Michelle. *The New Jim Crow: Mass Incarceration in the Age of Colorbindness*. New York: New Press, 2010.

Anderson, Benedict. *Imagined Communities: Reflections on the Origin and Spread of Nationalism*. London: Verso, 1983.

Anderson, Carol. *Eyes off the Prize: The United Nations and the African American Struggle for Human Rights, 1944–1955*. New York: Oxford University Press, 2003.

———. *White Rage: The Unspoken Truth of Our Racial Divide*. New York: Bloomsbury Press, 2016.

Andrews, William L. *To Tell a Free Story: The First Century of Afro-American Autobiography, 1760–1865*. Urbana: University of Illinois Press, 1986.

Baker, Anne. *Heartless Immensities: Literature, Culture, and Geography in Antebellum America*. Ann Arbor: University of Michigan Press, 2006.

Baker, Houston A., Jr. "Autobiographical Acts and the Voice of the Southern Slave." In *The Slave's Narrative*, edited by Charles T. Davis and Henry Louis Gates Jr., 242–61. New York: Oxford University Press, 1985.

———. "On Knowing Our Place." In *Richard Wright: Critical Perspectives Past and Present*, edited by Henry Louis Gates Jr. and K. A. Appiah, 200–225. New York: Amistad Press, 1993.

Baldwin, James. *Collected Essays: Notes of a Native Son, Nobody Knows My Name, The Fire Next Time, No Name in the Street, The Devil Finds Work, Other Essays*. Edited by Toni Morrison. New York: Library of America, 1998.

Beaulieu, Elizabeth Anne. *Black Women and the American Neo-Slave Narrative*. Westport, Conn.: Greenwood, 1999.

Beavers, Herman. *Geography and the Political Imaginary in the Novels of Toni Morrison*. London: Palgrave Macmillan, 2018.

Bell, Bernard W. *The Afro-American Novel and Its Tradition*. Amherst: University of Massachusetts Press, 1989.

———. *The Contemporary African American Novel*. Amherst: University of Massachusetts Press, 2004.

Bennett, Michael. "Anti-Pastoralism, Frederick Douglass, and the Nature of Slavery." In *Beyond Nature Writing: Expanding the Boundaries of Ecocriticism*, edited by Karla Armbruster and Kathleen Wallace, 195–210. Charlottesville: University of Virginia Press, 2001.

Berlant, Lauren. *Cruel Optimism*. Durham, N.C.: Duke University Press, 2011.

Bernier, Celeste-Marie. "'Frederick Douglass, the Freeman' and 'Frederick Bailey, the Slave': Private versus Public Acts of Letter-Writing in Frederick Douglass's Pre-Civil-War Correspondence." In *The Edinburgh Companion to Nineteenth-Century American Letters and Letter-Writing*, edited by Celeste-Marie Bernier, Judie Newman, and Matthew Pethers, 362–76. Edinburgh: Edinburgh University Press, 2016.

Beverley, Robert. *The History and Present State of Virginia, in Four Parts*. 4 vols. London: R. Parker, 1705.

Bhabha, Homi K. *The Location of Culture*. London: Routledge, 1994.

Billington, Monroe Lee, and Roger D. Hardaway. *African Americans on the Western Frontier*. Boulder: University Press of Colorado, 1998.

Blight, David W. *Frederick Douglass: Prophet of Freedom*. New York: Simon and Schuster, 2018.

Boles, John B. *Jefferson: Architect of American Liberty*. New York: Basic Books, 2017.

Boyd, Herb. *Baldwin's Harlem: A Biography of James Baldwin*. New York: Atria, 2008.

Brathwaite, Edward Kamau. *History of the Voice: The Development of Nation Language in Anglophone Caribbean Poetry*. London: New Beacon Books, 1984.

Brooks, Joanna. "Our Phillis, Ourselves." *American Literature* 82, no. 1 (2010): 1–28. https://doi.org/10.1215/00029831-2009-067.

Brückner, Martin. *The Geographic Revolution in Early America: Maps, Literacy, and National Identity*. Chapel Hill: University of North Carolina Press, 2006.

Brückner, Martin, and Hsuan L. Hsu, eds. *American Literary Geographies*. Newark: University of Delaware Press, 2007.

Burghart, David and Leonard Zeskind. "Racism, Anti-Semitism, and the Militia Impulse." In Tea Party Nationalism: A Critical Examination of the Tea Party Movement and the Size, Scope, and Focus of Its National Factions. New York: Institute for Research and Education on Human Rights, 2010: 57–67. http://www.irehr.org/news/special-reports/item/443.

Byerman, Keith. *Remembering the Past in Contemporary African American Fiction*. Chapel Hill: University of North Carolina Press, 2005.

Burke, Edmund. *Selected Letters of Edmund Burke*. Edited by Harvey C. Mansfield Jr. Chicago: University of Chicago Press, 2000.

Butler, Octavia. *Kindred*. Boston: Beacon Press, 1979.

———. *Parable of the Sower*. New York: Grand Central Publishing, 1993.

———. *Parable of the Talents*. New York: Grand Central Publishing, 2000.

Camp, Stephanie M. H. *Closer to Freedom: Enslaved Women and Everyday Resistance in the Plantation South*. Chapel Hill: University of North Carolina Press, 2004.

Carby, Hazel V. *Race Men*. Cambridge, Mass.: Harvard University Press, 1998.

Carrell, Severin. "Donald Trump Faces a Wall of Opposition as He Returns to Scotland." *The Guardian*, June 23, 2016.

Carretta, Vincent. *Equiano, the African: Biography of a Self-Made Man*. Athens: University of Georgia Press, 2005.

———. *Phillis Wheatley: Biography of a Genius in Bondage*. Athens: University of Georgia Press, 2011.

Cather, Willa. *My Ántonia*. Boston: Houghton Mifflin, 1918.

Chaney, Michael A. *Fugitive Visions: Slave Image and Black Identity in Antebellum Narrative*. Bloomington: Indiana University Press, 2008.

Child, Lydia Maria. *An Appeal in Favor of That Class of Americans Called Africans*. Edited by Carolyn L. Karcher. Amherst: University of Massachusetts Press, 1996.

Clifford, James. *The Predicament of Culture: Twentieth-Century Ethnography, Literature, and Art*. Cambridge, Mass.: Harvard University Press, 1988.

———. *Routes: Travel and Translation in the Late Twentieth Century*. Cambridge, Mass.: Harvard University Press, 1997.

Coates, Ta-Nehisi. *Between the World and Me*. New York: Spiegel and Grau, 2015.

Commander, Michelle D. *Afro-Atlantic Flight: Speculative Returns and the Black Fantastic*. Durham, N.C.: Duke University Press, 2017.

Cooper, James Fenimore. *The Prairie*. In *The Leather-Stocking Tales*. Edited by Blake Nevius. Vol. 1. New York: Library of America, 1985.

Cowan, William Tynes. *The Slave in the Swamp: Disrupting the Plantation Narrative*. New York: Routledge, 2005.

Craig, Maureen A., and Jennifer A. Richeson. "On the Precipice of a 'Majority-Minority' America: Perceived Status Threat from the Racial Demographic Shift Affects White Americans' Political Ideology." *Psychological Science* 25, no. 6 (2014): 1189–97. https://doi.org/10.1177/0956797614527113.

Danky, James P. "Reading, Writing, and Resisting: African American Print Culture." In *A History of the Book in America*, vol. 4, *Print in Motion: The Expansion of Publishing and Reading in the United States, 1880–1940*, edited by Carl F. Kaestle and Janice A. Radway, 339–358. Chapel Hill: University of North Carolina Press, 2009.

Davis, Thadious M. *Southscapes: Geographies of Race, Region, and Literature*. Chapel Hill: University of North Carolina Press, 2011.

Dawsey, Josh. "Trump Attacks Protections for Immigrants from 'Shithole Countries' in Oval Office Meeting." *Washington Post*, January 11, 2018.

Decker, William Merrill. *Epistolary Practices: Letter Writing in America before Telecommunications*. Chapel Hill: University of North Carolina Press, 1998.

———. "'Surely Cora Was Not Forgotten': Remembering Africa in the Leather-Stocking Tales." In *Reading Cooper, Teaching Cooper*, edited by Jeffrey Walker, 201–21. New York: AMS Press, 2007.

———. "Autobiography, Education: Henry Adams and the Definition of a Genre." *A/B: Auto/Biography Studies* 33, no 1 (2018): 47–63.

Dekker, George. *The American Historical Romance*. New York: Cambridge University Press, 1987.

DeLombard, Jeannine Marie. *Slavery on Trial: Law, Abolitionism, and Print Culture*. Chapel Hill: University of North Caroline Press, 2007.

———. "Apprehending Early African American Literary History." In *Early African American Print Culture*, edited by Lara Langer Cohen and Jordan Alexander Stein, 93–106. Philadelphia: University of Pennsylvania Press, 2012.

Delany, Martin R. *Blake; or, The Huts of America*. Edited by Floyd J. Miller. Boston: Beacon Press, 1970.

Deloria, Phillip J. *Indians in Unexpected Places*. Lawrence: University Press of Kansas, 2004.

Dixon, Melvin. *Ride Out the Wilderness: Geography and Identity in Afro-American Literature*. Urbana: University of Illinois Press, 1987.

Douglass, Frederick. *Autobiographies: Narrative of the Life of Frederick Douglass, An American Slave, Written by Himself; My Bondage and My Freedom; Life and Times of Frederick Douglass*. Edited by Henry Louis Gates Jr. New York: Library of America, 1984.

Downs, Donald A. "Government Censorship since 1945." In *A History of the Book in America*, vol. 5, *The Enduring Book: Print Culture in Postwar America*, edited by David Paul Nord, Joan Shelley Rubin, and Michael Schudson, 133–50. Chapel Hill: University of North Carolina Press, 2009.

The Dred Scott Decision: Opinion of Chief Justice Taney: A Machine Readable Transcript. Library of Congress. https://cdn.loc.gov/service/ll/llst/022/022.pdf.

Dubey, Madhu. *Signs and Cities: Black Literary Postmodernism*. Chicago: University of Chicago Press, 2003.

Du Bois, W. E. B. *The Autobiography of W. E. B. Du Bois: A Soliloquy on Viewing My Life from the Last Decade of Its First Century*. Edited by Henry Louis Gates Jr. and Werner Sollors. New York: Oxford University Press, 2007.

———. *Darkwater: Voices from Within the Veil*. Edited by Henry Louis Gates Jr. and Evelyn Brooks Higginbotham. New York: Oxford University Press, 2007.

———. *Dusk of Dawn: An Essay Toward an Autobiography of a Race Concept*. Edited by Henry Louis Gates Jr. and K. Anthony Appiah. New York: Oxford University Press, 2007.

———. *The Souls of Black Folk*. Edited by Henry Louis Gates Jr. and Arnold Rampersad. New York: Oxford University Press, 2007.

Edwards, Brent Hayes. *The Practice of Diaspora: Literature, Translation, and the Rise of Black Internationalism*. Cambridge, Mass.: Harvard University Press, 2003.

Ellison, Ralph. *Invisible Man*. New York: Vintage, 1952.

———. "Working Notes for *Invisible Man*." In *The Collected Essays of Ralph Ellison*, edited by John F. Callahan, 341–49. New York: Modern Library, 2003.

Emerson, Ralph Waldo. *Essays and Lectures*. Edited by Joel Porte. New York: Library of America, 1983.

Equiano, Olaudah. *The Interesting Narrative and Other Writings*. Edited by Vincent Carretta. New York: Penguin, 1995.

Erkkila, Betsy. "Phillis Wheatley and the Black American Revolution." In *A Mixed Race: Ethnicity in Early America*, edited by Frank Shuffleton, 225–40. New York: Oxford University Press, 1993.

Ernest, John. *Liberation Historiography: African American Writers and the Challenge of History, 1794–1861*. Chapel Hill: University of North Carolina Press, 2004.

Eyerman, Ron. *Cultural Trauma: Slavery and the Formation of African American Identity*. New York: Cambridge University Press, 2001.

Fandos, Nicolas. "Donald Trump Defiantly Rallies a New 'Silent Majority' in a Visit to Arizona." *New York Times*, July 11, 2015.

Fanon, Frantz. *Black Skin, White Masks*. Translated by Charles L. Markmann. New York: Grove Press, 1967.

———. *The Wretched of the Earth*. Translated by Constance Farrington. New York: Grove Press, 1963.

Finney, Carolyn. *Black Faces, White Spaces: Reimagining the Relationship of African Americans to the Great Outdoors*. Chapel Hill: University of North Carolina Press, 2014.

Fitzgerald, Charlotte D. "*The Story of My Life and Work*: Booker T. Washington's Other Autobiography." *Black Scholar* 21, no. 4 (2001): 35–40. https://doi.org/10.1080/00064246.1991.11412979.

Foley, Barbara. *Wrestling with the Left: The Making of Ralph Ellison's* Invisible Man. Durham, N.C.: Duke University Press, 2010.

Folsom, Ed. "Erasing Race: The Lost Black Presence in Whitman's Manuscripts." In *Whitman Noir: Black America and the Good Gray Poet*, edited by Ivy G. Wilson, 3–31. Iowa City: University of Iowa Press, 2014.

Foner, Eric. *The Story of American Freedom*. New York: W. W. Norton: 1998.

Foster, Frances Smith. *Written by Herself: Literary Production by African American Women, 1746–1892*. Bloomington: Indiana University Press, 1993.

Foucault, Michel. *The History of Sexuality.* Vol. 1, *An Introduction*. Translated by Robert Hurley. New York: Vintage Books, 1990.

———. "Of Other Spaces." Translated by Jay Miskowiec. *Diacritics* 16, no. 1 (1986): 22–27. https://doi.org/10.2307/464648.

Frank, Thomas. "Cornel West: 'He Posed as a Progressive and Turned Out to Be a Counterfeit. We Ended Up with a Wall Street Presidency, a Drone Presidency.' " *Salon*, August 24, 2014.

Franklin, Benjamin. *The Autobiography of Benjamin Franklin and Other Writings*. Edited by Ormond Seavey. New York: Oxford University Press, 1993.

Franklin, H. Bruce. *Prison Literature in America: The Victim as Criminal and Artist*. New York: Oxford University Press, 1989.

Fuller, Margaret. *Summer on the Lakes, in 1843*. Edited by Susan Belasco Smith. Urbana: University of Illinois Press, 1991.

Fultz, Lucille P. *Toni Morrison: Playing with Difference*. Urbana: University of Illinois Press, 2003.

Gaines, Kevin K. *Uplifting the Race: Black Leadership, Politics, and Culture in the Twentieth Century*. Chapel Hill: University of North Carolina Press, 1996.

Gardner, Eric. "Early African American Print Culture and the American West." In *Early African American Print Culture*, edited by Lara Langer Cohen and Jordan Alexander Stein, 75–89. Philadelphia: University of Pennsylvania Press, 2012.

Gates, Henry Louis, Jr. "Writing 'Race' and the Difference It Makes," *Critical Inquiry* 12, no. 1 (Autumn 1985): 1–20, https://doi.org/10.1086/448318.

———. *Figures in Black: Literary Theory and the Black Tradition*. New York: Oxford University Press, 1987.

———. *The Signifying Monkey: A Theory of African-American Literary Criticism*. New York: Oxford University Press, 1988.

Gayle, Addison, Jr. *The Addison Gayle Jr. Reader*. Edited by Nathaniel Norment Jr. Urbana: University of Illinois Press, 2009.

Genovese, Eugene. *Roll, Jordan, Roll: The World the Slaves Made*. New York: Pantheon, 1974.

Gilroy, Paul. *The Black Atlantic: Modernity and Double Consciousness*. Cambridge, Mass.: Harvard University Press, 1993.

Glass, Loren. *Counterculture Colophon: Grove Press, Evergreen Review, and the Incorporation of the Avant-Garde*. Stanford, Calif.: Stanford University Press, 2013.

Glissant, Édouard. *Caribbean Discourse: Selected Essays*. Translated by J. Michael Dash. Charlottesville: University Press of Virginia, 1989.

———. *Le disours antillais*. 1981. Reprint, Paris: Éditions Gallimard, 1997.

Goldsby, Jacqueline. *A Spectacular Secret: Lynching in American Life and Literature*. Chicago: University of Chicago Press, 2006.

Griffin, Farah Jasmine. *"Who Set You Flowin'?: The African-American Migration Narrative*. New York: Oxford University Press, 1995.

Hager, Christopher. *Word by Word: Emancipation and the Act of Writing*. Cambridge, Mass.: Harvard University Press, 2013.

Hall, David D. "Cultures of Letters, Cultures of Criticism." In *A History of the Book in America*, vol. 5, *The Enduring Book: Print Culture in Postwar America*, edited by David Paul Nord, Joan Shelley Rubin, and Michael Schudson, 223–32. Chapel Hill: University of North Carolina Press, 2009.

———. "Readers and Writers in Early New England." In *A History of the Book in America*, vol. 1, *The Colonial Book in the Atlantic World*, edited by Hugh Armory and David D. Hall, 117–51. Chapel Hill: University of North Carolina Press, 2007.

Hall, Michael Ra-Shon. "The Negro Traveller's Guide to a Jim Crow South: Negotiating Racialized Landscapes in United States Cultural History, 1936–1967." *Postcolonial Studies* 17, no. 3 (2014): 307–19. https://doi.org/10.1080/13688790.2014.987898.

Hall, Stuart. "Cultural Identity and Diaspora." In *Identity: Community, Culture, Difference*, edited by Jonathan Rutherford, 222–37. London: Lawrence and Wishart, 1993.

———. "Introduction: Who Needs Identity?" In *Questions of Cultural Identity*, edited by Stuart Hall and Paul du Gay, 1–17. London: Sage, 1996.

Hammond, Geordan. *John Wesley in America: Restoring Primitive Christianity*. Oxford: Oxford University Press, 2014.

Hartman, Saidiya V. *Lose Your Mother: A Journey along the Atlantic Slave Route*. New York: Farrar, Straus and Giroux, 2007.

———. *Scenes of Subjection: Terror, Slavery, and Self-Making in Nineteenth-Century America*. New York: Oxford University Press, 1997.

Harvey, David. *The Condition of Postmodernity: An Enquiry into the Origins of Cultural Change*. Oxford: Blackwell, 1989.

Hawthorne, Nathaniel. *Our Old Home: A Series of English Sketches*. Vol. 5, *Centenary Edition of the Works of Nathaniel Hawthorne*. Edited by William Charvat et al. Columbus: Ohio State University Press, 1970.

Hewitt, Elizabeth. *Correspondence and American Literature, 1770–1865*. New York: Cambridge University Press, 2004.

Hicks, Scott. "W. E .B. DuBois, Booker T. Washington, and Richard Wright: Toward an Eco-Criticism of Color." *Callaloo: A Journal of African Diaspora Arts and Letters* 29, no. 1 (2006): 202–22.

Higginbotham, Evelyn Brooks. Introduction to *Darkwater: Voices from Within the Veil*, by W. E. B. Du Bois, edited by Henry Louis Gates Jr. and Evelyn Brooks Higgenbotham, xxv–xl. New York: Oxford University Press, 2007.

Hinks, Peter P. *To Awaken My Afflicted Brethren: David Walker and the Problem of Antebellum Slave Resistance*. University Park: Pennsylvania State University Press, 1997.

hooks, bell. Belonging: A Culture of Place. New York: Routledge, 2009.

Hsu, Hsuan L. *Geography and the Production of Space in Nineteenth-Century American Literature*. New York: Cambridge University Press, 2010.

Hughes, Langston. *I Wonder as I Wander: An Autobiographical Journey*. Edited by Arnold Rampersad. New York: Hill and Wang, 1996.

Hutchinson, George. *The Harlem Renaissance in Black and White*. Cambridge, Mass.: Harvard University Press, 1995.

Irving, Washington. *The Sketch-Book of Geoffrey Crayon*. Edited by Susan Manning. New York: Oxford University Press, 1996.

Iton, Richard. *In Search of the Black Fantastic: Politics and Popular Culture in the Post–Civil Rights Era*. New York: Oxford University Press, 2008.

Jacobs, Harriet A. *Incidents in the Life of a Slave Girl*. Edited by Jean Fagan Yellin. Cambridge, Mass.: Harvard University Press, 1987.

Jameson, Fredric. *Postmodernism; or, The Cultural Logic of Late Capitalism*. Durham, N.C.: Duke University Press, 1991.

Jefferson, Thomas. *Notes on the State of Virginia*. Edited by William Peden. Chapel Hill: University of North Carolina Press, 1955.

Jennings, La Vinia Delois. *Toni Morrison and the Idea of Africa*. New York: Cambridge University Press, 2008.

Johnson, James Weldon. *The Autobiography of an Ex-Colored Man*. Edited by Jacqueline Goldsby. New York: W. W. Norton, 2015.

———. *Complete Poems*. Edited by Sondra Kathryn Wilson. New York: Penguin, 2000.

Joo, Hee-Jung Serenity. "Old and New Slavery, Old and New Racisms: Strategies of Science Fiction in Octavia Butler's Parables Series." *Extrapolation* 52, no. 3 (2011): 279–99.

Judy, Ronald A. T. *(Dis)Forming the American Canon*. Minneapolis: University of Minnesota Press, 1993.

Keizer, Arlene R. *Black Subjects: Identity Formation in the Contemporary Narrative of Slavery*. Ithaca, N.Y.: Cornell University Press, 2004.

Kidd, Thomas S. *George Whitefield: America's Spiritual Founding Father*. New Haven, Conn.: Yale University Press, 2014.

Kinnamon, Keneth. *The Emergence of Richard Wright: A Study in Literature and Society*. Urbana: University of Illinois Press, 1972.

Klammer, Martin. *Whitman, Slavery, and the Emergence of Leaves of Grass*. University Park: Pennsylvania University Press, 1995.

Kolodny, Annette. *The Land before Her: Fantasy and Experience of the American Frontiers, 1630–1860*. Chapel Hill: University of North Carolina Press, 1984.

Kranish, Michael. "FBI Releases File on 1970s Trump Housing Discrimination Case." *Washington Post*, February 15, 2017.

Kristeva, Julia. *Powers of Horror: An Essay on Abjection*. Translated by Leon S. Roudiez. New York: Columbia University Press, 1982.

Leeming, David. *James Baldwin: A Biography*. New York: Alfred A. Knopf, 1994.
Lefebvre, Henri. *The Production of Space*. Translated by Donald Nicholson-Smith. London: Blackwell, 1991.
Leonard, Elisabeth Anne. "Race and Ethnicity in Science Fiction." In *The Cambridge Companion to Science Fiction*, edited by Edward James and Farah Mendlesohn, 253–63. Cambridge: Cambridge University Press, 2003.
Levine, Robert S. *The Lives of Frederick Douglass*. Cambridge, Mass.: Harvard University Press, 2016.
———. "Circulating the Nation: David Walker, the Missouri Compromise, and the Rise of the Black Press." In *The Black Press: New Literary and Historical Essays*, edited by Todd Vogel, 17–36. New Brunswick, N.J.: Rutgers University Press, 2001.
———. Introduction and Notes to *Clotel; or, The President's Daughter, a Narrative of Slave Life in the United States*, by William Wells Brown. Boston: Bedford/St. Martin's, 2000.
———. *Martin Delany, Frederick Douglass, and the Politics of Representative Identity*. Chapel Hill: University of North Carolina Press, 1997.
Lewis, David Levering. *W. E. B. Du Bois: The Fight for Equality and the American Century, 1919–1963*. New York: Henry Holt, 2000.
Lewis, R. W. B. *The American Adam: Innocence, Tragedy, and Tradition in the Nineteenth Century*. Chicago: University of Chicago Press, 1955.
Lugo, Luis, et al. "Growing Number of Americans Say Obama Is a Muslim." Pew Forum on Religion and Public Life: Pew Research Center's Religion and Public Life Project, August 18, 2010. http://www.pewforum.org/2010/08/18/growing-number-of-americans-say-obama-is-a-muslim/.
Mahler, Jonathan, and Steve Eder. "'No Vacancies' for Blacks: How Donald Trump Got His Start, and Was First Accused of Bias." *New York Times*, August 27, 2016.
Malcolm X and Alex Haley. *The Autobiography of Malcolm X*. New York: Ballantine Books, 1999.
Malone, Christopher. *Between Freedom and Bondage: Race, Party, and Voting Rights in the Antebellum North*. New York: Routledge, 2008.
Marable, Manning. *Malcolm X: A Life of Reinvention*. New York: Viking, 2011.
Massey, Doreen. *For Space*. London: Sage, 2005.
———. *Space, Place, and Gender*. Minneapolis: University of Minnesota Press, 1994.
Matthiessen, F. O. *American Renaissance: Art and Expression in the Age of Emerson and Whitman*. New York: Oxford University Press, 1941.
Mayer, Jane. "Covert Operations: The Billionaire Brothers Who Are Waging a War against Obama." *New Yorker*, October 30, 2010.
McFeely, William S. *Frederick Douglass*. New York: W. W. Norton, 1991.
McHenry, Elizabeth. *Forgotten Readers: Recovering the Lost Histories of African American Literary Societies*. Durham, N.C.: Duke University Press, 2002.
McKittrick, Katherine. *Demonic Grounds: Black Women and the Cartographies of Struggle*. Minneapolis: University of Minnesota Press, 2006.
McKittrick, Katherine, and Clyde Woods, eds. *Black Geographies and the Politics of Place*. Toronto: Between the Lines Press, 2007.
McManus, Edgar J. *Black Bondage in the North*. Syracuse, N.Y.: Syracuse University Press, 1973.

Miles, Jan. *The Post-Racial Negro Green Book*. New Orleans: Brown Bird Books, 2017.

Morrison, Toni. *Beloved*. 1987. Reprint, New York: Vintage, 2004.

———. "Mourning for Whiteness." *New Yorker*, November 21, 2016.

———. *Playing in the Dark: Whiteness and the Literary Imagination*. Cambridge, Mass.: Harvard University Press, 1992.

———. *Song of Solomon*. New York: Knopf, 1977.

Moten, Fred. *In the Break: The Aesthetics of the Black Radical Tradition*. Minneapolis: University of Minnesota Press, 2003.

Nadel, Alan. *Invisible Criticism: Ralph Ellison and the American Canon*. Iowa City: University of Iowa Press, 1988.

Nelson, Robert K., et al.. "Mapping Inequality: Redlining in New Deal America." *American Panorama*. Edited by Robert K. Nelson and Edward L. Ayers. https://dsl.richmond.edu/panorama/redlining/#loc=11/40.7902/-73.9589&opacity=0.8&sort=98,197&area=D7&city=bronx-ny&text=bibliograph.

Nesbit, Jeff. "The Secret Origins of the Tea Party: How Big Oil and Big Tobacco Partnered with the Koch Brothers to Take Over the GOP." *Time*, April 5, 2016.

Norrell, Robert J. *Up from History: The Life of Booker T. Washington*. Cambridge, Mass.: Harvard University Press, 2009.

Olney, James. "'I Was Born': Slave Narratives, Their Status as Autobiography and as Literature." In *The Slave's Narrative*, edited by Charles T. Davis and Henry Louis Gates Jr., 148–75. New York: Oxford University Press, 1985.

Olson, Charles. *Call Me Ishmael*. New York: Grove Press, 1947.

Oubre, Claude F. *Forty Acres and a Mule: The Freedmen's Bureau and Black Land Ownership*. Baton Rouge: Louisiana State University Press, 1978.

Painter, Nell Irvin. *Exodusters: Black Migration to Kansas after Reconstruction*. New York: Knopf, 1976.

———. *The History of White People*. New York: W. W. Norton, 2010.

Patterson, Orlando. *Slavery and Social Death: A Comparative Study*. Cambridge, Mass.: Harvard University Press, 1982.

Perrin, Andrew J., Steven J. Tepper, Neal Caren, and Sally Morris. "Political and Cultural Dimensions of Tea Party Support, 2009–2012." *Sociological Quarterly* 55, no. 4 (2014): 625–52. https://doi.org/10.1111/tsq.12069.

Petry, Ann Lane. *The Street*. Boston: Houghton Mifflin, 1946.

Philip, M. NourbeSe. *Zong!* Middletown, Conn.: Wesleyan University Press, 2008.

Pratt, Mary Louise. *Imperial Eyes: Travel Writing and Transculturation*. 2nd ed. New York: Routledge, 2007.

Radway, Janice A. *A Feeling for Books: The Book-of-the-Month Club, Literary Taste, and Middle-Class Desire*. Chapel Hill: University of North Carolina Press, 1997.

———. "Learned and Literary Print Cultures in an Age of Professionalization and Diversification." In *A History of the Book in America*, vol. 4, *Print in Motion: The Expansion of Publishing and Reading in the United States, 1880–1940*, edited by Carl F. Kaestle and Janice A. Radway, 197–233. Chapel Hill: University of North Carolina Press, 2009.

Rampersad, Arnold. *Ralph Ellison: A Biography*. New York: Knopf, 2007.

Ramsey, Calvin Alexander, and Gwen Strauss. *Ruth and the Green Book*. Illustrated by Floyd Cooper. Minneapolis: Carolrhoda Books, 2010.

Redding, Arthur F. *Turncoats, Traitors, and Fellow Travelers: Culture and Politics of the Early Cold War*. Oxford: University Press of Mississippi, 2008.

Reed, Christopher Robert. *All the World Is Here! The Black Presence at White City*. Bloomington: Indiana University Press, 2000.

———. "The Black Presence at 'White City': African and African American Participation at the World's Columbian Exposition, Chicago, May 1, 1893–October 31, 1893." In the Paul V. Galvin Library Digital History Collection, Illinois Institute of Technology. http://columbus.iit.edu/reed2.html.

Rezek, Joseph. "The Print Atlantic: Phillis Wheatley, Ignatius Sancho, and the Cultural Significance of the Book. In *Early African American Print Culture*, edited by Lara Langer Cohen and Jordan Alexander Stein, 19–39. Philadelphia: University of Pennsylvania Press, 2012.

Rothstein, Richard. *The Color of Law: A Forgotten History of How Our Government Segregated America*. New York: Liveright, 2017.

Rowell, Charles H., and Octavia E. Butler, "An Interview with Octavia E. Butler." *Callaloo: A Journal of African Diaspora Arts and Letters* 20, no. 1 (Winter 1997): 47–66. https://www.jstor.org/stable/3299291.

Rowley, Hazel. *Richard Wright: The Life and Times*. New York: Henry Holt, 2001.

Rusert, Britt. *Fugitive Science: Empiricism and Freedom in Early African American Culture*. New York: New York University Press, 2017.

Rushdy, Ashraf H. A. *Neo-Slave Narratives: Studies in the Social Logic of a Literary Form*. New York: Oxford University Press, 1999.

Sandweiss, Martha A. *Passing Strange: A Gilded Age Tale of Love and Deception across the Color Line*. New York: Penguin, 2009.

Scholnick, Robert J. "Extermination and Democracy: O'Sullivan, the *Democratic Review*, and Empire, 1837–1840." *American Periodicals* 15, no. 2 (2005): 123–41. https://doi.org/10.1353/amp.2005.0020.

Schoolman, Martha. *Abolitionist Geographies*. Minneapolis: University of Minnesota Press, 2014.

Scruggs, Charles. *Sweet Home: Invisible Cities in the Afro-American Novel*. Baltimore: Johns Hopkins University Press, 1993.

Seiler, Cotton. "'So That We as a Race Might Have Something Authentic to Travel By': African American Automobility and Cold-War Liberalism." *American Quarterly* 58, no. 4 (2006): 1091–117. https://www.jstor.org/stable/40068407.

Sekora, John. "Black Message/White Envelope: Genre, Authenticity, and Authority in the Antebellum Slave Narrative." *Callaloo: A Journal of African Diaspora Arts and Letters* 32 (Summer 1987): 482–515. https://doi.org/10.2307/2930465.

Sexton, Jared. "Afro-Pessimism: The Unclear Word." In "Black Holes: Afro-Pessimism, Blackness and the Discourses of Modernity," edited by Dalton Anthony Jones. Special issue, *Rhizomes* 29 (2016). https://doi.org/10.20415/rhiz/029.

Sharpe, Christina. *Monstrous Intimacies: Making Post-Slavery Subjects*. Durham, N.C.: Duke University Press, 2010.

Shields, David S. "Eighteenth-Century Literary Culture." In *A History of the Book in America*, vol. 1, *The Colonial Book in the Atlantic World*, edited by Hugh Armory and David D. Hall, 434–76. Chapel Hill: University of North Carolina Press, 2007.

Smith, Henry Nash. *Virgin Land: The American West as Symbol and Myth*. Cambridge, Mass.: Harvard University Press, 1950.

Smith, Virginia Whatley. *Richard Wright's Travel Writing: New Reflections*. Jackson: University Press of Mississippi, 2001.

Smith-Rosenberg, Carroll. *Disorderly Conduct: Visions of Gender in Victorian America*. New York: Oxford University Press, 1985.

Soja, Edward W. *Postmodern Geographies: The Reassertion of Space in Critical Social Theory*. London: Verso, 1989.

Spaulding, A. Timothy. *Re-Forming the Past: History, the Fantastic, and the Postmodern Slave Narrative*. Columbus: Ohio State University Press, 2005.

Spillers, Hortense J. "Formalism Comes to Harlem." In *Black, White, and in Color: Essays on American Literature and Culture*, 81–92. Chicago: University of Chicago Press, 2003.

———. "Mama's Baby, Papa's Maybe: An American Grammar Book." In *Black, White, and in Color: Essays on American Literature and Culture*, 203–29. Chicago: University of Chicago Press, 2003.

Spivak, Gayatri Chakravorty. "Can the Subaltern Speak?" In *Marxism and the Interpretation of Culture*, edited by Cary Nelson and Lawrence Grossberg, 271–313. Basingstoke: Macmillan, 1988.

Stauffer, John. *The Black Hearts of Men: Radical Abolitionists and the Transformation of Race*. Cambridge, Mass.: Harvard University Press, 2001.

Stauffer, John, Zoe Trodd, and Celeste-Marie Bernier. *Picturing Frederick Douglass: An Illustrated Biography of the Nineteenth Century's Most Photographed American*. New York: Liveright, 2015.

Stepto, Robert B. *From Behind the Veil: A Study of Afro-American Narrative*. Urbana: University of Illinois Press, 1979.

Tally, Robert T., Jr. *Melville, Mapping, and Globalization: Literary Cartography in the American Baroque Writer*. London: Bloomsbury, 2009.

———. *Spatiality*. London: Routledge, 2013.

Taylor, Quintard. *In Search of the Racial Frontier: African Americans in the American West, 1528–1990*. New York: W. W. Norton, 1998.

Thaddeus, Janice. "The Metamorphosis of *Black Boy*." In *Richard Wright: Critical Perspectives Past and Present*, edited by Henry Louis Gates Jr. and K. A. Appiah, 272–84. New York: Amistad Press, 1993.

Thoreau, Henry David. *Collected Essays and Poems*. Edited by Elizabeth Hall Witherell. New York: Library of America, 2001.

Traubel, Horace. *With Walt Whitman in Camden*. Vol. 2. New York: Rowman and Littlefield, 1915.

Turner, Frederick Jackson. "The Significance of the Frontier in American History." In *The Frontier in American History*, 1–38. New York: Henry Holt, 1921.

U.S. Census Bureau. "U.S. Census Bureau Projections Show a Slower Growing, Older, More Diverse Nation a Half Century from Now." Press release, December 12, 2012. https://www.census.gov/newsroom/releases/archives/population/cb12-243.html.

Vlach, John Michael. *Back of the Big House: The Architecture of Plantation Slavery*. Chapel Hill: University of North Carolina Press, 1993.

Vogel, Todd, ed. *The Black Press: New Literary and Historical Essays*. New Brunswick, N.J.: Rutgers University Press, 2001.

Walker, David. *David Walker's Appeal, in Four Articles; Together with a Preamble, to the Coloured Citizens of the World, But in Particular, and Very Expressly, to Those of the United States of America*. Edited by Sean Wilentz. New York: Hill and Wang, 1995.

Wanzo, Rebecca. "Apocalyptic Empathy: A Parable of Postmodern Sentimentality." *Obsidian III: Literature in the African Diaspora* 6/7, no. 2/1 (2005–6): 72–86.

Warhol, Robyn R. "'Reader, Can You Imagine? No, You Cannot': The Narratee as Other in Harriet Jacobs's Text." *Narrative* 3, no. 1 (1995): 57–72. http://www.jstor.org.argo.library.okstate.edu/stable/20107043.

Washington, Booker T. *The Story of My Life and Work*. Toronto: J. L. Nichols, 1901.

———. *Up from Slavery: An Autobiography*. Garden City, N.Y.: Doubleday and Page, 1925.

Weiss, M. Lynn. "*Para Usted*: Richard Wright's *Pagan Spain*." In *The Black Columbiad: Defining Moments in African American Literature and Culture*, edited by Werner Sollors and Maria Diedrich, 212–25. Cambridge, Mass.: Harvard University Press, 1994.

Wells, Ida B. *Crusade for Justice: The Autobiography of Ida B. Wells*. Edited by Alfreda M. Duster. Chicago: University of Chicago Press, 1970.

———. *Southern Horrors and Other Writings: The Anti-Lynching Campaign of Ida B. Wells, 1892–1900*. Edited by Jacqueline Jones Royster. Boston: Bedford Books, 1997.

West, Cornel. Foreword to *The New Jim Crow: Mass Incarceration in the Age of Colorblindness*, by Michelle Alexander, ix–xi. New York: New Press, 2010.

———. *Race Matters*. Boston: Beacon Press, 1993.

Wheatley, Phillis. *Complete Writings*. Edited by Vincent Carretta. New York: Penguin, 2001.

Whitehead, Colson. *The Underground Railroad*. New York: Doubleday, 2016.

Whitman, Walt. "*Daily Eagle*, September 1, 1847." In *The Gathering of the Forces*. Edited by Cleveland Rodgers and John Black. 2 vols. New York: Putnam, 1920.

———. *Poetry and Prose*. Edited by Justin Kaplan. New York: Library of America, 1997.

Wilderson, Frank B., III. *Red, White and Black: Cinema and the Structure of U.S. Antagonisms*. Durham, N.C.: Duke University Press, 2010.

Wilkerson, Isabel. *The Warmth of Other Suns: The Epic Story of America's Great Migration*. New York: Random House, 2010.

Williams, Sherley Anne. *Dessa Rose*. New York: William Morrow, 1986.

Wilson, Ivy G. *Specters of Democracy: Blackness and the Aesthetics of Politics in the Antebellum U.S.* New York: Oxford University Press, 2011.

———, ed. *Whitman Noir: Black America and the Good Gray Poet*. Iowa City: University of Iowa Press, 2014.

Witte, Griff. "Trump Tried and Failed to Build a Wall in Ireland: That Could Mean Big Trouble for Europe." *Washington Post*, February 6, 2017.

Wong, Edlie L. *Neither Fugitive nor Free: Atlantic Slavery, Freedom Suits, and the Legal Culture of Travel*. New York: New York University Press, 2009.

Wright, Michelle M. *Physics of Blackness: Beyond the Middle Passage Epistemology*. Minneapolis: University of Minnesota Press, 2015.

Wright, Richard. "Blueprint for Negro Writing." In *Within the Circle: An Anthology of African American Literary Criticism from the Harlem Renaissance to the Present*, edited by Angelyn Mitchell, 97–106. Durham, N.C.: Duke University Press, 1995.

———. *Early Works: Lawd Today!, Uncle Tom's Children, Native Son*. Edited by Arnold Rampersad. New York: Library of America, 1991.

———. *Eight Men: Stories by Richard Wright*. New York: Harper Collins, 1996.

———. *Later Works: Black Boy (American Hunger), The Outsider*. Edited by Arnold Rampersad. New York: Library of America, 1991.

———. *White Man, Listen!* New York: HarperPerennial, 1995.

Yellin, Jean Fagan. Preface and introduction to *Incidents in the Life of a Slave Girl*, by Harriet A. Jacobs, edited by Jean Fagan Yellin, vii–viii and xiii–xxxv. Cambridge, Mass.: Harvard University Press, 1987.

Zernike, Kate. "N.A.A.C.P. Report Raises Concerns about Racism within Tea Party Groups." New York Times, October 20, 2010. http://www.nytimes.com/2010/10/21/us/politics/21naacp.html.

INDEX